Playing with Fire

Drawing on a rare cross-regional comparison of Kenya and India, *Playing with Fire* develops a novel explanation about ethnic party violence. Combining rich historical, qualitative, and quantitative data, the book demonstrates how levels of party instability can crucially inform the decisions of political elites to organize or support violence. Centrally, it shows that settings marked by unstable parties are more vulnerable to experiencing recurring and major episodes of party violence than those populated by durable parties. This is because transient parties enable politicians to disregard voters' future negative reactions to conflict. By contrast, stable party organizations compel politicians to take such costs into account, thereby dampening the potential for recurring and severe party violence. By centering political parties as key actors in the production of conflict, and bringing together evidence from both Africa and South Asia, *Playing with Fire* contributes new insights to the study of political violence.

Aditi Malik is Associate Professor in the Department of Political Science at the College of the Holy Cross. She studies political and gender-based violence, political parties, social movements and contentious politics, and ethnic and gender politics with regional specializations in Africa and South Asia. Malik has conducted fieldwork on these topics in Kenya, Rwanda, South Africa, Cambodia, India, and Nepal.

Playing with Fire

Parties and Political Violence in Kenya and India

ADITI MALIK
College of the Holy Cross

Shaftesbury Road, Cambridge CB2 8EA, United Kingdom

One Liberty Plaza, 20th Floor, New York, NY 10006, USA

477 Williamstown Road, Port Melbourne, VIC 3207, Australia

314–321, 3rd Floor, Plot 3, Splendor Forum, Jasola District Centre, New Delhi – 110025, India

103 Penang Road, #05–06/07, Visioncrest Commercial, Singapore 238467

Cambridge University Press is part of Cambridge University Press & Assessment, a department of the University of Cambridge.

We share the University's mission to contribute to society through the pursuit of education, learning and research at the highest international levels of excellence.

www.cambridge.org
Information on this title: www.cambridge.org/9781009444231
DOI: 10.1017/9781009444217

© Aditi Malik 2024

This publication is in copyright. Subject to statutory exception and to the provisions of relevant collective licensing agreements, no reproduction of any part may take place without the written permission of Cambridge University Press & Assessment.

First published 2024

A catalogue record for this publication is available from the British Library

Library of Congress Cataloging-in-Publication Data
NAMES: Malik, Aditi, author.
TITLE: Playing with fire : parties and political violence in Kenya and India / Aditi Malik.
DESCRIPTION: Cambridge ; New York, NY : Cambridge University Press, [2024] | Includes bibliographical references.
IDENTIFIERS: LCCN 2023045413 | ISBN 9781009444231 (hardback) | ISBN 9781009444248 (paperback) | ISBN 9781009444217 (ebook)
SUBJECTS: LCSH: Political parties – Kenya. | Political parties – India. | Political violence – Kenya. | Political violence – India. | Kenya – Politics and government. | India – Politics and government.
CLASSIFICATION: LCC JQ2947.A979 M35 2024 | DDC 324.254–dc23/eng/20240226
LC record available at https://lccn.loc.gov/2023045413

ISBN 978-1-009-44423-1 Hardback
ISBN 978-1-009-44424-8 Paperback

Cambridge University Press & Assessment has no responsibility for the persistence or accuracy of URLs for external or third-party internet websites referred to in this publication and does not guarantee that any content on such websites is, or will remain, accurate or appropriate.

For Nanu, Nani, Dada, and Dadi

Contents

List of Figures	*page* xi
List of Tables	xiii
Acknowledgments	xv
List of Abbreviations	xxiii

1. Parties and Political Violence — 1
   The Puzzling Phenomenon of Party Violence — 4
   Central Arguments and Scope Conditions — 6
   Existing Literature — 7
   Emerging Insights on Party Violence and the Contributions of This Book — 12
   Party Instability, Voter Sanctioning, and Elites' Incentives to Supply Party Violence — 16
   Party Violence in Kenya and India — 19
   Summary of Methodology — 23
   The Plan of This Book — 26

2. A Theory of Party Instability and Political Violence — 30
   The Sources of Elites' Time Horizons — 32
   Replacement Volatility as a Measure of Party Instability — 35
   A Supply-side Model of Party Violence — 37
   Endogeneity Concerns and Alternative Explanations — 45
   Summary and Conclusion — 49

3. The Development of Divergent Parties and Party Systems in Kenya and India — 51
   Party Development under Colonial Rule — 53
   Party Development after Independence — 59
   Summary and Conclusion — 74

4	Party Instability and Political Violence in Kenya	76
	Party Fragility, Elite Uncertainty, and Recurring Waves of Party Violence in Kenya	78
	Political Insecurity and Party Violence in the KANU Era (1992–2002)	79
	The Contours of Party Violence in the Post-KANU Era (2002–2013)	86
	Patterns of Party Violence under Kenya's New Constitution (2013–Present)	93
	Voter Knowledge about Party Violence in Kenya	97
	Summary and Conclusion	98
5	Party Fragility and Subnational Patterns of Violence in Kenya's Rift Valley and Coast Regions	100
	Vicissitudes in Party Violence in Kenya's Rift Valley (1992–2017)	101
	Vulnerabilities to Party Violence in the Kenyan Coast (1992–2017)	109
	Endogeneity Concerns	121
	Summary and Conclusion	124
6	Party Stabilization, Declining Riot Violence, and New Modalities of Political Conflict in India	126
	Party Politics, Elite Calculations, and Hindu–Muslim Riots in India	129
	Congress Dominance, Party Stability, and Relative Communal Calm in India (1950s–Late 1970s)	131
	Congress Defeat, Rising Party Instability, and Escalating Hindu–Muslim Riots in India (Late 1970s–Early 1990s)	134
	Party Re-equilibration, Declining Riots, and the Emergence of Everyday Communalism in India (Early 1990s–Present)	139
	Summary and Conclusion	141
7	Party Politics and Subnational Trajectories of Riot Violence in India's Hyderabad and Meerut Cities	142
	The Transition from Party Violence to Communal Quiescence in Hyderabad	143
	The Evolution from Regular Communal Violence to Relative Calm in Meerut	155
	Endogeneity Concerns	169
	Summary and Conclusion	171
8	Party Instability and Political Violence: Comparative Insights from Ghana and Turkey	173
	Stable Parties and Low-intensity Electoral Violence in Ghana (1992–Present)	175
	Unstable Parties and the anarşi *Crisis in Turkey (1976–1980)*	180
	Summary and Conclusion	186

Contents

9 Conclusion	188
Areas for Future Research	190
Policy Implications	191
Appendix A: National and Subnational Correlations between Replacement Volatility and Alternative Measures of Party Instability	193
Concepts, Descriptive Statistics, and Bivariate Relationships at the National Level in Kenya and India	193
Concepts, Descriptive Statistics, and Bivariate Relationships at the Subnational Level in India	196
Appendix B: Elite Interviews	199
Interviewee Recruitment and Data Collection Strategies	202
Interview Locations and Transcription Strategies	205
Interview Interpretation and Analysis	205
Positionality and Researcher Identity	207
Appendix C: The Development of Civil Society in Kenya and India	211
The Evolution of Civil Society in Kenya and India in Comparative and Historical Perspective	212
Evaluating the Civic Associations Claim in Kenya: Evidence from the Rift Valley	217
Evaluating the Civic Associations Claim in India: Evidence from Hyderabad and Meerut	221
Summary and Conclusion	222
References	225
Datasets	257
Index	259

Figures

1.1	Subnational research sites in Kenya	*page* 22
1.2	Subnational research sites in India	22
2.1	Initiating recurring and severe violence in unstable party settings	41
2.2	Refraining from organizing severe violence in stable party settings	42
2.3	The relationship between party instability, voters' reactions, and elites' decisions about violence	44
4.1	Ethnic party violence in Kenya (1992–2013)	80
4.2	Party and coalitional replacement volatility in Kenya (1992–2017)	82
5.1	Party and coalitional replacement volatility in Molo constituency (1992–2017)	102
5.2	Party and coalitional replacement volatility in Kapseret constituency (1992–2017)	108
5.3	Party and coalitional replacement volatility in Likoni constituency (1992–2017)	112
5.4	Party and coalitional replacement volatility in Garsen constituency (1992–2017)	119
6.1	Hindu–Muslim riots in India (1950–2000)	131
6.2	Mean replacement volatility in India (1951–2014)	132
7.1	Party and coalitional replacement volatility in Andhra Pradesh's Lok Sabha (1957–2014) and Vidhan Sabha (1955–2014) elections	146
7.2	Party and coalitional replacement volatility in Uttar Pradesh's Lok Sabha (1951–2014) and Vidhan Sabha (1951–2017) elections	156

8.1 Democratic longevity, party instability, and political violence in comparative perspective ... 174
8.2 Political party institutionalization and electoral violence in Ghana (1992–2018) ... 179
8.3 Political party institutionalization and the *anarşi* crisis in Turkey (1950–2018) ... 185

Tables

4.1	Incidence and proportion of deadly events and estimated death tolls from waves of ethnic party violence in Kenya (1991–2013)	page 79
5.1	2013 election results from Tana River County	121
A.1	Descriptive statistics and correlations between Pedersen volatility, party strength, and replacement volatility in Kenya and India	195
A.2	Descriptive statistics and correlations between party organization, Pedersen volatility, and replacement volatility in Andhra Pradesh and Uttar Pradesh	197
B.1	Breakdown of elite interviews in Kenya and India	201

Acknowledgments

In February 2002, when massive communal riots broke out in the Indian state of Gujarat, I was a school student in New Delhi. Far away from the horrific violence and secure in my parents' home, I would sneak into our den every night to follow news coverage of the riots on television. These reports – which were beamed into our homes by several intrepid journalists – drew my attention to two key realities. First, the riots had emerged out of careful engineering and planning by politicians. Second, the incumbent regime in Gujarat was likely to benefit from the violence in the upcoming state elections. The links between devastating ethnic conflict and electoral dividends – and how and when these accrue to parties – were not clear to me at that time, or indeed for a long time thereafter. But the events in Gujarat in 2002 did generate important questions for me, with which I would continue to grapple for many years to come.

As a college student, the 2007–2008 post-election crisis in Kenya forced me to return these questions with some urgency. I was fortunate to find an exceptional undergraduate mentor at my alma mater – Franklin & Marshall College (F&M) in Lancaster, PA – in Susan Dicklitch-Nelson. Susan was the first person to introduce me to the tools of comparative analysis in the study of politics. Over the years, she patiently responded to my countless questions by advising me to blend my big picture concerns with a granular understanding of political life. As I approached my senior year, Susan also encouraged to me apply to graduate school and to Northwestern University in particular.

There, William Reno took me under his wing early. Along with Rachel Beatty Riedl, Ana Arjona, and Sharath Srinivasan (at the University of Cambridge), he composed and steered a wonderful dissertation committee during my Ph.D. Like Susan, Will extended extraordinary kindness and grace to me, and continues to mentor me to this day. Not only did he champion the cross-regional comparison at the heart of this book, but Will – more than anyone else I know – models what meaningful, rigorous, and ethical fieldwork in challenging environments ought to look like. I am immensely proud and eternally humbled to be counted among his students. As one of the foremost experts on political parties and party systems in Africa, Rachel's insights were indispensable to developing this book. She has keenly followed its evolution over many years and has maintained a faith in the project that I was occasionally unable to summon. I could not have completed this research without her support. Ana is one of the finest scholars of political violence with whom I have had the good fortune of professionally crossing paths. Her incisive comments have shaped this project in ways both big and small. In fact, it was Ana who convinced me to go back to the field – even when I had completed more than 150 elite interviews – and to keep digging until more pieces of the puzzle started to come together. Finally, Sharath's encouragement was instrumental in orienting me to uncover ordinary citizens' *lived experiences* of politics. Over the years, his mentorship has been a constant reminder that political science research is most valuable when it helps us to imagine and conceive of a more just world.

Data collection for this book involved several rounds of fieldwork, none of which could have been conducted, far less completed, without the support of a legion of incredible individuals. In Kenya, I owe sincere thanks to Karuti Kanyinga, Humphrey Mathenge, Kennedy Mkutu, George Morara, Godwin Murunga, Adams Oloo, and Fabian Ongaya. The British Institute in Eastern Africa provided a welcoming and stimulating intellectual environment during my time in Nairobi. I am also grateful to Nic Cheeseman, Gabrielle Lynch, Peter Kagwanja, Musambayi Katumanga, and Ambreena Manji who took the time to meet with me and discuss this project on several occasions. To Kamanda Mucheke, thank you for the many conversations, contacts, and tips on how to effectively do research among Kenyan politicians. Your friendship is one that I deeply value. I am also thankful to Ilham Aboo and Njoki Wamai for the laughs that we shared and for providing me with much needed respite from the daily demands of fieldwork.

In Hyderabad, Meerut, and New Delhi, Warisha Farasat, Mazher Husain, Manjari Katju, Ajay Mehra, Aman Nayar, Jyotirmaya Sharma, P. D. Sharma, Sanjeev Sharma, and Sanjeev Vohra were not only expert guides but also caring mentors. Additionally, Professor Balveer Arora at the Centre for Multilevel Federalism within the Institute of Social Sciences in Delhi provided me with a range of invaluable contacts and several debriefing sessions every time I completed a handful of interviews. Our many conversations over cups of hot *chai* were crucial in guiding me to theoretically and empirically refine the core claims presented here. Finally, Sanchit Gaur and Pragya Singh were vital in helping me plan and complete fieldwork in Muzaffarnagar and Shamli.

This research would have been impossible without the insights of countless individuals in Kenya and India who took time out of their daily lives to speak with me about parties, elections, and political violence. I gratefully acknowledge the funding that I received from the Dispute Resolution Research Center at the Kellogg School of Management, the Program of African Studies, and

Acknowledgments

the University Research Grants Committee at Northwestern University as well as the Africana Research Center at the Pennsylvania State University, which enabled me to carry out the fieldwork necessary for this project. In addition, I am thankful to Andrea (Andie) Forsee and Tina Tang at Northwestern for helping me with many crucial data-analysis tasks. Institutional support at the College of the Holy Cross – in the form of Batchelor Ford Fellowships, Publication Awards, and funding for Research Associates – further helped me to sharpen this work. I thank Sara Axson, Alessandro (Alex) Campagna, Kayleigh Hoagland, Ava Klinge, and Samantha Peters for their diligent research assistance.

Holy Cross also supported me in organizing a book workshop to discuss an earlier version of this manuscript. I consider myself extremely fortunate to have received feedback at the workshop from Mai Hassan, Zachariah Mampilly, and Steven Wilkinson. They were each generous beyond measure in engaging with the entire book, and collectively, they pushed me to think bigger and better. I will always be grateful that such brilliant minds took the time and care to help me improve this work.

Over the years, several colleagues read key chapters of the manuscript and provided me with comments on everything from the theory to research design to empirics. I thank Margaret (Molly) Ariotti, Elizabeth Carlson, Christopher Chambers-Ju, Danilo Antonio Contreras, Jennifer Cyr, Ursula Daxecker, Madhavi Devasher, Raheel Dhattiwala, Matthew Gichohi, Matt and Sona Golder, J. Andrew Harris, Lauren Honig, Elena Gadjanova, Franklin Knight, Stephanie McNulty, Shivaji Mukherjee, Steven Rosenzweig, James Piazza, M. Anne Pitcher, Laura Thaut Vinson, Megan Turnbull, Beth Elise Whitaker, and Vineeta Yadav for their constructive feedback. This book also benefited from the feedback of audiences and participants at the African Studies Association, American Political Science Association, International Studies Association, Midwest Political Science Association, the American Political Science Association Africa Workshop, the Devolution Workshop at the Institut français de recherche en Afrique, and the Southwest Workshop on Mixed Methods Research. Chats with Erik Cleven proved especially fruitful in informing my organization of the literature as presented in Chapter 1. In addition, I must acknowledge Adrienne LeBas who has probably seen as many iterations of this project as I have, and has somehow responded to each version with a level of clarity that has always pushed me to strengthen my work. Likewise, Kim Yi Dionne championed this research from its early days. She also provided unparalleled advice – oftentimes getting on the phone with me at short notice – on how to navigate book publishing as a first-time author. In so doing, she demystified many processes that often felt overwhelming. I also gratefully acknowledge conversations with Kathleen Klaus, Susanne Mueller, Irfan Nooruddin, and Ken Opalo – all of which helped me to shape the main claims presented in these pages. Finally, Ashutosh Varshney's encouragement provided me with much assurance about several core elements of my work.

Parts of Chapters 4–7 previously appeared in *Commonwealth & Comparative Politics* and *Politics, Groups, & Identities*. The complete citations for these articles are: Malik, Aditi. 2018. "Constitutional Reform and New Patterns of Electoral Violence: Evidence from Kenya's 2013 Elections," *Commonwealth & Comparative Politics* 56(3): 340–359 and Malik, Aditi. 2021. "Hindu-Muslim Violence in Unexpected Places: Theory and Evidence from Rural India," *Politics, Groups, & Identities* 9(1): 40–58. Information from these articles is reprinted here with the permission of the publisher (Taylor & Francis Ltd., www.tandfonline.com). I am also deeply grateful to Rachel Blaifeder, Jadyn Fauconier-Herry, and Becky Jackaman at Cambridge University Press for their outstanding efforts on my behalf, and to Tahir Carl Karmali for providing me with a cover image that so seamlessly captured the central ideas I sought to communicate through this book. Three anonymous reviewers offered tremendous feedback on this work, and the expertise and remarkable editorial eye of Sarah Watkins helped me to transform the book in more ways than I can count. Finally, Kelsey Rydland provided vital GIS support to produce the maps included in these pages.

The list of acknowledgments presented here would be woefully incomplete if I did not give thanks to my other undergraduate mentors at F&M who shaped my worldview at an early and formative age. To Simon Hawkins and Michael Penn: thank you for showing me the intrinsic value in thinking and learning about the world. You personify the very best of what a liberal arts education offers to young minds, and I am eternally grateful for your mentorship and kindness.

The F&M community and I lost Stanley Michalak and Michael Billig while this manuscript was undergoing revisions. Along with Susan, Stanley and Michael played pivotal roles in my decision to go to graduate school. As the advisor to my senior thesis project, Stanley picked up on the fact that I was interested in studying political violence, and encouraged me for many months to pursue this goal. As an anthropologist and someone who knew my love for fieldwork – of which I had experienced a small taste due to F&M's remarkable support for undergraduate scholarship – Michael reassured me that I could become a political scientist and still prioritize field research. If it had not been for them discussing different graduate school programs with me – and helping me figure out everything from financial assistance packages to immigration formalities – I know I would have never found my way to Northwestern University. Stanley and Michael also steadfastly stood by me long after I left Lancaster and cheered me on during graduate school and the academic job market. Their influence is in every one of these pages (except any bad ones, of course), and I could not have done any of this without them.

At Holy Cross, Faisal Baluch, Sahar Bazzaz, Shreyashi Chakdar, Nancy Loyd Boyd, Vickie Langohr, Maria Rodrigues, and Ward Thomas have all been incredibly encouraging as I worked on this book for several years. I am also grateful for the support that I received from Daniel Klinghard, Ann Marie

Acknowledgments

Leshkowich, and Lorelle Semley, who each pored over reviewer reports and helped me think through where I wanted to take the project. Finally, none of this would have been possible without some of my favorite people: Alo Basu, Nadine Knight, Archana Parajuli, and Sanjog Rupakheti. In each of you, I have found an extraordinary group of friends and colleagues who I now consider family. Thank you for everything you do and for being all that you are.

I am also incredibly blessed to have a wonderful and fabulous group of women friends whose support and solidarity over the years have meant more than I can say. To Mallika Dua, Gözde Erdeniz, Alisa Kaplan, Khairunnisa Mohamedali, Keri Wong, and Nurjuanis Zara Zainuddin: thank you for always having my back. Gözde and Alisa, the friendships that I share with each of you – clocking in at well over a decade at this point – are truly the most amazing examples of sisterhood. I cannot thank you enough for all your support. To Srishti Nayak and Mrinalini Ranjan: the two of you deserve much praise for hearing me catastrophize about this manuscript on repeated occasions, and for never letting me lose faith that I would get it done one day. Our (crazy) WhatsApp group has been such a lifeline for me over the last few years; may it always be just as ridiculous!

I also thank Shamma Adeeb Alam, Rohan Arora, Elizabeth Baber, Dwai Banerjee, Anupam and Ranu Basu, Amiya Bhatia, Tarila Ebiede, Siddhartan Govindasamy, Moses Khisa, Jamie Merchant, Chaitanya Murti, Umer Piracha, Apekshya Prasai, Zain Rehman, Jeff Rice, Maxwell Ross, Shambhavi Tannir, Swati Sood Varma, Désirée Weber, and Cori Wielenga for providing much encouragement over many years and at several critical junctures. Avinash Uttamchandani expressed more enthusiasm for this book than I could humanly muster in the final phases, and for that I will always be deeply grateful. Thank you for being the shining, magical person you are, Avi. You brighten up so much of my world. In addition, I must acknowledge Tanmay Misra, with whom I first crossed paths in Kigali in 2010, and who has been a constant source of support ever since. Our friendship has thrived despite multiple moves – to and across different continents on both our parts – and grown richer every year. Tanmay, I am so excited to have you back in the U.S., and I look forward to many *gupshup* sessions in Boston, D.C., Delhi, and beyond!

On a personal note, my uncle and aunt – Sachin Malhan and Maria Clara Pinheiro – deserve a special mention in these pages for providing me with good food, many laughs, and countless pep talks to complete this project. Likewise, members of my extended family in North America have been crucial prongs of my support system over the last few years. In Boston, Sarita Kumar; Dr. Meenakshi Kumar and Neel Kumar; Dr. Vikram Sheel Kumar, Shweta Bagai, Kabir Kumar, and Meera Kumar have kept me grounded in community. In Toronto, Dr. Anupam Malik and Pradeep Malik opened their home to me during one frightfully unproductive summer and reminded me of the importance of self-care. I now know that this book would never have seen the light of day without all of their generosity and love.

Most importantly, completing this work would have been impossible without the unfailing support of my immediate family. My parents, Ashwin and Shuchi Malik, were tireless cheerleaders who consistently told me that I would someday submit the manuscript for publication even when I was overcome with grave doubts. My father is so many wonderful things all wrapped up in one: a sounding board for my ideas, proofreader extraordinaire, and the most progressive man I know. *Papa*, although you concealed it well, I know that the topic of this research and the associated fieldwork often left you feeling rather nervous. Yet, you never failed to support me and validate that my work matters. Indeed, without our frequent discussions about politics at the dining table, I know I would have never gone down this path. Thank you for instilling in me a thirst to explore and learn about the world. Thank you, also, for being the only member of our family who somehow manages to keep abreast of precisely what I am studying even as I insist on trotting around from one research setting to another.

Ma, thank you for always putting up with my moods. Your calming voice has helped me to maintain perspective during many stressful periods in life, but it was especially grounding when what was meant to be a short trip to India turned into five months of being locked down in Delhi during a pandemic. Despite the sheer tumult of those months and the many, many visa woes, there is remarkably a silver lining that marks my early to mid-2020: that is, all the quality time that I got to spend with you. Thank you for anchoring me, for ensuring that I put the laptop away at the end of the day, and for preparing copious amounts of *bhel puri* for me. Your care and love made pandemic writing a lot more tolerable. You are so the best!

My sister, Smiti Malik, and brother-in-law, Adhir Ghosh, provided levity and encouragement in equal measure throughout the lengthy writing and revision process. Smiti, in case you don't already know this (but also how could you not?), I consider it my greatest blessing in life to have you as a sibling. No one I know is able to extend as much empathy and understanding to others as you are, and coupled with your boundless wisdom, you somehow managed to see your eccentric *behena* through the significant emotional vagaries that accompanied this project – from its conception to completion. Thank you, also, to both you and BIL for all the beautiful music, and for keeping our family steeped in the arts. We could all use more art and wonder in our lives, and the two of you provide it in abundance.

This book is dedicated to my four extraordinary grandparents, who have left the greatest imprint on my life, and without whom nothing about the world would have ever made sense. My maternal grandfather, or *Nanu*, Mr. Kulbhushan Vohra spent much of his youth in Kashmir. When I was growing up, he shared many tales with me about Kashmir's beauty, its history, and its people, and thus ignited my perpetual fascination with the study of politics. He also patiently endeavored (and then gracefully gave up) on teaching me how to write in Urdu. But he never gave up on my other academic goals. Indeed, to

Acknowledgments

this day, *Nanu* somehow manages to locate and read every piece of scholarship I produce. I don't know how he does it, but I do know why: it's because of his immense love for his granddaughter, and I care about him just as much.

Nanu spent many decades of his life in an amazing partnership with my beloved *Nani*, the late Mrs. Urmila Vohra. *Nani* taught me so many things, but most fundamentally she showed me the value of education and the power of unconditional love. A beacon of strength, kindness, and grace, she took immense pride in my curiosity and intellectual development, even when I insisted on violating social norms and reading books at the dining table during family meals. Such behavior inevitably resulted in raised eyebrows and stern words from almost everyone else, but being an educator, my grandmother always spoke up for me in her own inimitable manner. I carry you in my heart, *Nani Ma*, and I miss you more than words can convey.

My wonderful maternal grandparents were matched by an equally incredible pair of paternal grandparents. My venerable paternal grandfather, or *Dada Ji*, the late and great Brigadier Shiv Charan Lal Malik expressed unwavering faith in me when I embarked on a PhD – something that I was woefully naïve about – at the age of 22. *Dada* and his family survived the Partition and left Sargodha, Pakistan with few material possessions. After resettling in Delhi, my grandfather rebuilt his life from scratch. And despite all the struggles that came his way, he never lost his grip on gratitude or his unyielding belief – one that he reiterated to all his grandkids countless times – that life's challenges have a way of working themselves out. *Dada*, no one I know better personifies what living a life of meaning entails. I think of you every single day.

Finally, my feisty *Dadi*, the late Mrs. Uma Malik, was a source of constant joy and laughter. She regularly teased *Dada* about the superiority of her hometown – cultured Lahore, as she put it – over my grandfather's humbler beginnings in Sargodha. Along with this, *Dadi* also claimed for years that my love for writing came from her. She was likely correct, as she was about so many things. But it is no less true that my work is not a patch on hers. Indeed, my *Dadi's* writing, her musical gifts, and her sense of style were all unparalleled. I spent countless afternoons with her on her balcony listening to her poems and short stories, completely awestruck by her ability to make magic through words. I can only hope that she derives some pride from the fact that after toiling for many, many years, her *poti* finally managed to do some writing as well. I miss you so very much, *Dadi*. There will never be anyone quite like you.

The four of you will always be my greatest role models. This book is for you.

Abbreviations

BULGARIA

NSDV	National Movement Simeon II

GHANA

CDD	Center for Democratic Development
NDC	National Democratic Congress
NDP	National Democratic Party
NPP	National People's Party

INDIA

ADM	Additional District Magistrate
AIMIM/MIM	All India Majlis-e-Ittehad'ul Muslimeen/Majlis-e-Ittehad'ul Muslimeen
AP	Andhra Pradesh
BJP	Bharatiya Janata Party
BJS	Bharatiya Jana Sangh
BSP	Bahujan Samaj Party
CM	Chief Minister
COVA	Confederation of Voluntary Associations
CPI	Communist Party of India
CSDS	Center for the Study of Developing Societies
CSP	Congress Socialist Party
ECI	Election Commission of India
INC	Indian National Congress
INC(I)	Indian National Congress (Indira)/Indian National Congress(I)

INC(U)	Indian National Congress (Urs)/Indian National Congress(U)
IPC	Indian Penal Code
JD	Janata Dal
JP	Janata Party
LKD	Lok Dal
MCC	Mandal Congress Committee
ML	Muslim League
MLA	Member of Legislative Assembly
OBC	Other Backward Class
PAC	Provincial Armed Constabulary
PM	Prime Minister
RSS	Rashtriya Swayamsevak Sangh
SC	Scheduled Caste
SIT	Special Investigation Team
SP	Samajwadi Party
SP	Superintendent of Police
SSP	Senior Superintendent of Police
ST	Scheduled Tribe
TDP	Telugu Desam Party
VHP	Vishwa Hindu Parishad

KENYA

ACK	Anglican Church of Kenya
CCM	Chama Cha Mwananchi
CIPEV	Commission of Inquiry on Post-Election Violence
CORD	Coalition for Reforms and Democracy
CRA	Commission on Revenue Allocation
DC	District Commissioner
DP	Democratic Party
DPC	District Peace Committee
FORD-A	Forum for the Restoration of Democracy-Asili/FORD-Asili
IPK	Islamic Party of Kenya
ISA	Internal Security Apparatus
JP	Jubilee Party
KADU	Kenyan African Democratic Union
KANU	Kenyan African National Union
KAU	Kenya African Union
KCA	Kikuyu Central Association
KED	Kenya Election Database
KHRC	Kenya Human Rights Commission
KNCHR	Kenya National Commission on Human Rights
KPU	Kenya People's Union
KVED	Kenya Violent Elections Dataset

List of Abbreviations

LDP	Liberal Democratic Party
LSK	Law Society of Kenya
NAMLEF	National Muslim Leaders Forum
NaRC	National Rainbow Coalition
NaRC-K	National Rainbow Coalition-Kenya
NASA	National Super Alliance
NCCK	National Council of Churches of Kenya
NCIC	National Cohesion and Integration Commission
ODM	Orange Democratic Movement
ODM-K	Orange Democratic Movement-Kenya
PA	Provincial Administration
PC	Provincial Commissioner
PCEA	Presbyterian Church of East Africa
PNU	Party of National Unity
SDP	Social Democratic Party
SPK	Shirikisho Party
TNA	The National Alliance
UDFP	United Democratic Forum Party
URP	United Republican Party
WDM-K	Wiper Democratic Movement-Kenya
YK '92	Youth for KANU '92
YKA	Young Kavirondo Association

TURKEY

AKP	Adalet ve Kalkınma Partisi/Justice and Development Party
ANAP	Motherland Party
AP/JP	Adalet Partisi/Justice Party
CHP	Cumhuriyet Halk Partisi/Republican People's Party
DEV-YOL	Revolutionary Way
DP	Demokrat Parti/Democratic Party
DYP	Doğru Yol Partisi/Truth Power Party
GKK	Provisional Village Guard
HP	Populist Party
MHP/NAP	Milliyetçi Hareket Partisi/Nationalist Movement Party
MLSPB	Marxist-Leninist Armed Propaganda Union
MNP/NOP	Millî Nizam Partisi/National Order Party
MSP	Millî Selâmet Partisi/National Salvation Party
NDP	National Democratic Party
PKK	Kurdistan Workers' Party
THKO	Turkish People's Liberation Army
THKO-C	Turkish People's Liberation Party-Front
TIKKO	Turkish Worker Peasant Liberation Party
TSK	Türk Silahlı Kuvvetleri/Turkish Armed Forces

LATIN AMERICA

APRA	American Popular Revolutionary Alliance (Peru)
FREDEMO	Frente Democrático/Democratic Front (Peru)
MBL	Movimiento Bolivia Libre/Free Bolivia Movement (Bolivia)
MNR	Movimiento Nacionalista Revolucionario/Revolutionary Nationalist Movement (Bolivia)
NFR	Nueva Fuerza Republicana/New Republican Force (Bolivia)
NUF	Frente de Unidad Nacional/National Unity Front (Bolivia)

SOUTH ASIA

CPN-M	Communist Party of Nepal-Maoist (Nepal)
CPN-UC	Communist Party of Nepal-Unity Centre (Nepal)

MISCELLANEOUS

ACLED	Armed Conflict Location and Event Dataset
CAS	Comparative Area Studies
CSO	Civil Society Organization
ICC	International Criminal Court
IDP	Internally Displaced Person
IPU Parline	Inter-Parliamentary Union Parliaments Online
IRB	Institutional Review Board
MP	Member of Parliament
NGO	Non-Governmental Organization
PGM	Pro-Government Militia
PO	Party Organization
PR	Proportional Representation
PS	Party Strength
SCAD	Social Conflict Analysis Database
V-Dem	Varieties of Democracy

1

Parties and Political Violence

TANA RIVER COUNTY, COAST PROVINCE, KENYA,
AUGUST 2012–FEBRUARY 2013

In August 2012, deadly communal clashes broke out between the pastoral Orma and agricultural Pokomo communities in Kenya's coastal Tana River County. The violence continued intermittently, in two waves, until January 2013, and resulted in the deaths of more than 180 individuals and the displacement of over 34,000 others (Human Rights Watch 2013a). Orma pastoralists together with herders from the Wardei community carried out the initial round of attacks in August and September. Subsequently, the Pokomos responded with a series of counterattacks in December and January.

In the wake of the clashes in Tana River, Kenyans expressed frustration and worry about the possibility of conflict around the upcoming March 2013 elections.[1] Their frustration emanated from the fact that after many fits and starts, the country had promulgated a new constitution in response to the devastating post-election violence of 2007–2008. This crisis had claimed the lives of over 1,100 individuals and resulted in the displacement of countless others. To lower the electoral stakes, the new constitution had replaced Kenya's largely unitary form of government with a devolved county system.[2] It had also altered the threshold for winning the presidency from a plurality to a simple majority: in addition to garnering more than 50% of the national vote, the triumphant candidate was now required to amass at least 25% of the votes cast in more than half of the country's 47 counties. Furthermore, all coalitions

---
[1] Interview with a human rights activist, Nairobi, February 2, 2013; interview with a human rights activist, Nairobi, February 4, 2013.
[2] Although provinces and districts formally existed prior to this time, power in pre-devolution Kenya was mainly concentrated in the presidency.

were now required to formally register themselves three months prior to the presidential poll.

Beyond these reforms, Kenyan authorities had appointed "prominent human rights activist Willy Mutunga as Chief Justice in 2011, vet[ted] judges in 2012, and establish[ed] a new electoral commission in 2011" (Lynch 2018: 35). Consequently, many citizens had approached the 2013 polls with greater confidence in important institutions (Lynch 2018) and with hope that the country might avoid severe violence. As an opposition stronghold, the Coast, in particular, was expected to maintain communal harmony. Yet not only did grave interethnic clashes break out in Tana River, but observers and experts alike agreed that local politicians had deliberately orchestrated the violence as a strategy to win votes in the upcoming county-level contests (Kenya National Commission on Human Rights 2012; Republic of Kenya 2013).[3]

The violence in Tana River, while lethal and destructive, proved to be politically effective, as Orma and Wardei candidates claimed all elected positions in the county-level elections, including the high-stakes governorship (Malik 2018). This was a historic change in electoral fortunes, as Pokomos had long held political power in the region (Pattison 2011; Kirchner 2013). Moreover, the elites who contributed to the 2012–2013 clashes either escaped without serious consequences, or worse, actually ascended to political office as a result of the violence.

Following the first wave of clashes, Dhadho Godhana, a Pokomo Member of Parliament (MP) from one of Tana River's parliamentary constituencies, was charged with inciting violence. However, by January 2013, all charges against him were dropped (Malik 2020). His rival, Yusuf Haji, was serving as the Internal Security Minister at the time. Haji was widely believed to have deployed militias and instrumentalized clashes to help an Orma candidate, Hussein Dado, win the gubernatorial seat (Ndonga 2012; Malik 2020). Due in part to the massive displacement of Pokomos from the area, Dado went on to win the mayoral position. Meanwhile, Haji secured the post of Senator from Garissa County in northeastern Kenya.

While journalists both inside and outside the country interpreted these results as evidence of widespread and continuing impunity (Ochami 2012; Al Jazeera 2013), the government established an official Commission, known as the Judicial Commission of Inquiry into Inter-Communal Violence in the Tana Delta, to investigate the clashes. However, the abduction of the Commission's Chair just days before it was due to submit its final report in January 2013 generated grave concerns about political interference with its work (Lynch 2018). Ultimately, the Commission only submitted its report on February 4.

---

[3] Interview with an academic, Nairobi, January 29, 2013; interview with a human rights activist, Nairobi, February 2, 2013; interview with a religious leader, Mombasa, October 4, 2013; interview with a TNA politician, Nairobi, October 17, 2013.

MUZAFFARNAGAR AND SHAMLI DISTRICTS, UTTAR PRADESH, INDIA, AUGUST 2013–MAY 2014

In early September 2013, Hindu–Muslim riots exploded across several villages in India's Muzaffarnagar and Shamli districts in the state of Uttar Pradesh (UP). These riots – the worst in the country since the Gujarat pogrom of 2002 – claimed the lives of over 60 individuals, mainly Muslims (Jain 2013). The violence emanated, in part, from the failure of the ruling Samajwadi Party (SP) to expeditiously control the situation, and became part of a longer SP record to tolerate and even oversee communal polarization in UP (Kirpal 2013; Unnithan 2013). As Saba Naqvi (2013) chronicles, since March 2012, at least "34 [Hindu-Muslim] clashes" had afflicted the state "in [the first] 16 months" of Chief Minister Akhilesh Yadav's regime.

Importantly, however, in the case of Muzaffarnagar and Shamli, the SP was not the only party that contributed to violence. Instead, both the Hindu nationalist Bharatiya Janata Party (BJP) and the Bahujan Samaj Party (BSP) actively "flare[d] up communal sentiments" as well.[4] In late August and early September, politicians from these parties organized two large *mahapanchayat* (grand village council) meetings at which they elevated communal matters. Whereas the BJP sought to bring attention to the task of "protecting Hindu women" from Muslims, BSP leaders emphasized biases in the criminal justice system that routinely resulted in the targeting of members of the minority community (Kirpal 2013). As existing research has shown, these meetings – for which local administrators had explicitly denied the organizers permission – nevertheless drew countless residents from Muzaffarnagar and the surrounding districts, and became critical precursors to the September riots (Pai and Kumar 2018; Malik 2021).

Despite the fact that multiple political parties tacitly and actively contributed to the riots, according to experts and observers alike, the BJP was the main provocateur of the violence. In fact, extant evidence reveals that for more than a year before these events, "local BJP leaders [had been] active in the rural parts of [Muzaffarnagar] district on a day-to-day basis" (Pai and Kumar 2018: 230). As part of their activities, they had politicized several local incidents to create a communally charged atmosphere. And yet, once the Muzaffarnagar and Shamli riots actually occurred, it was the BJP and only the BJP that benefited from this violence. In the 2014 general elections, the party amassed 71 out of 80 seats in UP, including the parliamentary seat from Muzaffarnagar constituency. In so doing, it bettered its 2009 performance by a whopping 61 seats. Meanwhile, the SP suffered a loss of 18 seats and the BSP failed to secure even a single seat in UP.

---

[4] Interview with an INC party leader, Muzaffarnagar, December 21, 2015; also see Kirpal 2013; Malik 2021.

THE PUZZLING PHENOMENON OF PARTY VIOLENCE

These events from Kenya and India raise important questions for the study of political violence. Why did elite involvement in devastating periods of conflict generate rich dividends for politicians in Tana River and BJP leaders in UP, but engender significant electoral costs for BSP and SP leaders? Furthermore, what can the above examples tell us more broadly about the costs and benefits of using parties as vehicles for conflict?

This book addresses these questions by examining the puzzling phenomenon of party violence. Despite the vital role that parties play in the healthy functioning of democracies, a small but growing literature shows that political parties and the elites who comprise them often engage in violence (Fjelde 2020; Staniland 2021; Siddiqui 2022). There is also much variation across space and over time in parties' involvement in conflict. In places such as Russia (Frye, Reuter, and Szakonzyi 2019) and many countries in Africa (Bekoe and Burchard 2017; Rauschenbach and Paula 2019), for example, voter intimidation has been a common form of party violence. Meanwhile, Pakistan and Guatemala have witnessed several assassinations of political rivals at the commands of party elites and their affiliates. Finally, as Niloufer Siddiqui (2022: 3) describes, parties have also contributed to violence by "ally[ing] with violent nonstate actors," as in Nigeria and "us[ing] state forces to carry out violence," as seen in Cambodia (Un 2019).

This book uses the terms *party-based violence* or *party-based conflicts* to refer to incidents of political violence in which politicians and political leaders use parties to directly organize or foment conflict. Such fomentation can take the form of elites publicly othering ethnic minorities as part of their party platforms, as seen among leaders of the extremist Serb Democratic Party in the former Yugoslavia (Maksić 2015), or exhorting partisan supporters to challenge and disrupt government procedures, as seen in the case of the January 2021 attack on the Capitol in the United States. I use the terms *party-sponsored violence* or *party-sponsored conflicts* for events in which party politics indirectly contribute to conflict. Elite sponsorship of such violence can involve outsourcing conflict to armed groups, as witnessed under the regime of Jean Bertrand Aristide of Haiti between 2001 and 2004 (Schubert 2015), or using gangs to assassinate or eliminate political rivals as seen in Indonesia (Tajima 2018).[5]

To date, many of our richest insights about party violence have come from the study of *electoral violence* (Kriger 2005; Shah 2012; Straus and Taylor 2012; Bob-Milliar 2014; Travaglianti 2014; Burchard 2015; Birch 2020;

---

[5] Recent research suggests that party-sponsored violence is far more common than party-based violence due to strong motivations on the parts of political elites to "obscure their role[s]" in political conflict (Birch 2020: 42). However, major events of party violence often involve both direct instrumentalization as well as outsourcing, and the empirical chapters shed light on the combination of these strategies in Kenya and India.

Klaus 2020; Rosenzweig 2023). In defining this phenomenon, some scholars have specified time periods within which violent events can be considered election-related. For example, according to Straus and Taylor (2012), violent events that occur six months before or three months after an election are incidents of electoral violence. Meanwhile, other scholars have cautioned that delineating these "bounded time frame[s]" is an arbitrary exercise (Klaus 2020: 11). These researchers have thus laid much more emphasis on election violence as a *process*. According to Sarah Birch, Ursula Daxecker, and Kristine Höglund (2020: 4), for instance, electoral violence is a strategy of political actors "to purposefully influence the process and outcome of elections" through "coercive acts against humans, property, and infrastructure."

Scholars of election-related violence have further illuminated a vast variety of forms as well as differing political logics that underpin such conflict. Studies of interparty clashes in both competitive (Okpu 1985) and dominant party systems (Wahman and Goldring 2020) – such as Nigeria and Zambia, respectively – have shown that such violence is primarily used to weaken the position, and limit the reach, of rival parties. Meanwhile, intraparty conflict, as seen in Venezuela (Coppedge 1993; Martz 1999) and Malawi (Seeberg and Wahman 2019), is typically used to influence the results of party primaries and nominations.

In addition to investigating inter- and intraparty violence, researchers have also studied the logics and contours of ethnic electoral conflict in many multiethnic societies. In India, for example, Steven Wilkinson (2004) has persuasively shown that communal riots – which disproportionately target Muslims and often occur around elections – are a strategy through which political elites seek to unite Hindus across caste lines. By contrast, studies of intraethnic electoral violence in places such as Burundi (Travaglianti 2014) and Sri Lanka (Shah 2012) have demonstrated that the purpose of such violence is to demobilize co-ethnic opposition candidates and coerce the support of co-ethnic voters.

Finally, the literature on election violence has helped to illuminate a number of institutional and socioeconomic variables that are associated with such violence. In the African context, for example, researchers have found that election-related conflict is more likely to occur in plurality or majoritarian electoral settings (Burchard 2015; Fjelde and Höglund 2016; Müller-Crepon 2022) and in places where an incumbent presidential candidate is running for reelection (Taylor, Pevehouse, and Straus 2017). Meanwhile, research from India has demonstrated that socioeconomic inequality – particularly high within-group inequality and low between-group inequality – can help to account for the outbreak of ethnic riots, which are often tied to elections (Bulutgil and Prasad 2023). According to Bulutgil and Prasad (2023: 630), this particular combination of inequality is associated with riots because it creates incentives for ethnonationalist elites to "reinforce the significance of ethnicity" as a means to weaken cross-ethnic coalitions.

Even as the growing scholarship on election violence has expanded to account for many different aspects of this phenomenon – from its varying forms to the institutional configurations that enable its instrumentalization – researchers have agreed that elites play a critical role in such conflict. As Kathleen Klaus (2020: 2) writes, for electoral violence to emerge, "elites must have an incentive to use violence." Similarly, Steven Rosenzweig (2023: 6) observes that "the most significant outbreaks of election-related violence tend to result from the maneuverings of political elites." Yet the place of *parties* themselves in the process of conflict production remains undertheorized with different scholars taking different approaches to locating parties in violent political events. Indeed, whereas some studies show that high levels of interparty competition incentivize politicians to engage in violence (Wilkinson 2004; Dhattiwala and Biggs 2012), others emphasize the role of "weak" party structures as enablers of electoral conflict (Mehler 2007; Mueller 2008; Höglund 2009; Wanyama and Elkit 2018).

These insights, while valuable, only tangentially contribute to interrogations of *party violence*.[6] After all, electoral violence is merely one form of conflict in which parties might become involved, and extant research has shed some light on other modalities of conflict in which parties feature as key actors. These modalities range from developing and sponsoring informal militias for counterinsurgency operations during civil wars (Peic 2014; Ahram 2016; Biberman 2018) to crafting and maintaining links with vigilante groups that then carry out anti-minority attacks at the behest, or at least with the knowledge, of members of majoritarian parties (Pai and Kumar 2018; Jaffrey 2021). Despite the emerging attention that scholars have started to pay to parties as key actors in political violence, it is also true that there are inherent difficulties involved in "go[ing] within," or opening up the black box, of party politics (Siddiqui 2022: 7). As a result, there is still much that we do not yet understand about when, how, and why elites can make use of political parties as instruments for conflict.

CENTRAL ARGUMENTS AND SCOPE CONDITIONS

Drawing on in-depth research on *ethnic* party violence in Kenya and India, this book proffers a systematic accounting of party violence. My emphasis herein is on the *supply* of violence, and my goal is to contribute to a growing instrumentalist literature on political conflict. This literature has persuasively shown that many forms of violence – including civil wars (Kalyvas 2006) and election-related conflict (Wilkinson 2004; Fjelde and Höglund 2016; Birch 2020) – hinge on the incentives and actions of politicians. By focusing closely on party violence, I aim to explain when and why politicians use parties to organize or sponsor violence, taking into account both the benefits and costs of this choice.

---

[6] Recent work by Hanne Fjelde (2020) and Niloufer Siddiqui (2022) are important exceptions here.

The central argument of the book is that *party instability* can crucially condition elites' decisions about supplying party violence as well as the scale at which to do so. In places where political leaders expect their parties to endure from one election to the next, longer time horizons and attendant fears of future sanctioning – particularly from voters – can disincentivize politicians from organizing or sponsoring conflict. Should political leaders choose to instrumentalize violence in stable party settings, I thus posit that they will usually do so at mild levels. By contrast, in places where parties are transient and fleeting, I argue that truncated time horizons will enable political elites to discount the possibility of incurring future punishment from voters, and thereby incentivize engagement with violence in the present. These truncated time horizons could also make it possible for politicians to repeatedly orchestrate major episodes of conflict.

The scope of these arguments extends to places where the rule of law is weak enough such that politicians can conceivably get away with using their parties as vehicles for violence. This is because I expect that "the real threat of legal penalty and/or social sanction" for violence will be sufficiently high in places where "accountability institutions are strong" (Birch 2020: 31). I thus argue that elites will face powerful incentives against organizing or sponsoring violence in places with strong accountability institutions. Put differently, my analysis *does not apply* to places where a robust rule of law and strong domestic legal systems might hold politicians to account for attempting or engaging in violent pursuits.

EXISTING LITERATURE

In developing and substantiating these arguments, I situate my claims in a vast body of work in comparative politics that has generated important insights about the conditions under which elite-driven ethnic violence can emerge. This scholarship includes studies of electoral violence (Wilkinson 2004; Müller-Crepon 2022) as well as research on communal war (Krause 2018). In the pages that follow, I discuss and organize existing studies into three broad, though overlapping, strands pertaining to the mobilization and restraint of violence, as well as scholarship on how and when divisive elite messaging resonates with ordinary individuals.

Theories of Mobilization

Researchers focused on mobilization have primarily sought to address the question of when and how ordinary individuals become involved in conflict. These scholars recognize that such involvement originates from elite provocations. Yet they also point out that not all elite provocations result in violence, and that even those that do often display varying logics and dynamics. How can we account for such variations?

Based on his extensive work on Hindu–Muslim riots in India, Paul Brass (1997, 2003b: xv) writes that an "institutionalized riot system" is "a central factor in the production" of violence. He holds that places marked by active riot systems are those where citizens are routinely persuaded to participate in conflict. This is because members of these systems – politicians, local administrators, vernacular journalists, and violence specialists – are able to give communal color to otherwise quotidian incidents, "mobilize crowds to threaten or intimidate persons from the other community," and more generally "let loose widespread violent action" (Brass 2003b: 258). In other words, Brass (2003b: 32) argues that ordinary citizens engage in violence when specialized members of the local riot system successfully exaggerate "a trivial, everyday incident" and place it into a "communal system of talk."

Also working on the topic of riots in India, Ward Berenschot (2011a, 2011b, 2011c) has emphasized the centrality of local patronage networks in spurring ordinary individuals to participate in violence. Based on neighborhood-level comparisons and ethnographic research conducted in Ahmedabad, Gujarat, Berenschot finds that citizens are most likely to respond to elites' calls for violence in places where "the[ir] dependency on local patronage channels is particularly intense" (Berenschot 2011b: 11). This is because working within these networks can offer residents access to scarce resources, including employment opportunities. For Berenschot (2011b: 11), then, riot production does not necessarily hinge on "institutionalized riot systems" or networks created for "the specific purpose of fomenting violence," but is shaped more proximately by "the difficulties that citizens face when dealing with state institutions" in India.

Moving beyond these qualitative insights, recent cross-national analyses of events of urban election-related violence in the Global South have shown that organized and unorganized actors contribute to such incidents in different ways (Thomson, Buhaug, Urdal, and Rosvold 2021). Even as the rates of urban social disorder have increased since the 1960s and elections have emerged as key focal points for these disturbances, researchers have found that different actors – organized and unorganized ones, respectively – play roles in pre-election versus post-election urban unrest (Thomson, Buhaug, Urdal, and Rosvold 2021). They further note that the involvement of organized groups such as parties and labor unions in events of election-related conflict is related to the fact that these actors are better equipped to assess the costs and benefits of such violence than their less organized counterparts. At the same time, organized actors possess "the organizational capacity to strategically ... mobilize supporters in demonstrations, rallies, canvassing, and other activities before voting" (Thomson, Buhaug, Urdal, and Rosvold 2021: 1528). In sum, this new research shows that there are distinct advantages with regard to both risk assessment and collective action that help to account for the primacy of organized groups as key mobilizers of election-related conflict in the Global South.

Theories of Restraint

Where theories of mobilization have sought to explain the conditions under which ordinary people will engage in violence, theories of restraint have focused more squarely on the ways in which conflict might be prevented or contained. In addressing this important matter, scholars have illuminated the roles of various kinds of leaders and elites, as well as the place of civilians in de-escalating violence.

For Steven Wilkinson (2004: 5), "whether violence is bloody or ends quickly depends ... primarily on the will and capacity of the government that controls the forces of law and order." In the Indian federation, Wilkinson documents that state governments control these forces. He thus argues that Hindu–Muslim riots will be contained when state-level politicians have the incentives to do so. These incentives are present "when minorities [i.e., Muslims] are an important part of the [ruling] party's current support base, or the support base of one of [its] coalition partners in a coalition government; or when the overall electoral system in a state is so competitive – in terms of the effect number of parties – that there is therefore a high probability that the governing party will have to negotiate or form coalitions with minority supported parties in the future, despite its own preferences" (Wilkinson 2004: 6–7).

Departing from theories that are anchored at the state level, Ashutosh Varshney (2002) suggests that city-level factors most proximately account for the containment of riot violence in India. His work specifically emphasizes the importance of interethnic civic associations in "polic[ing] neighborhoods, kill[ing] rumors, provid[ing] information to the local administration, and facilitat[ing] communication" between Hindus and Muslims in times of tension (Varshney 2001: 375). Where the production of violence thus turns on the activities of "institutionalized riot systems" for Brass, Varshney (2001: 378) holds that the maintenance of peace depends on the work of interethnic civic associations as constituents of "institutionalized peace systems."

Building on these insights, recent work has advocated for bridging the divide "between civil society and electoral incentives as the principal means" for preventing ethnic violence (Malik and Prasad 2022: 183). Research in this vein has thus emphasized the importance of "intentional state-society network[s]" for controlling conflict (Malik and Prasad 2022: 184). In Bhagalpur, Bihar, for example, new work has revealed that since the town's devastating 1989 riots, civil society leaders' connections with the state have helped them to resolve citizens' everyday problems and boosted their reputational capital such that residents have actually listened to appeals for peace during moments of tension (Malik and Prasad 2022). At the same time, working with trusted non-state actors has enabled state authorities to gather information necessary for defusing precipitating events over the last three decades.

Finally, research on the topic of communal war has shown that places within conflict zones that escape conflict-related violence are those where civilians successfully adapt and mitigate their vulnerability to violence through "continuous prevention efforts" (Krause 2018: 7). Communal war refers to "non-state armed conflict between social groups that results in casualty numbers that reach the civil war threshold" (Krause 2018: 6). Based on research on this topic in Jos, Nigeria, and Ambon, Indonesia, Jana Krause (2018: 51) has found that nonviolent or resilient communities emerged in those places where civilians exerted agency to "depolariz[e] ... social identities, establish social control within communities, and engage with external armed groups for negotiation and refusal to collaborate in attacks."

Linking Elite Provocations with Civilian Participation in Violence

In light of the considerable scholarship on the mobilization versus containment of ethnic and election-related violence, a number of recent studies have sought to provide clearer links between these two perspectives. These works ask: "how [do] the political objectives of elites interact with the motives and fears of ordinary citizens to shape the *process of mobilization* and *spaces of violent escalation?*" (Klaus 2020: 34).

As previously noted, cross-national evidence from Africa suggests that politicians will have stronger incentives – and find greater success in mobilizing citizens in violent conflict – under majoritarian electoral rules compared to proportional representation (PR) systems (Burchard 2015; Fjelde and Höglund 2016; Müller-Crepon 2022). Burchard (2015) holds that this is because of the winner-take-all nature of such contests as well as the relatively low thresholds for victory that plurality systems, in particular, demand. These low thresholds can render violence a tempting choice to influence electoral outcomes. At the same time, the fact that elections in such contexts create clear winners and losers can serve to persuade voters to respond to elites' calls for violence. In a related vein, Fjelde and Höglund (2016) argue that majoritarian voting rules are associated with higher electoral stakes and thereby incentivize the production of violence. Similarly, but squarely taking into account local ethnic demography and mobilization dynamics, Carl Müller-Crepon (2022) finds that ethnically polarized districts under majoritarian rules see substantively larger increases in the number of ethnic riots – as a specific form of electoral violence – than nonpolarized districts. He holds that this heightened increase is due to the fact that majoritarian rules mark the local level as the main arena of electoral competition. As a result, compared to nonpolarized districts, violent parties in polarized districts typically find greater success in mobilizing their supporters in pre-election riots. Importantly, such riots also help to demobilize those voters who are sympathetic to rival parties.

Beyond the focus on electoral institutions, scholars of inequality have demonstrated that ethnonationalist politicians have strong motives to organize riots in settings where cross-ethnic coalitions threaten their electoral prospects

Parties and Political Violence

(Bulutgil and Prasad 2023). Such coalitions are likely to emerge in contexts where within-group inequality is high and between-group inequality is low. Successfully mobilizing citizens in violence in these settings thus involves appealing to and reinforcing citizens' ethnic attachments over their class interests, as seen in the recent riots in Muzaffarnagar and Shamli.

In addition to the above studies, which rely on statistical data, a number of researchers have also brought qualitative insights to bear on the analytical task of linking elite provocations with civilians' participation in violence. According to Klaus, a scholar of electoral violence in Kenya, ordinary citizens come to participate in violence due to the mobilization of contentious land narratives. These narratives refer to "dynamic stories that help to define or reinforce a group's mode of identification and sense of entitlement, while serving as a strategic discourse for claiming or securing land" (Klaus 2020: 38). Klaus (2020: 7) further holds that "land narratives [act] as a mechanism linking inequality in tenure rights with the escalation of violence." In certain contexts, these narratives emerge as a "key device around which elites and citizens coordinate the use of violence" (Klaus 2020: 7). Simply put, then, contentious land narratives offer a frame through which violence becomes thinkable for ordinary individuals.

Other researchers, also working on the Kenyan case, have studied the interaction between elite tactics and civilians' engagement in violence by considering the role of the mass media, particularly vernacular radios. According to the scholarship of D. Ndirangu Wachanga (2011: 119, 122), these media outlets played a crucial part in both constructing "narratives of political and ethnic hatred" and imbuing these narratives with meaning such that they became a "rallying cry and a call to arms" for many listeners during the post-election crisis of 2007–2008. In a related vein, other scholars have shown that narratives of marginalization, victimization, and foreign occupation proved crucial in mobilizing citizens in violence during the crisis (Malik and Onguny 2020). These narratives, disseminated via vernacular radios, resonated most strongly with listeners when they "latched onto voters' pre-existing grievances against the government and/or their material incentives" to engage in conflict (Malik and Onguny 2020: 561).

Finally, and returning to his original emphasis on patronage networks, Ward Berenschot's (2020: 172) recent comparative and ethnographic scholarship from Gujarat, India, and North Maluku, Indonesia, has demonstrated that politicians succeeded in "fomenting violence in areas where citizens depend[ed] strongly on *ethnicized* patronage networks." By contrast, he finds that violence was averted in places "where state-citizen interaction was organized through networks that bridge ethnic divides" (Berenschot 2020: 172). Taken together, then, Berenschot (2020: 172; citing Horowitz 1985: 140) argues that by generating "both the infrastructure and incentives to organize violence," patronage networks resolve the question of "why followers follow."

EMERGING INSIGHTS ON PARTY VIOLENCE AND THE CONTRIBUTIONS OF THIS BOOK

As important as these accounts are, this book argues that they cannot fully account for elite decision-making about *party violence* because their emphasis is not on parties themselves. As Hanne Fjelde (2020: 152) documents, even in the "booming literature on electoral violence" and despite their central role in the "dynamics of electoral competition," political parties remain understudied in the broader literature on conflict. Similarly, Siddiqui (2022: 7) observes that "what is missing from our understanding of political violence is how parties themselves organize and structure violence."

There are, of course, notable methodological difficulties in studying party violence, particularly from the perspective of party leaders and workers. First, and as Andrea Ceron (2017: 7) describes, systematic interrogations of intra-party dynamics remain challenging because "assessing the preferences of politicians and party factions is [itself] a difficult task." Second, politicians have strong incentives to deny their roles in fomenting conflict, as such admissions could plausibly cost them their political positions.

Yet the lack of concerted attention paid to political parties in the scholarship on violence is significant because "parties and their movements are [key] transmission belts between individuals and political elites" (Fjelde 2020: 141). As previously discussed, recent research has also shown that parties hold distinct advantages in mobilizing urban election-related disturbances, partly because they are better able to assess the costs and benefits of this choice than less organized groups (Thomson, Buhaug, and Urdal, and Rosvold 2021). Taken together, then, it is now clear that violence in many different forms and across many different contexts cannot be adequately understood without directly incorporating parties and party elites into our frameworks. Given these developments, a few recent works – which are discussed below – have sought to squarely investigate the relationship between parties and conflict in different settings.

Based on research in Pakistan, Siddiqui (2022) has shown that three key factors – subnational incentives, costs, and organizational capacity – crucially influence the particular violence strategy that a party adopts. These strategies can take the form of direct involvement in conflict, outsourcing violence, forming electoral alliances with violent non-state actors, or refraining from violence altogether. In addition to capturing and accounting for different party strategies, Siddiqui's (2022: 8) framework is an important contribution to the study of party violence, as it "highlights the interaction between … parties, voters, violence specialists, and state actors" in the production of political conflict. A central insight of this work is that parties will directly mobilize violence when they face high incentives and low costs and possess strong organizational capacity. By contrast, when incentives are high, costs are low, and organizational capacity is also low, parties will outsource the organization of conflict to violence specialists. A key implication of this research is that parties operate as rational actors; they engage in direct or indirect strategies of violence when they face low costs for doing so.

In a similar vein, Daxecker and Rausenbach's (2023) study of subnational pre-election violence in Zimbabwe finds that parties and political leaders pay close attention to the costs and benefits of conflict when making decisions about where to organize violence. These scholars further show that because costs and benefits differ by election type, with national-level considerations dominating in presidential elections and district-level considerations dominating in legislative contests, pre-election violence in Zimbabwe follows distinct patterns. Specifically, incumbent politicians target opposition strongholds with conflict before presidential elections, but they direct conflict toward competitive constituencies before legislative contests. This is because parties' "first and foremost preoccup[ation is to] direct violence at the 'correct voters'" (Daxecker and Rausenbach 2023: 3). In seeking to get things right in these ways, parties try to ensure that they maximize the benefits accrued from violence while simultaneously minimizing any potential risks or costs.

Whereas Siddiqui and Daxecker and Rausenbach highlight the careful and strategic decisions that parties make in order to attain this balance, Rosenzweig's (2023: 12) research from Kenya holds that "accurately inferring the effects of different electoral tactics – [including violence] – is a much more difficult task for politicians than the literature tends to assume." He further argues that, as opposed to the efficacy of violence as an electoral tactic, it is elites' misperceptions about the upshots of conflict that account for the commonality of election-related violence around the world. Because such misperceptions lead politicians to overestimate the returns that can be accrued through conflict, election-related violence sometimes occurs even in contexts where it can plausibly generate backlash from voters.

In keeping with these larger concerns about costs and benefits, a few scholars of party violence have sought to investigate precisely the kinds of parties – in terms of their internal characteristics – that are likely to become embroiled in conflict. Fjelde's (2020) cross-national analysis of electoral violence, for example, has demonstrated that strong parties are associated with peaceful electoral dynamics. She further suggests that robust party organizations reduce the risks of conflict by constraining both party leaders and grassroots politicians from carrying out violence and offering less costly ways of mobilizing voters. In a related vein and focusing squarely on the electoral authoritarian regimes of Tanzania, Kenya, and Cameroon, Yonatan Morse (2019: 32) has argued that credible ruling parties – those that cultivate "regular and predictable exchanges with supporters" – are key to reining in incumbents' strategies of electoral manipulation, including their reliance on violence. Morse (2019: 18) finds that "credibility produces longer time horizons" and enables parties to contest "elections with confidence." Such confidence further encourages politicians to "use manipulation … strategically rather than systematically"

(Morse 2019: 18). Finally, a recent study of Hindu–Muslim riots in India has uncovered that higher levels of party system volatility are positively associated with episodes of communal violence (Suhas and Banerjee 2021). This research from Prashant Suhas and Vasabjit Banerjee proposes that instability in the party system serves to encourage ethnic outbidding on the part of political parties and thereby helps to facilitate violence.

Given its emphasis on the relationship between parties and violence, the arguments of this book align with, and build on, key claims about electoral violence as well as more recent arguments about party conflict. To begin with, Wilkinson's (2004) model of elite incentives and his claims about electoral competition are certainly compatible with my arguments about party instability. In fact, it is plausible that the closest electoral races – those around which Wilkinson (2004: 25) argues elites will dedicate scarce resources to "highlight ethnic cleavages" – could be contexts of truncated time horizons.

My work also shares Siddiqui's concern with opening up political parties and detailing a supply-side framework for understanding elites' decisions about violence. I engage seriously with the claim – proffered by both Siddiqui and Daxecker and Rauschenbach – that parties care about maximizing the payoffs from violence while minimizing the costs. At the same time, I agree with Rosenzweig that politicians and party leaders can miscalculate the efficacy of violence as an electoral strategy. In Chapter 7, I show that these miscalculations contributed to seat losses for the SP and BSP after the Muzaffarnagar and Shamli riots. Finally, I do not dispute Fjelde, Morse, or Suhas and Banerjee's findings that weak, noncredible, or unstable party contexts are associated with higher risks of violence.

Despite these broader areas of agreement, however, my arguments and core concerns differ from these prior works in some important respects. First, compared to Siddiqui, who studies different strategies of party violence in one country, my research investigates a shared form of party conflict across two countries. I also adopt a narrower approach to the potential costs of party violence than Siddiqui does and focus specifically on voter sanctioning. This choice is motivated by the fact that we now have considerable evidence, which shows that "large majorities of citizens" in many parts of the world "express disapproval of violence in any form" (Rosenzweig 2023: 61). I marry this focus on voter sanctioning – and the relationship between parties and voters – with a rare cross-regional comparison of cases. These cases help to generate broad insights about elite decision-making as it pertains to political conflict. They also reveal that many major episodes of ethnic party violence in Kenya and India have involved both direct fomentation of conflict as well as outsourcing. Taken together, then, while I focus less on the varied ways in which parties might become involved in conflict, my emphasis on party instability helps to explain how elites reach decisions about whether or not to engage in violence as well as the scale at which to do so.

Parties and Political Violence

Second, compared to Daxecker and Rausenbach as well as Rosenzweig – who all study election-related conflict – the outcome of interest in this book is the wider category of party violence. As Siddiqui (2022: 10) discusses, "parties ... frequently engage in violence for nonelectoral reasons." My decision to study party violence broadly conceived is thus informed by the fact that we need to look beyond electoral conflict if we are to fully grasp the conditions under which parties play a part in political violence.

Third, whereas Fjelde and Suhas and Banerjee's studies propose – but cannot test – the mechanisms through which strong and stable parties disincentivize violence, the data presented in this book help to carefully probe elite decision-making about conflict in contexts of varying party instability. Finally, while Morse focuses on the decisions of electoral autocrats as they pertain to manipulation broadly conceived, my research squarely contends with how politicians at various rungs of the party apparatus make choices about violence.

Taken together, the arguments, cases, and approach of this book make several important contributions to the literature on political violence. First, by focusing on the *supply* of violence, this research moves us beyond existing demand-side perspectives about political conflict. These demand-side perspectives – many of which have emerged from experimental studies – have rightly helped us to uncover the potential costs of violence (Gutiérrez-Romero and LeBas 2020; Horowitz and Klaus 2020). Yet, they cannot fully parse out the circumstances in which politicians will need to incorporate such costs into their decision-making. Indeed, by virtue of their experimental designs, elite involvement in conflict is assumed in these studies. If we are to become better equipped to prevent or contain party violence, however, the supply of violence ought to be explained. In developing a supply-side framework, this book proffers one crucial factor – party instability – that stands to influence politicians' decisions about organizing or sponsoring violent conflict.

Second, the cross-regional comparison at the heart of this book contributes in important ways to the field of comparative area studies (CAS) (Ahram 2011; Ahram, Köllner, and Sil 2018). This research agenda is motivated by the study of "general questions that bear on cases from different areas" (Köllner, Sil, and Ahram 2018: 4). The main country cases that I examine here – Kenya and India – are rarely put together in the study of comparative politics. Yet, it is precisely through their careful comparison that this book is able to develop a novel theory about how party instability informs elites' choices about violence. Future research on important social and political phenomena could similarly benefit by comparing a small number of cases from different regions of the world.

Third, and in a related vein, the comparison between Kenya and India also helps to illuminate when and how dominant parties can become embroiled in conflict. Conventional theories about elites' incentives for conflict – many of which focus on the closeness of elections – might suggest that violence in hegemonic party settings will be limited due to low levels of electoral competition. However, as Chapters 4–7 will reveal, the Kenya African National Union (KANU) and, at various points, the Indian National Congress (INC) both resorted to violence despite their status as hegemonic parties in Kenya and India, respectively. Beyond these two countries, we know from contexts such as South Africa (Gottschalk 2016) and Burundi (Travaglianti 2014) that dominant party systems are no strangers to party violence. The findings of this book and its consideration of party instability thus help to show that even dominant parties can become involved in conflict when they are uncertain about their future survival.

Finally, a party instability framework is useful for explaining the involvement of parties in some forms and modalities of violence that might otherwise seem surprising to researchers. Fjelde (2020: 145), for instance, grants that there are several examples of "highly institutionalized parties that have used their organizational strength as vehicles for illegal electoral manipulation – including violence – in order to win elections." The BJP in India is a key case of one such party. Its electoral prominence over the last decade has not averted the party from engaging in conflict, though the evidence shows that party leaders are now carefully instrumentalizing or supporting violence in new sites, such as rural areas, or in low-intensity forms (Pai and Kumar 2018; D. Basu 2021; Jaffrey 2021; Malik 2021). Large-N cross-national studies cannot fully account for such cases or developments, but a party instability framework and granular qualitative data make it possible to show that these sites and forms of conflict are being deliberately chosen to mitigate the possibilities of future backlash against violence.

PARTY INSTABILITY, VOTER SANCTIONING, AND ELITES' INCENTIVES TO SUPPLY PARTY VIOLENCE

I argue that party instability incentivizes elites to engage in violence by shortening their time horizons and enabling them to discount the future costs of conflict. This is not to say that party instability always explains violence or is the sole determinant of politicians' time horizons. Given the complexity of elite decision-making around various issues, including violence, proposing a monocausal explanation along these lines would be unrealistic. Indeed, many different factors – including a politician's age or the willingness of the party leadership to ignore conflict, as well as the strength of the judiciary or the press – might affect elites' time horizons and their decisions about conflict. I discuss these factors in greater depth in Chapter 2.

Nevertheless, I argue that party instability is an underappreciated factor in the broader instrumentalist literature on conflict. Instability matters because it can make the selection and deployment of violence less costly and risky for elites. As Sarah Birch (2020) suggests, due to their lower costs and risks, politicians generally prefer illicit strategies such as vote-buying and misconduct to

Parties and Political Violence

carrying out violence. In fact, leaders typically keep "violence – or the threat of violence – ... as an *additional* strategy to be deployed as and when required" (Birch 2020: 28). Drawing on Birch as well as Morse – who holds that the use of manipulation provides vital information about the credibility of autocratic parties – I propose that parties that routinely turn to organizing conflict tell us something fundamental about their instability. I also posit that severe episodes of direct or indirect party violence are likely to emerge in settings marked by unstable parties.

In developing this theory, my work argues that party instability can plausibly serve to lower one important cost that might be associated with violence – the possibility of garnering sanctioning from voters. Existing studies have already discussed how punishment from domestic courts (Höglund 2009) as well as international tribunals (Hafner-Burton, Hyde, and Jablonski 2014) can constrain elites from gambling with political conflict. Indeed, recent instances of former heads of state who have faced trials for contributing to large-scale episodes of political violence include Saddam Hussein of Iraq, Hosni Mubarak of Egypt, and Laurent Gbagbo of Côte d'Ivoire. Collectively, these cases suggest that there are real risks of prosecution to which leaders might expose themselves if they orchestrate or support conflict in their societies. We might also expect that places with a robust media that is capable of "naming and shaming" conflict-wielding elites might deter politicians from turning to violence. Likewise, in some contexts, we might see legislators become involved in holding their fellow politicians accountable for violence. In the United States, for example, Donald Trump was impeached for a second time following the January 6 insurrection. Finally, it is possible that parties themselves might serve to dampen political incentives for violence by hauling up nefarious subleaders or constituency-level politicians who engage in conflict.

Despite these various quarters from which violent elites might incur punishment, I focus on the role of voters because violence is fundamentally destabilizing to the lives of ordinary citizens. According to extant research, politicians often target voters with violence based on partisan or ethnic identities (Wilkinson 2004; Rauschenbach and Paula 2019; Klaus 2020). But major episodes of party violence also generate broader consequences – including revenue losses and curfews or shutdowns – that affect both in-groups and out-groups. When such effects emerge, violence has the potential to trigger an electoral backlash even among those voters who are not directly victimized or attacked (Rosenzweig 2023). Indeed, scholarship drawn from many different countries has illustrated how conflict can limit access to essential services (Dupas and Robinson 2010, 2012; Pyne et al. 2011; Doctor and Bagwell 2020) and weaken social capital (Dercon and Gutiérrez-Romero 2012) across communities. In keeping with these insights, one political expert from Nairobi described the consequences of the 2007–2008 post-election crisis in grave terms:

Nobody could move ... up to February 2008. People were stuck in their homes; people couldn't go to the places they loved to go; they couldn't eat the kind of food they loved to eat because they couldn't go out to shop. I think that [is when the] wake-up call that, "Gosh, violence affects *all of us*!" arrived.[7]

Likewise, a civil society leader who hailed from Kenya's Mijikenda community – a group indigenous to the country's Coast – recounted the effects of ethnic violence that engulfed the division and constituency of Likoni and the district of Kwale over ten years earlier:

In 1997, the Coastal people were drawn into violence.... They were convinced by our political leaders who [were] basically manipulating them, knowing exactly what the goal of the KANU regime was ... [for] Moi to win the general election.[8] When you've been so distressed and so disenfranchised, and you are told by the people in government and in power that "this is the time ... You can now take over the region..." People bought into that. The violence was devastating for this area, and the election result [did] not make a difference in addressing the Coastal problems of land, marginalization, and discrimination. [Instead,] a whole manner of brutality [followed].... The people felt that they were ultimately cheated.[9]

Finally, a Hindu interviewee from Bhagalpur, Bihar, discussed the aftermath of the town's 1989 riots – which claimed the lives of more than 1,000 individuals, mostly Muslims – as follows:

I not only saw the riot, but [I] also saw people's suffering. It was so frightening.... People were even starving for a drop of water, you can forget [about] food.[10]

Given these cross-community destabilizing effects, this book centers voters not simply as violence participants (Brass 1997, 2003b; Berenschot 2011a, 2011b), but also as actors who can choose to hold leaders accountable *after* conflict. This emphasis is crucial for recovering the agency of ordinary citizens and for better understanding how elites' choices about conflict can be influenced by voters' reactions. It is also supported by the insights of recent experimental studies of violence, which have shown that political leaders who use conflict as an electoral strategy generally *do not* elicit intended reactions from voters. Rather, both in-group and out-group voters exposed to divisive messages or active conflict are typically either unmoved by, or punishing of, violence-wielding elites (Gutiérrez-Romero and LeBas 2020; Horowitz and Klaus 2020; Rosenzweig 2021, 2023).[11] In some cases, moreover, the

---

[7] Interview with a political expert, Nairobi, December 3, 2013; emphasis added.
[8] The 1997 election was the second election to take place in Kenya after the restoration of multiparty competition. The incumbent, Daniel arap Moi, contested the presidency on a KANU ticket.
[9] Interview with a civil society leader, Mombasa, September 25, 2013.
[10] Interview with a civil society leader, Bhagalpur, July 15, 2016.
[11] Daxecker and Fjelde's (2022) experimental work on partisan responses to election violence in West Bengal, India, uncovers a different finding from the above studies. Specifically, they show

magnitude of this backlash against politicians is strong and significant enough to undermine the effectiveness of conflict-mobilizing strategies themselves (Rosenzweig 2021, 2023).

Insofar as this book argues that unstable parties can incentivize political leaders to repeatedly organize or sponsor party violence – including at a high intensity – it does not hold that elite success in mounting conflict will necessarily rest on party fragility. Rather, it recognizes that factors other than party instability – including politicians' abilities to appropriate ethnic cleavages or latch onto pre-existing grievances between social groups – can crucially inform the outbreak and scale of such violence. Even in contexts of highly unstable parties, in other words, my model proposes that we should expect to see variation in *how* and *where* violence breaks out. For example, I note that developments that reveal new ethnic fault lines can serve to alter elites' calculations about the most opportune locations for organizing or sponsoring conflict. By contrast, in places with relatively stable parties, I argue that major events of party violence will be relatively rare. When violence does occur in these settings, I suggest that elites will seek to organize it in forms, scales, and locations so as to minimize backlash from voters. Taken together, then, I do not claim that party instability on its own *causes* violence; instead, I argue that it can *incentivize* elites to engineer or sponsor violence.

PARTY VIOLENCE IN KENYA AND INDIA

This book centers Kenya and India as the main country cases for comparison due to similar background factors but key differences in their larger trajectories of party violence. In pairing these cases, it also contributes in a methodological sense to the growing field of CAS. Even though "small-N comparative studies that span multiple areas are not new" in the social sciences, it remains true that most social scientific qualitative research is focused on the study of "particular countries or compar[ing] cases within a single area, even for research problems and phenomena that cut across world regions" (Köllner, Sil, and Ahram 2018: 4).[12]

---

that while partisan voters object to violence carried out by a rival party, they endorse violence organized by their party, viewing it as necessary. Importantly, however, this study involves treatment conditions where violence occurred at a low intensity. It thus remains plausible that partisan voters could sanction co-partisans in severe violence contexts. This is because it is in these settings that conflict would generate broad consequences that negatively affect both partisans and nonpartisans.

[12] Indeed, a recent analysis of articles published in eight leading U.S.-based political science journals revealed that between 1965 and 2017, "approximately 60% of papers involving cross-national, case-based comparisons focused on countries within the same region" (Strohm 2019: 2). Analogously, an appraisal of books reviewed in *Perspectives on Politics* between March 2006 and March 2013 found that "cross-regional comparison represent[ed] no more than 15% of the literature" (Köllner, Sil, and Ahram 2018: 17).

At the same time, however, we also know that "comparisons of countries that are not usually paired together can be a fruitful source of new insights" (Strohm 2019: 6). For example, seminal studies that have leveraged such comparisons have productively interrogated wide-ranging political questions such as the roles of different classes in democratization efforts across space and time (Collier 1999), the strategies used to terminate violent insurgencies (Wood 2000), and the varied success of state-directed development policies in postcolonial countries (Kohli 2004). More recently, work in the vein of CAS has put forth novel findings about the failure of peasant reforms and land reform policies in agrarian societies (Banerjee 2019), the contributions of women to postconflict reconstruction efforts (Berry 2018), and civilians' responses to communal conflicts (Krause 2018). Through a cross-regional comparison of Kenya and India, this book aims to similarly advance our understanding of a global phenomenon – political violence – and illuminate the central place of parties as vehicles in such conflict.

Beyond this broader methodological goal, my substantive reasons for selecting Kenya and India as the main cases for investigation are threefold. First, these countries shared important historical experiences under British colonialism, including divide-and-rule policies that privileged specific communities – namely, upwardly mobile non-Kikuyus (Throup and Hornsby 1998; Branch 2006) and middle-class, professional, mainly Hindu "Moderates" (Tudor 2013b) – in their respective societies. After independence, ethnicity thus emerged as a salient cleavage in Kenya and India alike, as evidenced, among other factors, by the ubiquity of ethnic parties in each nation (Barkan 2004; Chandra 2004; Posner 2007). Today, these parties continue to shape electoral politics by engaging in efforts to craft and deploy *cross-ethnic appeals* (Devasher and Gadjanova 2021). Second, and as previously noted, Kenya and India have witnessed analogous types of party violence in the form of ethnic clashes and communal riots, respectively. These conflicts have taken shape as "highly patterned events" marked by discernible logics of mobilization and victimization in each country (Horowitz 2001: 1).

Third, and despite these initial similarities, Kenya and India's *trajectories* of party violence make for an important cross-regional comparison. Kenya exemplifies a case where unstable parties repeatedly incentivized violence in the 1990s and 2000s. Recently, however, even as parties have remained unstable, the strengthening of other institutions such as the Supreme Court has helped to deter conflict. Meanwhile, India exemplifies a case where the stabilization of parties themselves has contributed to significant declines in the frequency and intensity of Hindu–Muslim riots. Even as democratic erosion has weakened other safeguards such as the press, stable parties and the ability of voters to sanction politicians for severe violence has helped to deter elites from orchestrating major episodes of conflict. Thus, while violence certainly has not disappeared from India – and is marked by an observable shift to low-level and targeted attacks against ethnic minorities (Pai and Kumar 2018; A. Basu 2021;

Parties and Political Violence 21

D. Basu 2021; Jaffrey 2021) – the enduring nature of parties has helped to disincentivize politicians from organizing severe riots over the last three decades.

This book pairs the cross-regional comparison of Kenya and India with subnational comparisons within the two countries. In so doing, it contributes to the growing literature on the subnational dimensions and logics of conflict (Daxecker 2020; Turnbull 2020; Wahman and Goldring 2020; Wahman 2023). These studies have persuasively argued that large-N cross-national comparisons are poorly suited to explaining subnational patterns of violence since such comparisons hold national-level variables constant across subnational units. The research design adopted in my work contributes to this scholarly agenda but also departs from it by offering new insights about the subnational logics of party violence in two countries from different regions.

In Kenya, one of my main research sites is the Rift Valley, a setting marked by recurring ethnic violence as evidenced by the severe clashes that broke out in this area around the 1992, 1997, and 2007 elections. Within this region, I illuminate patterns of party conflict in Nakuru and Uasin Gishu counties. In addition, I incorporate findings from Coast Province, where vulnerability to party conflicts has been more variable. Specifically, whereas Mombasa and Kwale counties fell prey to severe party conflict around the 1997 election, mild clashes broke out in Mombasa during the 2007–2008 post-election crisis, and Tana River succumbed to a significant period of party violence in the run-up to the 2013 elections.

Interview data collected over six months of fieldwork in 2013 – in Nakuru (Nakuru County), Eldoret (Uasin Gishu County), and Mombasa (Mombasa County) – serve as the foundation of the main claims presented in this book about Kenya. In addition to these research sites, and as shown in Figure 1.1, I also conducted considerable fieldwork in the country's capital, Nairobi. Due to the timing of my fieldwork, I was unable to conduct on-the-ground research in Tana River. However, I draw on conversations with respondents from this county, which occurred mainly in Mombasa and Nairobi, to explain the ethnic clashes of 2012–2013.

In the Indian case, and as depicted in Figure 1.2, I primarily compare the trajectories of Hindu–Muslim violence in Hyderabad, Andhra Pradesh (AP), and Meerut, UP.[13] Between 1950 and 1995, these cities emerged as the third and fourth most riot-prone sites in the country, respectively (Varshney 2002; Varshney-Wilkinson dataset 2004). More recently, however, both Hyderabad and Meerut have experienced dramatic declines in riot violence. Indeed, compared to the 1950–1995 period when these cities amassed riot-related death tolls of 314 and 268, respectively, their fatality figures dropped to 16 and 5

---

[13] The entire period of riot violence in Hyderabad with which I am concerned in this book occurred before the creation of the state of Telangana in 2014. As such, I mainly focus on the politics of AP in studying this case, though it is important to note that Hyderabad is today the largest city and capital of Telangana.

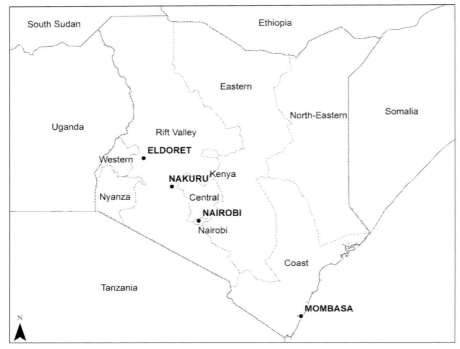

FIGURE 1.1 Subnational research sites in Kenya

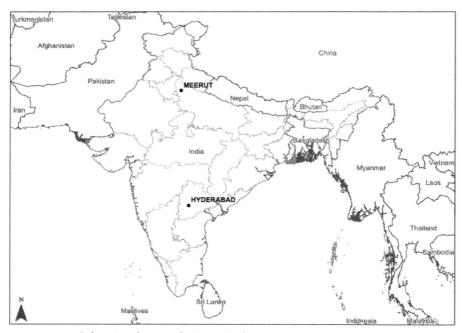

FIGURE 1.2 Subnational research sites in India

for the 1996–2010 period (Varshney-Wilkinson dataset 2004; Mitra-Ray dataset 2007; author's extension). In addition to carrying out fieldwork in Hyderabad and Meerut, I also conducted a handful of elite interviews in the Indian capital, New Delhi. Finally, two years after the 2013 riots ended, I traveled to Muzaffarnagar and Shamli to better understand this period of party violence in UP.

SUMMARY OF METHODOLOGY

I build the theory outlined above by drawing on three different sources of data. I adopt a mixed-methods approach, which allows me to leverage the strengths of both quantitative and qualitative data in the study of violence (Thaler 2017). First, I use event data from Kenya and India to operationalize my dependent variable of ethnic party violence. Second, I rely on original quantitative data on party volatility, specifically replacement volatility (Birch 2001, 2003; Powell and Tucker 2014), to measure party instability. These data sources are used descriptively to (1) capture variations in party violence across space and over time; and (2) chart longitudinal changes in party instability levels in my two country cases and main subnational sites. Third, I draw on insights from over 200 original and in-depth interviews conducted during fieldwork in Kenya and India. These interviews illuminate the motives of politicians to use parties as vehicles for conflict. They demonstrate the impact of party instability on the time horizons of political leaders as well as their associated incentives to drive, support, or avoid party violence. I also conducted a smaller number of interviews with ordinary citizens in the two nations, and I draw on these interviews to shine a light on the possibilities of voter sanctioning in Kenya and India. The pages that follow discuss these data in further depth.

Event Data on Party Violence

Scholars working on Kenya have variously described the kind of violence with which I am concerned in this book as "ethnic" (Klopp 2001), "inter-ethnic" (Rutten and Owuor 2009), or "communal clashes" (Adeagbo and Iyi 2011).[14] To capture ethnic party violence in the Kenyan case, I compiled an original dataset, known as the Kenya Violent Elections Dataset (KVED), for this research (Malik 2023). This dataset covers ethnic or communal clashes that occurred in the country between 1991 and 2015. The sources used to compile KVED include government commission reports, such as the Akiwumi and Commission of Inquiry on Post-Election Violence (CIPEV) reports; nongovernmental organization (NGO) reports from organizations like the Kenya Human

---

[14] During fieldwork, some respondents also referred to such violence as "tribal clashes." However, in this book, I mainly use the terms ethnic, interethnic, or communal clashes and only describe party conflicts as "tribal clashes" when directly quoting my interviewees.

Rights Commission (KHRC), Kenya National Commission on Human Rights (KNCHR), and Human Rights Watch; newspaper reports; and travel advisory reports from a global health and security services firm known as International SOS for the period between January 1, 2013, and December 31, 2015. In coding and including events in KVED, I triangulated incidents of violence, to the extent possible, across multiple sources. I also sought to match events to constituencies to the best of my ability.[15] In total, KVED includes data on 445 events of ethnic party violence.[16]

In India, my work focused on the study of ethnic or communal riots between Hindus and Muslims (Varshney 2002; Brass 2003b; Wilkinson 2004). To measure this form of violence and to select subnational sites for comparison, I drew on the seminal Varshney-Wilkinson (2004) dataset as well as the Mitra-Ray (2007) extension to these data. While Varshney and Wilkinson's (2004) original compilation covered Hindu–Muslim riots between 1950 and 1995, Mitra and Ray (2007) subsequently extended these data from 1996 to 2000. After selecting my subnational cases, I compiled newspaper reports from the *Times of India* and other prominent dailies as well as NGO and scholarly sources to further extend the riot data for my chosen locations through December 31, 2010.

Replacement Volatility Data

I measure party instability in this research using original data on replacement, or Type A, volatility. A subtype of total party system volatility or the Pedersen index (Pedersen 1979), replacement volatility specifically "measures shifts in vote [or seat] shares among parties that [have] entered [or] exited competition" between two consecutive elections (Cohen, Kobilanski, and Zechmeister 2018: 1018–1019).[17] As such, this form of volatility is directly attributable to the birth of new parties and the death of existing parties (Powell and Tucker 2014).

---

[15] Despite the importance of these data in offering a disaggregated and subnational accounting of party violence, KVED does have some limitations. First, because I was unable to secure reliable and complete access to Kenyan newspaper reports published in the 1990s and early 2000s, the dataset cannot provide a day-by-day record for incidents of violence that occurred before 2013. Second, several of the sources used to compile KVED, particularly government commission and NGO reports, often provided information – such as the names of roads or farms – that could not be reliably matched to constituencies. In these cases, I coded incidents of violence into KVED at higher administrative levels, such as at the county or district levels, as appropriate.

[16] A detailed description of these data is also available in Malik (2018). The figures listed in this book, however, are slightly different from those presented in the 2018 article due to subsequent updates that I made to the dataset.

[17] The broader measure of Pedersen volatility captures "the net change within the electoral party system resulting from individual vote [or] seat transfers" (Pedersen 1979: 3). Meanwhile, the second subtype of total party system volatility, known as vote switching, stable party, or Type B volatility, measures "volatility in vote [or seat] share among established parties" (Cohen, Kobilanski, and Zechmeister 2018: 1019).

Parties and Political Violence

In this book, I rely on replacement volatility rates as an ex-ante proxy for elites' time horizons, and I use the terms replacement volatility, party entry and exit volatility, or party birth and death volatility when referring to Type A volatility. To the extent that party instability *conditions* politicians' decisions about violence, we should expect that transformations from low to high levels of party replacement can begin to change the ways in which elites think about the costs versus benefits of conflict. In particular, I propose that politicians operating in unstable party contexts will be more likely than their durable party counterparts to repeatedly turn to organizing severe episodes of violence.

The replacement volatility measure that I use in this book is positively correlated with the Pedersen index and negatively correlated with the individual party and system-level measures of party organization (PO) and party strength (PS), respectively (Chhibber, Jensenius, and Suryanarayan 2014; Fjelde 2020). Despite these broader correlations, which are all in the expected directions and discussed in detail in Appendix A, I specifically rely on Type A volatility in this work due to its close association with party system instability (Powell and Tucker 2014). I adopt a 0% threshold to code parties as replaced.[18] For parliamentary elections in Kenya and national (i.e., Lok Sabha) and state-level (i.e., Vidhan Sabha) elections in India, I measure entry and exit volatility using party seat share information.[19] Meanwhile, I rely on vote share data to compute party birth and death for constituency-level and national presidential elections in Kenya. Finally, following Mainwaring and Scully (1995) and Kuenzi and Lambright (2001), I use the scale below to categorize volatility levels in the two countries:

0–10% = quite stable
11–20% = moderately stable
21–30% = quite unstable
>30% = extremely unstable[20]

---

[18] Compared to other studies that have used a 2% threshold (Powell and Tucker 2014; Cohen, Kobilanski, and Zechmeister 2018; Heath and Ziegfeld 2018), I make this modification because adopting a 2% threshold would lead me to overstate the extent of party exit in Kenya. This is because owing to the country's highly fractionalized party system, numerous small and marginal parties routinely capture less than 2% of parliamentary seats and amass less than 2% of the vote in contests for the presidency. Although these parties carry little individual weight, they can collectively impact the fates of larger parties as members of coalitions. I thus set a more difficult task for myself in establishing Kenya as a country with highly transient parties using the stricter 0% threshold in this book.

[19] My replacement volatility data for Hyderabad includes computations for Vidhan Sabha contests held in both AP and Telangana. However, in the empirical analyses, I mainly rely on the AP data since Telangana had only held two assembly elections, in 2014 and 2018, at the time of this writing.

[20] In their research, Mainwaring and Scully (1995) and Kuenzi and Lambright (2001) applied this scale to rank total system volatility using the Pedersen index. I adopt the same scale to rank party entry and exit volatility levels in this book.

Qualitative Interviews

My third source of data comes from over 200 in-depth interviews. I conducted these interviews with politicians and political party leaders, members, and functionaries; policy and security sector experts; human rights activists and civil society leaders; ethnic and religious elites; academics; journalists; police officers; and local residents in my subnational research sites in Kenya over six months in 2013. In addition, in the run-up to the 2017 elections, I conducted interviews with several church leaders from the Rift Valley region via Skype. In India, I interviewed the aforementioned groups of respondents over multiple rounds of fieldwork between 2013 and 2016.

My interviews with politicians and political party leaders and functionaries specifically sought to probe *how*, *when*, and *why* elites have utilized parties as vehicles for violence. Despite the accepted wisdom that party-based and party-sponsored conflicts owe their origins to deliberate political instrumentalization, relatively few studies have relied on interviews with political elites to arrive at this finding.[21] Instead, existing research has typically proxied political incentives by either using quantitative data on party competition (Wilkinson 2004; Dhattiwala and Biggs 2012) or by conducting interviews with violence participants (Brass 1997; Cleven 2013) and civilians affected by conflict (Klaus 2020).

Of course, in carrying out my fieldwork, I was aware that politicians and political party leaders would have strong motivations to deny involvement in violence. As Morse (2019: 28) suggests in his work on electoral authoritarian parties, some actors, especially political elites, "have an incentive to … obscure" nefarious activities. Yet, it is also true that "the extent of fieldwork and the time spent developing relationships with interview subjects" can help to overcome some of these hurdles (Morse 2019: 18). I discuss my approach to navigating these challenges in Appendix B. It is also worth noting that my interviews with policy and security sector experts, human rights activists, civil society leaders, ethnic and religious elites, academics, journalists, police officers, and local residents in both Kenya and India sometimes helped me to verify the information that political elites shared with me. In addition, these conversations enabled me to uncover discrepancies or evasions in elite accounts so as to arrive at a fuller understanding of the relationship between parties and violence. As such, the individual quotes that I cite in this should be read as representations of viewpoints that I was able to corroborate across multiple respondents.

THE PLAN OF THIS BOOK

In developing and substantiating my theory about the relationship between party instability and violence, the remainder of this book is organized as

---

[21] Siddiqui (2022) and Rosenzweig (2023) are important exceptions here.

follows. In Chapter 2, I detail my theory: I begin by discussing various factors that can affect elites' time horizons and propose party instability as an important and understudied variable in this mix. I then present my theoretical model, focusing first on elites' decisions and then on voters' reactions to violence. Within this discussion, I highlight how expected party lifespan stands to impact leaders' decision-making about violence – with respect to both whether or not to engage with conflict as well as the scale at which to do so. I argue that, conditional on voter attitudes and the level of political competition, elites' projections about party survival can affect their choices about violence by elongating or truncating their time horizons. When operating with short time horizons, I suggest that politicians can more easily discount the possibilities of voter sanctioning and choose to orchestrate or sponsor conflict, including at a high intensity. By contrast, I argue that politicians with large "shadow[s] of the future" (Axelrod 1984) can be expected to consider the likelihood of garnering such backlash more carefully and might accordingly steer clear of organizing or supporting severe episodes of violence. Simply put, then, I hold that the effect of party instability is *conditioning* rather than determinative: on its own, party instability does not *cause* violence. However, it can *incentivize* elites to engineer or sponsor violence in certain contexts. Finally, while levels of party instability can serve to inform *when* politicians might deploy violence, demographic variables, the strength of local grievances, and the interplay between these factors can help them to decide *where* to organize or sponsor party conflicts. I conclude Chapter 2 by discussing potential endogeneity concerns and theoretically addressing these concerns.

In Chapter 3, I trace political party development in Kenya and India from a comparative and historical perspective. Specifically, I show that despite many shared experiences as British colonies, nationalist parties with transoceanic connections to one another, and dominant party structures that endured for several years after independence, party development in the two countries took very different routes in the medium and long terms. In Kenya, the Kenya African National Union emerged as a narrow, divisive, and ethnically-oriented party whose leaders oversaw a transition to a de facto one-party state in the late 1960s. Even after the era of one-party politics ended in the early 1990s, the precedents set by KANU led to a mimicking of its leaders' choices and a reproduction of the party's organizational logic on the part of new electoral entrants. In addition to producing parties that relied on ethnic mobilization, these strategies contributed to the frequent birth and death of parties in the nation, as narrow parties constantly sought to undercut and outbid one another. In contrast to KANU, the Indian National Congress developed deep societal roots, penetrated rural areas, and sought to unite Indians across caste and ethnic divides. Congress leaders also prioritized party organization and championed democracy in India, and their strategies created pressures for new parties to attain stability and build multi-ethnic bases of support. These divergent trajectories further generated differing incentive structures for instrumentalizing political violence in Kenya versus India. Contrary to the Kenyan case, and even though the INC failed to dampen the salience of the Hindu–Muslim cleavage, I show that Indian elites shared strong incentives to avoid orchestrating major episodes of ethnic party violence in the initial decades after independence.

In Chapter 4, I use national-level violence and volatility data along with in-depth elite interviews to demonstrate the relationship between short projected party lifespans and recurring bouts of ethnic party violence in multiparty Kenya. I organize this discussion in three phases from the KANU era to the period after the promulgation of the country's new constitution. My findings reveal that although Kenyan voters are not lacking in information about the political nature of party conflicts and actually reject violence-wielding politicians, high levels of party replacement and attendant changes in coalitional arrangements tend to prevent them from holding these leaders to account.

In Chapter 5, I turn to studying subnational patterns of party violence in Kenya's Rift Valley and Coast Provinces and offer insights from chosen constituencies in Nakuru, Uasin Gishu, Mombasa, and Tana River counties to support my core arguments. My research from these sites helps me to incorporate additional subnational variables that are relevant to accounting for elites' specific engagements with conflict, including information on candidates' anxieties over MP seats, demographic data, and fine-grained information on grievances used to instrumentalize violence. My findings from Tana River also help me to show how reforms such as devolution have done little to stabilize parties at their fundament and have instead generated new ethnic fault lines in some areas that are conducive to the organization of subnational conflict in the Kenyan context. Finally, the chapter empirically evaluates concerns about endogeneity.

In Chapter 6, I illustrate the relationship between politicians, parties, and communal conflict in India. I organize this discussion in three phases from the era of Congress dominance in the 1950s through the late 1970s to the period following the re-equilibration of political parties in the late 1980s. The chapter shows that it was after the INC started to weaken and was eventually voted out of national office in the late 1970s that riot violence escalated across many parts of India through the 1980s. Although voters gradually became aware of elites' roles in such conflicts, it was not until parties stabilized in the late 1980s that politicians began to take the prospects of voter sanctioning seriously. Since then, however, severe riots have dramatically declined in India, as the risks of provoking such violence have become prohibitive for many political parties. However, other forms of conflict – including rural clashes and targeted low-level attacks against Muslims – have escalated in recent years under the BJP. The chapter suggests that these newer modalities of conflict are part of the same recalibrated elite strategies that have contributed to declines in major communal riots even as Hindu nationalists have simultaneously sought to redefine India as a fundamentally Hindu society (Pai and Kumar 2018).

Building on this national-level analysis, Chapter 7 offers a subnational accounting of patterns of riot violence in Hyderabad in AP and Meerut in UP. It shows that, much like at the national level, these cities fell prey to repeated and severe riots when party instability incentivized conflict on the part of both Congress elites as well as politicians from its emerging electoral rivals. However, following the restoration of relative party stability in the late 1980s, both Hyderabad and Meerut have witnessed communal quiescence. My discussion of UP in this chapter enables me to return to the cases of Muzaffarnagar and Shamli with which I began this book. In accounting for these rural riots, I find that elites' eagerness to avoid sanctioning from urban voters seemed to inform their decisions to organize violence in villages in 2013. The chapter concludes by addressing endogeneity concerns in the Indian context.

Chapter 8 extends the main arguments of the book beyond Kenya and India. In so doing, it evaluates the alternative account of democratic longevity as a potential explanation for party violence. The chapter draws on research on electoral violence in multiparty Ghana and party-sponsored conflict during Turkey's 1976 to 1980 *anarşi* crisis to assess this rival claim. Taken together, these cases not only serve to probe the generalizability of the book's main arguments but also help to extend the cross-regional scope of this work.

Chapter 9 concludes. It reviews the central arguments and empirics, maps out areas for future research, and discusses the policy implications of the book's findings.

2

A Theory of Party Instability and Political Violence

According to Nicolas van de Walle (2003: 298), political parties are "the single most important organizations in electoral politics." They form the government and opposition, provide structure to the electoral process, aggregate and channel citizens' preferences, and shape public opinion (Stokes 2001; Cyr 2016). In addition, parties play a central role in promoting democratic accountability (Powell 2000).

Yet recent research underscores a darker side to party politics, highlighting the roles of parties and politicians as the primary protagonists in episodes of political conflict around the world (Staniland 2014, 2021; Fjelde 2020; Siddiqui 2022). Parties and their constituents can directly contribute to violence by delivering divisive speeches (Klopp 2001; Ezeibe and Ikeanyibe 2017; van Klinken and Aung 2017) or by provoking attacks and leading mobs during pogroms and riots (Berenschot 2009; Banerji 2012; Pai and Kumar 2018; Malik 2021). Indirectly, furthermore, global evidence shows that it is not uncommon for party members to appropriate different state and nonstate actors – including bureaucrats, militias, vigilantes, armed groups, and criminal gangs – to do their bidding (Hassan 2020; LeBas 2013; Mutahi 2005; Ahram 2016; Berenschot 2009, 2011b; Kakar 1996; Tajima 2018; Siddiqui 2022).

Despite the plethora of ways in which parties contribute to political conflict, party violence remains understudied as a phenomenon. Why, where, and when do political leaders make use of parties as vehicles for violence? Several scholars hold that the choice to organize or sponsor conflict is best understood with reference to the benefits of this decision (Höglund 2009; Hickman 2009; UNDP 2011), particularly for those elites who compete in weakly institutionalized settings (Barron 2019; Birch 2020; Fjelde 2020; von Borzyskowksi and Kuhn 2020). Relatedly, extant research also suggests that politicians rely on parties for violence in order to reduce uncertainty (Fjelde 2020).

I argue, however, that the current emphasis on the benefits of violence understates the *costs* associated with this choice. These costs can take the form of international prosecutions (Hafner-Burton, Hyde, and Jablonski 2014) or various unwanted domestic outcomes, such as garnering punishment from courts (Höglund 2009) or the media or incurring blame from voters themselves (Toros and Birch 2021). Previous research has established that credible information is crucial for empowering voters to attribute blame to politicians for unscrupulous behaviors (Pande 2011; Klašnja 2017). In some cases, the attribution of such blame has led voters to turn their backs on conflict-wielding elites, as seen in contexts such as Kenya (Gutiérrez-Romero and LeBas 2020; Horowitz and Klaus 2020; Rosenzweig 2021, 2023), India (Susewind and Dhattiwala 2014; Malik 2021), and South Africa (de Kadt, Johnson-Kanu, and Sands 2023).[1] Cumulatively, then, there is now an emerging consensus that elites and parties must think carefully about conflict due to its potential negative impacts on the attitudes and choices of voters.[2]

Given these insights, my theory starts from the premise that as rational actors, conflict-wielding elites will try to minimize the negative consequences of violence whenever possible. As previously described in Chapter 1, since violence fundamentally destabilizes the lives of citizens – from generating property damage to causing loss of life and livelihood – I focus primarily on the likelihood of voter sanctioning in developing a model of elite decision-making about violence. I propose that varying levels of party instability can crucially condition politicians' choices about violence by (1) shortening their time horizons and enabling them to discount the possibilities of future punishment in settings marked by unstable parties; or (2) lengthening their time horizons and sensitizing them to the prospects of incurring sanctioning from voters in stable party contexts. I further argue that politicians competing with truncated time horizons will be more likely to repeatedly gamble with severe episodes of conflict while those operating with lengthy time horizons will typically refrain from conflict altogether or contribute to mainly mild incidents of violence.

In developing these claims, this chapter proceeds as follows: I begin by discussing various sources of elites' time horizons and offer party instability as an important factor within this mix. I then illuminate the difference between

---

[1] These findings are consistent with the insights of a large body of work on voters' negative reactions to, and sanctioning of, corrupt (Klašnja and Tucker 2013; Mares and Young 2016; Klašnja 2017; Klašnja, Lupu, and Tucker 2020; de Kadt and Lieberman 2020), criminal (Banerjee et al. 2011; Dutta and Gupta 2014), and wealth-accumulating (Chauchard, Klašnja, and Harish 2019) elites.

[2] Two key exceptions in this regard have emerged from studies of partisan responses to violence and voters' reactions to political assassinations. According to new research from West Bengal, India, partisan voters endorse low-level incidents of conflict organized by their co-partisans. Meanwhile, new scholarship from South Africa shows that targeted attacks on political candidates appear to neither affect voter turnout rates nor influence citizens' decisions at the polls (Pierson 2021).

replacement and vote-switching volatility, using examples from Latin America and Europe to highlight how imminent party birth and death maps onto party instability. After this discussion, I put forth my supply-side model of violence in two stages, beginning with elites' actions and then proceeding to voters' reactions. To conclude, I address potential concerns about endogeneity, evaluate the alternative account about democratic longevity and quality, and provide a brief theoretical discussion about why party instability offers a better explanation for elite decision-making about violence than a rival account that focuses on civic associations.[3]

THE SOURCES OF ELITES' TIME HORIZONS

There is a wealth of work in comparative politics about the effects of politicians' time horizons on their decision-making. Researchers have shown that time horizons can influence decisions about corruption (Campante, Chor, and Do 2009), rent extraction and distribution (Collier 2009; Hughes et al. 2015; Barma 2016), government spending on health (Dionne 2011), the disbursement of aid (Wright 2008), and violence (Bates 2008). Together, these studies demonstrate that predatory or extractive elite behaviors are more likely to emerge in contexts of truncated time horizons. As Naazneen Barma (2012: 292) documents in her work on postconflict reconstruction, elites who face "very short time horizons" tend to "increase predation in the present time period [and] erode social cohesion" in order to retain power.

Given the importance of lengthy time horizons for desirable social and political outcomes, a related literature has underlined the factors that can influence – and increase – the size of leaders' shadows of the future. This body of work has emphasized that politicians associated with credible and programmatic parties typically operate with long time horizons. As Morse (2019: 33) suggests, "credibility makes elites ... put aside immediate material opportunism and forces them to take a longer-term perspective" toward their careers. Meanwhile, Paul Kenny (2020: 264) suggests that programmatic parties are "deeply institutionalized and expect to outlive any particular leader or government." Due to the "greater procedural constraints on leaders that exist within such parties," members of programmatic parties are understood to be less likely to engage in behaviors that undermine democratic norms (Kenny 2020: 264). By contrast, contexts marked by "weak institutions – of which fluid party systems are a prime example – are associated with shorter time horizons, with more frequent changes in the rules of the game, with less effective provision of public goods, and with greater propensity for corruption" (Mainwaring 2018: 72).

---

[3] In Appendix C, I also proffer a historiography of the development of civil society in Kenya and India, as well as qualitative interview data to show the empirical limitations of this explanation in these settings.

Despite this broad consensus on the relationship between credibility and programmaticity on the one hand and elites' lengthy time horizons on the other, research is mixed on the impact of clientelism on the size of politicians' shadows of the future. Scholars such as Kenny (2020: 264) argue that clientelistic parties, much like programmatic ones, "have an institutional life expectancy that extends beyond a single leader." Furthermore, these parties depend "to a significant degree on maintaining the support of brokers … who control the party's vote banks" (Kenny 2020: 264). Ward Berenschot and Edward Aspinall (2020: 3) similarly argue that clientelism alone need not be associated with short-term orientations: in settings marked by "resilient parties," they find that longer-term and relational forms of exchange can tie politicians, their agents, and voters together. Put differently, then, even though scholars recognize that the mechanics of voter mobilization differ considerably between programmatic and clientelistic parties, one strand of research suggests that members of clientelistic parties can, in fact, be oriented toward the future.

However, other scholars argue that clientelism tends to emerge in places where "politics are relatively unpredictable, and there are low degrees of institutionalization, accountability, and constraint on power" (Barma 2014: 260). In these places, patron–client relationships are understood to reflect truncated elite time horizons. To quote Karl Jackson and Lucian Pye (1978: 349), patronage-based systems are marked by an "abbreviated time horizon [and] a foreshortened time perspective." In these systems, "patrons [can not only] abandon clients according to changing circumstances and opportunities, [but] clients [too] can switch [to] patrons" who are better positioned to provide them with resources and state access (Jackson and Pye 1978: 349).

Recent work on the relationship between patronage and elite time horizons has significantly advanced the above debate by demonstrating that rather than being a function of clientelism alone, it is the interaction between patronage and context that influences the size of politicians' shadows of the future. Studies in this vein have shown that it is specifically in settings marked by "competitive clientelism" – where elections pose credible threats to the power of ruling elites and where patron–client connections are pervasive – that politicians tend to be oriented toward the short term (Abdulai and Hickey 2016; Tyce 2019). These insights are largely in keeping with extant scholarship on the truncating effect of electoral competition on elites' time horizons (Schedler and Santiso 1998; Bates 2008; Lupu and Riedl 2013).

Beyond macro-level variables – such as the strength and nature of institutions – that stand to influence the size of leaders' shadows of the future, individual-level factors can also impact whether politicians are oriented toward the short or long term. We might imagine that elites who are close to the end of their careers due to advanced age, for example, will be less concerned with the future effects of their decisions (see, e.g., Horowitz, McDermott, and Stam 2005). Likewise, the head of an executive who is coming to the end of her term due to a procedural constraint such as a term limit might be less worried about the future than someone who either does not face a term limit or is up for re-election. By contrast, it is conceivable that politicians who have put in considerable efforts to develop reputations of trust and respect among constituents and colleagues will tend to be more invested in their legacy.

Despite the attention that scholars have paid to these individual-level considerations, there is not yet clear agreement in the literature on the kinds of political leaders who will operate with long time horizons. In a recent study of party brands in Latin America, for instance, Noam Lupu (2016: 31) has argued that party subleaders or constituency-level candidates "are more likely to consider the long-term implications of their choices," since these are the individuals who are trying to build "a future career in politics." However, other studies have focused on the time horizons of higher-up politicians, including the leaders of parties and heads of executives, and argued that since it is often their decisions that determine government policies (see, e.g., Sridharan 1991; Dionne 2011), these individuals are likely to operate with lengthy time horizons.

In making a case for party instability as a factor that impacts elites' time horizons, this book does not dispute the importance of the institutional or individual-level variables that other scholars have proposed. Rather, I acknowledge that party instability works alongside other variables to influence how heavily leaders value the future relative to the present. For example, I grant that leaders or subleaders with strong individual reputations might steer clear of violence even when they are affiliated with fleeting or unstable parties. I further recognize that the time horizons of politicians who face a term limit might shorten in the run-up to the end of their term even if these leaders belong to durable party entities. It also follows that heads of executives in their final term might lack the motivation to stay engaged in politics for better or worse. The impact of party instability, as per my model, is thus *conditioning* rather than determinative of elites' time horizons and their attendant decisions about violence.

Nevertheless, as I introduced in Chapter 1, instability matters because it can enable politicians to discount the future costs or risks of conflict, such as garnering punishment from voters. I further posit that aside from a few exceptional circumstances, unstable parties can incentivize violence on the part of party subleaders and higher-up politicians alike. This is partly because local and national-level elites from disintegrating parties can face difficulties in switching out of such organizations. For subleaders in particular, I expect that while elites with their own resources – in terms of money and/or muscle (Vaishnav 2017) – might be able to abandon declining parties and still contest elections, candidates tied to parties due to a sense of loyalty or a lack of individual resources will likely stick with such parties even as they crumble. Under such circumstances, subleaders might come to use violence – including at a high intensity – to reduce uncertainty at the ballot box. Likewise, national-level leaders whose careers are tied to particular organizations might be unwilling to make the switch to other parties. In the midst of imminent or

A Theory of Party Instability and Political Violence

expected party decline, these leaders might gamble with violence as a means of holding on to power. I also expect that in hierarchically organized parties facing replacement, party leaders' decisions to engage with conflict could have broader reverberating effects that might encourage subleaders to behave in a similar manner.

Given my focus on understanding elites' decision-making about violence, it is beyond the scope of this book to identify the factors that contribute to party replacement. However, I do expect that both subnational and national-level factors could affect elites' perceptions of party durability. For instance, we might imagine that in a nationally declining party organization, the presence of strong subleaders and party branches could keep an organization relevant at the subnational level and thereby disincentivize the use of conflict locally. Likewise, national leaders who are invested in the future of their organizations might direct resources to help struggling branches and thereby diminish subleaders' proclivities toward violence. However, in places where expectations of party decline pervade both leaders and subleaders' calculations – and where ethnic cleavages or pre-existing grievances are ripe for the taking – my theory holds that elites across party ranks may come to use parties as vehicles to drive or sponsor violence. Under such circumstances, we might also expect that the scale of party violence will be severe.

REPLACEMENT VOLATILITY AS A MEASURE OF PARTY INSTABILITY

As described in Chapter 1, this book relies on original data on replacement volatility to measure party instability in Kenya and India. Replacement or Type A volatility measures "shifts in vote [or seat] shares among parties that [have] entered [or] exited competition" between two consecutive elections (Cohen, Kobilanski, and Zechmeister 2018: 1018–1019). Meanwhile, Type B, vote-switching, or stable party volatility measures "volatility in vote [or seat] share among established parties" (Cohen, Kobilanski, and Zechmeister 2018: 1019).

The cases of Bolivia, Peru, and Bulgaria help to highlight the central differences between these two forms of volatility. Even though they fall outside the regions investigated in this book, I rely on these examples here for a few reasons. First, they help to advance the cross-regional and comparative goals of my research. Second, and more importantly, these contexts are useful sites for probing instability in party politics, a concept core to my arguments. In Latin America, Levitsky, Loxton, and Van Dyck (2016: 1) have expertly documented the reality of party fragility, noting that "major parties have dramatically weakened or collapsed altogether in Argentina, Bolivia, Colombia, Costa Rica, Ecuador, Guatemala, Peru, and Venezuela" since 1990. It is thus not surprising that this region has received much attention from scholars of party volatility and collapse (Morgan 2011; Seawright 2012; Cyr 2017).

In a related vein, researchers working on the Bulgarian case have observed that the country's entire "post-1990s period has been characterized by instability" (Kolarova and Spirova 2019: 87). Taken together, the selection of Bolivia, Peru, and Bulgaria offers a rich array of insights to inform our understanding about different kinds of party volatility. I discuss each of these cases below in turn.

In Bolivia's 2002 general elections, the center-right Nueva Fuerza Republicana (New Republican Force or NFR) party captured 27 of 130 seats in the Chamber of Deputies or lower house of the legislature and two of 27 seats in the Senate or upper house. However, three years later in 2005, its seat shares in both houses plummeted to zero, thereby marking an important instance of party death or exit. Crucially, the NFR's demise also contributed to considerable instability in the country's party system (Morgan 2011; Cyr 2017).

Around the same time that the Nueva Fuerza Republicana fell apart, a new center-left party known as the Frente de Unidad Nacional (National Unity Front or NUF) formed. Founded in late 2003, the NUF emerged as the third largest party in the 2005 elections, capturing eight seats in the Chamber of Deputies and one seat in the Senate. Its performance in this election thus marked a key instance of party birth. Finally, six years after the NUF's birth, the Movimiento Nacionalista Revolucionario (MNR or Revolutionary Nationalist Movement) – long considered Bolivia's "most important party" – entirely exited the country's party system (Cyr 2017: 19; Lupu 2016).[4] This example underlines the reality that even influential parties can attenuate and, in some instances, collapse completely. For the purposes of my broader argument, I hold that all else equal, elites from such disintegrating parties can turn to violence – including at a high level – owing to truncated time horizons that enable them to discount the possibilities of sanctioning down the line.

Data from Peru, routinely classified as one of the most unstable party systems in Latin America (Dietz and Myers 2007; Levitsky 2018), also helps to clarify the concept of replacement volatility. In this case, comparisons between the 1985 and 1990 election results are especially useful for illuminating the dimension of party birth. In 1990, the Cambio 90 party, led by Alberto Fujimori, emerged triumphant in the polls following a run-off for the presidency. In claiming this victory, Fujimori defeated Mario Vargas Llosa of the Frente Democrático (Democratic Front or FREDEMO) party. Of critical note here is the fact that neither of these parties existed at the time of the 1985 election, as they were only formed in 1989 and 1998, respectively. Meanwhile, the incumbent American Popular Revolutionary Alliance (APRA) party finished in third place in the first round of the polls despite being one of the oldest parties

---

[4] The MNR recently re-entered the electoral playing field in 2019 and put forth Virginio Lema as its candidate for the presidency. However, it failed to win a single seat in the Chamber or Senate and only amassed 0.69% of the vote.

A Theory of Party Instability and Political Violence

in Latin America (Graham 1992) and "perhaps [the] best known of Peru's traditional parties" (Seawright 2012: 38).

Whereas data from Bolivia and Peru help to illuminate the concept of replacement volatility, the Bulgarian experience aids in capturing the dynamics of stable party or vote-switching volatility. As Lyubka Savkova (2005: 1) has chronicled, between 2001 and 2005, "small parties in Bulgaria [succeeded in] gain[ing] votes at the expense of … the [ruling] National Movement Simeon II" (NSDV). Together, these parties also contributed to the incumbent's defeat. Contrary to the NFR and MNR, however, the NSDV did not entirely collapse in Bulgaria. Nevertheless, it suffered considerable declines in electoral influence, as it went from holding 120 of 240 seats in the National Assembly in 2001 to 53 seats in 2005.

Even though Pedersen volatility or total party system volatility combines replacement and stable party volatility, logically we should expect vote-switching volatility to be 0 in settings where replacement volatility is 100%. This is because if all seats (or votes) in an election are won by parties that did not exist in the previous election, then there will be no vote-switching among existing parties. Similarly, if vote-switching volatility is 100%, then entry and exit volatility must be 0. This is because in an election in which all seats (or votes) change hands among existing parties, new party birth and existing party birth will be nil. Taken together, then, and as shown in Appendix A, although Pedersen and replacement volatility are strongly and positively correlated in my country cases of Kenya and India, I rely on Type A volatility to measure party instability in this book because it is "much more closely associated with party system instability" (Powell and Tucker 2014: 124). Compared to settings marked by moderate to high levels of Type B volatility, moreover, where we could be reasonably confident about "who the relevant political actors are likely to be over the medium term," high levels of Type A volatility make for a truly unstable party system (Powell and Tucker 2014: 124). Such parties, I further contend, stand to incentivize violence – including severe clashes – on the part of politicians by shortening their time horizons and making it possible for them to discount the possibility of sanctioning in the future.

A SUPPLY-SIDE MODEL OF PARTY VIOLENCE

Having discussed a number of sources of elites' time horizons and clarified the difference between Type A and Type B volatility, I now develop my model about the conditions under which politicians will resort to using their parties as vehicles for violence. I proceed in two stages, focusing first on elites' decisions and then on voters' reactions. My model begins with elites due to the broad scholarly consensus on the central role of political leaders in organizing and sponsoring conflict (Wilkinson 2004; Staniland 2014; Birch 2020; Klaus 2020; Rosenzweig 2023). Within this first stage, I focus specifically on politicians' decisions to *initiate* violence and discuss the scale at which they might do so. This emphasis differentiates my approach from the work of scholars such as Steven Wilkinson (2004), who mainly study the *restraint* of violence. While I agree with Wilkinson that certain coalitional arrangements – particularly those whose survival hinges on the support of ethnic minorities – can serve to dampen elites' incentives for violence, I also hold that stable parties can play this role by directing the attention of politicians to the possible costs of conflict down the line. After laying out the elite-level stage of my model, I discuss voters' reactions to violence and detail how these reactions can impact leaders' decisions.

In centering voter sanctioning as a response to violence that politicians might need to take into account, I position voters among the police, courts, media, and parties themselves as actors who can dampen elites' incentives for conflict. Chapters 4–7 of this book thus offer some examples of how actors beyond Kenyan and Indian voters can influence leaders' decisions about violence. In addition, to the extent that parties are embedded in broader institutional contexts, I acknowledge that elites affiliated with unstable parties could choose *not to* organize or sponsor violence if they believe that they might suffer backlash from these other institutions, as seen in the Kenyan case, covered in Chapters 4 and 5, in 2022. For the reasons previously discussed, however, I maintain a focus on voter sanctioning as a key form of backlash in my theory. Finally, because party instability exerts a conditioning, rather than determining, effect on politicians' time horizons and their choices about conflict, my model recognizes that elites can make mistakes in deciding where and when to supply violence. Indeed, the literature is replete with examples of leaders miscalculating the consequences of their political choices (Eisenstadt 2003; Gherghina 2013), including decisions about repression and violence (Gautam 2005; Rosenzweig 2023). Chapter 7 briefly features these realities in the case of the 2013 Muzaffarnagar and Shamli riots in Uttar Pradesh, India (Pai 2014; Malik 2021). For the moment, however, I simply note that insofar as my model proposes that politicians will try to account for the possibility of future sanctioning in making decisions about the costs and benefits of violence, they will not always arrive at the most accurate assessments. Instead, because elite decision-making is a complex phenomenon that is influenced by a variety of factors, I expect that political leaders will make mistakes in deploying violence from time to time.

Stage 1: Elite Choice

Given my interest in understanding the *supply* of violence, politicians are the first movers in my model. I posit that fleeting or transient parties can encourage political elites to initiate violence by reducing the costs and risks associated with this choice. More concretely, I hold that unstable parties can contribute to truncated time horizons among politicians and thereby incentivize the instrumentalization or sponsorship of violence. I further propose that compared to

A Theory of Party Instability and Political Violence

their counterparts from stable parties, politicians associated with transient parties will be more likely to initiate recurring and high-intensity violence.

Importantly, however, I expect that violence in unstable party contexts will exhibit spatial variations. In particular, I suggest that elites will try to spark conflict in those places where they can draw on manipulable ethnic cleavages or tap into pre-existing grievances among citizens. Such sentiments might be particularly easy to exploit in settings where "similarity in demographic proportions" among two or more groups creates real or perceived competition over resources (Varshney 2002: 8). In subnational sites with significant Muslim concentrations in India, for example, Varshney (2002: 8) has shown that Hindu nationalist politicians have often peddled arguments about "Muslim appeasement" and other alleged threats posed by the community to drive wedges between Hindus and Muslims. In his more recent study of pre-election ethnic riots in Africa, Müller-Crepon has made an analogous case for the importance of comparable sizes of key ethnic groups in making violence possible. He notes that such configurations are necessary to raise the salience of ethnic identities and also help to mount riots due to the "broad demographic basis" that undergirds these incidents (Müller-Crepon 2022: 244). Finally, in contexts such as the United States (Olzak, Shanahan, and McEneaney 1996) and Indonesia (Barron, Kaiser, and Pradhan 2004), a number of scholars have affirmed the importance of demography in predisposing some subnational sites to violence.

Where ethnic demography can thus be one factor that can give rise to opportunity structures – including the crafting of manipulable grievances – that are conducive to mobilizing conflict, it is not a necessary condition for violence. Indeed, constructivist insights tell us that such grievances can also be present or fashioned over time in places where local or regional ethnic composition may not predict conflict. Boone (2011), for example, chronicles that state-allocated land rights in Kenya are central to understanding the subnational spatial distribution of election violence in the 1990s. These land rights crucially "structured the geographic pattern of land-related grievances, defined rival constituencies of land claimants, and created opportunities and incentives for ruling elites to manipulate existing land grievances and land-tenure relationships for electoral gain" (Boone 2011: 1313). In a similar vein, Klaus (2020: 260) holds that it is "the histories of land control and distribution of land rights" in Kenya – as opposed to subnational ethnic composition – that have rendered ethnic arrangements relevant for mobilizing violence in some locations over others.

Finally, a few scholars have argued for the interplay between demographic variables and grievances in predicting where violence might occur. Kimuli Kasara's (2017) research in Kenya has persuasively shown that ethnic segregation increases community-level vulnerabilities to conflict. Combining data on ethnic composition and violence across 700 localities in Rift Valley Province, her work finds that segregation increased communal violence during the 2007–2008 post-election crisis by decreasing interethnic trust among residents. Similarly, in studying the Indian case, Rikhil Bhavnani and Bethany Lacina (2015) have shown that domestic migration prompts nativist riots in states that lack political alignment with the center. Because such states receive fewer resources from the national government, Bhavnani and Lacina find that they are often unable to control in-migration and therefore face violence that targets migrant communities.

Chapters 5 and 7 of this book discuss the demographic composition and relevant local grievances that have helped to propel violence in my subnational research sites. For the moment, however, my argument simply holds that it is in settings where unstable parties incentivize violence on the part of politicians – and conducive demographic or contextual factors are present on the ground – that elites' attempts to organize conflict will often find success. This is not only because social or ethnic fault lines and/or pervasive intercommunal grievances will make for readily combustible contexts for violence, but also because restraining conflict will be difficult in such circumstances. Scott Straus's (2012: 344) work on genocide, for example, has previously established that it is precisely in settings where "voices of restraint [are] marginalized, overwhelmed, or destroyed" that mass violence emerges. Likewise, Berenschot's (2011b: 168–169) ethnographic research on the Gujarat riots in India has unearthed several instances of the marginalization of restraining mechanisms, including a case where the speech of one individual who tried to appeal for calm was met not with consideration or respect, but with stone-throwing from an angry crowd. Finally, Krause (2018: 5) has acknowledged that the nonviolent communities she studies in Nigeria and Indonesia are "exceptional." Her work has further shown that their success in avoiding violence hinged on the development of social orders that sought to "prevent killings," as well as "prevention strategies," that civilians continuously modified in order to maintain peace (Krause 2018: 5).

Given these difficulties in controlling conflict across various contexts, I argue that once the match for violence is lit, even minor clashes can quickly escalate into large conflagrations. In the case of Ambon, Indonesia, for example, journalists and practitioners have chronicled how a relatively quiet two years were broken in 2004 when Christians and Muslims clashed with one another following incitement by military elites and opposition politicians (Al Jazeera 2004; International Crisis Group 2004). Once the violence began, it rapidly spread from the town center to different parts of the city and the island, ultimately claiming the lives of 36 civilians over the course of six short days (Pelletier and Soedirgo 2017).

In light of the very real possibilities of violence spiraling after its initiation, it stands to reason that elites will seek to organize or support conflict in a manner that maximizes its benefits and minimizes its costs. All else equal, my model proposes that places and periods marked by unstable parties will make it possible for politicians to attain this balance. This is because these settings will enable elites to discount the potential future costs of violence, including

A Theory of Party Instability and Political Violence

costs associated with severe episodes. Moving from the party system to individual parties, moreover, I propose that politicians situated within transient parties will be especially likely to resort to conflict. In sites and epochs marked by relatively stable and durable parties, by contrast, I argue that the future costs of violence could be high enough to disincentivize conflict. An observable implication of this claim is that we should expect to see no or mainly low-level violence in such settings.

Taken together, the first stage of my model – and the variations in time horizons that I expect to see in stable versus unstable party contexts – gives rise to two claims, laid out below. Whereas the first claim describes the kinds of elites and party structures with strong incentives to drive political conflict, the second lays out how these incentives can change over time.

(1) Politicians who hold low expectations of party durability will be more likely to resort to violence, including at severe levels, than their counterparts who expect their parties to endure in the long term.
(2) As long-standing, stable parties start to erode and politicians' time horizons begin to shorten, the scale and frequency of party-based violence will increase.

From a cross-national comparative perspective, the first claim further generates the following third expectation:

(3) Places marked by unstable political parties will be more vulnerable to repeated episodes of high-intensity party conflict than places where stable parties abound.

Finally, my model holds that whereas levels of party instability help to explain *when* politicians might resort to violence, subnational factors pertaining to demography and inter-communal grievances serve to account for *where* violence might be organized. As shown in Figures 2.1 and 2.2, I expect that elites will be more likely to latch onto ethnic fault lines and intercommunal grievances in their efforts to initiate recurring and severe violence in settings marked by fleeting, rather than stable, parties. Tapping into local ethnic demography

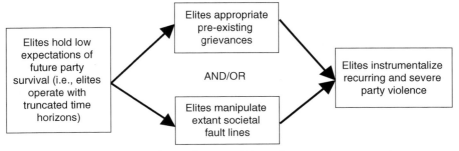

FIGURE 2.1 Initiating recurring and severe violence in unstable party settings

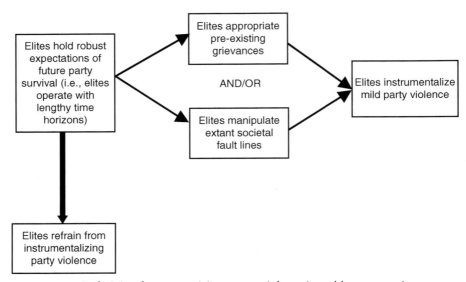

FIGURE 2.2 Refraining from organizing severe violence in stable party settings

and subnational grievances would thus be the means through which conflict could be mobilized. By contrast, in places populated by stable parties – and as shown in Figure 2.2 – elites will either bypass these local factors that support violence or make use of them to instrumentalize or sponsor low-level conflict.

Stage 2: Voters' Reactions

I now move to the second stage of my model, which hinges on voters' reactions. After politicians initiate violence, they open up possibilities for voters to respond. Furthermore, voters' ability to react to conflict rests on their learning and processing of information about elites' actions. We should thus expect that there will be some lag between an event of party-based or party-sponsored violence and voters' responses. I also acknowledge that voters can learn about violence through various channels, ranging from community leaders, politicians themselves, or investigatory commission or media reports. Some of these sources will seek to provide information to voters in neutral or unbiased ways while others will disseminate information in a manner that suits their interests. For instance, we might imagine that opposition elites will exaggerate claims about incumbent-driven violence in order to delegitimize ruling politicians. Likewise, leaders who already occupy power might try to displace blame for violence onto their rivals in an effort to shield themselves from potential backlash.

Regardless of the channels through which voters learn about conflict, I propose that major events of violence will motivate citizens to punish the leaders and parties responsible. Experimental research on this topic has already highlighted a strong tendency among voters to sanction elites for violence irrespective of their ethnic or partisan affiliations (Horowitz and Klaus 2020; Gutiérrez-Romero and LeBas 2020; Rosenzweig 2021, 2023).[5] As highlighted in Chapter 1, during fieldwork in Kenya and India, I found a similar intolerance toward violence among voters, who routinely emphasized the costs of major episodes of conflict to their families, livelihoods, and communities. For example, a Kikuyu resident of the Pipeline Camp for Internally Displaced Persons (IDPs) on the outskirts of Nakuru shared the following information with me:

I came here [to the camp] from Kipelion [in the Rift Valley]. That place was occupied mainly by Kalenjins. During the [2007–2008] violence, my business, a big hotel, was burned down. I can never go back there now. It is too difficult to start over.[6]

Similarly, a civil society leader from the Hindu community in Meerut recounted the consequences of the city's massive 1987 riots in the following words:

When the violence took place here in 1987, it continued for quite a long time … for approximately four to six months. During that time, all the businesses were destroyed. I was still young then, [and] these are old matters now, but what was seen was that the people from both communities [and] from all fields were worried.[7]

While the postulations of the second stage of my model are thus consistent with the insights of many experimental studies on violence, I contend that not all voters will be capable of sanctioning elites and parties responsible for conflict. Specifically, I hold that settings marked by unstable parties will make it difficult for voters to punish violent politicians. This is because when parties crumble in such settings, they can result in violence-wielding elites exiting the electoral arena entirely. For leaders who do survive party decline, moreover, they might affiliate with parties or coalitions in ways that preclude sanctioning. In Kenya, for example, unstable parties have not only made for unstable alliances, but these alliances have sometimes also formed in a manner that has led to an alignment – rather than an opposition – between the interests of previously violent elites and certain groups of voters. I discuss these dynamics in greater detail in Chapters 4 and 5.

In settings marked by stable parties, by contrast, voters armed with information about violence will be in a better position to sanction the political actors responsible. Depending on the kind of election in which they are participating as well as the nature of executive-legislature relations, I expect that voters could direct such punishment toward individual candidates or toward

---

[5] Daxecker and Fjelde's (2022) findings on partisan responses to violence are an important exception here.
[6] Interview with a resident of an IDP camp, Nakuru, October 26, 2013.
[7] Interview with a leader of the Boolean Jewelry Traders Association, Meerut, August 22, 2013.

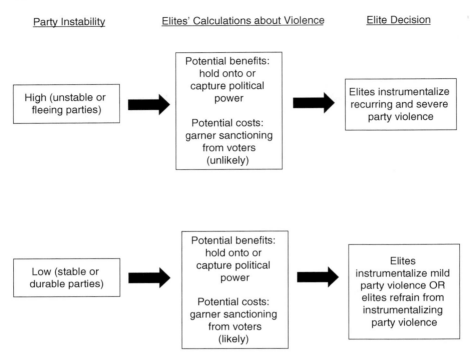

FIGURE 2.3 The relationship between party instability, voters' reactions, and elites' decisions about violence

the party as a whole. In subnational legislative elections in parliamentary or presidential regimes, for example, granular information about the involvement of constituency-level elites could enable voters to directly punish such leaders. Similarly, given the prominence of personalities in national presidential contests, voters could conceivably direct sanctioning toward specific leaders. By contrast, because many voters may live outside the constituencies of violence-wielding elites, we might see citizens penalize *parties*, rather than candidates, responsible for violence in national legislative elections in parliamentary or presidential systems.

The logic of backward induction supports my prior claims about how party instability stands to condition elites' decisions about violence. First, I expect that given how unstable parties can make it difficult for citizens to hold violent leaders to account, elites in these settings will be in a position to discount the possibilities of future voter sanctioning and routinely gamble with violence, including at a severe scale. Second, and by contrast, I posit that those competing in stable party settings can be expected to steer clear of organizing or sponsoring high-intensity conflict for fear of garnering punishment from voters down the line. These postulations are further depicted in Figure 2.3 above.

A Theory of Party Instability and Political Violence

ENDOGENEITY CONCERNS AND ALTERNATIVE EXPLANATIONS

This book holds that variations in party instability impact elites' decisions about violence by shortening or elongating their time horizons. It further posits that the size of politicians' shadows of the future matters because these shadows enable or prevent elites from discounting the possibility of incurring future sanctioning from voters, among other costs.

Could it be the case, however, that political violence actually affects party birth and death rates? To address this important concern about endogeneity, I first consider the conditions under which violent political parties might witness outright party collapse. I then examine the pathways and processes through which a period of political conflict might give rise to new parties. Overall, I find that neither of these scenarios are as compelling as my argument that party birth and death rates impact elites' incentives for violence.

I also evaluate the alternative explanation that democratic longevity might better account for variations in party violence across space and time. Finally, I briefly discuss the rival claim that the composition of civil society – as opposed to elites' incentives – most proximately captures the outbreak of party violence. Compared to each of these accounts, I argue that projected party lifespan and elites' time horizons offer a superior explanation for politicians' decisions to drive or sponsor conflict.

Endogeneity Concerns

There are two scenarios in which political violence could conceivably impact party entry and exit rates. First, parties that commit or support conflict in the present might find themselves subject to such extreme levels of voter sanctioning that they come to face outright party collapse around the next election or closely thereafter. Second, a sustained period of political violence might create opportunities for the rise of new parties down the line.

Bolivia's MNR party approximates the first scenario. The MNR faced severe sanctioning from voters in 2005 after it repressed violent demonstrations opposing the export of natural gas in 2003 (Assies and Salman 2005). In fact, the sanctioning was so severe that the MNR's presidential candidate, Michiaki Nagatani Morishita, only amassed 6% of the vote in the 2005 polls (Lupu 2018: 374). This figure marked a decrease of 16 percentage points from its 2002 performance when the MNR had competed in an alliance with the center-left Movimiento Bolivia Libre (MBL or Free Bolivia Movement). In addition, the party suffered a loss of 29 in the Chamber of Deputies and ten seats in the Senate.

Notwithstanding this dramatic change in electoral fortunes, it is important to note that even this case did not rise to the standard of outright party death as defined in this book. In fact, I am not aware of any examples of parties that have faced a complete demise for organizing or sponsoring conflict. Even in cases where leaders have miscalculated the consequences of violence, outright party death has been an extremely rare outcome. Indeed, both observational and experimental research finds that voter sanctioning in the aftermath of conflict generally engenders vote-switching rather than party replacement (Susewind and Dhattiwala 2014; Gutiérrez-Romero and LeBas 2020; Rosenzweig 2021).[8] Thus, whether violence is committed in error or purposefully deployed, existing evidence does not support the claim that the costs of political conflict are severe enough to lead to party exit.

The second major pathway through which violence might impact party replacement is by contributing to party birth. Under this scenario, conflict in the present could contribute to the rise of new parties around the next election or thereafter. The extant literature on rebel-to-party transformations offers some evidence for this dynamic (Manning 2007; Sörderberg-Kovacs 2007; de Zeeuw 2008; Reilly, Nordlund, and Newman 2008; Reno 2011). This body of work shows that rebel groups are especially likely to transition into political parties in cases where end-of-war peace negotiations include "electoral participation provisions" for insurgent organizations (Matanock 2017a, 2017b). Indeed, in countries such as Burundi (Speight and Wittig 2018) and Nepal (Ishiyama and Widmeier 2013), the historical record reveals that rebel groups have not only transitioned into political parties but even won elections and attained party longevity in the postconflict era.

However, such cases remain rare. As one expert on the metamorphosis and political mainstreaming of the Maoist insurgents in Nepal[9] summarized, "there have been insurrections around the world and very, very rarely does [one see] a smooth, or almost a smooth, transition from being an armed insurrection into government and political power."[10] Beyond civil wars, furthermore, there is little evidence to suggest that party violence stands to encourage the birth of new political parties. Thus, while my research does not dispute the fact that political conflict can motivate a fresh breed of politicians or animate new issues (Harmel and Roberston 1985) conducive to party birth, I also

---

[8] A notable exception here is the fate of the BSP, which failed to capture even a single seat in the 2014 Indian general elections. This poor performance was at least partly on account of some party leaders' involvement in the 2013 Muzaffarnagar and Shamli clashes (Pai 2014; Malik 2021).

[9] Following a decade-long civil war between 1996 and 2006, Nepal's Maoists reinvented themselves as a political party known as the Communist Party of Nepal-Maoist (CPN-M) and re-entered the political mainstream. Two years later in 2008, the CPN-M attained a victory in Nepal's constituent assembly elections, which catapulted its leader, Prachanda, to the position of Prime Minister. Prachanda recaptured this post for a second term in 2016. Even in this case, however, it bears stating that the party itself wasn't entirely new. Rather, it had first emerged in 1994 following a split from the Communist Party of Nepal-Unity Centre (CPN-UC). Two years after its emergence on the electoral stage, the party transformed into an armed group under the leadership of Prachanda and other senior Maoists.

[10] Telephonic interview with a former Indian Ambassador to Nepal, New Delhi, May 6, 2020. This interview was conducted for an unrelated project on rebel-to-party transformations. It was held over the phone due to the COVID-19 pandemic.

A Theory of Party Instability and Political Violence

argue that party formation resulting from such processes does not guarantee electoral support from voters. For these reasons, I hold that the direction of the relationship proposed thus far-from party birth and death rates to elites' incentives for violence-is more plausible than the reverse claim.

Alternative Explanations

Democratic Longevity

I now turn to discussing democratic longevity as an alternative explanation for party violence. This explanation holds that compared to levels of party instability, the youth of some democracies more proximately accounts for elites' incentives to drive or sponsor violence. There is already a well-established literature documenting the deficiencies that young democracies suffer in arenas such as legislatures (Huber, Reuscheyer, and Stephens 1997; Alabi 2009; Barkan 2009; Rakner and van de Walle 2009), legal and security institutions (O'Donnell 1998; Schedler, Diamond, and Plattner 1999; Serra 2016), and political parties (Caramani 2000; Mainwaring and Zoco 2007; Lupu and Riedl 2013). Related work also shows that the age of democracy bears some association with democratic consolidation, as older democracies tend to be more consolidated (Brender and Drazen 2007). Consequently, prodemocracy cultures and attitudes in these places are usually stronger than those found in immature democracies (Anderson 1998). Moreover, such cultures appear to play a part in protecting well-established democracies from succumbing to electoral manipulation and elite malpractices such as violence (Aluaigba 2016; Schedler 2002).

In light of these findings and given the two country cases under investigation in this book, a logical question that emerges is whether the difference in Kenya and India's democratic ages might provide a superior account for the observed disparities in their vulnerabilities to party violence than my proposed explanation of party instability. After all, following nearly three decades of authoritarian rule, multiparty elections only returned to Kenya in the early 1990s. Moreover, according to some experts, the country only achieved true multiparty democracy in 2002 when the long-reigning Kenya African National Union (KANU) party was voted out of office (Brown 2001; Barkan 2004). Meanwhile, with the exception of the Emergency years under Indira Gandhi in the mid-to-late 1970s and the country's more recent democratic weakening (Alizada et al. 2021), India maintained an enviable democracy throughout her post-independence years. Another way to articulate these ideas, then, is that as democracy matures in Kenya, elites' incentives to drive and sponsor party violence will accordingly diminish.

Chapters 3 and 8 grapple with this alternative explanation. In Chapter 3, I chronicle important historical reasons – separate from democratic age – that account for differences in elites' incentives to organize and support violence in these nations. Specifically, I trace Kenyan and Indian politicians' incentives for conflict to the decisions of nationalist and early postcolonial leaders who sowed the seeds for dramatically different party systems with dissimilar rates of party instability. These arguments, in the Kenyan case, build directly on the work of scholars such as Ken Opalo (2019) and Mai Hassan (2020: 17) who have both documented KANU elites' use of the Provincial Administration (PA) – "the largest administrative and security apparatus" in the country – in managing regime threats. Meanwhile, other scholars have shown how party weakness during the Kenyatta years emerged as a consequence of a neglect of party politics (Good 1968; Throup and Hornsby 1998). With regard to the Indian case, the arguments I present in Chapter 3 draw on the scholarship of Patrick Heller (2000: 504), Kanchan Chandra (2005), and Maya Tudor (2013a, 2013b), who have all credited the Indian National Congress (INC) for putting the country "firmly on the road to democracy" and setting a precedent for the rise of stable political parties from the nationalist period onward.

Taken together, these insights show that one of the central reasons for Kenyan and Indian politicians' diverging incentive structures for violence – that is, considerable differences in levels of party instability – can be located in the choices of their respective founding leaders. I further argue in Chapters 4 and 5 that Kenya's recent avoidance of severe violence – seen most recently in 2022 – can be attributed to the strengthening of institutions beyond political parties. By contrast, my empirical materials in Chapters 6 and 7 show that the stability of Indian parties and the electoral risks posed by severe violence are key to understanding the decline in significant Hindu-Muslim riots in cities and the rise of newer sites and forms of conflict, including rural clashes and targeted low-level attacks against Muslims.

In Chapter 8, I further illuminate the limitations of democratic age as an explanator for party violence, drawing on evidence from Ghana and pre-Erdoğan Turkey. This comparison between a young democracy with stable political parties and a more mature democracy with highly volatile parties, respectively, helps to underscore the primacy of party (in)stability in preventing high levels of electoral violence in Ghana and enabling an intense and brutal period of conflict – known as the *anarşi* crisis – in Turkey between 1976 and 1980.

Civil Society and Social Networks

A second explanation that might account for variations in elites' incentives for violence pertains to the role of civil society and social networks. As Varshney (2001: 374) has documented in the case of India, places with "preexisting local networks of civic engagement" between Hindus and Muslims tend to weather the precipitants of communal riots, such as rumors and minor skirmishes, much better than settings where associational life is ethnically segregated. Thus, it is plausible that differences in the strength and composition of civil society organizations (CSOs) better explain elites' incentives for violence than my proposed model of party instability.

A Theory of Party Instability and Political Violence

I hold, however, that the argument about civic associations is most useful for identifying *where* politicians' efforts to instrumentalize violence are likely to find success. As previously discussed, I expect that subnational ethnic demography and/or the availability of local grievances – which may in turn be associated with the extent of ethnic segregation in associational life – help to inform elites' decisions about where to supply violence. As such, I posit that the civic associations framework does not offer as much direct insight into the factors that actually stand to generate incentives for conflict. This is because rather than explicitly articulating when and why leaders might resort to violence, Varshney's model assumes the existence of such tendencies. These important differences in our research questions thus limit the relevance of civic associations for understanding elite decision-making as it pertains to initiating political conflict.

SUMMARY AND CONCLUSION

Parties are among the most important institutions for democracies to survive and thrive. Yet global evidence shows that politicians now frequently use parties as instruments to drive violence. This chapter has developed a new theory about the conditions under which parties can be appropriated toward such ends. Focusing on the *supply* of violence, I have argued that party instability can incentivize the use of conflict – including severe conflict – on the part of elites by shortening their time horizons and enabling them to discount the future costs of violence such as incurring punishment from voters. My theory further holds that insofar as major episodes of conflict are destabilizing to communities across partisan and ethnic divides, ordinary citizens should be motivated to punish elites responsible for such events. However, the *ability* to sanction politicians rests on the durability of parties themselves. In places where parties are fleeting or transient, informed voters are typically unable to hold leaders to account, which in turn renders them vulnerable to experiencing repeated and severe episodes of conflict. By contrast, in places where parties are stable and long-lasting, real possibilities of future voter sanctioning stand to dampen elites' incentives to engage in violence in the present.

Chapters 3–7 provide support for this theory by drawing on evidence from Kenya and India. Whereas Chapters 4 through 7 offer evidence by drawing on both quantitative party volatility data as well as qualitative interviews, Chapter 3 begins by developing the cross-regional comparison between these countries in the tradition of comparative historical social science (Skocpol 1979; Skocpol and Somers 1980; Tilly 1984; Mahoney and Rueschemeyer 2003). This approach is a powerful framework for carrying out macro-level comparative analyses, illuminating contrasts across different contexts, and interrogating the temporality of social and political change. As such, before we can study the particular ways in which Kenyan and Indian parties have engaged with political violence – tasks to which I turn in Chapters 4 through 7 – the tools of comparative historical analysis can provide us with crucial insights to better understand the dissimilar development of these parties.

In this regard, Chapter 3 shows that whereas KANU emerged as a weakly institutionalized party – and set the stage for a fragile, divided, and authoritarian party system in Kenya – the INC not only sought to usher in democracy in India but also offered a model to newer parties for building stable organizations and crafting broad bases of electoral support. The chapter further demonstrates that these different modes of party development generated dissimilar incentives for elites to supply violence in the two nations. Concretely, while the onset of multiparty competition in the 1990s enabled an insecure KANU to resort to its prior record of violence in managing new regime threats, India managed to avoid major bouts of party conflict until the late 1970s and early 1980s due to relatively low rates of party instability. The central claims of this chapter thus offer a path-dependent framework (Pierson 2000) for making sense of subsequent variations in elites' incentives for violence in Kenya and India.

3

The Development of Divergent Parties and Party Systems in Kenya and India

> [Political parties] in Kenya are not historical entities. Since the KANU years, there has been no historical precedent to say that parties themselves are even viable. [Party members hold] no loyalty to parties at all. Joining a party is about personalities. It is about deals on power sharing. It is about access to money and influence. It is about tribal grouping. This is an extremely fragile setting in which to be holding competitive electoral politics. There is very little that one can say in terms of longevity for most parties in the country.
> – Interview with a policy expert, Nairobi, October 17, 2013

> People can say what they would like about the [Indian National] Congress. Obviously, the party is facing major challenges right now. But what the Congress did for centrism, moderation, and stability in the party system must be acknowledged as well.
> – Interview with an academic, Hyderabad, July 22, 2013

The interviews above underscore crucial differences between political parties in contemporary Kenya and India. They reveal that nationalist-era parties, namely, the Kenya African National Union (KANU) and the Indian National Congress (INC, or the Congress), established highly dissimilar party systems with deviating rates of stability and moderation. They further highlight that the precedents set by these parties largely endure to the present day. This endurance is particularly noteworthy in the face of the major political changes that both countries have witnessed over the last few decades: on the one hand, the transition to multiparty competition in Kenya in the early 1990s followed by the promulgation of a new constitution in 2010, and on the other hand, the decline of the "Congress system" (Kothari 1964) in India and the related rise of Hindu nationalism.

In this chapter, I trace the differing logics of party organization in Kenya and India from a comparative and historical perspective. This macro-political and macro-sociological approach (Skocpol and Somers 1980; Tilly 1984) helps to carefully reveal how parties developed in dissimilar ways both before and especially after the critical juncture of decolonization. I argue that this dissimilar development in turn generated a distinct set of elite calculations about the utility of conflict in the two countries. I organize the chapter chronologically, beginning with the colonial period and proceeding to the postcolonial period. My core finding is a path-dependent one (Pierson 2000): concretely, I demonstrate that leaders' decisions from the colonial and early postcolonial periods put Kenya and India on radically different tracks of party development. Although both the Kenya African National Union and Indian National Congress emerged and held power as dominant parties in the initial decades after independence, KANU elites oversaw the development of a more fragile, divided, and autocratically-oriented system. By contrast, politicians from the INC not only secured enviable organizational depth for their party (Tudor 2013a, 2013b), but they also modeled the adoption of a "centrist position" for other parties (Reddy 2005: 277; Rudolph and Rudolph 1980). These elite decisions further played a significant role in helping India emerge as a democracy and maintain regime stability for several decades after independence (Tudor 2013a, 2013b). In addition, the two countries' dissimilar party systems gave rise to differing elite incentive structures and calculations about political violence: where KANU leaders took to repression early in the postcolonial period and extended these strategies into the autocratic era, their INC counterparts sought to accommodate many differing voices and resorted to the use of force more selectively.

In articulating these arguments, I build on the recent insights of several scholars of African and South Asian politics. Research on institutional development in these regions – on parties (LeBas 2011; Tudor 2013a, 2013b), party systems (Riedl 2014), and legislatures (Opalo 2019) alike – has shown how critical junctures related to nationalist movements, decolonization, and transitions to multiparty competition put in place legacies that persisted long past these windows. In Kenya, for example, Hassan's (2020: 9) research on the Provincial Administration (PA) has held that "vestiges of authoritarianism continued to linger within state institutions" well after independence was achieved and contributed to the rise of weak parties as well as difficulties in consolidating democracy. While Hassan focuses on the PA – an important entity through which KANU elites sponsored violence in Kenya – my effort in this book is to open up political parties for the reader. I thus also draw on Maya Tudor's (2013a, 2013b) path-dependent analysis of democratization and regime maintenance in India, and extend her insights from the nationalist phase and early postindependence era into subsequent decades. This extension allows me to show how the development of stable political parties served to dampen elites' incentives for organizing and sponsoring violence well into the 1970s.

This chapter proceeds as follows. I begin by discussing party development in the Kenya Colony and under the British Raj. Specifically, I show that while

Divergent Parties and Party Systems in Kenya and India

colonial administrators devised comparable ethnic wedges and sought to nurture similar kinds of "loyalist" leaders in both places, KANU leaders exhibited a disinterest in party organization during the anti-colonial period itself. By contrast, their counterparts in the INC sought to develop differentiated structures within the nationalist movement and mobilize mass support for independence. I then detail party development after liberation from British rule, highlighting differences in leaders' initial priorities that only became starker after colonial rulers departed. The cumulative impact of these deviating choices not only resulted in radically divergent ruling parties in Kenya and India but also gave rise to opposing regime-types. Taken together, then, the historiography presented in this chapter provides the crucial foundation upon which to make sense of many subsequent elite decisions about party violence in these countries.

PARTY DEVELOPMENT UNDER COLONIAL RULE

The roots of divergent party and party system development in Kenya and India were set in crucial ways during the colonial period. During this era, the British relied on some common strategies to administer the Kenya Colony and British India. Central among these was the politicization of particular axes to manufacture, or at least encourage, social tensions among colonial subjects (Subrahmanyam 2006).

At the same time, and as several scholars have documented, there were also robust transnational connections between the Indian and East African anti-colonial movements (Aiyar 2011, 2015; Frenz 2013). Indeed, according to Margaret Frenz (2013: 152, 160), "the realization of nationalism not only involved communicating ideas of *swaraj* [political independence], *uhuru* [freedom], and self-determination, but also [entailed the provision] of [vital] material means" to support these struggles. Since India attained her independence first, her leaders such as Prime Minister Jawaharlal Nehru and members of the South Asian diaspora in Kenya contributed significant sums of money to back movements against British rule in East Africa (Frenz 2013). Despite this South-South exchange, however, party development in Kenya and India unfolded along divergent paths, and a number of differences in leaders' priorities emerged during the nationalist period itself.

Intra-elite Divides and the Rise of a Weakly Institutionalized Ruling Party in Kenya

Beginning with the cleavages that colonial administrators sought to politicize in each of these countries, it is important to note that the British initially adopted a race-based approach to divide-and-rule politics in Kenya (Subrahmanyam 2006). From there, they slowly shifted to emphasizing ethno-linguistic and class-based fault lines (Subrahmanyam 2006). This transition, as Amanda

Robinson (2014: 717) holds, amounted to "a policy of reifying local languages and customs." The instruments used for this project were vast and wide-ranging: they included "maps, the establishment of colonial museums ... and even physical artifacts [that] were assigned a unique tribal identity and physical location" (Berman 1998: 321).

Critically, after establishing the Kenya Colony in 1920, the British also sought to radically alter Africans' relationships to their land (Berman and Lonsdale 1980). First, they pushed local pastoral communities and indigenous groups out of the fertile Central and Rift Valley regions where they had long lived, and allocated much of the land in these areas for European settlers (Kanogo 1987; Okoth-Ogendo 1991; Kanyinga 2009; Elischer 2010; Lynch 2011). In so doing, they "relegated [Kenyans] to their specific ethnic group's 'Native Reserves,' land set aside for each of the colony's forty-plus ethnic groups on a fraction of their historic homeland" (Hassan 2020: 58). Second, and owing to the small size of the European settler community, they recruited members of the majority Kikuyu and Luo populations to fulfill the "labor needs of the new White Highlands – as well as coastal plantations and emergent industries" (Lynch 2011: 37).

These policies virtually transformed the land and labor market. Coupled with population growth, they led to a major shortage in access to land for ordinary Kenyans. This shortage was particularly acute "in the densely populated Kikuyu reserves in Central Province, most of which were clustered around settler plantations" (Klaus 2020: 76). Although some wealthy Kikuyu were able to buy land within Native Reserves, they were in a small minority. Consequently, by 1950, it is estimated that "around 25% of this group were [reduced to] working as 'squatters,' or tenant farmers without formal title deed, on European land" (Hassan 2020: 60).

Ultimately, the intra-Kikuyu fault line that emerged during this period found expression in the rise of the Land and Freedom Army or "Mau Mau." This movement, which took on the colonial state and its African collaborators between 1952 and 1960, "resulted in the deaths of approximately 25,000 Kenyan Africans" (Klaus 2020: 77; Branch 2009). It received considerable backing from the rank-and-file members of the "squatter" community (Kanogo 1987: 131). In addition, the movement drew support from countless women who vehemently objected to British officers and their African agents' decisions to remake social relations by using women's bodies as "sites for the elaboration of political and moral order" in the colony (Thomas 2003: 101). Taken together, the formation of Mau Mau not only marked a rejection of the colonial state but also of "the Kikuyu leadership that many ... people viewed as negligent" in failing to provide land to young men (Klaus 2020: 77).

In order to manage the Mau Mau insurgency, the British devised three key strategies. First, they articulated a distinction between "loyalists" – largely upwardly-mobile and educated non-Kikuyus – and Mau Mau fighters and

Divergent Parties and Party Systems in Kenya and India

their sympathizers who they termed "traitors."[1] Second, they groomed "loyalists" to contest the Colony's 1957 Legislative Council election, the first election under colonial rule in Kenya in which Africans could stand for political office and ordinary citizens could choose their representatives (Branch 2006; Engholm 1956; Barkan and Okumu 1978). In nurturing "an African educated and moderate political elite" as "part of the solution to the Mau Mau war," colonial authorities also restricted the 1957 vote in deliberate and predictable ways (Angelo 2020: 67). In Central Province and Nairobi in particular – areas of support for Mau Mau – they limited registration to "those who could prove their loyalty to the regime" (Branch 2006: 27). As Branch and Cheeseman (2006: 19) have shown, this amounted to a mere "7.4% of the adult population of Central Province" being registered to cast their ballots in the 1957 vote. Third, administrators "came to rely heavily ... on the Provincial Administration [PA] to maintain control over the colony amid unrest by the indigenous population" (Hassan 2020: 60). As the "main organ of security, administration, development," the PA not only "adjudicated land disputes both among indigenous Kenyans and between Kenyans and white settlers," but also "approved candidacy papers, supervised campaigns, determined voter eligibility, and tabulated the results" after elections were introduced in the Kenya Colony (Hassan 2020: 60–61).

Recent research by Ken Opalo (2019: 143) has demonstrated that at the time of independence on December 12, 1963, Jomo Kenyatta – who had spent much of the 1950s in prison – "inherited the PA intact." Concurrently, he also found himself leading a "weakly institutionalized elite party" – KANU – of which he was not a founding member and over which he wielded only "tenuous control" (Opalo 2019: 135, 151; Tamarkin 1978). Founded in 1944 as the Kenya African Union (KAU), a political organization dedicated to achieving independence for Kenya, the colonial government banned KAU in 1953 during the Mau Mau movement. In 1960, when this ban was lifted and while Kenyatta was still imprisoned, a number of nationalist leaders resurrected KAU as KANU. Days before its official founding, elites associated with the organization agreed to convert district associations, located across the country, into KANU branches (Odinga 1968: 193). By the end of the following year, the party had amassed some 500,000 members spread over 30 branches (Good 1968: 116).

Despite this promising start, Kenyan leaders chose to circumscribe KANU's role in the liberation struggle. In fact, the party's first policy manifesto, published during Kenyatta's internment in 1960, explicitly held that whereas

---

[1] During the course of the conflict, colonial administrators altered the parameters of these categories in ways that suited them. As Daniel Branch (2006: 32) writes, between 1952 and 1962, they variously cast Kikuyus, as well as members of the Meru and Embu communities – with whom the Kikuyu share cultural ties (Parsons 2012) – as "Mau Mau, loyalist, and all things in between."

"parties may be necessary for the working of a democracy ... [they] were not necessary in the fight for freedom" (Good 1968: 117). The early momentum toward developing a "grass-root[s] organization[al]" structure for the party thus quickly crumbled (Odinga 1968: 200).

Against this background, one of KANU's earliest challenges came in 1960 itself, when Ronald Ngala, a leader from the coastal Mijikenda group, left. Ngala held that his departure emanated from grave concerns about Kikuyu and Luo domination – two key communities that comprised KANU's leadership – after independence. As the founder of the Kenya African Democratic Union (KADU), he also persuaded Masinde Muliro, a member of the Luhya community, and Daniel arap Moi from the Kalenjin group to join him.[2] This splintering of parties along ethnic lines marked an important pre-independence blow to KANU. To make matters worse, between 1960 and 1963, many KANU branches disintegrated, and the party also failed to recruit new members and collect the requisite membership dues (Odinga 1968). Indeed, the structural and fiscal woes of KANU multiplied so rapidly that when journalists asked its treasurer, Joseph Murumbi, questions about the party's organization and finances in early 1963 – mere months before the country's independence – he admitted that "they [simply did not] exist" (Good 1968: 118).

In light of KANU's many deficiencies and the considerable strengths of the inherited administrative apparatus, it is unsurprising that Kenyatta appropriated the PA as his main instrument for managing regime threats after independence. As Opalo (2019: 137) writes, "KANU [simply] was not a viable option" for this purpose. At the same time, it is also true that the first president's inability, or at the very least unwillingness, to develop a party-based means of consolidating power was partly the result of his own disinterest in strengthening the organization. To quote Opalo (2019: 152) again, "Kenyatta had agency, and could have invested in strengthening KANU instead of relying on the PA," but did not.

His "benign neglect" of KANU came through in a number of ways (Opalo 2019: 152). First, in a reversal of the position laid out in the previously mentioned 1960 manifesto, Kenyatta stated in an interview with the *Daily Nation* newspaper that "actual Party organization is not [as] important, perhaps, as the discipline in thought-lines which KANU must learn" (Good 1968: 271). These statements were reassuring to the British: they indicated that departing colonial officials had handed over power to a set of "reliable [and] conservative allies" in Kenya, as intended (Anderson 2005: 335). Second, even though KANU was not exclusively comprised of "loyalists," the "cadre of colleagues

---

[2] Owing to the colonial state's encouragement of "more moderate [and] pro-British ['loyalist']" individuals to compete in Legislative Council elections in the Kenya Colony, Ngala, Muliro, and Moi had all clinched the African constituencies for which they competed in 1957 (Throup and Hornsby 1998: 10). In doing so, they had emerged as three among eight non-Kikuyu Africans to be elected to the Legislative Council in this historic election (Branch 2006; Angelo 2020).

Divergent Parties and Party Systems in Kenya and India

that Kenyatta assembled around himself at the top of the party remained steadfastly moderate, and anti-Mau Mau, for several years" (Anderson 2005: 334–335). Such arrangements, as subsequent pages detail, not only affected Kenyatta's treatment of ex-Mau Mau members within the party postindependence but also generated downstream consequences for party organization in the nation as a whole.

Inclusive Nationalism and the Emergence of a Strongly Institutionalized Party Apparatus in India

These events from the Kenyan case – achieving freedom with a weak and divided party and an executive largely unconcerned about party strength – differ in considerable ways from the development of party structures in India under colonial rule, where the Congress was the "main vehicle of for nationalism" (Johnson 2005: 5). Established as an independence movement by urban and educated Indian elites in 1885, it turned to mass politics during the 1920s under Mahatma Gandhi's leadership (Tudor 2013a). Rather than falling prey to divisive colonial-era tactics, Congress leaders typically tried to bridge differences between ethnic communities wherever possible. Their intentions around this issue, to be clear, were not always well-meaning; nor were their efforts always successful. As John McLane (1988: 47; also see Sarkar 2002) writes, "Congress leaders [did not act] consistently for the common good or in a disinterested manner because they did, indeed, act sometimes as partisan spokesmen for sectional interests, such as landlords, moneylenders, or university graduates."

During the nationalist phase, for example, even though "communalism was the 'other' against which the Congress arrayed itself ... many Congressmen deployed Hindu symbols as they attempted to mobilize the masses" (Staniland 2021: 95–96). Furthermore, Staniland (2021: 98) points out that INC elites never fully resolved the Hindu–Muslim question. This cleavage would both come back to haunt the Congress in the run-up to independence and would also later feature quite prominently in INC leaders' efforts to drive political violence. Yet the Congress went much further on the issue of caste. Indeed, when it came to opposing the caste system, several INC leaders not only preached "equality in intercaste interactions," but also modeled "egalitarian public behavior" by cleaning toilets and carrying out other menial chores, tasks that were typically relegated to members of the untouchable community (Tudor 2013a: 262; Tudor and Slater 2016: 41).

These campaigns on the part of the INC were largely a response to the strategies of the British to latch onto and exacerbate caste and religious differences in India (Chatterjee 2004; Subrahmanyam 2006). In 1871, the colonial census had taken the "unprecedented step of enumerating group identities, including religion [which was now] defined in terms of the singular categories of Hindus, Muslims, Sikhs, and Christians" (Lieberman and Singh 2017: 13). Subsequent decisions – including the 1905 Partition of Bengal, which bifurcated the province along religious lines, and the 1909 passage of the Indian Councils Act, which established separate electorates for Muslims – further sought to drive wedges between Hindus and Muslims. While such measures found varying success – the British were forced to reverse the Partition of Bengal in 1911 following widespread protests from Bengalis – together, they critically weakened "cross-community networks" between the two communities (Hasan 2019: 13).

In addition to implementing the above policies, the British also sought to weaken the nationalist movement in India. As in the Kenyan case, their strategy to divide elites in South Asia focused on exacerbating differences between "Moderate" (or reformist) and "Extremist" anti-colonial leaders. Concerned about the increasing popularity of the "Extremists," colonial officers initially took it upon themselves to amplify moderate Congress voices. When this strategy proved insufficient, they launched a "wide attack on the Extremist leadership [and] jail[ed] and deport[ed] many of its leaders" in 1907 (Tudor 2013b: 53). In so doing, they "effectively end[ed] the 'Swadeshi' movement" for economic self-sufficiency in colonial India (Tudor 2013b: 53).

Despite the deployment of these common strategies in the Kenya Colony and during the British Raj, the INC emerged as a strong party with a coherent distributive coalition at its core, a commitment to a set of programmatic principles, and robust intraparty organizational structures (Tudor 2013a, 2013b). Indeed, according to Tudor (2013a, 2013b), the Congress achieved these markers of party strength well *before* independence. Its transition to a mass movement against colonial rule in the 1920s was a vital turning point: not only did this transition help the Congress to "successfully advance electoral reforms," but it also generated the impetus for settling and pursuing crucial party priorities (Tudor 2013a: 257).

In 1920, INC leaders thus adopted a new constitution in which they detailed the organization's internal structures. These structures would include "[a] President, three General Secretaries, the All-Indian Congress Committee, the Working Committee (after 1921), the Provincial Congress Committees, the District, Taluka, and Town Congress Committees [as well as] other recognized associations" (Krishna 1966: 414). The multi-level apparatus promulgated and subsequently established by the INC enabled the movement to penetrate the Indian countryside and harness mass discontent against British oppression. Indeed, so extensive was the reach of the Congress that even outspoken critics of the INC and its leadership – including Dr. B. R. Ambedkar (1946: 157), who held that the movement's anti-caste campaigns had amounted to little more than "a formal recognition of the problem" (Keer 1971: 165) – admitted in his writings that the party organization "cover[ed] every town and every village in the country." Following the creation of this grassroots structure, during two short years between 1921 and 1923, the Congress went on to raise more than Rs. 13 million under Gandhi's leadership to carry out various anti-colonial activities (Krishna 1966: 414).

Taken together, by the time that Kenya and India realized their goals of independence in 1963 and 1947, respectively, they were already poised with considerably different founding parties. These differences became even starker in the postindependence period, further setting apart elites' incentives to organize or sponsor party violence.

PARTY DEVELOPMENT AFTER INDEPENDENCE

After independence, a fundamental divergence in KANU and the INC's development – which produced broader consequences for the party systems of the two countries – emerged in the Kenya African National Union's failure to evolve into a mass party and the Congress's attainment of predominant party status with "mass party structural features" (Singh 1981: 28). KANU Secretary General Tom Mboya summed up the confusion over the organization's future role in November 1966, when he argued that it was "but a nationalist movement" (Good 1968: 128). By contrast, the INC not only developed "national and state party organizations ... with a fair degree of branch-type structural formalization and articulation, [but also established] district and subdistrict local party organizations [of the] 'machine-type' [variety]" (Singh 1981: 28–29).

Despite realizing such organizational heft and differentiation, it is worth noting that the transformation of the Congress into a political party was not entirely uncontroversial. Indeed, Gandhi himself believed that the INC should not participate in competitive elections (Weiner 1967; Rudolph and Rudolph 2010). He thus attempted to "prevent the Congress from becoming the governing political party in a newly-independent India," and in late January 1948, 24 hours before his death, wrote that it "should be dissolved and ... replaced by a *Lok Sevak Sangh*, a people's service organization" (Rudolph and Rudolph 2010: 140, 142). However, other voices in the organization won out, and the Congress not only transformed into a political party but took on the crucial tasks of nation-building and governance postindependence.

One possible explanation for this difference in KANU and the INC's trajectories at the critical juncture of liberation from British rule may lie in the nature of the respective nationalist movements themselves. As Branch and Cheeseman (2006: 21) chronicle with regard to the Kenyan case, "even prior to Mau Mau, the varied impact of colonialism according to geographical and economic considerations had led to an uneven mobilization of African political communities" for independence. Likewise, Carl Rosberg (1963: 3–4) argues that the colonial state's "regulations to restrict African political organizations to the local, tribal level" meant that by the late 1950s, Kenyan nationalism amounted organizationally to "nothing than a collection of separate, locally based parties, knit together by the common objective of African self-determination and the symbolism of Kenyatta's past and promised leadership."

By contrast, in India, the INC succeeded in organizing a national independence movement. It did so, as Tudor (2013a: 260) documents, by building "a coherent distributive coalition ... composed of segments of the middle class that shared an interest in gaining control of the colonial state through a mass" agitation for freedom. Efforts to develop this mass base first began in 1920 with a focus on reaching the relatively wealthy peasantry. This group was considered key to bringing in the poorer peasantry in turn. Over time and during the 1930s in particular, heterogenous groups of dominant peasants came to view the "nationalist movement as an appropriate platform through which to express localized grievances" (Tudor 2013a: 266). As a result, agitations against colonial rule took on "a more widespread national tendency" (Tudor 2013a: 260).

This macro-level difference in KANU's failed transition into a mass party and the INC's achievement of predominant party status further revealed itself in six major, though interrelated, ways: (1) the state of party finances; (2) the organizational capacity of the two entities; (3) elites' approaches to ethnic politics; (4) the logics of political patronage; (5) intraparty dynamics and approaches to dispute resolution; and (6) preferences and decisions about regime-type. In the pages that follow, I discuss each of these characteristics of the postindependence Kenya African National Union and Indian National Congress parties to chart the core distinctions between them.

The State of Party Finances

Following Murumbi's 1963 admission about the dire state of KANU's party finances, the fiscal woes of the organization only increased in the early postindependence years. Indeed, by early 1966, the matter became so urgent that John Keen, the organizing secretary, described the Kenya African National Union's circumstances as "appalling" and "deplorable" (Good 1968: 125; Buijtenhuijs 1945–1975: 59). He further held that KANU "was £20,000 in debt," with telephones that had "been cut off at party headquarters, and staff [who] had not been paid for seven months" (Goldsworthy 1982b: 238–239). In a similar vein, Opalo (2019: 151–152, citing Government of Kenya 1965) quotes from the 1965 annual report of the District Commissioner (DC) of Nyeri in Rift Valley Province, who wrote, "The Union [KANU] closed its offices toward the end of 1964 or beginning of 1965 due to financial difficulties."

In stark contrast to the exigent financial condition of the Kenya African National Union, the Indian National Congress found itself in a healthy fiscal position postindependence. This is in large part because Congress leaders followed in Gandhi's footsteps to build and maintain the organization's material base. As Stanley Kochanek (1987: 1287) writes, "all major Congress party leaders collected funds" for the INC. He further notes that between 1951 and 1969, they used a number of different sources – including "party membership fees, contributions [from] candidates and their friends, [levies] on parliamentary income," and inputs from the business community – to raise election funds. Over time, the task of raising money for the party became more decentralized. Under this new system, "whereas certain central ministers collected funds in western India ... influential leaders took care of collections in their respective areas" (Kochanek 1987: 1287). Taken together, it is thus clear that within a few years of Kenya's and India's independence from British rule, the Kenya African National Union and Indian National Congress found themselves in radically different financial positions.

Organizational Capacities

The fiscal circumstances described above had a direct bearing on KANU and the Congress's organizational capacities. As previously described, less than two years after independence, the Kenya African National Union was forced to close its branch office in Nyeri. In bringing the party to this point, KANU officials' decisions about key aspects of party organization had played a pivotal role: specifically, leaders from the Kenya African National Union had opted to maintain British colonial precedents by pursuing political organizing at the district, rather than national, level (Elischer 2010). This "loose organization[al]" structure – in which branch and district coincided – "meant that KANU Headquarters had little control over the district branches" (Opalo 2019: 151). Even though "constituencies formed the sub-branches of the party," Opalo (2019: 151) chronicles that "KANU sub-branches almost never existed throughout Kenyatta's tenure, and the National Governing Council seldom met."

During the course of the June 1972 parliamentary debates, which were dedicated to discussing the new budget, John Keen – now the Under-Secretary of State for Public Works – once again "sounded the alarm" (Buijtenhuijs 1974–1975: 59). This time, he warned that "the country was heading for disaster if an immediate reorganization of KANU was not effected" (Buijtenhuijs 1974–1975: 59). Based on his extensive observations of the Kenya African National Union in the mid-1970s, Robert Buijtenhuijs (1974–1975: 73) similarly wrote that the party's "organization [left] much to be desired." However, insofar as "Kenyatta eschewed an important role for KANU" (Tordoff 2002: 131), and party organizing continued to take place along district lines, the Kenya African National Union "lacked any strong connections with voters, many of whom remained primarily loyal to their specific district (ethnic) political patrons" (Opalo 2019: 152).

In India, by contrast, postindependence INC elites not only sought to maintain the grassroots structures of the nationalist-era Congress, but they also worked hard to strengthen party organization and extend party reach wherever possible. Indeed, in order to better understand his constituents' needs, Prime Minister Jawaharlal Nehru himself went so far as to hold "a public audience at his home every morning" (Tharoor 2003: 222). These interactions were not always easy. As the *New York Times* journalist A. M. Rosenthal (1964), who observed a number of such forums, described: Nehru "sometimes talked angrily to his India" and "shrieked at it" for being "just impossible." At other times, however, he passionately "courted his India, laughed with it, and was merry, delicate, and understanding" (Rosenthal 1964).

Beyond the difficulties that the INC faced in building connections with voters, her leaders also encountered some challenges in strengthening party organization. In fact, according to W. H. Morris-Jones (1967: 113–114), it was only after Nehru stepped down from the party presidency and U. N. Dhebar took his place in 1955 that "the party began the process of remedying a dozen years of organizational neglect … suffered [during] wartime restrictions and the preoccupations of independence." The creation of the Mandal Congress Committees (MCCs) helps to highlight this priority. In 1957, Dhebar "firmly established" (Morris-Jones 1967: 117) these new units – comprised of "one member for each thousand inhabitants of an area with a population of 20,000" (Kochanek 1967b: 63; Franda 1962) – as the base layer for the party. The MCCs went on to play a significant role in candidate selection procedures for the 1962 general elections (Kochanek 1967a). Thus, as with party finances, the early years of postindependence party politics in Kenya and India revealed considerable differences in these founding parties' organizational capacities.

Elites' Approaches to Ethnic Politics

As previously described, KANU elites' decision to maintain district-level organizing principles inherited from the colonial era directly lent itself to ethnic, as opposed to national, logics of political mobilization (Okoth-Ogendo 1972; Elischer 2010; Fjelde and Höglund 2018; Opalo 2019). Sebastian Elischer (2013), for instance, argues that the persistence of KANU's early choices helps to explain the paucity of *nonethnic* parties in the country to this day. Meanwhile, other scholars have variously described the consequences of KANU's decisions as engendering "uncivil nationalism" (Berman 1998) and an "exclusionary" (Fjelde and Höglund 2018) and a "negative" (wa Wamwere 2003) form of ethnic politics.

During the course of fieldwork, several respondents discussed such matters with me. As one interviewee put it, owing to the decisions of KANU elites, "tribalism itself [became] a political resource" in Kenya.[3] Another respondent cast further light on the consequences of the party's leadership decisions, emphasizing the ways in which these choices set a precedent for the ethnic splintering of newer parties as well:

---

[3] Interview with an academic, Nairobi, December 3, 2013.

Divergent Parties and Party Systems in Kenya and India

So, actually, [in Kenya] it is "negative ethnicity" that precedes the party because the elites organize themselves along ethnic lines. This has to do with our history. Let me explain: negative ethnicity or what other people might call "tribalism" was actually used for the first time by the British. They used negative ethnicity very effectively as a tool of divide and rule. I'm sure it is the same thing that they [the British] did in India. *And at the time of independence, one would have thought that the founding fathers would have seen the need to eradicate this ideology. But, instead, they decided to keep it and use it*.... And so, before we knew it, people were no longer being organized along class lines but [along] ethnic lines. And the parties ended up ... even the ones that had formed before independence, they ended up becoming tribal parties.... And negative ethnicity slowly began to take over from class ideology as a weapon of mass mobilization.[4]

By contrast, Congress leaders in India largely sought to extend their nationalist-era strategies, mobilizing broad coalitions of urban and rural middle-class voters (Tudor 2013a, 2013b). This focus helped them to achieve a key feature of postindependence Indian politics, namely its "centrist equilibrium" (Rudolph and Rudolph 1987). As per the observations of a former bureaucrat from Hyderabad, the INC's efforts to maintain its grassroots infrastructure and bridge ethnic divides in India were intertwined pursuits:

They [Congress elites] made some mistakes ... but still, the party was everywhere. Everywhere you went, people from the poorest to the richest person, [they] knew about the party. That was the kind of reach it enjoyed... It was everywhere ... in all the districts and villages of this country. And everywhere, the Congress leaders talked about democracy and national unity.[5]

Yet, as acknowledged earlier, there were ethnic wedges – centrally, the Hindu–Muslim divide – that Congress leaders never fully resolved. Worse still, a number of the INC's postindependence decisions arguably failed to convince Muslims of the organization's claims that it was a "truly 'national' party" (Guha 2019: xxii).

Two policies warrant particular attention within this discussion. First, the Indian constitution, promulgated in 1950, abolished minority electorates and guaranteed minority seats (Wilkinson 2000). In so doing, members of the Constituent Assembly aligned with the position of Ambedkar who had rallied since the late 1920s against "the evil of communal electorates" (Government of India 2014: 338; Khosla 2020). In place of these electorates, the constitution put in place the "mutable category [of] backwardness" (Khosla 2020: 148). This new concept ensured that "any scheme of reservations would have to be sensitive to the principle of equality of opportunity" (Khosla 2020: 148). Before the 1949 vote on this matter, Congress leaders went to considerable lengths to ensure that their preferences would prevail: they warned "their

---

[4] Interview with a CCM politician, Nakuru, October 23, 2013; emphasis added.
[5] Interview with a former bureaucrat, Hyderabad, August 5, 2013.

own minority members to remain silent during the debate" and "also tried to cajole several Muslim representatives to speak up in favor of the abolition" (Wilkinson 2000: 780). Thus, even though the final version of the constitution provided political safeguards to the Scheduled Caste (SC) and Scheduled Tribe (ST) communities and empowered state and central governments to set up similar policies for Other Backward Classes (OBCs) (Chandra 2005), this was mainly seen as a reflection of the fact that "lower-caste groups ... needed protection at the time" (Khosla 2020: 148). But the constitution did not afford such protections to religious minorities (Bajpai 2000). Second, although Congress elites continued to shun practices such as untouchability after independence, they tolerated the enumeration of religion in the Indian census (Lieberman and Singh 2012, 2017).

According to Staniland (2021: 96, 98), policies of this nature were core to the ideological project of the INC, which viewed "tribal peoples ... as a distinct social category worthy of special treatment" but did not see the elimination of "either Hindu traditionalism or nationalism in the broader political system and society" as necessary. Even so, it is true that when compared to their KANU counterparts in Kenya, Congress leaders in India pursued a considerably different strategy with regard to institutionalizing ethnicity. As extant scholarship has shown, KANU politicians relied on the largely *overlapping* cleavages of language and ethno-regional grouping to mobilize social groups and organize political competition (Miguel 2004; Posner 2007). According to recent research from Samantha Balaton-Chrimes (2021: 44), they further codified this narrow approach to ethnicity in the postindependence census, which they then wielded as a tool of both "demographic posturing" and the "recognition of minorities," as they saw fit. Meanwhile, INC leaders adopted a *multidimensional* position on reifying ethnic categories (Chandra 2005). In addition to devising affirmative action policies for marginalized caste and tribal communities, they also drew state boundaries along linguistic lines (Stuligross and Varshney 2002; Staniland 2021). As Varshney (1998: 43) describes, these decisions gave rise to a largely "dispersed ethnic configuration," which diluted the salience of ethnicity in national politics. With the exception of the Hindu–Muslim cleavage, most ethnic identities in the country thus became "regionally or locally specific" (Varshney 1998: 43). Likewise, Chandra (2005: 238) has argued that policies of the early postindependence years created pressures for other parties in India's party system, including national parties, to "moderate [their] platforms."

The Logics of Political Patronage

One characteristic around which there was some resemblance between KANU and the INC relates to their reliance on political patronage to establish themselves as dominant parties after independence. However, the specific contours of clientelism in the two countries differed in some important respects. In

Divergent Parties and Party Systems in Kenya and India

Kenya, KANU politicians largely embraced an ethnic logic to distributing the state's largesse. This modality began with Kenyatta, who developed "a complex neo-patrimonial system" to consolidate power (Throup and Hornsby 1998: 17). His successor and Kenya's second president, Daniel arap Moi (1978–2002), further extended this system. Indeed, it is notable that even though Moi tried to strengthen KANU and used it, and not the PA, as "the focal point for negotiating intra-elite power sharing," he nevertheless relied extensively on clientelism to maintain his regime (Opalo 2019: 159). As Steeves (2006: 213) writes, Moi is even rumored to have kept "briefcases full of money or 'chai' (tea) on hand to reward key allies." By contrast, whereas INC leaders certainly used patronage to build up the "mass base of the party" in India, they developed this system around less exclusionary criteria (Kenny 2017a: 69).

Under Kenyatta, fellow Kikuyu became the main beneficiaries of the state's bounty. Beyond doling out key cabinet positions to co-ethnics, Ken Omolo (2002: 214) notes that the country's first president also made arrangements so that "the head of the central bank ... the head of the civil service, the police, and most other public service and parastatal positions" all became "the preserve of the Kikuyu." In addition, he allocated "the lion's share of government spending" to the projects of his Kikuyu allies. This policy led to the accumulation of considerable wealth on the part of his loyalists. For example, J. M. Kariuki – who served as Kenyatta's personal secretary between 1963 and 1969 and subsequently as a Member of Parliament (MP) from Nyandarua North constituency in Central Province between 1974 and 1975 – is said to have amassed "assets worth more than £50,000" during his association with the president (Good 1968: 133). Meanwhile, another politician, Dr. Julius Kiano, came to be known as "Mr. Ten Percent" for his tendency to take kickbacks (Good 1968: 132). As Good (1968: 133) suggests, Kiano was "surely not unassociated with the rule and policies of Kenyatta."

Beyond political elites themselves, Kenyatta also developed relationships with bureaucrats on a neo-patrimonial basis. He started by ensuring that key administrators reported directly to him. As Throup and Hornsby (1998: 18) write, Provincial and District Commissioners became squarely "responsible to the Office of the President, rather than to the new political class, local authorities, or KANU headquarters" under Kenyatta's founding regime. Likewise, Hassan (2020: 117) highlights that even though most top-level bureaucrats in the PA – namely Provincial Commissioners (PCs) and DCs – "were not [the President's] co-ethnics, the loyalty of these high-ranking officers was sustained through patronage." Being "among the highest paid in the state," PCs and DCs were "allowed to use their position to predate extensively" and most "benefit[ed] from the president's continued rule, regardless of their ethnicity" (Hassan 2020: 117).

After Daniel arap Moi ascended to the presidency in 1978, the state's reliance on clientelism became stronger still. Moi began his rule by crafting "a new ethnic coalition" – comprised of Kalenjins (his co-ethnics), Coastals (i.e., Mijikenda elites), Luhyas, and Kenyan Asians – to further ensconce himself in power (Throup 2020: 57). He also helped groups within his alliance secure key political positions, lucrative business contracts, civil service posts, as well as jobs in the internal security apparatus (ISA) (Hassan 2017; Throup 2020). In so doing, he decisively kept Kikuyus from accessing these posts. Within the PA, Moi's budgetary allocations similarly followed a clientelist logic, as "co-ethnic areas receive[d] a larger share than their proportion of the population would suggest" and came to "enjoy higher levels of public goods" in general (Hassan 2020: 150).

Over time, such policies gave rise to a veritable "language of consumption," as Kenyan voters came to view the office of the President as the domain from which they could secure their "turn to eat" (Branch and Cheeseman 2010: 1). Recent research on the topic of voter behavior has usefully shown that the country's elections should not be studied as ethnic censuses (Bratton and Kimenyi 2008). This is because even though parties themselves are often organized along narrow ethnic or personalistic lines – or as one respondent argued, "all parties are aligned to tribes"[6] – and although Kenyans "vote defensively in ethnic blocs, [they do] not [do so] exclusively" (Bratton and Kimenyi 2008: 272). Nevertheless, it is worth noting that during the course of fieldwork, respondents frequently talked about the state as the source through which they could access political patronage. As one interviewee in Mombasa put it:

The problem in Kenya is that the president who wins, first of all, he promises that his area, his province, his town, his people will be taken care of. And so, people from other communities start to worry…. This is why ethnic voting has a lot of strength remaining up to now. People think: "why shouldn't we vote our own so that we can also have our turn to eat?"[7]

Across the Indian Ocean, the Congress also heavily relied on clientelism to consolidate its political position in postindependence India. Kothari (1964: 1167), for example, writes that the party created a system that allowed it to achieve "a concentration of resources [and] a monopoly of patronage." Indeed, so extensive was the patronage-based system of the INC – connecting the national organization to regionally and locally influential brokers (Kohli 1994) – that one recent scholar has described it as "infamous" (Kenny 2017a: 16). Likewise, another has documented the significant downstream consequences that emerged from this arrangement and demonstrated that anything in India – from hastening the bureaucratic process to attaining the issuance or withdrawal of criminal charges to obtaining permits for contracts and building projects – "can be achieved through contacts" (Jensenius 2011: 394).

[6] Interview with a WDM-K party official, Nairobi, October 15, 2013.
[7] Interview with an ODM/NAMLEF politician, Mombasa, October 10, 2013.

Divergent Parties and Party Systems in Kenya and India

Taken together, then, even in the face of some recent insights about the weakening of patron-client linkages between elites and voters in certain parts of the country (Krisha 2007; Dasgupta 2011), India's status as a quintessential "patronage democracy" in the Global South remains intact (Chandra 2004). Furthermore, not only is patronage "generally rampant in the public sector" today, but its endurance as a system-wide force can crucially be traced back to the early policies of the Congress (Kenny 2017b: 154). Yet, compared to the Kenyan case, key constitutional constraints on the discretion of individual politicians in India, along with the broader logics of electoral politics, limited the extent to which patronage could be largely doled out along ethnic lines in the postindependence era.

To begin with, Congress leaders were required to abide by constitutional rules and ensure proportional representation of SCs and STs in "national, state, [and] local legislatures [as well as] in government institutions, including the civil services and police force" (Chandra 2005: 240). Even today, such policies along with the "relative sanctity of the secret ballot" appear to be keeping "brokers and politicians highly constrained in their ability to monitor voters" (Auerbach et al. 2022: 259).

In addition, in order to maintain dominant party status, postindependence Congress elites had to integrate "localized caste-based voting blocs ... into *multi-ethnic coalitions*" (Auerbach et al. 2022 255; emphasis added). Indeed, "ethnicity [still] does not always neatly overlap with political preferences" in India, partly because clientelism does not strictly follow an ethnic logic in the country (Auerbach et al. 2022: 255). This reality is particularly worth noting in the face of major transformations in India's party system since independence. These transformations include the collapse of the "Congress system" in the late 1970s (Kothari 1964); the splintering of parties along ethnic (Chandra 1999) and regional lines (Ziegfeld 2012, 2016), coupled with significant increases in their electoral influence in the late 1980s and early 1990s; and the virulent rise of Hindu nationalism on the national stage in recent years. Owing to such developments, while it is certainly true that some parties have taken to relying on identity-based cleavages to mobilize voters, it has also become clear that different ethnic axes matter across and even within different states in India. As one respondent from Meerut put it:

The [current] system is very fractured and all these small, small regional parties have come up. You can take the case of UP, for instance: here, we have Mayawati [of the BSP] who woos the Dalits, the SP that woos the Yadavs, [and] then you have the Congress. And all these parties want to win over Muslims also. Finally, you have the BJP with its slogans of "Hindu, Hindi, Hindustan." So, what has happened is that there is not a single leader who has influence over the majority of communities in India…. Politics in India is all about *realpolitik* now and about combining the support of different communities.[8]

---

[8] Interview with an academic, Meerut, March 2, 2013.

Despite these broader shifts, we also know that "some ethnic groups in India are remarkably heterogenous in the expression of their political preferences" (Auerbach et al. 2022: 259). As a result, it is not entirely surprising that during their conversations with me, Indian voters did not typically describe their relationship with the state in ethnic terms. In short, contrary to the consumption-based language that KANU's patronage decisions seem to have generated in Kenya, the INC's construction of a clientelist system does not seem to have produced the same lexicon in India.

Intraparty Dynamics and Approaches to Dispute Resolution

In addition to Kenyan and Indian postindependence elites' diverging decisions about party organization and ethnic politics, KANU and Congress leaders also developed radically different systems for resolving disputes within their parties. As Anderson (2005: 334) suggests, Kenyatta "had no wish to join a party that might ... succumb to the influence of Mau Mau's hooligans." In order to keep KANU intact, he thus sought to swiftly handle "the divisions of the past," mainly by silencing and sidelining the voices of those who might challenge him (Anderson 2005: 335). His successor, Moi, followed this precedent but also extended it in crucial ways. By contrast, Nehru and his senior colleagues in the INC prioritized "cohesion and consensus" as two core principles of their party (Hasan 1979: 64). This approach, as Zoya Hasan (1979: 64) writes, helped them to establish "a system of mutual trade-offs and alliances" within the organization.

In dealing with the divisions – between former "rebels" and "loyalists" – that he had inherited within KANU, Kenyatta initially took on the role of *Muigwathania* or the Reconciler (Anderson 2005: 335). He thus "acknowledged the part the freedom fighters had played in the struggle" for independence (Anderson 2005: 335). Yet, "he never once made any statement that conceded to them any rights or any genuine compensation" (Anderson 2005: 335). Moreover, he used certain public appearances to make his position on the movement amply clear. At a September 1962 rally in Githunguri town in Central Province, for example, Kenyatta proclaimed: "We shall not allow hooligans to rule Kenya. Mau Mau was a disease, which has been eradicated and must never be remembered again" (Kenyatta 1968: 189, cited in Anderson 2005: 336). Declarations of this nature were followed by the removal of ex-Mau Mau from the party. In June 1964, for example, Kenyatta promptly dismissed former Mau Mau leader Bildad Kaggia from KANU after he denounced the government for engaging in corruption.

Notably, he did not merely reserve such treatment for ex "rebels" alone, but applied it to anyone who dared to challenge his decisions. The case of Luo leader Oginga Odinga – a man who had engaged in a long public campaign for Kenyatta's release from prison – is especially instructive. In the early postindependence years, Odinga had raised the crucial matter of intraparty democracy and representation. "With Kenyatta at the helm" of KANU, he had cautioned that the country's Kikuyu elite could become "the true inheritors of the state" (Omolo 2002: 214). Despite his long association with the party – going back to its founding in 1960 – Odinga was sidelined from the organization and lost his position as party Vice President following a series of rigged internal elections in March 1996 (Elischer 2010). He left KANU soon thereafter and went on to form the rival Kenya People's Union (KPU).

Other objecting voices within the organization were more violently quashed during Kenyatta's rule. These include Kenyan journalist and politician Pio Gama Pinto; Tom Mboya, who served as the Minister of Justice and Constitutional Affairs between June 1, 1962 and December 12, 1964, and who had agitated along with Odinga for Kenyatta's release from detention; as well as the previously mentioned J. M. Kariuki, once a loyalist of the President.

Born to Goan immigrant parents in Nairobi, Pinto had played a key part in the anti-colonial struggle. As Frenz (2013: 161) writes, he "draft[ed] programmes, memoranda, and manifestos" and raised funds for the movement by leveraging his "transnational links across empires." Following the country's independence, he was rewarded for his commitment to KANU and elected to the National Assembly as a special representative in 1964. In August of that year, however, Pinto raised concerns about the silencing of dissenting voices within the party and started to draft "a motion of 'no confidence'" against KANU in the National Assembly (Angelo 2020: 201). He was assassinated in 1965. Likewise, a few years after Mboya began to call for sub-branch elections in mid-1964 – amidst broader "demands for reform within the party" – he was gunned down in Nairobi's Central Business District after visiting a pharmacy (Good 1968: 119). These two killings, as several scholars have argued, took place "at the behest of individuals close to the president" (Holmquist, Weaver, and Ford 1994: 79; also see Goldsworthy 1982b; Branch and Cheeseman 2006). Finally, J. M. Kariuki met his demise in 1975. Killed by two bullets in early March, Kariuki had mysteriously "gone missing" from his home the week prior (Otzen 2015). Despite his earlier close relationship with Kenyatta, by the 1970s, Kariuki had reportedly emerged as a thorn in the president's side and was viewed as a would-be challenger of the regime (Otzen 2015). As Branch and Cheeseman (2006: 27) suggest, his repeated allegations that Kenyan elites had failed "to support the advancement of others" had not gone down well with Kenyatta.

Following Kenyatta's demise and Moi's ascension to power in 1978, the possibilities for expressing dissent against the party and the regime shrank even further. This is in part because Kenya's second president effectively presided over the construction of what Jennifer Widner (1992: 27) has described as a "party-state" – an arrangement in which the functions of the ruling KANU party were fused with the "administrative responsibilities of the state." In crafting this system, Moi strengthened the organizational capacity of the party but also sought to ensure that it became "a vehicle for transmitting the views of the president to the grassroots" (Widner 1992: 158; Opalo 2019). Put differently, he turned the party into "an adjunct" for "the office of the president," and both KANU and the nation as a whole thus became his "personal fief[s]" (Widner 1992: 5; Barkan 2004: 89). The increased lack of transparency under Moi also meant that party leaders could loot the nation with impunity and pressure other public servants – including election commission officers – whose behaviors they sought to influence around the 1992 and 1997 elections (Adar 2000; Barkan 2004). Finally, the construction of the "party state" enhanced the possibilities for deploying political violence in the country. In addition to several high-profile assassinations during Moi's tenure – including the 1990 murder of Foreign Affairs Minister Robert Ouko, a "known opponent of official corruption" (Chege 2008: 128; Branch and Cheeseman 2006) – Moi came to rely "on the Provincial Administration to neutralize popular dissent against him" (Hassan 2020: 156). As Hassan (2020: 156) finds, whereas the largesse of the state was directed toward co-ethnic areas, he ensured that bureaucrats would be "most active in *coercing* dissidents in majority-Kikuyu and majority-Luo areas" – communities that opposed his rule – during the 1970s and 1980s (Hassan 2020: 156; emphasis added).

This intolerance for dissenting voices under the autocratic regimes of Kenyatta and Moi contrasts considerably with the INC's "consensus" model for resolving intraparty disputes (Weiner 1957: 281). Importantly, the Congress arrived at this model out of prior experiences in overcoming factional tendencies during its nationalist phase. During the 1930s, a number of "left-wing factions" had evolved within the organization (Staniland 2021: 97). These included the Socialists who organized themselves as the Congress Socialist Party (CSP) within the broader INC structures in 1934 (Weiner 1957), as well as "Nehruvians who attempted to straddle different parts of the party" (Staniland 2021: 97). At the same time, and "arrayed against the Left within the Congress were industrialists and merchants," who formed its right wing (Staniland 2021: 97). In the party presidential elections of 1948, the conservative wing fielded Purshottamdas Tandon, "an orthodox Hindu from Uttar Pradesh [who held] very strong views on communal problems" and whose campaign was financed by the industrialist G. D. Birla (Kochanek 1967b: 15). This contest, in which there were three other contestants, was marked by sharp divisions – not unlike those that the Congress had seen in prior periods – on "ideological, sectional, and organizational" grounds (Konchanek 1967b: 14). But such divisions were tolerated and managed within the organization.

In handling intraparty disputes, both before and after independence, Congress leaders prioritized compromise. In the 1930s, for example, the party leadership forged "an intra-Congress bargain," which enabled "a role for left-wing politics with the Congress … but with the substantial protection of private property and economic elite power" (Staniland 2021: 97). After independence, "a core group of Congress leaders, generally longstanding members of parliament, government ministers, and chief ministers served regularly in the Working Committee, the body responsible [among other items] for managing internal party conflict" (Reddy 2005: 294; also see Brass 1990).

Although the routinization of these roles played a crucial part in helping the party promote intraorganizational democracy, they did not completely eliminate factionalism. On the contrary, and as Kothari (1964: 1163) describes, the Congress "function[ed] through an elaborate network of factions ... which were built around a functional network consisting of various social groups and leader-client relationships." Patronage thus became vital to the Congress, not only in drawing in groups from the countryside but also in managing its factional components. Compared to KANU, however, the broader point is that the postindependence INC ultimately honed a structure in which compromises could be reached. Indeed, as Chapters 6 and 7 will show, it was the collapse of this "consensus" model (Weiner 1957) – mainly under Nehru's daughter Indira Gandhi – that opened the door for politicians to organize and sponsor party violence. In other words, once the painstakingly assembled "Congress system" fell apart and party leaders started to worry about their electoral survival, resorting to conflict emerged as a strategy to try and hold onto power (Kothari 1964).

Preferences and Decisions about Regime-Type

The cumulative impact of these deviating choices about party organization, ethnic politics, and dispute resolution is reflected in postindependence Kenyan and Indian politicians' decisions about regime-type. Specifically, whereas Kenyatta crafted a "dominant-authoritarian party system" in Kenya, which Moi then consolidated as an outright one-party state, INC leaders established a "dominant umbrella party" with "genuinely democratic conditions" in India (Farooqui and Sridharan 2016: 335).

For his part, Kenyatta began to move the needle toward authoritarianism soon after independence. In November 1964, for example, his government passed Kenya's first constitutional amendment, which replaced the extant parliamentary system with a presidential one (Okoth-Ogendo 1972). With an executive presidency achieved, in a March 1966 address, Kenyatta openly advocated for the creation of a one-party state (Good 1968). Most of his party colleagues embraced this proposal, and the one-party system thus quickly came to be framed as "the most effective way of promoting national unity" in the country (Welsh 1996: 484–485). Then, in June 1966, another constitutional amendment – known as the Preservation of Public Security Act of 1966 – empowered the Office of the President to detain Kenyan citizens without trial (Widner 1992: 67; Okoth-Ogendo 1972). It also transferred emergency powers, previously vested in parliament, to the president.

Following the approval of this law, the KANU government first used the Preservation of Public Security Act to arrest several prominent trade union leaders and regime opponents in August 1966 (Conboy 1978). Over the next few years, it further deployed the Act to haul up a number of opposition leaders and detain them without trial. Next, in 1969, the government banned the country's last remaining opposition party, the KPU; KADU had already dissolved in 1964. Finally, in crafting the neo-patrimonial state that Throup and Hornsby have detailed, Kenyatta developed a system that was "both pre-determined and personal": key decisions were now made and handed out by those at the top, and politicians who sought to challenge these policies were either removed from political office or rapidly neutralized, as previously described (Good 1968: 132). Taken together, the core strategies of the Kenyatta regime amounted to a veritable extension of the "structure of the inherited state" (Maloba 2017: 4).

The policies passed under Moi only served to further strengthen autocracy in Kenya. To begin with, insofar as Moi, too, relied on clientelist networks to secure his rule, he also took away patronage-based rewards just as quickly as he disbursed them. In 1979, for example, he used his networks to engineer an MP path for former Attorney General Charles Njonjo (Goldsworthy 1982a). Following a successful run, he promptly granted Njonjo the portfolio of Minister for Home and Constitutional Affairs (Goldsworthy 1982a). However, in the wake of a 1982 coup attempt against his rule, Moi purged the party of his cabinet and several detractors, including the former Attorney General. He then dragged Njonjo through a lengthy judicial inquiry and eventually forced him to resign in 1983 (Feldmann 1983).

In 1982, Moi's government also passed Section 2a of the constitution, which banned "the formation of [any and all] opposition parties" (Throup 2020: 6). As one interviewee explained:

Moi came to be known as *"nyayo,"* which means "footstep" or "footprint" in Swahili, because he followed in the footsteps of the first president of the country, Jomo Kenyatta. You see, Kenyatta had already banned political dissent and curbed the opposition a lot during his rule, but Moi was the one who formally turned the country into a one-party state.[9]

Next, in 1988, Moi "unilaterally amended the Kenyan constitution … terminated judicial independence, [and] extended the time that an individual could be jailed without charges" (Fredland 1989: 4). Compared to Kenyatta, his regime was thus marked by a significantly wider use of violence and repression, which he often deployed to target lawyers, university lecturers, students, and civil society leaders (Sabar-Friedman 1995; Mueller 2014b). Ironically, individuals who sought to bridge ethnic divides were cast as "tribalist[s]" and "anti-unity" activists (Sabar-Friedman 1995: 433). Finally, in addition to using repression to silence elite threats, Moi also appropriated the PA to shut down collection action against his regime (Hassan 2020).

[9] Interview with a human rights activist, Nairobi, February 2, 2013.

Divergent Parties and Party Systems in Kenya and India

In contrast to their counterparts in Kenya, postindependence Congress politicians in India crucially underwrote "the social accord necessary for 'democracy'" (Barlas 2019: 3). Prime Minister Jawaharlal Nehru had long viewed democracy as "a structure of society in which economic and social equality [would] gradually be attained" (Smith 1958: 59). In order to achieve this vision in independent India, he placed considerable emphasis on the principle of tolerance. For Nehru, "democracy meant tolerance ... not merely of those who agree, but of those who do not agree" as well (All India Congress Committee 1954: 34, cited in Smith 1958: 64). He also supported a constitutional framework that would be "growing, adaptable, and flexible" in responding to the nation's needs (Nehru 1954: 525, cited in Smith 1958: 141). However, as opposed to Kenyatta and Moi, Nehru did not treat the constitution as a utilitarian document through which to entrench his rule; in fact, he argued that the constitution was a key *prerequisite* through which other core principles for India – such as secularism – could be realized (Smith 1958).

In addition to the values and policies that Nehru espoused, senior Congress leaders also helped to promote democracy in the country. By reconciling "different points of view" within the party (Weiner 1957: 281) and "institutionalizing the phenomena of general elections in five-year intervals" (Jalal 1995: 18), they not only encouraged elite behaviors that would foster democracy but also created crucial avenues for acculturating voters and ordinary citizens to its norms and procedures. At the same time, they carefully sought to manage extra-organizational threats that other parties posed to their dominance.

Within a year of the founding of India's republic in 1950, Weiner (1957: 16) documents that "four major blocks of parties" had emerged in the country. These included the Congress, which represented a center-left orientation; the Communist Party of India (CPI), which variously "fluctuated between contemptuous hostility ... and eagerness for cooperation" with the INC (Varkey 1979: 881), but largely "stake[d] out a distinct space for the Congress" (Staniland 2021: 96–97); the Jana Sangh and Hindu Mahasabha, which held that India should be a "nation of Hindus" (Jaffrelot 1996: 44); and entities representing "provincial and communal interests" such as the Akali Dal, the Scheduled Caste Federation, the Tamilnad Congress, and the Jharkhand Party (Weiner 1957: 16). According to Staniland (2021: 107–108), although INC leaders initially "differed in their views of the severity of the threat from the Left," once the CPI "abandoned the revolutionary road," Nehru largely agreed to let it operate as an independent organization. However, both the Hindu nationalist forces and the Sikh agitation in Punjab by the Akali Dal presented severe enough ideological threats to the goals of the Congress that any "accommodation with them was seen as unacceptable" (Staniland 2021: 100). The unwillingness of the INC to compromise with Hindutva forces, in turn, enabled Hindu nationalists to "carve out a resilient niche in India's politics" (Staniland 2021: 100). Meanwhile, in dealing with the Akali Dal and Sikh mobilization more generally, Congress leaders oversaw a consistent policy of resistance throughout the 1950s, 1960s, and 1970s (Staniland 2021). This policy ultimately resulted in a bloody and brutal confrontation with Sikh separatists in the early 1980s.

Taken together, then, it is certainly true that postindependence INC elites in India refused to tolerate entities that threatened their vision of "how the Indian nation should be constructed" (Staniland 2021: 100). Indeed, they sought to manage and confront these threats as necessary, including through the use of force. However, compared to the policies of KANU politicians – who presided over the creation and maintenance of a one-party state – Congress leaders crafted a system in which dominance and competition coexisted (Morris-Jones 1966). They also remained steadfast in their pledge to usher ordinary citizens into democratic politics after independence. For example, despite some reservations (Shani 2018), they did not renege on their commitment to universal suffrage, a matter around which they had previously mobilized mass support during the nationalist movement (Tudor 2013a). In addition, and contrary to KANU elites, who turned to bureaucrats to advance authoritarianism, INC leaders empowered administrators in India to prepare the country's first draft electoral roll. In sum, a democratic constitution, universal franchise, and a hegemonic party system – all of which the Congress supported – put India on the path to emerging as an instructive case of democratization in the Global South (McMillan 2008).

SUMMARY AND CONCLUSION

Through a comparative and historical analysis, and with an eye toward illuminating macro-level developments, this chapter has shown that elite decisions forged during the colonial and early postcolonial periods put Kenya and India on radically different paths of party and party system development. Whereas key KANU leaders undermined the role of political parties from the nationalist phase itself, Congress elites not only sought to build an anti-colonial movement with mass appeal but also developed an organization with grassroots-level penetration. Following liberation from British rule, the choices of these leaders – with regard to party finances, organizational capacities, approaches to ethnic politics, logics of political patronage, methods of intraparty dispute resolution, and preferences about regime-type – only diverged further. Owing to these differences, this chapter has demonstrated that where violence came to be a tried and tested strategy of the Kenya African National Union, Indian politicians from the Congress carried out careful calculations about its use during the early postindependence years.

Over the last few decades, there have, of course, been major transformations in the politics of these nations – from the transition to multiparty competition and the more recent promulgation of a new constitution with a stronger judiciary in Kenya to the rise of Hindutva politics at the national level in India. Even so, I find that the initial models established by KANU and the INC have

Divergent Parties and Party Systems in Kenya and India

persisted in important ways: parties in Kenya continue to largely operate as narrow ethnic entities with short lifespans, while their Indian counterparts display considerably more longevity. These differences in party organization also exert an influence on the logics of driving or sponsoring party violence in these nations. As I demonstrate over Chapters 4–7, while elite-orchestrated party violence continues to occur with some frequency in Kenya, Indian politicians have been forced to make more calibrated calculations about the benefits and especially *costs* of violence. This consideration of costs and benefits, I argue, not only serves to explain the decline in riot violence witnessed since the early 1990s but also helps to account for recent transformations in conflict, including the rise of low-level anti-minority attacks.

4

Party Instability and Political Violence in Kenya

> The violence [in 2007–2008] was premeditated. And there was a deep hatred that was inculcated into people's minds. There was a perception that was propelled in the minds of Kalenjins that the Kikuyus are positioning themselves to take power again. And it was done very systematically. The politicians did it. And yes, you can say that there wasn't violence this time [in 2013] but even now we can fight. If the right conditions are there, we can be made to fight.... If you think about a man who was displaced, whose properties were torched, and his child was killed, of course he can be made to fight [again]. The wounds are still fresh, and so if some important person asks him to fight, he will fight. If the parties or party bosses want conflict again, politicians can make the people fight.
> – Interview with a civil society leader, Nakuru, October 21, 2013

The interview excerpt above highlights two important truths about party violence in Kenya. First, it reveals the central role of elites in provoking such violence. Second, it suggests that in the presence of conducive conditions, major conflicts could return to the country in the future. As Gabrielle Lynch (2018: 23, 51) has argued, although a "peace-at-all-costs" narrative has prevailed in Kenya since 2007–2008, this campaign has come at the cost of carrying out the "substantive political change[s]" that would be necessary for preventing future outbreaks of party violence. Likewise, Susanne Mueller (2011: 99) has held that "the root causes of violence still persist, have not been addressed, and could be easily reignited."

This chapter accounts for these ongoing risks of party violence in Kenya and discusses the broader patterns of conflict observed in the country thus far. Focusing on the period since the restoration of multiparty competition, it argues that the country's unstable and fragile parties have played a key part in making Kenya vulnerable to violence.[1] These parties have enabled

---

[1] I draw on data from the African Elections Database, the Inter-Parliamentary Union (IPU Parline), and the Kenya Election Database (KED) to capture the instability of political parties

politicians to discount the *costs* of conflict, including voter sanctioning, and opt for violence as a means of influencing electoral outcomes. Importantly, such proclivities for conflict have held even in the face of key continuities in presidential candidates, as continuously unstable parties have enabled politicians to repeatedly bet on violence. My research further shows that the rise of coalitional politics has not served to ebb elites' incentives for conflict, as unstable parties have made for fleeting coalitions. Understood in this light, the chapter holds that the moments in which political alliances have held conflict at bay in Kenya – as seen in the 2013 presidential election (Lynch 2014; Malik 2016) – have amounted more to convenient biproducts of elite decision-making rather than a fundamental reshaping of leaders' relationship with violence as a power-seeking strategy.

To illustrate these core arguments, Chapters 4–5 draw on both qualitative and quantitative data. First, I rely on the Kenya Violent Elections Dataset (KVED) to document incidents of violence across space and over time in Kenya. Second, I use novel data on party replacement as an ex-ante proxy for elites' expectations of party survival. Insofar as my theory holds that party instability can incentivize politicians to resort to violence, the Kenyan case demonstrates how relatively high levels of party replacement have made the country vulnerable to repeated bouts of severe conflict. Third, I draw on interviews with politicians and political party leaders, members, and functionaries; policy and security sector experts; human rights activists and civil society leaders; ethnic and religious elites; academics; journalists; police officers; and local residents to show how unstable parties have generally given rise to truncated time horizons among the country's political elites. Taken together, readers of this book should thus interpret the quantitative data on party replacement as proffering a snapshot of the size of leaders' shadows of the future in a given moment and should look to the qualitative interviews for in-depth accounts of the choices that politicians actually made with respect to instrumentalizing or sponsoring conflict in Kenya.

This chapter proceeds as follows. Focusing on the national level and on the period since the restoration of multipartyism, I begin with a broad overview of spatial and longitudinal patterns of party violence in Kenya. I then discuss these patterns in detail in three epochs: the KANU era (1992–2002), the early post-KANU era (2002–2013), and the period after the post-election crisis and implementation of constitutional reforms (2013–present). This approach helps me to highlight that while much of the violence in the 1990s was organized by the incumbent and increasingly insecure KANU regime, since its defeat in 2002, several other parties – both in the government and the

---

and alliances in Kenya. I also thank Karen Ferree (2010) for providing me with her data on party volatility in African countries, which covered the 1992–2002 parliamentary elections for the Kenyan case.

opposition – have engaged with conflict as well. The comprehensive discussion of various waves of party violence also offers important insights about periods of Kenyan politics during which significant conflict occurred despite relatively low levels of party volatility as well as timeframes when widespread violence was avoided despite highly unstable parties, as seen in the 1990s and since 2013, respectively. The chapter concludes by providing evidence of voters' knowledge about elite participation in party violence and demonstrating how party instability prevents citizens from acting on this knowledge. Taken together, these insights set the stage for the subnational analyses provided in Chapter 5.

PARTY FRAGILITY, ELITE UNCERTAINTY, AND RECURRING WAVES OF PARTY VIOLENCE IN KENYA

A rich literature on political violence in Kenya has underlined the central place of elites in driving or sponsoring conflict. With regard to the clashes of the 1990s, for instance, Lynch and Anderson (2015: 85) have chronicled that these conflicts "were promoted across the Rift Valley and parts of Western Province by advocates of President Moi's 'KANU zone.'" In the Mount Elgon region, in particular, "the local Member of Parliament Wilberforce Kisiero, local councilors, and other prominent" leaders all played a part in mobilizing violence (Lynch and Anderson 2015: 85).

Despite nearly three decades of multiparty competition in Kenya, the proclivities of elites to engender political conflict persist. In 2022, for instance, presidential aspirant Raila Odinga's decision to challenge the results of the election in the Supreme Court contributed to tensions in the country (Wadekar 2022). In fact, in the political contests held during the twenty-first century, leaders associated with the ruling party and the opposition have both contributed to violence. During the 2007–2008 post-election crisis, for example, Uhuru Kenyatta – then the MP from Gatundu South constituency – is alleged to have financed and funded "pro-Kikuyu organized gangs" in Central Province (Kenya National Commission on Human Rights 2008: 113). Meanwhile, opposition leaders and party activists – including current President and former Vice President William Ruto – are known to have made explicit claims about alleged vote-rigging. According to the Pre-Trial Chamber of the International Criminal Court (2011: 9), Ruto also "established a network of perpetrators [from] the Kalenjin community" to "punish [Party of National Unity] (PNU) supporters in the event that the 2007 presidential elections were rigged." Less than five years after this period of sustained violence, in March and April 2012, over 500 families were displaced from their homes in Isiolo County in deadly fighting between the Turkana, Borana, and Somali communities. Subsequent investigations uncovered political incitement at the heart of these clashes (The New Humanitarian 2012; Human Rights Watch 2013a; Malik 2020).

TABLE 4.1 *Incidence and proportion of deadly events and estimated death tolls from waves of ethnic party violence in Kenya (1991–2013)*[2]

Election year	Number of deadly events of ethnic violence	Proportion of deadly events (%)	Estimated death toll
1992	30	10.79	1,500
1997	73	26.25	1,500
2002	8	2.87	404
2007	121	43.52	1,133
2013	46	16.54	744
Total	278		5,281

Beyond these particular episodes, a comprehensive analysis of KVED reveals that out of 445 total incidents of ethnic violence, 372 or 83.60% have directly or indirectly stemmed from elite involvement. Furthermore, these data – summarized in Table 4.1 – show that while the 2007 election witnessed the highest incidence of lethal ethnic clashes, the 2002 election was the least violence-ridden.

In addition to these fluctuations in the incidence and intensity of violence over time, Kenya has also witnessed important spatial variations in conflict. As Figure 4.1 demonstrates below, while some counties consistently experienced violence across the 1992, 1997, 2007, and 2013 elections, others only succumbed to conflict around one or two contests.[3]

POLITICAL INSECURITY AND PARTY VIOLENCE IN THE KANU ERA (1992–2002)

In accounting for these longitudinal and spatial patterns, the present chapter builds and extends the analysis previously presented in Chapter 3. As shown therein, the Kenya African National Union set the precedent for political violence by using conflict as a strategy to crowd out other parties and dissenting actors. In the autocratic period, the relationship between the dominant party, KANU, and rival organizations thus crucially came to define the contours for conflict.

During the authoritarian era, ruling elites sought to handle these threats through a range of strategies, including constitutional amendments, clientelism,

---

[2] As previously discussed in Chapter 1, these figures are slightly different from those presented in Malik (2018) due to subsequent updates that I made to KVED. The cumulative figures shown in the column for estimated death toll are as reported in reports such as Akiwumi, CIPEV, and Africa Watch/Human Rights Watch.

[3] I use counties rather than constituencies to show violence-affected areas in Figure 4.1, because counties are key administrative units in present-day Kenya. I also exclude the 2002 election from this image because while this contest was not entirely peaceful, it saw considerably lower levels of violence than the four elections depicted here.

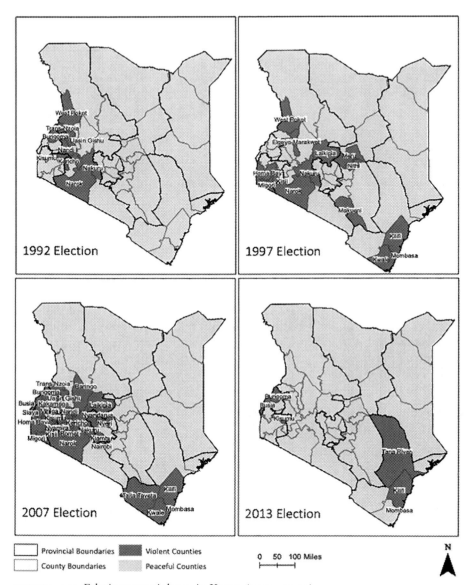

FIGURE 4.1 Ethnic party violence in Kenya (1992–2013)

and a reliance on the PA. Compared to Kenyatta before him, Moi did make some sincere efforts to strengthen KANU. These efforts were motivated by a desire to turn to a party-based means for balancing elites and effectively managing the factional disputes that had afflicted KANU under Kenyatta (Widner 1992; Opalo 2019). As Morse (2019: 120) writes, after ascending to the presidency in 1978, Moi "reintroduce[d] internal elections" and oversaw the creation of "new party branches, with grassroots nomination of candidates for five rather than two-year limits." In addition, he sought to "reinvigorate[e] KANU's moribund infrastructure" and stipulated that all 281 party branches raise the party membership fee, "open bank accounts [and] submit financial statements to the party's treasurer" (Morse 2019: 120). Yet, KANU never transformed into a credible or strong party; instead, it turned into an instrument of coercive control and largely "remained a collection of patrons" (Cheeseman 2006: 226; Morse 2019; Opalo 2019). Indeed, it actually became more common under Moi "for the administration to deny KANU party meetings" (Morse 2019: 121).

Beginning around 1992, the party "fell into [yet another] period of decay, [as] KANU party branches declined in strength, and party donations and recruitment ... decreased" (Hassan 2020: 180). Around the same time, the restoration of multipartyism generated new and important considerations for Moi and his colleagues, as "the most serious popular threat" to KANU's rule now came from the ballot box (Hassan 2020: 176).

To compensate for the weakness of the party in a context marked by "increased political uncertainty," KANU politicians and party leaders doubled down on predatory behaviors such as corruption, clientelism, and violence (Branch and Cheeseman 2008: 4). As Branch and Cheeseman (2008: 12) describe in their work on state informalization, "the increasing likelihood of electoral defeat resulted in senior figures within the Moi government seeking to accumulate wealth at an accelerated rate in order to secure their 'retirement.'"

Likewise, in his study of property rights formalization in Kenya, Alexander Dyzenhaus (2021: 9) documents that "competition in the form of elite challenges to power as well as the [arrival] of competitive multiparty elections introduced extreme uncertainty for the new autocratic administration, which contributed to short time horizons for Moi" and his colleagues. This uncertainty made the distribution of patronage even more critical to KANU's survival. In order to "preserve political stability," the Moi regime began to illegally allocate land – without formal title – to groups that remained unaligned with existing political factions (Dyzenhaus 2021: 10). The goal of this strategy was simple: it was meant to "control [the] political behavior" of ethnic communities, such as landless Kamba in Eastern Province, on whose votes KANU's future could now very well rest (Dyzenhaus 2021: 9).

Finally, in his work on political violence in Africa, Robert Bates (2008: 116) shows that the loss of foreign patrons and mounting "threats at home" led to a shortening of elites' time horizons. Writing about the Kenyan case and the Moi regime, specifically, Bates (2008: 116–117) notes that the president and his allies made extensive use of "the coercive powers at [their] command ... to jail political opponents [and] arrest, torture, and detain ... opposition politicians." In short, while there might be theoretical reasons to expect that patronage and violence could be substitutable strategies in some contexts,

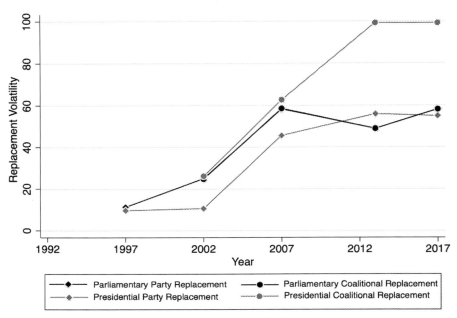

FIGURE 4.2 Party and coalitional replacement volatility in Kenya (1992–2017)

evidence from Kenya reveals that in a "competitive clientelist" sense (Abdulai and Hickey 2016), KANU elites' reliance on both tactics only became stronger in the multiparty era as part of a desperate attempt to cling to power.

Ethnic Party Violence in 1992

In keeping with these insights about the political uncertainties wrought by the restoration of multipartyism, the quantitative data collected for this project also underscores the real risks of political exit that leaders close to Moi urgently encountered during the 1990s, despite dominant party status. Specifically, by 1997, party replacement in parliamentary elections had already crept into the domain of only moderate stability, clocking in at 11.25%. As shown in Figure 4.2, this number as well as replacement volatility for the presidency would increase further over the next several elections, and thereby engender sustained incentives for elites to instrumentalize violence. In fact, since 2007, replacement volatility for individual parties and electoral coalitions has stood at more than 30%, above the threshold of extreme instability.

Where these data offer ex-ante suggestions of the truncated time horizons with which Kenyan elites were likely operating, interviews from fieldwork reveal that KANU politicians organized ethnic party violence during the 1990s in a deliberate attempt to hold onto power. Importantly, these admissions not

Party Instability and Political Violence in Kenya

only came from voters but also from political leaders, including those affiliated with the Kenya African National Union. As one KANU leader in Nakuru admitted:

> [Before multipartyism], when KANU was ruling, there was a bit of dictatorship because the leaders didn't want to release power. But then in the 1990s, the multiparty elections came and many KANU elites became worried.... And [so] these clashes [were] geared politically.[4]

In a similar vein, a party leader affiliated with the Party of National Unity (PNU) in Nakuru held:

> 1992 was very high stakes for KANU. 1992 is when the Kikuyu opposed the government and they said that they were not going to vote for KANU. [They said,] "we want to go for multiparty government." And the first minister resigned – that was Kenneth Matiba.[5] And that brought in the opposition in a big way. So, KANU was falling apart because a lot of leaders were leaving and there were all of these opposition parties and the ordinary people who were fed up with the government.[6]

Finally, an ethnic leader from Eldoret noted:

> I was not a member of KANU in terms of political alignment. [But we] could tell [some things] from the outside manifestations, from violence or statements or so forth.... You see, competitive politics in Kenya introduced an element that was not known to us, and this competition was not produced in a healthy manner. It's like a game that has been agreed upon, but the rules are not there. So, you play the game the way you want and you devise your own rules and play according to those rules and you [c]ouldn't care less about the other person.... I guess, there must [have] been some rules that govern[ed] elections [in the 1990s], but no one honored them. So, KANU had to devise ways and methods of capturing [the political] leadership and they chose violence.[7]

Against this background, and consistent with the theoretical propositions of this book, the earliest incidents of violence in multiparty Kenya broke out in October 1991 in several multiethnic districts of Rift Valley Province where land-related grievances were ripe for the taking (Africa Watch/Human Rights Watch 1993; Klopp 2009). The Meteitei farm in Nandi district was the first site to fall prey to ethnic conflict on October 29. The violence at Meteitei directly targeted "non-Kalenjins" (Africa Watch/Human Rights Watch 1993: 31). From there, conflict quickly spread to Baringo, Kericho, Nakuru, Uasin Gishu, Trans Nzoia, and West Pokot districts of the Rift Valley as well as Kisumu and Bungoma districts of Nyanza and Western provinces, respectively.

---

[4] Interview with a KANU party leader, Nakuru, October 24, 2013.
[5] After resigning from Moi's KANU-led government in December 1988, Matiba contested the 1992 presidential election on a FORD-Asili (FORD-A) ticket and finished in second place.
[6] Interview with a PNU party leader, Nakuru, October 29, 2013.
[7] Interview with an ethnic leader, Eldoret, November 5, 2013.

In many of these places, KANU stalwarts such as Paul Chepkok, Nicholas Biwott, and William Ole Ntimama latched onto grievances about land distribution as well as broader concerns about belonging and resources to mobilize violence. They delivered inflammatory speeches at various election rallies in which they openly vilified "outsiders" – that is, members of the Kikuyu, Luo, and Luhya communities (Africa Watch/Human Rights Watch 1993; Klopp 2001, 2009; Klaus 2020). At a speech in Kericho district, for example, MP Chepkok exhorted his supporters to "take up arms and destroy dissidents [Kikuyu] on sight" (Klopp 2009: 185). Likewise, Maasai MP Ntimama openly painted "all Kikuyu in Narok [district] as alien despoilers of Maasai land" (Klopp 2001: 490). All the while, national elites issued strong warnings about how multipartyism would be "bad for Kenya" (Richburg 1991). In a statement to the *Washington Post*, for instance, a senior Moi aide singled out ethnic violence as an acute risk for the country and stated that "it [was] threatening everything" (Richburg 1991). On this issue, specifically, one of my respondents recalled:

Before opening up, Moi had predicted ... he had said that the multiparty system would bring about ethnic violence. And ... to guarantee the fulfillment of his prophecy, he actually organized communities that were supporting the government to attack communities that wanted change.[8]

After beginning in October 1991, conflict in the Rift Valley continued until December 1992 when voters finally took to the polls. By this time, however, the clashes had given KANU "better than a fighting chance" to run away with the election (Mutua 1992: 36). Although we might not be able to attribute the results of this contest to violence alone, it is important to note that Moi ultimately amassed 36.35% of the total votes cast for the presidency and held on to his position (African Elections Database 2021). Likewise, Chepkok, Biwott, and Ntimama continued as MPs from Keiyo North, Keiyo South, and Narok North constituencies, respectively.

Ethnic Party Violence in 1997

In the run-up to the 1997 elections, KANU leaders deployed this playbook once again. Rosenzweig's (2023: 13) recent work has held that "the tactics used by winners of founding elections" – including violence – "become the conventional wisdom about what works." This appears to be consistent with the behavior of KANU in 1997. For Moi and his close associates, organizing and sponsoring ethnic conflict ahead of these elections made good sense for three key reasons. First, ethnic conflict seemed to have brought electoral benefits to the party in 1992. Second, the Kenya African National Union continued to face grave challenges with regard to its organizational capacity and future survival. As Jeffrey Steeves (1999: 72) writes, by early 1997, "KANU had

---

[8] Interview with a CCM politician, Nakuru, October 23, 2013.

Party Instability and Political Violence in Kenya

fractured between two groups – 'KANU A,' a moderate, reform group [and] 'KANU B,' a conservative group of hardliners." Even though Moi had sought to "sharpen party strategy and discipline," it wasn't entirely clear that the organization would hold together, as "the resiliency of district-based politics" and "internal factional politics" both endured in the organization (Steeves 199: 72; Opalo 2019: 160). Third, compared to 1992, Moi faced considerably more pushback in the months leading up to the 1997 election, as the "opposition presence in parliament and a revitalized civil society" both agitated vigorously for constitutional reform (Steeves 1999: 72).

Taken together, violence thus offered a viable strategy through which the influence of the opposition could be checked in 1997. Rather than limiting themselves to the Rift Valley, Nyanza, and Western regions, ruling politicians expanded their instrumentalization efforts to the Kenyan Coast – and particularly to Mombasa and Kwale districts – where subnational grievances about land distribution, historical marginalization, and unemployment were available for elite appropriation. Much like in 1992, moreover, they entered the 1997 election with short time horizons, and subsequently not only instrumentalized violence but also painted it as an inevitable offshoot of multipartyism. As two respondents explained:

Don't forget 1992 was a turnaround for this country. It was when multipartyism was first implemented. So, there was a bit of excitement here and there: everybody coming in, everybody talking about reform, and KANU getting worried. So, I think 1997 was a follow-on of 1992. It was more of the same [in that the] occupational hazards of survival were still there ... [The] political occupational hazards. "If I don't like you, I look at excuses to get rid of you. I either chase you back to where you came from or I [try to] kill you." That's what happened in 1992 and it happened again in 1997 because the future was [still] unknown.[9]

[Again], in 1997, he [Moi] said, "I told you multiparty politics would bring violence in this country." And of course, he ha[d] now to make it look real and he did. They [KANU elites] were worried that they might not win again, so they decided to cause trouble.[10]

Meanwhile, a civil society leader from the Coast discussed the specific issues that were used to drive conflict in this region as follows:

[It was a] question of political strategy by the political class. The KANU regime ... by that time [1997], they had already reaped benefits from the clashes in the Rift Valley. So, now they also moved to the Coast. And they started telling the indigenous communities to chase away the upcountry people: the Kikuyus and the Luos.... And so, a lot of people fought.... When you've been so distressed and so disenfranchised, and you are told by the same people in government and in power that this is the time that you can now take over your region as before, then [people] bought into that.[11]

---

[9] Interview with a WDM-K party leader, Nairobi, October 15, 2013.
[10] Interview with a political expert, Nairobi, December 3, 2013.
[11] Interview with a civil society leader, Mombasa, September 25, 2013; also see Human Rights Watch (2002).

Finally, a leader associated with the United Democratic Forum Party (UDFP) discussed why elite narratives about land reclamation and historical marginalization resulted in violence in Likoni constituency in Mombasa and in Kwale district in particular:

> In 1997, there were clashes in the Coast. Again, it was over the land issue. Again, KANU was in power. Kikuyus have taken a lot of land – fairly or unfairly – in the Coast region. So again, it was the issue of land [and] the solution was to chase them ["outsiders"] away since "they have had your land." So, the land issue was used to "do away with these people and you will have your land back." So, if you notice the clashes in the Coast were where Kikuyus were many – in Likoni and Kwale.[12]

Eventually, the result of the 1997 election was the same as the outcome witnessed five years earlier: Moi held onto the presidency, this time with 40.12% of the total votes cast (African Elections Database 2021).

THE CONTOURS OF PARTY VIOLENCE IN THE POST-KANU ERA (2002–2013)

Following two violent elections and two KANU victories in the multiparty era, the 2002 contest "marked an important break from the past, [as] the KANU regime was defeated by a significant margin" (Klaus 2020: 15). According to Steeves (1999: 78), the possibilities for a KANU loss were already looming on the horizon in 1997 when "the new parliament saw [the ruling party's] standing [considerably] weakened" compared to its 1992 performance. As opposed to the contests of the 1990s, the 2002 election was also notable due to the absence of extensive violence that accompanied it. However, five years later, Kenya fell prey to its worst period of party violence, which claimed the lives of more than 1,100 individuals.

Opposition Coordination and the Avoidance of Widespread Violence in 2002

KANU's loss generated a marked increase in party instability, as Type A volatility in parliamentary contests rose from 11.25% in 1997 to 24.95% in 2002. Despite the shakiness of parties, however, a number of important variables militated against the organization of widespread violence at this time. First, even though they had failed to unite against Moi in the past, "opposition parties show[ed] strength" in 2002 (Steeves 1999: 78). In fact, in an effort to unseat the president, several of his rivals came together to forge the multiethnic, and ultimately triumphant, National Rainbow Coalition (NaRC). In so doing, these leaders – including Charity Ngilu from the Kamba community, Mwai Kibaki from the Kikuyu group, and Raila Odinga from the

---

[12] Interview with a UDFP party leader, Nairobi, October 18, 2013.

Luo community – ushered Kenya into its era of coalition politics (Cheeseman 2008). Second, as he was up against a term limit himself, the incentives for Moi to gamble with conflict were severely diminished. As one KANU party leader explained during an interview:

> 2002 was the last term for President Moi, who was a long-time KANU chairman. And the constitution was dictating that he could not go for any further term. So, it was seen as the correct time for other groups now to take up power. So, in that scenario, there was little need to generate these clashes again.[13]

Similarly, another respondent held:

> [By 2002] the constitution had been changed to put [in term] limits, so [Moi] was serving [his] second and last term. So really, the stakes, again, were not that high for the status quo. Moi was going anyway. It could have been very, very serious if maybe Moi was again contesting. But he wasn't, and so that's why I think the KANU leaders decided that they could forgo violence.[14]

While Moi's imminent exit dampened his motivations for conflict, there were also powerful reasons for politicians vying for the presidency to avoid violence in 2002. Crucially, the two leading candidates – Kibaki of NaRC and Uhuru Kenyatta of KANU – both hailed from the Kikuyu community. This configuration dampened the utility of violence as a political strategy. As one interviewee held, "[B]oth the candidates were from the same – Kikuyu – community. With so many Kenyans wanting change, KANU may not have been able to swing people's votes through violence."[15] Similarly, another explained:

> The politicians play a very vital role in bringing up these tribal clashes. Whoever were the presidential aspirants … both of them were from the same tribe. I think that's why it [violence] never happened in 2002…. So, they didn't have some stories or some ways [for] how to bring it [conflict]. Moi was at his term limit, so KANU didn't care for violence. The NaRC leaders had gone around saying that they were different from KANU, so they couldn't use tribalism. So, in 2002, it was much more peaceful.[16]

Taken together, the 2002 election emerged as a prime case wherein coalitional arrangements and the arrival of a presidential term limit disincentivized widespread violence even amidst unstable party conditions. Insofar as the alliance forged by NaRC was a multiethnic one, it operated in a manner consistent with Wilkinson's argument about the dampening effects of such arrangements on elites' incentives for conflict. Yet, to say that the 2002 election was entirely free of conflict would be an overreach. As Lynch (2018: 31; Mutahi 2005: 73) describes, this contest "was [actually] characterized by a level of electoral violence that would be shocking in most other contexts," as hundreds of people

---

[13] Interview with a KANU party leader, Nakuru, October 23, 2013.
[14] Interview with a policy expert, Nairobi, November 29, 2013.
[15] Interview with a civil society leader, Mombasa, September 25, 2013.
[16] Interview with a resident of an IDPs camp, Nakuru, October 26, 2013.

were "killed in political conflicts linked to electoral logics in the year running up to the polls." One of the sites that fell prey to significant violence during this time was Tana River district, a place that will receive greater attention in Chapter 5.

Ethnic Party Violence during Kenya's Post-election Crisis

There is considerable suggestive evidence that Kenya's descent into the 2007–2008 post-election crisis was conditioned by rising rates of party instability. Specifically, where party birth and death rates in 2007 stood at 58.29% and 45.58% in the parliamentary and presidential contests, respectively, coalitional replacement stood at 58.52% for the parliamentary election and 62.2% for the presidential race. Taken together, uncertainty about party survival seemed rife in the party system.

These uncertainties can be traced to a number of intervening developments between 2002 and 2007. Core among them was NaRC's vulnerability to "internal schisms," particularly between Kibaki and leaders of the Liberal Democratic Party (LDP) led by Raila Odinga (Khamisi 2011: 51). These gulfs ultimately led to the collapse of the coalition in 2005, a mere three years after it had ousted KANU from power. In discussing NaRC's disintegration, several respondents emphasized the fragility of the alliance from its founding, especially its susceptibility to interpersonal disputes and its absence of a shared vision about governance.[17] As one official from the organization explained:

We [in NaRC] did not have common interests. The main thing was to fight Moi.... They [alliance leaders] only made sure that they wanted to bring an end to the twenty-four years of Moi's rule and they brought him down.... We only campaigned for 90 days.... And immediately after we won and Moi was thrown out of power, NaRC died.... In the following year, it was no longer there.... It was really weakened because [in the] following electioneering year [of 2007], we only got two Members of Parliament.[18]

Another political leader discussed the short-lived nature of coalitions in Kenya more broadly:

In terms of political affiliations ... they are very weak and they change like [the] weather. You can never predict your tomorrow comfortably under any coalition. [There are always] alignments and realignments, new organizations, people running away, some joining each other, some planning things. This is just how things are.[19]

---

[17] Interview with a DP official, Nairobi, October 18, 2013; interview with a NaRC party official, Nairobi, December 5, 2013.
[18] Interview with a NaRC party official, Nairobi, December 5, 2013. Parliamentary election results reveal that NaRC actually captured three parliamentary seats in 2007 in Kitui Central, Kitui West, and Nyaribari Chache constituencies (Kenya Election Database 2021).
[19] Interview with a WDM-K party leader, Nairobi, October 15, 2013.

Party Instability and Political Violence in Kenya 89

Even though NaRC was effectively out of the running, Mwai Kibaki – one of its founders and the president of the country – still competed in the 2007 polls. This time, however, he ran on the ticket of the PNU, which was essentially "a coalition of parties with additional allied parties" (Lynch 2008: 552). His main rival in the presidential race was his former NaRC colleague, Raila Odinga, who led the Orange Democratic Movement (ODM). Compared to the PNU, which produced a manifesto "bereft of principles and any ideological foundation but the person of Kibaki," ODM was marked by "coherence as a single party" and an 80-page manifesto with "pledges of redistribution, devolution, correction of historical injustices, and job creation" (Wanyama 2010: 89; Lynch 2008: 544, 552). In addition, Odinga succeeded in incorporating five politicians from different ethnic communities to head the campaign of the Orange Democratic Movement (Lynch 2008). This group, which came to be known as the "pentagon," included Luhya leader Musalia Mudavadi, Coastal leader Najib Balala, Kalenjin politician Ruto, Kamba politician Charity Ngilu, and Mbeere leader Joseph Nyaga. The buy-in from these leaders visibly helped Odinga's electioneering efforts, as they often joined or represented him at public rallies; by comparison, Kibaki frequently "appeared as a sole campaigner" (Lynch 2008: 552).

Combined with rising party instability levels, which generated considerable political uncertainty and shortened the time horizons of many established politicians, the ethnic configurations centered by the 2007 presidential contest made renewed violence possible in Kenya. As Tom Wolf (2009: 280, citing Atieno-Odhiambo 2004) describes, the "two main candidates represent[ed] the most deeply rooted divide in Kenyan public life: that between the Kikuyu and the Luo." In addition, key to the eventual precipitation of widespread conflict was Kibaki's unexpected victory. Klaus (2020: 15) documents that "anger over perceived electoral fraud committed by the incumbent regime" proved vital to mobilizing violence in various parts of the country. Indeed, so strong was the perception of electoral fraud that a Gallup poll conducted some six months after the election found that whereas "57% of Kenyans believed that Odinga had won, only 25% stat[ed] that they thought that Kibaki had" (Wolf 2009: 280).

Qualitative interviews provide support for each of these factors – short time horizons, a salient ethnic cleavage available for manipulation, and grievances pertaining to perceptions of electoral fraud – which coalesced to generate violence in 2007–2008. With regard to the short-term orientations of key elites, one respondent spoke of Kibaki's decisions as follows:

[I]n 2002, it was NaRC. NaRC is still there as a party [not a coalition], but Kibaki jumped ship in 2007 and went to PNU, which was formed as a vehicle for [him] to sail to retain power. So [he] discarded NaRC. That alignment again was an alignment with very minimum cohesion and Kibaki walked into PNU.[20]

---

[20] Interview with a WDM-K party leader, Nairobi, October 15, 2013.

This interviewee further noted that even though Odinga's ODM represented a more coherent entity than the PNU, ultimately, his thinking too was: "now let me look for other alliances that will get me to where I want to."[21]

In discussing the impact of ethnic configurations in enabling violence in 2007, a party leader from Nairobi explicitly compared this contest to the 2002 election, and argued:

At that time [in 2002], the Kikuyus and Luos were on one side.... Now, 2007 was a different case: Luos and Kalenjins were on one side and Kikuyus were on the other side, and that was dangerous.[22]

Meanwhile, a political expert who strongly implied that the incumbent regime had stolen the vote also emphasized that ethnic divisions were available for the taking:

The PNU and the ODM election of 2007 was the most polarized in terms of ethnicity to the extent that when one team lost and then stole the vote, they then saw this as, "It's ours to keep. Nobody is going to take it away from us." I can put the whole blame on politicians.[23]

In a related but more detailed vein, two politicians who had campaigned on the side of the PNU discussed both the ethnic cleavages central to the elections as well as the role of perceived electoral fraud in enabling violence. Unsurprisingly, these leaders expressly placed the blame for the post-election crisis on opposition politicians' shoulders:

Now in 2007, the violence which was there was not really a question of Kikuyu and Kalenjin ... I campaigned. I was very involved in those campaigns. I really campaigned at the presidential level across the country. I really campaigned very hard for him [Kibaki] because I believe he had made serious changes.... The violence broke out because, and I squarely blame it on ODM. ODM was the opposition political party.... [T]hey cultivated the idea in the minds of Kenyans that it was Kikuyus versus everyone else. So, that was very negative campaigning, and at that time we didn't have laws to prosecute incitement. [The] electoral laws were very weak and the electoral commission was also not reformed so they could get away with it.... [This was] an extremely bad way of campaigning and then creating false expectations among the people that "we have won, we have won!" [Then when] the facts were released, they had lost. So, they set the stage for a violent confrontation.[24]

The 2007 violence was mainly in Rift Valley, Nyanza, and Western provinces. The violence occurred because ODM thought they had won the election and it was robbed. Why did they think this way? I was also in the middle of the action at that particular time because I was defending my seat. What actually happened, I must tell you, [is] that

---

[21] Interview with a WDM-K party leader, Nairobi, October 15, 2013.
[22] Interview with a DP official, Nairobi, October 18, 2013.
[23] Interview with a political expert, Nairobi, December 3, 2013.
[24] Interview with a TNA politician, Nairobi, October 17, 2013.

Party Instability and Political Violence in Kenya

that election was rigged – not by the government per se or by Kibaki, but by the same people who created that violence. That is, [by] Raila and company [who] convinced themselves [that] they must win [the] election.[25]

By contrast, an official affiliated with ODM argued that the violence was attributable to PNU's machinations and the grievances engendered by a rigged election:

I was part of that union – ODM – [and] I participated in that election…. The election was largely peaceful until the day that they [PNU] realized that they were losing. And I can tell you very confidently that president Kibaki never won [that] election in 2007. He never won. We can talk other stories about maybe these other matters, but this one of 2007, he never won. But the matter was so grave for them that some people thought that "if we allow this change in terms of governance, then we are likely to be victims." That is why they fought also: to retain power. So, as others fought to take power, others fought to retain power. And since they were the government at that time, we could see how they manipulated the agencies that you know, that dealt with security … even the swearing in, the judiciary, and all that matter. And that's how it became. So, people now resorted to violence because they were saying "now, we have nowhere else to go. The people in leadership are violating the law with impunity!" I'm sure you have heard of this word in Kenya many times: impunity. It's just a very simple word that you just ignore the law and you say, "Go to hell. What will you do? I'm this person." And that's what basically Kibaki did with his cronies at that time … [and] unfortunately Kenyans died.[26]

Insofar as the displacement of blame in this manner is expected of political elites who hail from rival camps, the scale of violence in 2007–2008 warrants consideration. Beyond exploding across several districts and constituencies in the Rift Valley, Nyanza, and Western regions, the crisis also claimed the lives of Kenyans in Nyeri, Nyandarua South, and Kiambu West districts of Central Province, as well as Mombasa, Kilifi, and Kwale districts in the Coast (Malik 2023). At the provincial level, this spatial distribution is consistent with the theoretical claims of the book, as many regions with diverse populations and long-standing interethnic grievances fell prey to the 2007–2008 post-election crisis. Drilling down to locations, for example – which are the second smallest administrative unity in Kenya – in the multiethnic Rift Valley, Kasara (2017) shows that ethnic segregation often enabled violence by eroding trust among noncoethnics.

Crucially, the post-election crisis involved both explicit incitement and indirect sponsorship of party violence. In places such as Nakuru district, elites' contentions about electoral fraud tapped into the anger of many local residents and precipitated ethnic conflict (Klaus 2020). As one PNU official explained, "once all these allegations began … that the election had been

---

[25] Interview with a former MP, Mombasa, September 24, 2013. This respondent did not permit me to report his prior party affiliation in my writing.
[26] Interview with an ODM party official and former MP, Nairobi, December 10, 2013.

stolen ... [there was] violence."²⁷ In Sotik (Kenya National Commission of Human Rights 2008) and Naivasha (Klaus 2020) constituencies, respectively, politicians also appropriated pre-existing "infrastructures for violence"²⁸ – such as gangs and ethnic militias – and transported violence specialists to do their bidding. Compared to the intense scale of violence in the Rift Valley – where over 700 individuals lost their lives (Republic of Kenya 2008) – conflict was relatively mild in the Kenyan Coast. This is because Luo residents and communities indigenous to the area all flanked behind ODM, which left mainly Kikuyu voters vulnerable to attacks in the post-election period.

In stark contrast to the devastating consequences that violence generated for ordinary citizens in 2007–2008, the two main contenders for the presidency fared much better. Indeed, whereas Kibaki emerged victorious, negotiations to end violence – overseen by Kofi Annan – helped to create the nonexecutive position of Prime Minister for Odinga. In addition, the mediation process resulted in the formation of a Grand Coalition cabinet between PNU and ODM. According to one interviewee, the benefits garnered through violence were clear: "Who was the beneficiary of that violence? It was Raila. He became Prime Minister and got 50% of the government."²⁹

As opposed to Kibaki and Odinga's fates, Uhuru Kenyatta and William Ruto faced indictments from the International Criminal Court (ICC) for their roles in organizing violence. The levying of these charges raised grave questions about fairness among some communities and interviewees, as shown below:

You know the proceedings at the Hague are televised live: in Kenya, everybody sees it.... And so, Kalenjins [are] like: "Huh? We are being crucified! Hello? Why isn't there any Luo [charged]?" That [is] the question. "Didn't the Luos participate [in violence]?" And then, they said, "Raila shielded these Luos and then allowed the Kalenjins and the Kikuyus to be taken there [to the Hague]."³⁰

In 2007, it was Raila and Kibaki who [had] contested over the presidency. So, the responsibility over the violence is supposed to be borne by the two. But the investigations by the Waki Commission [the official commission established to investigate the post-election crisis] ended up with Ruto and Uhuru's names and these are now matters at the ICC. So, the question is: why is Raila's name not in the envelope? Why is Kibaki's name not in the envelope?³¹

Even as respondents asked such questions about the post-election crisis, Kibaki's arrival at his term limit considerably attenuated his incentives to organize or sponsor violence in 2013, the contest to which I now turn.

---

²⁷ Interview with a PNU official, Nakuru, October 29, 2013.
²⁸ Interview with a human rights activist, Nairobi, February 2, 2013.
²⁹ Interview with a WDM-K political leader, Mombasa, October 5, 2013. The respondent here is referring to power-sharing in the Grand Coalition cabinet, wherein portfolios were allocated in keeping with the relative power of parties in parliament.
³⁰ Interview with an elections expert, Nakuru, October 29, 2013.
³¹ Interview with a NaRC-K party official, Nairobi, September 16, 2013.

PATTERNS OF PARTY VIOLENCE UNDER KENYA'S NEW CONSTITUTION (2013–PRESENT)

Following the devastation caused by the post-election crisis, Kenya promulgated a new constitution in 2010. This constitutional arrangement was first put to the test in the electoral domain in 2013. Since then, it has remained the framework under which the elections of 2017 and 2022 were conducted. Importantly, these exercises have all resulted in lower rates of party violence than those witnessed in the 1990s and in 2007–2008. However, the evidence also shows that there are new domains in which elites might organize such conflict in Kenya today, including around county-level contests.

Party Violence under a New Constitution in 2013

The 2013 election – the first held in the country since the post-election crisis – took place amidst "constitutional reforms, political realignments, daily struggles for advancement and survival, and an array of peacebuilding efforts" that emphasized the place of "individual Kenyans" in contributing to "early warning [systems], peacebuilding, and conflict resolution" (Lynch 2018: 55). However, because these programs largely focused on influencing the behavior of civilians rather than politicians, they did not quell elites' incentives for violence.

The clearest evidence of these enduring proclivities for conflict was revealed in the severe clashes that exploded across Tana River County in 2012–2013. Beyond this site, deadly violence was also recorded in the months preceding and immediately following the March 2013 polls in Kilifi County in the Coast, Kisumu County in Nyanza, Garissa County in Northeastern Province, and Busia and Bungoma Counties in the Western region (Malik 2023). Noticeable in this pattern is the fact that the Rift Valley maintained calm throughout. This is despite the fact that party replacement in the parliamentary and presidential elections stood at more than 45% and 55%, respectively, and coalitional volatility in the presidential poll approached 100%.

As in 2002, important shifts in coalitional arrangements helped to spare the Rift Valley from violence in 2013. In particular, Uhuru Kenyatta and William Ruto's decision to forge the Jubilee Alliance and mobilize Kikuyus and Kalenjins together rendered the instrumentalization of conflict between the two groups an unwise choice. As one politician explained:

The only two communities [that have held power in Kenya] have been brought together. They [Uhuru and Ruto] needed to tamper with the higher stakes with respect to competition for power....[32] So, [there has been] an arrangement between them [Kalenjins] – with

---

[32] The respondent here is referring to the more demanding requirements for winning the presidency under Kenya's new constitution. These requirements include amassing more than half of the votes cast as well as at least 25% of the total votes in more than half of the country's 47 counties.

William Ruto – and the Kikuyu community. [So,] Ruto and Uhuru [had to] stay away from that ethnicization of [the Kikuyu-Kalenjin cleavage of] Kenyan political matches.[33]

In the wake of Jubilee's subsequent victory, scholars and analysts explained the triumph of the alliance in a number of interrelated ways. Some placed emphasis on Jubilee's "well-funded and coordinated campaign" (Lynch 2014: 95). Others held that while the broader campaign certainly mattered, it was the two leaders' messaging around the intervention of the ICC that proved pivotal (Lynch 2014; Malik 2016). This messaging, according to several interviewees, framed the court as an unjust institution and thereby helped Uhuru and Ruto to build a broad Kikuyu-Kalenjin alliance.[34]

Regardless of the factors that brought about Jubilee's eventual win, it is worth noting that mere months after the election, some respondents expressed uncertainty about its long-term survival. To quote an elections expert from Nakuru:

It is too early to say anything about Jubilee because it's just months down the line since they came to power, but as a political coalition.... Yes, it has its challenges, and yes, it [has] some risks to manage.... Notable among those risks is ... that they should never ever, ever break up because one even doesn't want to imagine the consequences of such a break-up. So, those are the risks and the potential risks for that manner, which they themselves must try to manage.[35]

Echoing these broader ideas, a leader affiliated with the coalition noted that efforts directed at its maintenance and institutionalization were ongoing in late 2013:

We are working on this coalition not to die because we still have another term to run.... We are working on this coalition to hold together. That is why we are sitting down and we want to form the coalition structures. When we get the coalition structures, we will have the Chairman maybe from TNA, we will have the Secretary General maybe from NaRC, we will have maybe another person from the post-coalition parties. That way we will get a Secretariat. When we get a Secretariat, that way we are keeping watch on each of the political parties.... That way it [the coalition] will stand. But if we do not have those structures, we might have other coalitions before we get to 2017.[36]

Finally, others warned that even if the alliance held together, it wasn't entirely clear that the 2017 polls would, in fact, be peaceful:

---

[33] Interview with a WDM-K politician, Mombasa, September 27, 2013.
[34] Interview with a WDM-K political leader, Mombasa, October 5, 2013; interview with a DP leader, Nairobi, October 18, 2013; interview with a UDF party leader, Nairobi, October 18, 2013.
[35] Interview with an elections expert, Nakuru, October 29, 2013.
[36] Interview with a NaRC party leader, Nairobi, December 5, 2013. The Jubilee Alliance was comprised of the National Alliance (TNA), United Republican Party (URP), Republican Congress (RC), and NaRC parties.

Party Instability and Political Violence in Kenya

You can hear the language [already]. It's like they [politicians] are taunting [voters], "If you *dare not* elect us, you *dare not* elect this team ..." And that, to me, is more dangerous ... because that taunting prepares people. It's like a war cry, you start slowly. By the time the day comes, all you need to do is say, "Go!" and everybody will then do whatever.[37]

The claims of this interviewee are similar to those presented by Lynch (2018; also see Elder, Stigant, and Claes 2014: 13) who argues that the pre-election peace narrative wielded by Jubilee in 2013 demanded certain behaviors from ordinary citizens. Should they disagree with its premise – maintaining peace above all else – they stood to be cast as troublemakers (Lynch 2018: 52). But politicians still appeared to have the latitude to stir up violence if they so wanted. In a country where many previous elections had given rise to violence, it thus became difficult, if not impossible, for citizens to be "*against* peace, reconciliation and order," particularly in places such as Rift Valley Province, even as other areas like parts of the Coast experienced significant conflict (Lynch 2018: 55). I further discuss the Coast's descent into conflict in Chapter 5.

Enduring Party Instability and Opportunities for Party Violence in 2017 and 2022

Since 2013, Type A volatility levels have continued to climb in Kenya, reaching more than 55% in the parliamentary and presidential polls in 2017, respectively. This is despite the fact that Kenyatta and Odinga contested for the presidency once again – albeit as leaders of new entities in the form of the Jubilee Party (JP) and the National Super Alliance (NASA), respectively – and the pact between Uhuru and Ruto stayed in place. The rise of these organizations was squarely in keeping with the 2013 statements of a party leader from Nairobi:

> Come to 2013 [and] there was no PNU, no NaRC. We came into something else called Jubilee and some other coalitions: A, B, C, D. And I can assure you, come 2017, we will have some other animal coming on board.[38]

Importantly, even though Kenyatta and Ruto managed to maintain their prior arrangement and Uhuru and Raila competed against each other again, the 2017 election was not entirely peaceful. At the same time, the contours of conflict shifted in some key ways. First, many parties succumbed to violence during the primaries and nomination cycles (Raleigh 2022). Second, following procedural irregularities, the Supreme Court nullified the August 2017 results in which Uhuru Kenyatta had been proclaimed victorious. Two months later, NASA boycotted the October re-run and called on its supporters to do the same. As opposition supporters' faith in electoral integrity deteriorated, several counties – including Bungoma, Homa Bay, Kisumu, Mumias, and Siaya – fell

---

[37] Interview with a policy expert, Nairobi, December 3, 2013.
[38] Interview with a WDM-K party leader, Nairobi, October 15, 2013.

prey to violent protests and riots in the weeks preceding the re-run (Raleigh 2022; Republic of Kenya 2017a, 2017b).

Despite these manifold uncertainties, Kenyatta ultimately won his second term as president in 2017. For citizens and researchers with an eye toward the future, the possibilities for political violence in 2022 thus stood to turn not so much on the president's personal stakes in the contest, but on his treatment of and decisions about Ruto's future (Magu 2018).[39] On this matter, in December 2013, one party official already made clear that even "if Uhuru goes for two terms, when the last term is coming ... it is not ... automatic that Ruto [will] land up at State House."[40] Writing in January 2018, Opalo argued that there might be good reasons for the president to continue to work with Ruto and further suggested that weakening the Vice President would require Kenyatta to take "overt steps." Two months later in March, however, accusations and counter-accusations from each camp escalated, signaling a clear breakdown in the two leaders' relationship (Kiruga 2020). By June, the journalist Macharia Gaitho (2020) noted that the "Kenyatta team" was actively trying to "cut Ruto down to size" by "purg[ing] his acolytes in Jubilee." The shroud over the president's forthcoming decision was lifted quickly enough, as the door on Ruto's succession was slammed shut in mid-2020 (Kiruga 2020) and Uhuru backed his former rival – Odinga – for the country's top job in March 2022 (Al Jazeera 2022).

Although these events generated some cause for concern, voters and analysts drew hope from three other developments that violence could be avoided in 2022. First, even though some divisive language was deployed in the campaigns ahead of the elections (Khalid 2021) – with Ruto casting the contest as one between "dynasties" and "hustlers" so as to distinguish himself from Odinga and Kenyatta – the main presidential candidates ultimately exercised restraint and pledged to uphold peace (Mungai 2022). There were also important instances of state-society partnerships in historically violence-prone regions such as the Rift Valley, which indicated a broad commitment to peace (Cherono 2022). Second, citizens expressed faith in the Supreme Court as the country proceeded toward the elections. This faith was suggestive of a maturing of political institutions other than parties that could serve to deter elites from engaging in violence. Third, class issues such as the cost of living, rising inflation, and food shortages seemed to matter more to many Kenyans in 2022 than ethnic considerations (Angar and Klaus 2022). These realities were also reflected in the electioneering efforts of the leading presidential contenders, both of whom explicitly emphasized economic and class-based considerations during their campaigns. As Opalo (2022: 2) suggests, while it would be premature to conclude from these developments that we have arrived at "the end of ethnicity as the predominant logic of voter mobilization" in Kenya, it is now

---

[39] Skype interview with a religious leader from the Global Empowerment Christian Center in Eldoret, March 24, 2017.
[40] Interview with a NaRC party official, Nairobi, December 5, 2013.

Party Instability and Political Violence in Kenya

clear that economic and institutional factors played key roles in reducing the salience of ethnicity in 2022 (Opalo 2022: 2).

Even amidst all these positive developments, as per the Armed Conflict Location and Event Dataset (ACLED), Kenya witnessed nearly 400 riot events between January and August 2022, as well as a spike in "violent demonstrations and mob violence during the party primaries" in April and May (Raleigh 2022: 2). In addition, Raila Odinga's refusal to concede defeat in the wake of the August 9 polls generated some concerns about the possibilities for renewed conflict in the country.

VOTER KNOWLEDGE ABOUT PARTY VIOLENCE IN KENYA

Insofar as a central claim of this book is that party instability has emboldened Kenyan politicians to repeatedly organize and sponsor violence by shortening their time horizons and enabling them to discount the costs associated with conflict – including potential punishment from voters – it is important to highlight that ordinary citizens are aware of and opposed to politicians' roles in violence. Indeed, research has established that voters understand that elite tactics frequently lead to conflict in Kenya (Elder, Stigant, and Claes 2014; Bekoe and Burchard 2017). Newer work on this topic has further revealed that citizens generally reject politicians who organize violence (Gutiérrez-Romero and LeBas 2020; Horowitz and Klaus 2020; Rosenzweig 2021, 2023).

My qualitative data finds that voters' awareness about elite roles in conflict has developed over time. In discussing the violence of the 1990s, for instance, a number of interviewees held during fieldwork that politicians had essentially "manipulated" unsuspecting voters to mount and participate in ethnic clashes.[41] One interviewee from the Coast, for example, explained civilians' participation in party-based clashes in 1997 in the following words:

> The people of the Coast [have long felt] underprovided for by the system. The underprovision is in the sense [of] jobs or opportunities, facilities, educational facilities, health facilities, and the worst of them all [is] the land. Most of the land here ... most of the land in the Coast is owned by outsiders. [These are] the issue[s] that created that kind of bitterness and that is why violence erupted in the Coast, including the lower Coast [in 1997].... The young men, most of them, followed by the young women, [felt] that "why are [we] neglected? Why are [we] sidelined?" And so, it was very easy to incite them into violence. I don't think many of them ever thought things would get so bad. But the violence was very bad here, as you know. It all escalated quickly and then the people were left wondering, "how did this happen?"[42]

In contrast to the 1990s when citizens were left somewhat puzzled about the elite origins of violence, they seemed to grasp its genesis after the post-election

---

[41] Interview with a civil society leader, Mombasa, September 25, 2013; interview with a CCM politician, Nakuru, October 23, 2013.
[42] Interview with a URP politician, Mombasa, September 24, 2013.

crisis much more clearly. As a resident of an internally displaced persons (IDP) camp in the Rift Valley recalled:

> In 2007–2008, it's like the country was divided. So, they [politicians] could make people fight. But now we know, now we know. In fact, even before [the] election, those of us who were living in areas dominated by ODM or simply with Kalenjins, we started feeling unsafe. The area started developing some kind of tension. We just felt that we were not in the right place. So, even from then, the politicians started using some other terminology of hatred.... So, we could tell, there are things that are happening that are being planned. In fact, in 2007, things started coming up openly, because by then you felt that there are some ... young men who you are maybe used to seeing in town or other areas. Now it's as if they were pulled up.... They were somewhere [else]. It's later that we came to discover that they were being trained somewhere.[43]

Compared to experimental studies, however, which find broad support for voter sanctioning, I argue that voters are unable to consistently punish elites for conflict because of the unstable nature of political parties. In Kenya, party fragility can sometimes result in the outright exit of violent elites from the electoral arena. The journey of Suleiman Rashid Shakombo – a politician from Likoni in the Coast who will receive greater attention in Chapter 5 – is illustrative of this trend. Briefly, Shakombo's case reveals the following: despite his involvement in instrumentalizing violence in Likoni in 1997, he eventually lost his MP seat in 2007 not due to this record but because he joined hands with the wrong party, PNU. This party was not competitive in the Coast and only captured two Coastal MP seats in 2007. At other times, and due to the fleeting nature of coalitions, political elites with a hand in violence might find themselves working with and mobilizing previously rival communities together, as witnessed in the pursuit of a Kikuyu-Kalenjin alliance in 2013. In such circumstances, sanctioning a violent leader from a different party – but one within the coalition in question – could also negatively impact the prospects of a voter's preferred politician and drive down the overall support for the alliance. An important policy implication of these findings, then, is that paying more attention to stabilizing political parties could serve to disincentivize conflict in Kenya going forward. This is because stable political parties would not only enable voters to respond to politicians based on their understanding about elites' roles in violence – facilitating the punishment of such politicians around future contests – but would also force leaders to take the potential of such sanctioning into consideration as part of their decision-making.

SUMMARY AND CONCLUSION

Based on a combination of quantitative and qualitative data and with a focus on national-level patterns, this chapter has highlighted the crucial place of

---

[43] Interview with an IDP camp resident, Nakuru, October 26, 2013.

party instability in incentivizing violence on the part of political elites in Kenya. Specifically, I have shown that unstable parties have contributed to truncated time horizons, which have in turn enabled leaders to discount the costs that violence can generate, such as voter sanctioning. The chapter has further demonstrated that these truncated time horizons are reflected in both the activities of dominant KANU party elites, who instrumentalized violence in the initial multiparty contests of 1992 and 1997, as well as in the involvement of newer parties such as the ODM and PNU, whose leaders incited and sponsored ethnic clashes in 2007–2008. I also find that these incentives for violence have persisted even though Kenya has transitioned to an era of coalitional politics since 2002; many leaders have repeatedly contested for the presidency; a new constitution has brought forth important reforms such as devolution, which has in turn reduced the stakes of presidential elections; and voters have learned about, and come to reject, violence. At the same time, there is evidence that the strengthening of institutions beyond political parties – such as the Supreme Court – has helped to check elites' appetites for conflict around recent contests. Having laid the groundwork with this national-level analysis, I now turn to offering subnational analyses of party violence in the Rift Valley and Coast regions of Kenya in Chapter 5.

5

Party Fragility and Subnational Patterns of Violence in Kenya's Rift Valley and Coast Regions

Building on the broader arguments of this book as well as the national-level evidence presented in Chapter 4, I turn to explaining and accounting for subnational patterns of party violence in Kenya's Rift Valley and Coast regions. in this chapter. In each area, I focus on two constituencies and two counties: namely, Molo (Nakuru County) and Kapseret (Uasin Gishu County) in the Rift Valley, and Likoni (Mombasa County) and Garsen (Tana River County) in the Coast. In addition to event data, party replacement data, and in-depth qualitative interviews, I also draw on newspaper reports and constituency-level election information in my discussion of these cases. Collectively, these data allow me to carefully trace the fates of politicians who organized conflict in the above sites. Consistent with my overall theory, I find that many violence-wielding politicians in Kenya have been able to compete in subsequent elections; rather than facing significant sanctioning for conflict, they have been able to maintain their political careers or reshape them as they see fit.

I also incorporate subnational data on party instability in this chapter for another key reason: we might imagine that politicians' decisions to drive violence in particular places are not merely conditioned by the state of the party at the national level but also by candidates' insecurities about holding onto their seats. Turning to the subnational level facilitates the inclusion of this important factor; in addition, the case studies presented herein enable me to speak to the place of ethnic demography and local-level grievances. Taken together, then, this chapter serves to comprehensively illuminate the subnational variables that make party violence in Kenya possible.

This chapter proceeds as follows. I begin my analysis with the Rift Valley, where I lay out the relationship between party instability and elites' incentives to drive violence in Molo constituency and Nakuru County, as well as Kapseret constituency and Uasin Gishu County. I then turn to discussing and analyzing patterns of party violence in Coast Province, focusing on Likoni constituency and Mombasa County, as well as Garsen constituency and Tana River County. My findings from this region reveal that while devolution has reduced presidential stakes (Opalo 2022), it has not entirely staunched elites' proclivities toward conflict. Rather, by transferring the incentives for violence to the county level, this institutional reform has rendered a new set of subnational sites vulnerable to party conflict. I conclude the chapter by addressing concerns about reverse causality.

VICISSITUDES IN PARTY VIOLENCE IN KENYA'S RIFT VALLEY (1992–2017)

Molo and Nakuru

> Before 1992 ... the stakes were not high. There was only one party in the country: KANU. And there had been one party since 1969. [T]herefore, because the stakes were not high, everybody [knew that] no matter what, it [was] KANU that [was] going to win. But then with multiparty politics, the stakes became very high. And all throughout KANU – from top to bottom – these people realized that to win the election, they needed to dislodge the Kikuyus in particular areas like the Rift Valley so that they [were] nowhere to vote on that day.[1]

This interview excerpt underscores the fact that the Rift Valley was the first region where elites orchestrated violence after the restoration of multiparty competition in Kenya. Located in Kikuyu-majority Nakuru County – where there are also sizeable Kisii and Kalenjin populations present (Republic of Kenya 2008; Malik 2018) – Molo constituency's ethnic demography rendered it an opportune site for instrumentalizing party conflict at the micro level. Like many other parts of the Rift Valley, Molo had witnessed an influx of Kikuyu settlers from Central Province in the early postindependence era (Maupeu 2008). Owing to this ingress, by the early 1990s, "most land belonged to Kikuyus" in locations such as Likia (Boone 2012: 87). At the time of the restoration of multipartyism, this issue had evolved into a veritable "powder keg of grievances" that elites from the Kenya African National Union could exploit for their power-seeking goals (Boone 2012: 89). In addition, the early years of multiparty competition generated acute worries for various subleaders, but especially KANU politicians, about the prospects of losing their seats in Molo.

Type A volatility data provides a helpful proxy to understand these anxieties. As shown in Figure 5.1, since the restoration of multiparty competition, party replacement rates in parliamentary races in Molo have consistently exceeded the threshold of extreme instability (30%). In fact, in 2007, replacement volatility in Molo reached its zenith of 95.90% before settling back down to 36.23% as of 2017.

---

[1] Interview with a policy expert, Nairobi, December 3, 2013.

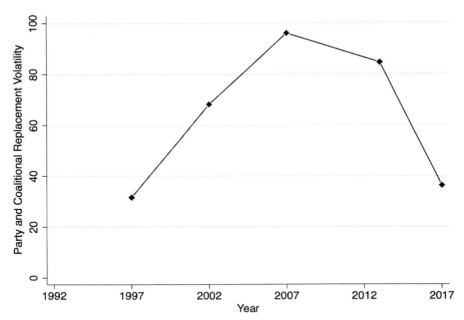

FIGURE 5.1 Party and coalitional replacement volatility in Molo constituency (1992–2017)[2]

Following the restoration of multipartyism, this constituency recorded some of its earliest reverberations from violence in late 1991 after hundreds of thousands of displaced Kikuyus from nearby Elgeyo-Marakwet district flooded into the area. Nicholas Biwott, the MP from Keiyo South constituency in Elgeyo-Marakwet, had reportedly built a "private army" to clear the Rift Valley of "people from other provinces," and the actions of these groups had a downstream effect on Molo residents (Africa Watch/Human Rights Watch 1993 42–43). In addition, several clashes originated in Molo itself and a good number continued into 1993. For example, the Akiwumi Report (Republic of Kenya 1999) chronicles that even though some of the earliest incidents of violence in the constituency were documented on March 14, 1992, the ground for conflict had been prepared well in advance. This period of preparation had involved, among other elements, the distribution of handwritten leaflets in Swahili, which had ordered "mainly the Kikuyu and the Kisii [to] leave the area or else ... be killed" (Republic of Kenya 1999: 45). Likewise, according to Mwangi Kimenyi and Njuguna Ndung'u (2005: 130–131), key factors

---

[2] In the four constituencies detailed in this chapter, electoral coalitions have fully captured the birth and death of constituent parties. Thus, the data depicted in the associated figures represent exit and entry volatility at the level of both parties and coalitions.

favoring violence – including disputes over cattle, land, and pasture – emboldened politicians to actively provoke conflict. Finally, Africa Watch/Human Rights Watch (1993: 51) has detailed four days of violent conflict in Molo in August 1993 when Kalenjins reportedly "attacked and selectively torched over 200 [Kikuyu] houses."

A few years later, violence returned to Molo once again. According to Marcel Rutten (2001), on January 25 and 26, 1998 – weeks after the 1997 election – Kalenjin raiders burned down some 40 Kikuyu homes. Kikuyu residents then organized a series of counterattacks, claiming the lives of countless civilians in turn (Republic of Kenya 2008; Kimenyi and Ndung'u 2005).

As with the clashes of the early 1990s, investigations into the events of late January 1998 found political planning at the heart of the initial arson incidents (Rutten 2001). However, even as evidence against KANU leaders started to mount, some "41 Rift Valley MPs" strategically pointed the finger at the Democratic Party (DP) (Rutten 2001: 543). These leaders accused the opposition of using violence to try and "topple Moi" (Rutten 2001: 543).

According to interviewees, there were important reasons why KANU appeared to be particularly worried about the DP in 1997. As one respondent put it:

A lot of chaos came out.... A lot of politicians were wondering, "how do we get enough votes from that side?" The DP wanted to take power. The president wanted to [stay] back.... All of these new parties were there. So, there was a lot of chaos, and the chaos ... led to violence.[3]

Candidate-level information helps to further illuminate these anxieties. In 1997, the incumbent MP John Mungai, previously of FORD-Asili, was contesting on a KANU ticket, but he lost his seat to the DP's Dickson Kimani (Kenya Election Database 2021). As such, it is possible that at least some of the post-election violence in Molo broke out as a reaction to his defeat. Furthermore, insofar as changes in party affiliation can be indicative of leaders who are trying to find the best possible vehicle to rise to political office, it also stands to reason that those affiliated with insecure parties, such as KANU, could have opted for violence as a part of a broader set of power-seeking strategies.

Ten years later, during the post-election crisis, Molo succumbed to a seemingly "endless cycle" of conflict (Human Rights Watch 2008: 53). The fact that it could be especially susceptible to political violence had been known for some time to be sure, as ethnic clashes had been recorded in the constituency since 2006 (Republic of Kenya 2008). However, the sheer scale of the violence – which entailed "house sackings and burnings, destructions of shops and schools, killings, [and] land invasions" – was staggering (Boone 2012: 91). According to the Commission of Inquiry on Post-Election Violence (Republic of Kenya 2008: 340), over 1,500 houses were torched in the area.

---

[3] Interview with a human rights activist, Nakuru, October 21, 2013.

In speaking about party violence in Molo and in the Rift Valley more generally, respondents laid blame at the feet of political elites, as demonstrated in the opening excerpt to this section. Importantly, however, their claims did not simply relate to the clashes of the 1990s. Instead, they extended these arguments to the period of the post-election crisis and held that both the incumbent regime and the opposition outsourced the production of violence during this time. As one interviewee stated:

Most of the clashes were organized and state-sponsored. The PNU side used Mungiki and ODM used the Kalenjin militias in the Rift Valley. So, you see, they [parties] all had their links with the gangs.[4]

In 2013, the rise of the Jubilee Alliance helped to shield Molo, and Nakuru more broadly, from violence. Indeed, volatility and conflict data together reveal that party violence in Nakuru County has generally escalated as party replacement rates have increased over time. With the exception of the 2002, 2013, and 2017 elections, when accommodationist alliances dampened the possibilities for organizing conflict in the area, Nakuru has witnessed repeated bouts of severe violence since the restoration of multiparty competition.[5] In fact, as per the Kenya Violent Elections Dataset (Malik 2023), ethnic clashes in this county claimed the lives of more than 200 individuals around the 1992 election, over 90 individuals around the 1997 election, and more than 200 individuals during the 2007–2008 post-election crisis.[6]

In her research on Nakuru County, Klaus (2020: 160–161) highlights that two kinds of contentious narratives – pertaining to land injustice and land insecurity – proved pivotal to instrumentalizing violence in 2007–2008. Yet, she also finds that while these narratives helped to mobilize conflict among land-insecure communities in Mauche and Likia, they did not generate conflict in sites such as Ogilgei and Kerma where residents are land-secure. In a similar vein, my work finds that land-based grievances have varying effects on party conflict. However, I focus more closely on understanding the deliberate choices of political *elites* to elevate this issue in some moments but not others.

As previously discussed, Molo is a site where land-related grievances are ripe for elite appropriation. In accounting for politicians' decision-making about when to use this matter as a tool for driving violence, two respondents talked about the core elements as follows:

---

[4] Interview with a human rights activist, Nairobi, February 2, 2013.
[5] The 2022 election in the Rift Valley also concluded without active violence. Rather than coalitional arrangements, however, this time it appears that structural and institutional factors reduced the salience of ethnic considerations in the election campaigns (Opalo 2022). In addition, the absence of a Kikuyu presidential candidate helped to diminish elites' incentives for conflict.
[6] These figures are slightly different from those presented in Malik (2018) due to subsequent updates that I made to KVED.

Party Violence in Kenya's Rift Valley and Coast Regions 105

Personally, I am born in Molo. That is where I was born and brought up. My parents were moved from Central Province to Molo in the 1940s.... The land was occupied by the Europeans. [It] was sold on a "willing-buyer-willing-seller" basis. The Kikuyus bought about 1,000 or 2,000 acres of this land from the Europeans. The Kalenjin also bought some land.... [But] then, when it came to 1992, they [KANU politicians] used an excuse of "this is our land; you must move out!".... They used it to make violence.[7]

The politicians take the issue of land and make it a campaign agenda when the two communities [Kikuyus and Kalenjins] are backing different candidates. Honestly, at the back of their minds, they know that there [is] a historical issue where land allocation and ownership is concerned. So, every time the two main communities living in the Rift Valley backed different candidates, the issue of land [has] come strongly because that is what elicit[s] emotions. With that, they [politicians] know that they would excite the electorate to listen to their agenda that "once you give me the votes, your land will be restored to you, your land will be wholly yours. These other people who invaded our area will surely go." Now, with that kind of a political language, you can be sure that it would elicit very bitter emotions and the culmination of that was usually electoral violence or violent confrontation.[8]

Contrary to these periods of conflict, and because the Kikuyu-Kalenjin divide was not salient to the 2002 and 2013 elections, politicians seemed to sidestep land-related matters on these occasions. With reference to the 2013 contest in particular, one respondent explained their choices in the words below:

The situation on the ground is still the same. The land issue is still unresolved. The competition is still there, and in fact in some parts of the Rift Valley – like in Nakuru – there is fierce competition even politically among the Kikuyu and the Kalenjin, but they're not killing each other.... The Kikuyu and the Kalenjin are at each other's throats over the issue of land, but when it suits the leaders who have a common interest – which Ruto and Uhuru clearly have now – then those community interests can become secondary. No one is talking about land right now.[9]

Altogether, then, my data from Molo and Nakuru reveal four major findings. First, and most broadly, they show that amidst high rates of party instability, political elites have repeatedly organized violence in these places. Second, I find that in the early years following the restoration of multipartyism, fears of losing one's seat seemed to factor into the decisions of some subleaders to gamble with political conflict. Third, I demonstrate that elites have frequently latched onto the issue of land distribution to drive violence in Molo and Nakuru. Fourth, insofar as unstable parties have made for a number of different coalitions across elections, some of these coalitions – such as Jubilee – have disincentivized the instrumentalization of violence in particular moments.

---

[7] Interview with a PNU party leader, Nakuru, October 29, 2013.
[8] Interview with an elections expert, Nakuru, October 29, 2013.
[9] Interview with a WDM-K political leader, Mombasa, October 5, 2013.

However, it would be premature to conclude that the lack of active conflict in Molo and Nakuru over the last few elections is a guarantor of peace going forward. As one interviewee explained:

> [T]he parties themselves keep changing, [so politicians] don't usually have to think twice about the use of negative ethnicity. It's a given for most of them. That's why you also see that all these coalitions only last for a short time.... Again and again, they [elites] realize that negative ethnicity can help them to get votes and so the alliances just come and go.[10]

In other words, because the main elements that have enabled violence in these sites in the past – including unstable parties, unresolved historical grievances, and conducive ethnic and demographic factors – continue to be in place, it is not inconceivable that conflict could conceivably return to Molo and Nakuru in the future. To this end, it is also worth noting that Type A volatility levels continued to indicate extreme rates of party instability – at 36.25% – in Molo in 2017.

Kapseret and Uasin Gishu

> [There are] two ethnic communities in this area: first of all, the indigenous owners of [land in] the region – the Kalenjin people – and those who have come in.... The majority of those who have come in and settled in Uasin Gishu are the Kikuyu people.... The point here is, in a way, there is a camp ... sort of where they [Kalenjins] think: "maybe the only way to destabilize these people [Kikuyus] so that they can go back to their original, ancestral land is you know, you create a very unhealthy environment politically." And the best way to do it is if they are in this camp and look at each other with suspicion and a lot of enmity. And so, if someone makes a volatile statement, the thing [can] erupt.... Our politicians have [also] shown us that they are very capable of making these volatile statements. They have done this over and over again because it is very inexpensive for them. It [violence] has become a matter of convenience.[11]

The interview excerpt above reveals that Uasin Gishu County in the North Rift is another site where elite machinations can generate violence. Within this county, Kapseret constituency – previously known as Eldoret South – is a place where the relationship between parties and violence can be productively probed. Kapseret, a Kalenjin-dominated area, experienced several ethnic massacres between 1992 and 1993. During this time, Youth for KANU '92 and various Kalenjin armed groups carried out targeted attacks against Kikuyu residents (Maupeu 2008). In fact, in September 1991, the MP for Eldoret South, Joseph Misoi – a man who has also been named in official government reports for illegally acquiring public land in the Rift Valley (KHRC 2011) – issued

---

[10] Interview with a Chama Cha Mwananchi (CCM) politician, Nakuru, October 23, 2013.
[11] Interview with an ethnic leader, Eldoret, November 5, 2013.

Party Violence in Kenya's Rift Valley and Coast Regions

a chilling message to voters. He warned that "unless those clamoring for political pluralism stop," KANU would "devise a protective mechanism" to ensure its survival (Oucho 2002: 89).

Like Chepkok, Biwott, and Ntimama in other Rift Valley constituencies, Misoi held on to his seat in 1992 with 65.21% of the total votes cast (Kenya Election Database 2021). Although he subsequently lost this post in 1997, by 2011, he switched affiliations to the Orange Democratic Movement (ODM) and held the position of Chairman of the National Elections Board of the opposition party (KHRC 2011). In an ironic twist, later that year, Misoi also appealed to his co-ethnic Kalenjin to "shun tribal alliances" (Damary 2011).

Following its experience with party violence in 1992, Kapseret attained notoriety once again when it succumbed to significant levels of conflict during the 2007–2008 post-election crisis. In fact, between late February and early March 2008, the Kenya National Commission for Human Rights (KNCHR 2008: 68) reported that police violence had claimed the lives of 23 individuals from the constituency. In addition, there is some evidence that subleaders' insecurities about retaining their seats played a part in incentivizing violence in this constituency. In 2007, the incumbent MP from Kapseret was David Kiptanui Koros (Kenya Election Database 2021). Previously affiliated with KANU in 2002, Koros had joined ODM in the run-up to the 2007 polls. However, following considerable chaos during the November 2007 party nominations process, he defected to ODM-Kenya (ODM-K) party and finished in second place in the 2007 MP race (Lynch 2008; Kenya Election Database 2021).

Like many other politicians in the Rift Valley, Koros is a "credible land patron" in Uasin Gishu and is perceived by voters to hold "the political power and will to follow through on land-based appeals" (Klaus 2020: 223). Importantly, he is also known to have organized political violence (Klaus 2020). My research indicates that beyond his ability to draw on existing land narratives to drive conflict, his insecurities over holding on to his seat on the flank of a relatively new and young party also could have led him to opt for violence in 2007.[12]

In addition to these candidate-level details, quantitative data on party and coalitional volatility rates show that party instability has been on a consistent upswing in Kapseret since the restoration of multiparty competition. In fact, as depicted in Figure 5.2, replacement volatility in this constituency stood at more than 90% in 2017, and further analyses uncovered that KANU is the only entity to have secured votes in Kapseret in every local MP race held since 1992.

Meanwhile, at the level of county politics in Uasin Gishu, the evidence suggests that rates of party replacement have worked alongside favorable demographic conditions and local-level grievances to make violence possible. As a

---

[12] ODM-K split from ODM in August 2007, and Koros joined this breakaway entity a few months later. In the 2007 elections, ODM-K finished in third place in the parliamentary and presidential polls, considerably behind both PNU and ODM.

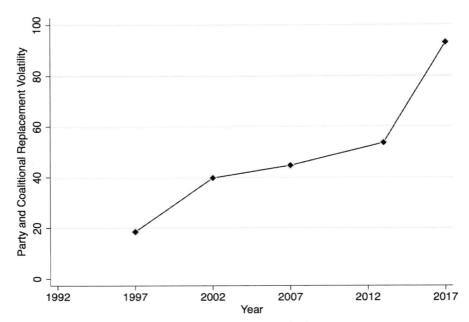

FIGURE 5.2 Party and coalitional replacement volatility in Kapseret constituency (1992–2017)

"predominantly Kalenjin [region] with a significant Kikuyu presence" (Human Rights Watch 2013b), Uasin Gishu is a site where politicians have frequently used the "message of evicting Kikuyu[s]" to mobilize Kalenjins in ethnic conflict (Linke 2022: 190). Much like in Nakuru, narratives about reclaiming ancestral lands have loomed large in these efforts. As one human rights activist explained:

> These politicians use [ordinary] people telling them, "When you vote for me, this land comes to you." I think that is the easiest way to convince people. This is how they [politicians] started bringing conflict between the residents of the area [in the 1990s]. They affected [places like] Molo and Eldoret very badly.... In '92 and '97, they [clashes] were mostly where the Kikuyus were ... because [that is where] these leaders tried to incite their tribesmen.[13]

Beyond the elections of the 1990s, academic research and policy reports also show that politicians made use of grievances around land to organize conflict in Uasin Gishu in 2007–2008. A survey by Klaus (2017: 55), for instance, found that among 162 respondents in this country, 41% – or 66 individuals – recalled the use of polarizing land appeals by candidates to mobilize voters. This was also the election around which replacement volatility peaked in the

[13] Interview with a human rights activist, Nakuru, October 21, 2013.

Party Violence in Kenya's Rift Valley and Coast Regions

county, clocking in at 58.52%. Given these extreme levels of party instability, favorable demographic factors, and manipulable land-related grievances, it is not entirely surprising that the Armed Conflict Location and Event Dataset (ACLED) found Uasin Gishu to be the second deadliest county per capita, behind only Nakuru, during the post-election crisis (Linke 2022: 188–189).

A few years earlier and later than this troubling time, however, local politicians' appropriation of land-based grievances appeared to be considerably weaker. Commenting upon the circumstances in 2002, one interviewee explained the relative absence of divisive land narratives as follows:

> Because it [land] is an unresolved issue, it is available to be used. It is very easy to [escalate] emotions [with] respect [to] land, very quickly, very quickly. It [does not] take too much effort because the grievances – whether true, real, or imagined – are just beneath the surface, so anything can [serve as a] trigger. But in 2002, there was a constitutional moment. The incumbent was not allowed by the constitution to defend his seat. He agreed with that position. He didn't resist the constitutional position. And then the opposition formed in such a way that there was a counterweight to the land question, which [prevented] the land thing from being at the top. And so, neither side spoke about land much.[14]

Similarly, a respondent from Eldoret accounted for elites' avoidance of invoking land-based grievances in 2013 in the words below:

> It [the land issue] wasn't brought up because that issue will always be a contest between the Kikuyu and Kalenjin. [But] now [in 2013], they found themselves in a very awkward position where they were voting together.[15]

Ultimately, however, at the time of fieldwork in 2013, interviewees agreed that insofar as Jubilee appeared to amount to a "coalition of convenience," they could not rule out the possibility of violence returning to this part of the Rift Valley in the future.[16] In this vein, recent party replacement rates in Kapseret could present an additional cause for concern, as the constituency recorded a Type A volatility level of 93.09% in 2017.

VULNERABILITIES TO PARTY VIOLENCE IN THE KENYAN COAST (1992–2017)

Likoni and Mombasa

> In 1997 ... the violence was ... KANU thought it was going to lose. You see what I mean? In 1997, they thought [they were going to lose] because people were entitled about democracy, about multiparty[ism]. You know, in 1992

---

[14] Interview with a bureaucrat, Nairobi, November 25, 2013.
[15] Interview with a human rights activist, Eldoret, November 1, 2013.
[16] Interview with an IDP camp resident, Nakuru, October 26, 2013; interview with a human rights activist, Eldoret, November 1, 2013.

is when we started the first multiparty elections, so people did not so much understand this whole issue. But in 1997, people understood that we needed to have change and that we must change this rule.... You know, the Moi era ... was a long one and people were tired of it. People were fatigued with it and all those things. And services were not being provided for the public.... I think KANU was losing [in 1997]. They thought they were losing in [the] Coast. That's why the violence began. The government instigated the violence.... The issue was in 1997, KANU thought ... they were not getting good votes maybe in the Coast region. So, the only way they could really amass votes was by instigating violence.[17]

The interview above shows that as in the Rift Valley, there is now a clear understanding in the Kenyan Coast that party violence owes its escalation to elites' actions. Compared to the Rift Valley, however, where such conflict first occurred in the run-up to the 1992 election, the origins of political violence in the Kenyan Coast are slightly more recent. Nevertheless, the major factors that have enabled conflict in this region are broadly similar to those seen in the Rift Valley, and include high rates of party instability; incumbents' fears about losing parliamentary seats, particularly in early multiparty contests; a historic sense of marginalization; inequality in land ownership; and localized grievances about land distribution in several multi-ethnic constituencies. Indeed, Klaus (2020: 215) documents that land inequality in the Coast is "more profound" than in the Rift Valley, as "the majority of Coast residents, most of whom identify as Mijikenda, have no formal land tenure rights." Rather, title deeds for the area's "prime agricultural and commercial land belong to the region's elite," namely communities from "'upcountry' Kenya, ... prominent Arab families, Indians, [and] Swahilis" (Klaus 2020: 215). To highlight the interplay between these key factors, I focus my analyses in this section on the cases of Likoni constituency in Mombasa County and Garsen constituency in Tana River.

During the 1990s, Likoni emerged as a key site of political conflict in the Coast. According to estimates from that time, 80% of Likoni's half a million residents hailed from the Mijikenda community, while the other 20% identified as Kikuyu, Luo, Luhya, or Kamba, or members of various "upcountry" groups (Republic of Kenya 1999: 2). As a multiethnic constituency, Likoni thus fulfilled the base demographic criteria for a place where elites with short time horizons might be tempted to organize violence. Moreover, the constituency and Mombasa County more broadly are also sites where a "defining feature of Coastal politics" – a historic sense of marginalization – has long been present (Willis and Chome 2014: 116). In fact, Likoni is the poorest part of relatively cosmopolitan Mombasa and thus stands out as a place where grievances about state neglect are particularly acute.[18]

---

[17] Interview with a civil society leader, Mombasa, September 25, 2013.
[18] Interview with an ODM/NAMLEF, Mombasa, October 10, 2013; also see Baah 2014.

Party Violence in Kenya's Rift Valley and Coast Regions

As one interviewee explained, the broader sentiment about historical neglect of the Coast can be traced to important postindependence policies, many of which were implemented during the Kenyatta years:

> At independence, Coastals embraced and cherished the *majimbo* or federal form of government because we were convinced that that was the form of government that would secure our right and preserve our self-determination and self-governance, and also protect our resources from exploitation by other communities. So, when the Kenyatta regime brought in the so-called unitary form of government, the Coastal people realized that, "now [we] are out for our own deal because we are now deprived of our right of governance on our resources, our land."[19]

In a similar vein, scholars have documented that the Kenyatta regime "designated nearly 30% of settlement schemes in [the Coast] region for the resettlement of Kenyans from other regions, notably Kikuyu[s] from Central Province" (Klaus 2020: 98).[20] But the neglect of this area did not end with these policies alone, as respondents also noted that subsequent governments under Moi, Kibaki, and Uhuru Kenyatta failed to take the necessary steps to address the scarcity of jobs, education, and health provisions that residents routinely encounter.[21]

Following the restoration of multiparty competition, ruling politicians chose not to instrumentalize violence in the Coast in 1992. According to interviewees, this was largely because KANU leaders expected Moi to defeat his presidential rivals and capture the votes of indigenous communities from this region. As one respondent explained:

> At that time, Moi was in KANU, Kibaki was in DP, and Matiba was in FORD-Asili. So, basically, they [KANU elites] thought that the Kikuyus in the Rift Valley would not have voted for Moi. They would have voted for the Kikuyus, either Matiba or Kibaki. And at that time also, winning the big province was important. The Rift Valley is the biggest [province] and it was [vital] for KANU. But that same threat didn't exist in the Coast because Matiba and Kibaki didn't resonate.[22]

Another interviewee similarly explained that since the days of Jomo Kenyatta's rule, Coastal voters had held acute "anxiet[ies]" about having another "Kikuyu in power," which rendered Moi more attractive than Kibaki and Matiba in 1992.[23]

---

[19] Interview with a civil society leader, Mombasa, September 25, 2013.
[20] In the Kenyan context, "a settlement scheme refers to land that the government purchases and then subdivides into plots for farming or residential purposes, with each scheme typically ranging from 100 to 20,000 acres" (Klaus 2020: 84).
[21] Interview with a URP politician, Mombasa, September 24, 2013; interview with a civil society leader, Mombasa, September 25, 2013; interview with an ethnic leader from Tana River, Mombasa, October 5, 2013.
[22] Interview with a UDF party leader, Nairobi, October 18, 2013. In addition to Kibaki and Matiba, the Luo politician Oginga Odinga also contested for the presidency in 1992, and respondents similarly held that they did not expect him to present a major threat to Moi in the Coast.
[23] Interview with a WDM-K politician, Mombasa, September 27, 2013.

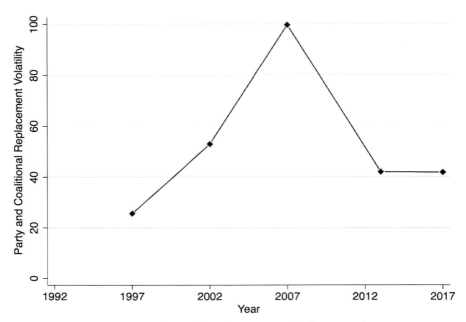

FIGURE 5.3 Party and coalitional replacement volatility in Likoni constituency (1992–2017)

Despite these expectations, the 1992 polls were not a clean sweep for KANU in the Coast. In Likoni, for instance, KANU candidate Hashim Mwidau failed to grab the MP seat, which triggered fears about a similar loss in 1997 (Klaus 2020: 217; Kenya Election Database 2021). Moreover, as shown in Figure 5.3 above, by the time of this particular contest, replacement volatility in the constituency already stood at the quite unstable rate of 25.59%, and thereby created important circumstances conducive to the instrumentalization of violence.

Amidst these broader machinations and activities, Likoni became the first site to succumb to active violence in the run-up to the 1997 polls when raiders from the Digo community (part of the broader Mijikenda group) attacked a police station on August 13 (Human Rights Watch 2002). This assault resulted in 13 deaths and led to a wave of conflict in Mombasa and Kwale districts that continued well into December (Malik 2023). During an interview, a journalist familiar with the clashes highlighted the central role that politicians played in the violence:

The Coast ha[d] been peaceful in those times [in 1992]. You understand, it [violence] is a strategy that can come up after some time. Again, it depends [on] who is looking for [what] seat[s]. So, maybe in 1992, that motive of using violence [in the Coast] was not there. But then in 1997 it came up. So, to ensure that they retain the seats ... you can say

Party Violence in Kenya's Rift Valley and Coast Regions

that KANU's staunch supporters and financiers decided to employ violence. They had seen that violence had worked for them in the Rift Valley, so now they also organized clashes in the Coast.[24]

Key among these "staunch [KANU] supporters and financiers" was a man named Omar Masumbuko.[25] According to Human Rights Watch (2002: 22), four years earlier, president Moi and other "KANU officials at the highest level" had supported Masumbuko as part of an effort to "counter the influence of the nascent [and] unregistered Islamic Party of Kenya (IPK)" in the Coast. This decision had proved to be somewhat effective: in 1992, three of the four successful MP candidates in Mombasa district had received support from the IPK's leader, Sheikh Balala (Oded 1996). However, by 1994, the party had split into two factions due to its founders' concerns about Balala's leadership (Oded 1996).

Given the vital assistance that Masumbuko had offered to KANU in the past, ruling politicians deliberately "used [him] to ... actually finance ... violence [in an effort to] retain the[ir] seats" in various parts of the Coast in 1997.[26] As one political leader explained, "Moi was a master tactician, [so he] called Omar Masumboko [again] in 1997."[27] In addition, KANU elites also relied on Masumbuko to try and recapture seats in constituencies such as Likoni. The deployment of violence in this manner – to retain and reclaim seats – suggests that many politicians from the Kenya African National Union were operating with short time horizons, as discussed in the interview excerpt below:

The issue was ... in 1997 [that] KANU thought they were going to lose elections and they were not getting good votes maybe in the Coast region. So, they started to think in the short-term, and it was concluded that the only way they could really amass votes was by instigating violence so that people [experience] fear and ... vote [for] the, you know, government in power.[28]

The involvement of elected KANU leaders such as Boy Juma Boy and Kassim Mwamzandi – the MPs from Matuga and Msambweni constituencies, respectively – provides further evidence of these short-term orientations. Three days before the Likoni attack, Juma Boy had sought to whip up sentiments among indigenous communities by arguing that "'upcountry' residents were taking all the money from jobs and tourism" in the region (Human Rights Watch 2002: 26). Likewise, the Akiwumi Report (Republic of Kenya 1999) noted that some two weeks after the assault in Likoni, the Matuga MP was known to be in touch with some of the raiders. Meanwhile, a witness who testified at the Akiwumi Commission explicitly named Juma Boy, Kassim Mwamzandi,

---

[24] Interview with a journalist, Mombasa, October 3, 2013.
[25] Ibid.
[26] Ibid.
[27] Interview with a WDM-K political leader, Mombasa, October 5, 2013.
[28] Interview with a human rights activist, Mombasa, September 25, 2013.

and Suleiman Rashid Shakombo – who was vying for a KANU ticket from Likoni – as the chief conspirators who had "sponsored and financed the military training of the Digo youths to attack and drive away the upcountry people" (Republic of Kenya 1999: 40). Other political leaders whose names appear as organizers of political conflict in these reports include Suleiman Kamole, who was seeking a KANU ticket; Mwalimu Masoud Mwahima, who was the KANU Chairman for Likoni constituency; and Rashid Sajjad, who was coordinating the party's political campaign in the Coast (Human Rights Watch 2002; Republic of Kenya 1999).

In this broader cast of characters, Juma Boy was one of the few politicians who suffered electorally for provoking violence. In 1997, he lost the KANU ticket to Suleiman Kamole who went on to clinch the MP seat from Matuga in Kwale district (Shiundu 2014; Kenya Election Database 2021). In a 2014 interview with a journalist from *The Standard* newspaper, Juma Boy recalled that he then spent more than a decade in "political oblivion" after being allegedly "scapegoat[ed]" for the clashes (Shiundu 2014). He stated, "I was perceived to be the man behind those atrocities. They looked at me as the mastermind, the cause of all the problems for the party" (Shiundu 2014). Despite being forced into political exile, his involvement in violence did not terminate his political career. Indeed, in 2013, Juma Boy made his way back into elected office when he won the Senatorship from Kwale County (Shiundu 2014).

Much like Juma Boy, Shakombo's role in organizing violence in Likoni was also wide-ranging: he was accused of supplying weapons to local gangs, paying three militia leaders 3,000 Kenyan Shillings to mount clashes in the constituency, using the police to harass and intimidate voters in the run-up to the election, and plotting the assassination of the reigning Likoni MP, Mwidau (Mumo and Mayoyo 1998; Republic of Kenya 1999; Human Rights Watch 2002). At the same time, his political fate in the wake of these actions was also instructive. Although he failed in his quest to clinch the KANU ticket, Shakombo contested the election as the candidate from the newly formed Shirikisho Party (SPK) and ultimately won the Likoni parliamentary seat (Human Rights Watch 2002; Kenya Election Database 2021). He then held onto this seat in 2002, by which time he had switched affiliations to KANU (Makali 2002). Even though he was "not a political heavyweight," as one journalist reported, and had been accused of instrumentalizing violence in 1997, KANU was willing to adopt him (Makali 2002). Notably, Shakombo also served as National Heritage Minister between 1997 and 2007 when he finally lost his MP seat to the ODM's Masoud Mwahima (Mudi 2011). The collapse of NaRC by 2005 – of which KANU was a key member – largely seems to have sunk his fate. Yet, even this defeat did not faze him for long, and in 2011, he announced his intentions to re-enter electoral politics, promising "reconciliation [and] ways [for] mak[ing] Likoni go forward" (Mudi 2011).

Although Shakombo has not been able to regain an elected position since 2007, he has contested for the MP seat from Likoni on two occasions – in 2013

Party Violence in Kenya's Rift Valley and Coast Regions

and 2017 – from the United Republican Party (URP) and Wiper Democratic Movement-Kenya (WDM-K), respectively. Furthermore, in 2013, President Uhuru Kenyatta appointed him to serve as chairman of the Board of Directors of the Kenya Petroleum Refineries, a post to which he was reappointed in 2015. Even though Shakombo was eventually removed from this position in 2020 (Lang'at and Nyassy 2020), his broader trajectory suggests that he suffered few penalties – from parties, voters, or powerful politicians – for his role in fomenting violence in Likoni in 1997.

These examples of Juma Boy and Shakombo's career trajectories offer crucial evidence of how politicians in Kenya can benefit from political violence. It further bears noting here that insofar as Juma Boy was forced out of politics for some time, his exiling appears to be due to developments within KANU itself rather than direct punishment from voters (Shiundu 2014).

Altogether, conservative estimates suggest that the clashes in the Kenyan Coast in the late 1990s claimed the lives of over 120 individuals – mostly Kikuyu and Luo residents – and resulted in the displacement of thousands of others from their homes (Kimenyi and Ndung'u 2005). Five years later, however, Likoni maintained peace, as "the determination [of] the opposition to unite and defeat Moi" resonated with voters.[29] One political leader from Mombasa County explained the circumstances around the 2002 contest thusly:

… The opposition realized that they'd made a mistake and they came together. In 1992, Moi divided them. In 1997, Moi divided them. In 2002 … it was all of us against Moi. We had a common enemy as a united front, and 2002 was a sudden recognition that if we don't unite, we'll lose again.[30]

In a similar vein, Mbaruku Vyakweli (2005: 351) has chronicled that "the formation of the National Rainbow Coalition (NaRC) in the run-up to the 2002 General Elections [served as] … an opportunity for the entire Coast region to fully capitalize on voting out KANU."

Subsequently, however, during the post-election crisis, Likoni once again emerged as a site of violence when significant destruction of property was reported here in the wake of Kibaki's unexpected victory (Republic of Kenya 2008: 228–229). This was also the time at which Type A volatility peaked in the constituency, reaching 99.63%. As in other parts of Kenya where voters were anticipating an Odinga win, the declaration of the results of the presidential race triggered much of the violence in the Coast. As one interviewee explained, "Before the elections, everything was calm. Everyone here thought that ODM would win. [But] after the results came out, then there were some disturbances."[31] As with prior episodes of conflict, elite incitement also

---

[29] Interview with a religious leader, Mombasa, October 4, 2013.
[30] Interview with a WDM-K political leader, Mombasa, October 3, 2013.
[31] Interview with a journalist, Mombasa, October 3, 2013.

contributed to these clashes, and a number of interviewees laid the blame for violence at the doorstep of ODM elites and affiliates.[32]

However, as opposed to the clashes that the Coast had witnessed a decade earlier – in which "upcountry" groups had been the main targets – this time around, violence was expressly directed toward members of the Kikuyu community and was therefore milder in scale. The logic of this narrower targeting pattern was because the creation of Raila Odinga's "pentagon" had effectively transformed the broader master cleavage between indigenes and "upcountry" communities in the Coast to a Kikuyu/non-Kikuyu fault line. As a politician from the The National Alliance (TNA) described:

> Raila picked and created kingpins from all the eight provinces and called it the pentagon. That was brilliant! Raila had to find somebody to say that the Coast is also included. So, the 2007 election was 42 [ethnic groups] versus one [the Kikuyus].[33]

Likewise, another explained, "Raila by then had a lot of following in the Coast from the South Coast to the North Coast. He had more support, much more support, from the indigenous groups."[34] Finally, a third political leader explained that the shift in ethnic and electoral divisions helped to spare the Coast of the levels of violence seen in other areas such as the Rift Valley:

> You see, the Coast was largely ODM in 2007, it was overwhelmingly ODM. So, the clashes weren't really clashes. We didn't really have clashes in the Coast. We had attacks on businesses and supporters of the PNU side. It was Kikuyu businesses that were burned down and things like that. But when you talk about clashes, it is like what happened in the Rift Valley where people took bows and arrows and [attacked] the opposite tribe. We didn't have that here.[35]

Taken together, Likoni thus emerges as a key subnational case where coalitional and ethnic arrangements helped to militate against severe violence even in the midst of high rates of party replacement in 2007.

Subsequently, in 2013 and 2017, Coastal voters once again rallied behind Odinga's Coalition for Reforms and Democracy (CORD) and National Super Alliance (NASA), respectively. Despite extremely high levels of party instability, these patterns of consistent support helped to more or less shield Likoni and Mombasa County from political conflict. Indeed, my data reveal that Type A volatility levels for parties in parliamentary and presidential elections in Mombasa have clocked in at more than 45% since 2007. Yet, the Coast's status as an opposition stronghold has protected much of Mombasa County from severe violence in recent years.

---

[32] Interview with a former MP, Mombasa, September 24, 2013; interview with a journalist, Mombasa, October 3, 2013.
[33] Interview with a TNA politician, Nairobi, October 17, 2013.
[34] Interview with a former MP, Mombasa, September 24, 2013.
[35] Interview with a WDM-K politician, Mombasa, October 5, 2013.

Party Violence in Kenya's Rift Valley and Coast Regions

Nevertheless, the enduring instability of parties, alongside other conducive factors, has contributed to considerable events of party violence outside electoral windows. For example, over the last few years, places such as Lamu and Mombasa counties have seen a troubling rise in sectarian conflicts in which political elites, police, and security sector officials have all played key roles (Akwiri 2014; Anyadike 2014; Human Rights Watch 2014, 2015). National-level politicians such as Uhuru Kenyatta have attributed these incidents to "well planned, orchestrated, and politically motivated" efforts of their rivals to "profil[e] and evict" Kikuyus from the region (Anyadike 2014). Meanwhile, others have argued that the rise of new vigilante groups, such as Funga Five and Forty Brothers (Kemboi 2017), coupled with a "long-standing crisis of second-class citizenship" (Anyadike 2014), are the main pathways through which elites with favorable incentives have been able to instrumentalize conflict in the Coast.

During fieldwork, respondents who discussed violence in this region warned against attributing too much weight to inequality and marginalization and emphasized the need to consider elite incentives much more closely. One interviewee, for example, stated:

People raise issues about inequalities: you know, the issue of land, the issues of marginalization, the issues of other historical [forms of neglect]. These inequalities exist and have always been existing. But how do they generate [violence]? Why do they come [up] only sometimes? It's because politicians decide when to use these things ... to create, you know that tension among communities.... In 2007 [for example], the Coast voted [for] ODM, and they voted [for] ODM because they were told, "The land that had gone with KANU and all those people. The land that was taken from you will be given back to you." That was the promise from ODM.... So [it is the] politicians who use the[se] issues of inequalities [when it suits them].[36]

In keeping with this directive to foreground politicians' motivations for conflict, this book argues that high rates of party instability have received inadequate attention in existing research on party violence in the Coast. In places such as Likoni constituency, for example, there is evidence that fleeting party organizations contributed to political conflict by enabling elites to operate with truncated time horizons in the 1990s. Amidst these short-term orientations, political leaders then tapped into indigenous communities' grievances about inequality and historic marginalization to orchestrate violence in places such as Likoni. Finally, although the Coast's status as an opposition stronghold has shielded sites such as Mombasa from election-related party violence in recent years, emerging evidence suggests that other factors conducive to conflict – including the rise of new specialists in violence, enduring sentiments of state neglect, and unstable party structures – persist in the region. As a result, conflict outside electoral windows continues to occur from time to time.

---

[36] Interview with a civil society leader, Mombasa, September 25, 2013.

Garsen and Tana River

> This violence was clearly linked to the election. It [the violence] was all about making sure the pastoral communities could come to power at the county level.[37]

The interview above highlights how the 2012–2013 clashes in Tana River were directly tied to the new and high stakes of county-level competition. Located on the banks of the Tana River, Garsen is one of three parliamentary constituencies in Tana River County. According to existing estimates, approximately 28% and 40% of the county's residents identify as members of the pastoral Orma and agricultural Pokomo communities, respectively (Burbidge 2015; Malik 2020), while a majority – 81.4% – identify as Muslim (Republic of Kenya 2019). As a semi-arid area, much of the county is "susceptible to drought conditions," and economic competition and communal rivalries over access to resources have contributed to clashes here since the colonial period (Martin 2012: 169, 172).

Despite this longer history of violence and the considerable clashes that broke out in 2012–2013, Garsen and Tana River first reported ethnic conflict in the multiparty era in the run-up to the 2002 polls. As Pilly Martin (2012) documents, even as much of the Coast maintained calm and rallied behind NaRC, local contests for power in Tana River pitted the agricultural Pokomo against the pastoral Orma and Wardei. Martin (2012: 174) further notes that a contentious December 2000 land adjudication scheme, which aimed to provide local Pokomo farmers with title deeds, exacerbated this fault line. Meanwhile, my data reveals that party volatility in Garsen constituency clocked in at 49.25% in 2002, thus plausibly incentivizing politicians to gamble with violence.

Amidst these circumstances, a group of armed pastoralists killed "a Pokomo farmer who was clearing his farm and reinforcing his farm boundaries in Ngao village [in] Garsen" on March 7, 2001 (Martin 2012: 175). From this incident, violence rapidly escalated throughout Tana River, and ultimately claimed the lives of more than 180 individuals (Malik 2023). Academic research on this period of conflict suggests that "incitement by politicians" played a key part in the violence (Martin 2012: 184). As one interviewee put it, "the problem in Tana River is something that has been simmering for quite some time … for more than a decade."[38]

Despite these underlying tensions, during the post-election crisis, Garsen constituency managed to avoid active conflict even as Type A volatility levels – depicted in Figure 5.4 – rose to 70.04%. In fact, apart from a peaceful demonstration against the presidential election results, much of Tana River maintained calm throughout this time (Mghanga 2010: 73). Qualitative interviews suggest that the dominance of the Kikuyu/non-Kikuyu

---

[37] Interview with a religious leader, Mombasa, October 4, 2013.
[38] Interview with an ethnic leader from Tana River, Mombasa, October 5, 2013.

Party Violence in Kenya's Rift Valley and Coast Regions

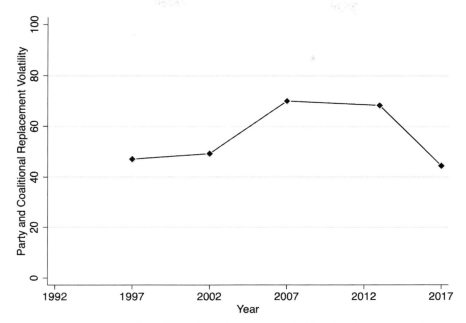

FIGURE 5.4 Party and coalitional replacement volatility in Garsen constituency (1992–2017)

cleavage over local divisions between farmers and herders contributed to this quiescence.[39] However, the worst for Garsen and for the county as a whole was still to come, as Tana River fell prey to massive clashes in the run-up to the 2013 polls.

Much like the violence witnessed in 2002, political conflict in 2012–2013 brought the divide between the agricultural Pokomo and the pastoralist Orma and Wardei back into sharp focus, as initial attacks by members of the herder community were succeeded by counterattacks by Pokomo farmers and their supporters. This time, however, rather than competition over parliamentary seats, it was hostilities over grabbing newly created *county-level* positions that generated conflict. The fiscal component of devolution appears to have been especially relevant to this calculus, as the formula of the Commission on Revenue Allocation (CRA) – a body established under the new constitution – stipulates that larger and poorer counties such as Tana River receive higher allocations in the form of unconditional grants for development from the national government than their smaller and richer counterparts (Cheeseman, Lynch, and Willis 2016; Scott-Villiers 2017; Malik 2018, 2020).

---

[39] Interview with a civil society leader, Mombasa, September 25, 2013; interview with an ethnic leader from Tana River, Mombasa, October 5, 2013.

With the stakes this high and with party replacement in Garsen hovering at the extremely unstable rate of 68.33%, subleaders and national-level politicians both began to plot and organize conflict. Dhadho Godhana, for example, the MP from Tana River's Galole constituency, purportedly delivered several inflammatory speeches in the run-up to the 2013 polls, which amounted to "criminal offences of hate speech, incitement, and related offences" (Republic of Kenya 2013: 176–177). Meanwhile, Yusuf Haji reportedly ordered "police officers to attack ... Pokomo[s]" in September 2012 (Volisi 2019: 53; Kirchner 2013).

Ultimately, much of the 2012–2013 violence in Tana River targeted members of the Pokomo community. Respondents familiar with these clashes held that they were organized as such with a clear "electoral purpose" – to "create a false sense of unity among the pastoral groups and [to] remove the agricultural Pokomos [who held key political positions] from power."[40] Meanwhile, others spoke extensively about the impact of devolution on animating grievances, incentivizing violence in Tana River County, and potentially contributing to conflict in other parts of Kenya in the future. Consider, for instance, the two excerpts below:

There is this perception from the other community, the pastoralist community, who [have] been claiming that the farmer community had been dominating their community. There are historical issues that need to be addressed in that particular place [Tana River]. And the government has been neglecting those [pastoral] communities. When they raise their concerns, when they lecture their people at the national level, they don't feel like their concerns are being addressed. So, now with devolution and with all of the changes in the parties and the alliances, all these things came up. The aspiring candidates from the Pokomo side were always saying, "We should ensure that we throw away the pastoralists." Same for also these other guys [Orma and Wardei politicians] because they were also saying, "We need to dominate the resources in the county."[41]

In the future, given the way the county governments are moving, we are likely to see a more diluted role for the national state. [This is] because the counties have grants [that they can] use for development of their own areas.... People have realized that the counties are the main avenues [for] development now. So, we will see people minimizing the role of the president and they will start voting very strongly for the governor.[42]

These interviews also support Peter Kagwanja's (2009: 384) position, who holds that "'decentralization' ... might not actually deliver [for] Kenya." In fact, as with many prior episodes of political conflict, violence in postdevolution Tana River largely proved to be politically effective: as shown in Table 5.1, not

---

[40] Interview with an SDP politician, Nairobi, October 13, 2013; interview with a TNA politician, Nairobi, October 17, 2013. In the 2007 parliamentary elections, for example, two of the three MP seats in Tana River had fallen to Pokomo politicians.
[41] Interview with a human rights activist, Mombasa, September 25, 2013.
[42] Interview with an academic, Nairobi, December 12, 2013.

TABLE 5.1 *2013 election results from Tana River County*

Name	Position	Ethnic Group
Tuneya Hussein Dado	Governor	Orma
Ali Abdi Bule	Senator	Wardei
Halima Ware Duri	Women's Representative	Orma
Ibrahim Ahmed Sane	MP (Garsen Constituency)	Wardei
Hassan Abdi Dukicha	MP (Galole Constituency)	Wardei
Ali Wario	MP (Bura Constituency)	Orma

only did Orma and Wardei candidates capture plum county-level positions, but they also claimed all three seats in the National Assembly. Meanwhile, even though Godhana failed to retain his MP position from Galole, four years later in 2017, he returned to political power as the Governor of Tana River County.

At a subnational level, then, it appears that highly unstable parties have provided a consistent incentive for political elites to instrumentalize violence. With the exception of elections around which coalitional arrangements have dampened local fault lines favorable to conflict, Tana River has repeatedly fallen prey to party-based violence. In this regard, it is especially worth noting that even though devolution introduced a new variable relevant to understanding ethnic clashes in the county in 2012–2013, amidst unstable parties and alliances, violence-wielding elites did not simply get away with conflict but actually reaped electoral benefits from some of these entanglements.

More recently, in 2017, notable changes in the coalitions and affiliations of long-time local elites contributed to a transformation of the Orma-Wardei alliance into a cross-ethnic coalition between the Pokomo and Wardei groups. In so doing, these configurations diminished the incentives for elites to organize violence in Tana River along the farmer-herder cleavage (Mwakwaya 2017). In fact, as far as I am aware, the county only recorded one event of political conflict in 2017 at a vote-tallying center in Galole town, which claimed the life of an election official as well as two perpetrators of the attack (Reuters 2017). However, like other regions detailed in this chapter – including Nakuru, Uasin Gishu, and Mombasa, where party instability rates remain extremely high – and in light of the considerable developmental grants that are up for grabs in Tana River – it would be premature to interpret recent quiescence as a sign of enduring peace going forward.

ENDOGENEITY CONCERNS

Overall, my findings support the claim that replacement volatility levels have impacted politicians' decisions about orchestrating party violence in Kenya rather than the other way around. First, the evidence shows that high levels of party instability have usually preceded, rather than followed from, waves of political conflict in the country. Indeed, Chapter 3 has demonstrated that the pathway for the emergence of transient party entities was paved well before ethnic clashes first broke out in the early 1990s. Second, to the extent that the restoration of multipartyism led to an explosion of party births, this book has revealed that the entry of these new entities threatened KANU's survival and thereby incentivized violence around the 1992 elections.

As discussed in Chapter 4, my qualitative research also finds that Kenyan citizens are well-attuned to political leaders' roles in instrumentalizing party conflicts and have developed these insights over time. Nevertheless, it is important to acknowledge that as per public opinion data, the economy, the implementation of the new constitution, employment, security, and corruption all feature far more prominently than political violence in the minds of Kenyan voters. In the seventh round of Afrobarometer (2018) surveys, for example, respondents ranked corruption, unemployment, the management of the economy, and health as their most urgent concerns. Likewise, income inequality, food shortages, and the country's deteriorating economy emerged as some of the most pressing issues in 2022, as citizens continued to struggle with the lingering effects of the COVID-19 pandemic, the Ukraine war, and drought (International Crisis Group 2022; Angar and Klaus 2022).

Despite the importance of these matters, the evidence suggests that Kenyan voters are largely intolerant of violence. This is because conflict brings considerable destruction to their lives. During fieldwork, several interviewees discussed these realities with me and also shared that they were aware of the benefits politicians had garnered through violence. One respondent recalled the consequences of the 1991–1993 clashes in the Rift Valley in the following terms:

… People [politicians] managed to politicize the issue of land, and it was too much. I had just left [for] college during that time. I was a young boy, and I saw that it was tough. So many people were just left without anything. I come from the Rift Valley myself, so I could see what has happening. It was clear who was suffering and who was benefiting.[43]

Meanwhile, another respondent described the origins and impacts of the violence in the Coast as follows:

… The elites [involved the] Coastal people in fighting [by] saying, "you have to get rid of the upcountry people." In the end, KANU benefited but the indigenous Coastals and the *wabara* communities all suffered. *Wabara* is the Swahili term to refer to "upcountry" communities in Kenya That became clear to the people in the aftermath of the clashes.[44]

For their part, political elites also acknowledged that previous episodes of conflict had devastated communities across the country. In discussing the

---

[43] Interview with an elections expert, Nakuru, October 29, 2013.
[44] Interview with a civil society leader, Mombasa, September 25, 2013.

Party Violence in Kenya's Rift Valley and Coast Regions

consequences of the post-election crisis in the Rift Valley, for instance, a PNU leader explicitly noted:

There were people who benefited, there were people who were paid, [and] there were people who were burned. The Kikuyu, the Kalenjin, and the Luo elites: they were the people who capitalized during the elections. They made their money during the election. But not the common *wananchi*, not the common Kalenjin [and] not the common Kikuyu....[45] There were people who benefited from those clashes who organized them. But the ordinary citizens suffered. And they are always the ones to suffer from such violence. And they know this too. They know that the elites organize the violence but [it is] the people [who] suffer.[46]

Even in the face of such knowledge, I find that Kenyan politicians have been able to repeatedly organize – and have largely gotten away with – severe episodes of violence because unstable parties have provided them with crucial avenues for doing so. Contrary to the findings of recent experimental studies, then – which offer broad evidence of backlash and sanctioning (Rosenzweig 2021, 2023; Gutiérrez-Romero and LeBas 2020; Horowitz and Klaus 2020) – my research shows that persistent party instability presents a real hurdle to the country's citizens in holding nefarious politicians to account. Put differently, because political parties rapidly mushroom, disintegrate, and forge new alliances, voters have limited opportunities to actually engage in sanctioning. A respondent from Mombasa described these constraints in the following words:

In Kenya, anything can happen. You cannot hope that the alliance will last forever because each and every time, depending on the conditions or depending on the situation in the country, new parties spring up and new parties come to lead. We had the NaRC government in 2002. In 2007, we had the PNU leadership. And now, [in] 2013, we have the Jubilee government. Each came up as a result of the conditions at that particular [time]. So, you cannot say that a party that is existing can be strong [in the future] and take the leadership at any given time because you find that parties in Kenya are not solid because they have no structures. They have no permanent structures, and it is because of this that clashes happen. The parties [can] make voters fight and very often the people are helpless.[47]

Despite the continued fragility of parties and the ways in which they incentivize violence, recent developments in Kenya suggest that there might be other entities that could keep conflict from escalating. In this vein, we should take particular note of the strengthening of the Supreme Court, as this institution has exerted considerable weight on politicians' incentives and encouraged them to steer clear of violence. Even as the evidence about devolution remains mixed in other words – with diminished stakes around presidential contests but new possibilities for violence in key subnational sites – the 2022 elections

---

[45] *Wananchi* is the Swahili term for citizens.
[46] Interview with a PNU party leader, Nakuru, October 29, 2013.
[47] Interview with a journalist, Mombasa, October 3, 2013.

in particular offered hopeful signs about the roles that institutions other than political parties can play in keeping the prospects for political conflict at bay. To the extent that parties could be stabilized in Kenya going forward, political leaders' proclivities toward conflict might be controlled even further by empowering voters to sanction violent politicians and sensitizing leaders to this credible possibility.

SUMMARY AND CONCLUSION

Drawing on an array of qualitative and quantitative data, this chapter has shown how party instability has incentivized elites to organize and sponsor violence in the Rift Valley and Coast regions of Kenya. Extending the analyses previously presented in Chapter 4, it has highlighted how politicians' insecurities about political survival interacted with subnational demographic factors and local-level grievances to make conflict possible in these places. Contrary to one of its intended objectives to diminish elites' incentives for violence, the chapter has also shown how devolution has actually created opportunity structures for instrumentalizing conflict in subnational sites such as Tana River County. Finally, marrying the larger data sources at the heart of this book with constituency-level information on the political fates of violence-wielding candidates, the preceding pages have demonstrated that politicians responsible for organizing violence have largely escaped sanctioning from voters for these actions.

Despite these challenges, there are reasons to be hopeful that renewed and severe conflict might be kept at bay in Kenya in the future. In particular, it is now clear that the strengthening of institutions beyond parties has made instrumentalizing violence politically riskier in some parts of the country.

Having examined the Kenyan case in detail, I now proceed to my analyses for India in Chapters 6 and 7. I first discuss the relationship at the national level between party instability and riot violence in Chapter 6. Thereafter, I study the subnational trajectories of Hindu–Muslim riots in Hyderabad in Andhra Pradesh (AP) and Meerut in Uttar Pradesh (UP) in Chapter 7. Broadly speaking, these chapters show that party replacement levels in India escalated precipitously between the late 1970s and mid-1980s – with some differences in volatility trajectories in AP and UP – before settling back down at the end of that decade. After various parties started to exhibit this instability, their leaders and subleaders started to provoke and sponsor political violence. For their part, as in the Kenyan case, ordinary citizens in India slowly grasped that national and subnational politicians had contributed to several major episodes of conflict in the country. However, following the re-equilibration of the party system in 1989, the frequency and intensity of communal riots drastically decreased. In fact, the forthcoming chapters show that in the present day, Indian politicians must carefully consider both the benefits and costs of political conflict before committing to this choice. This is because voter sanctioning is a real possibility in the country, and emerging evidence points to voters' willingness to punish violence-wielding parties and politicians after major riot episodes (Susewind and Dhattiwala 2014; Malik 2021). Finally, to the extent that India is now witnessing important transformations in violence – including the rise of targeted anti-minority attacks – Chapters 6 and 7 argue that these developments can also be partially explained by the keenness of politicians to avoid sanctioning for severe episodes of communal conflict.

6

Party Stabilization, Declining Riot Violence, and New Modalities of Political Conflict in India

> We had a continuous period of fifteen to twenty years of communal riots in Hyderabad ... from 1968-1969 until 1983, [I believe]. Fifteen years of continuous riots in Hyderabad.... Now, what has happened since the mid-1990s, I would say from around 1994, is that people have started saying "enough is enough." After all, no one likes to fight on the basis of religion on a day-to-day basis. There may be flash riots or some pent-up feelings that could be taken out in small incidents. But these big riots? No one wants to go through that.... So, now people know how the politic[al game] is being played ... that is, it is these parties – Congress, MIM, BJP that incite them. Now, you know in Hyderabad, MIM leaders were arrested, BJP leaders were put [under] arrest.[1] And the way they have started to conduct themselves, no riots are taking place. Why aren't riots taking place? Because political parties know that people won't get used in the same ways anymore. They won't participate in riots.
> – Interview with a journalist, Hyderabad, July 23, 2013

The interview excerpt above highlights three important truths about party violence in India. First, it reveals the central place of elite involvement in severe Hindu–Muslim riots. Second, it shows that urban locations such as Hyderabad have witnessed considerable declines in major riots since the 1990s. Third, the respondent suggests that Indian politicians have been forced

---

[1] The mention here of the detention of BJP leaders actually relates to their participation in agitations for the creation of a separate state of Telangana in the summer of 2013 rather than their involvement in mobilizing communal violence (India Today 2013). By contrast, a Majlis-e-Ittehadul Muslimeen (MIM) politician was charged under the country's penal code in 2013 for making a divisive speech in late 2012. Despite these differences, and as subsequent pages will show, both the MIM and BJP share strong incentives against instrumentalizing large-scale riots in contemporary Hyderabad.

to turn away from such violence due to the unwillingness of city dwellers to participate in communal clashes, as well as the sanctioning of some elites by law enforcement authorities.

Admittedly, since the time of this interview, much has changed in the fabric of Indian politics. The rise of the Bharatiya Janata Party (BJP) to national political office less than a year after this conversation has resulted in notable democratic erosion (Varshney 2019, 2022; Alizada et al. 2021; Biswas 2021). With reference to the core concerns of this book, moreover, this macro-level change has given rise to key transformations in the "landscape of communal violence," wherein rural incidents of conflict, vigilante violence, and targeted attacks against ethnic minorities have replaced urban Hindu–Muslim riots (Jaffrey 2021: 232; A. Basu 2021; D. Basu 2021). As Amrita Basu (2021: 277) describes, the issues that now provoke violence in the country range from "concerns like prohibiting beef consumption, conversion out of Hinduism, and interfaith marriage."

Yet it is also true that the BJP is a durable and strong party (Fjelde 2020). Consequently, even though communalism, as Basu suggests, has emerged as an everyday lived reality in different parts of the country, Hindu nationalist politicians have simultaneously sought to instrumentalize "carefully calibrated communal incidents [and] avoid large-scale riots" (Pai and Kumar 2018: 29). According to Sudha Pai and Sajjan Kumar (2018: 28), these new forms of violence – which are increasingly occurring across rural locations – are the "product[s] of conscious selection [and] plan[ning]" on the part of Hindutva elites. Drawing on and further expanding upon such insights, while my work deeply shares concerns about escalating anti-minority attacks (Jaffrelot 2019; A. Basu 2021; D. Basu 2021; Jaffrey 2021) and the growing liberal deficits in democratic governance in India (Varshney 2019, 2022), I also hold that the relatively stable nature of parties is deterring elites from instrumentalizing and sponsoring major riots.

I develop these arguments through an interrogation of Hindu–Muslim riots between 1950 and 2000, as well as analyses of more recent forms of conflict in the country in this chapter. Collectively, my data show that key developments in party politics help to explain these shifts. Following several years of fairly high levels of party stability, I find that urban India witnessed significant increases in communal riots in the late 1970s and throughout the 1980s due to a marked rise in unstable parties. This era of party instability led to a shortening of elites' time horizons and enabled politicians across various parties to gamble with political violence. In the early 1990s, however, the Indian party system began to revert to being relatively stable once again. As a result, politicians became reoriented to the future and started to shift away from organizing major riots. It is this shift that also helps to account for new forms of anti-minority violence in the country, which present lower risks to political parties than instrumentalizing severe Hindu–Muslim clashes.

I demonstrate these central claims by drawing on a combination of quantitative and qualitative data. I use the Varshney-Wilkinson (2004) and Mitra-Ray (2007) datasets to chart incidents of Hindu–Muslim riots in India. I then rely on original data on party replacement to measure party instability levels.[2] Throughout this chapter, I use these data descriptively to offer a snapshot of levels of party volatility across different eras of postindependence Indian politics. As party instability can *condition* politicians to turn to violence, my work suggests that we should expect epochs marked by more unstable parties to result in greater levels of conflict than those when parties are relatively stable. This does not mean that an increase in party volatility will immediately set off elite-driven violence, but that politicians' calculus about the utility of conflict may change over time. Finally, I incorporate insights from interviews with politicians and political party leaders, members, and functionaries; policy experts; human rights activists and civil society leaders; ethnic and religious elites; village leaders; academics; journalists; police officers; and local residents to trace the impact of party instability on elites' time horizons and their attendant decisions about political conflict.

I organize this chapter as follows. Focusing on the national level, I trace the relationship between levels of party replacement and the incidence of Hindu–Muslim riots in India in three phases: the era of Congress party dominance when major incidents of communal violence were relatively rare (1950s to late 1970s); the period immediately following the 1977 defeat of the Congress and the rise of new national and regional competitors when riots increased dramatically (late 1970s to early 1990s); and the period following the re-equilibration of parties after which the frequency and intensity of riot violence decreased even as new forms of conflict began to escalate in recent years (early 1990s to present). In each of these sections, I discuss changing levels of party replacement in conjunction with key episodes of party violence. To highlight the involvement of parties and politicians in major riot incidents, I also include case studies of two major riots – the 1980 Moradabad riots and violence in Uttar Pradesh (UP) around BJP leader L. K. Advani's *rath yatra* in 1990 – in the section on party politics and conflict between the late 1970s and early 1990s. This discussion shows that while the increasingly insecure Congress became willing to engage with conflict during the 1980s, especially in the middle of that decade, the emerging BJP also became involved in instrumentalizing communal riots. Finally, for the period of party politics since the early 1990s, I draw on qualitative interviews with both voters and politicians to show how the stabilization of parties has helped to turn elites away from organizing severe riots while also enabling them – especially those affiliated with the BJP – to embrace other forms of communal conflict.

---

[2] My computations of party and coalitional volatility rates for national elections in India are based on the records of the Election Commission of India (ECI) and cover the period until 2014.

PARTY POLITICS, ELITE CALCULATIONS, AND HINDU–MUSLIM RIOTS IN INDIA

In the extensive literature on Hindu–Muslim riots in India, scholars have long established that such conflict stems from elite instrumentalization. Varshney (2002: 10), for example, has squarely made his case for the importance of interethnic associations by arguing that these groups can help to mitigate *political leaders'* divisive actions: "If politicians insist on polarizing Hindus and Muslims for the sake of electoral advantage," he claims, "they can tear the [very] fabric of everyday engagement apart through the organized might of criminals and gangs." Thus, as per this account, intercommunal civic networks matter not only because they can withstand "exogenous communal shocks," but also because they can "constrain local politicians in their strategic behavior" (Varshney 2002: 10).

Micro-level accounts of riot violence from investigatory commissions, journalists, and academics have similarly revealed the key roles of politicians during major riot episodes. In the December 1992–January 1993 riots in Bombay, for instance, which claimed the lives of over 750 individuals (Varshney-Wilkinson dataset 2004), Pramod Navalkar, a leader of the Hindu nationalist Shiv Sena and a member of the upper house of Maharashtra's state assembly, openly admitted that his "boys were involved in the rioting" (Engineer 1993: 20). Beyond the Shiv Sena, a faction of the ruling Congress party reportedly also fueled the riots as part of a deliberate attempt to delegitimize the regime of Chief Minister Sudhakar Rao Naik (Engineer 1993). Likewise, in his documentation of the 2002 Gujarat pogrom, journalist Nagendar Sharma (2009) of the *Hindustan Times* has written about BJP MLA Mayaben Kodnani's distribution of swords to rioters and her firing of pistol shots to prepare the ground for massacres in the Naroda suburb of Ahmedabad city. Similarly, Berenschot (2011c: 223) has chronicled the prominent role of BJP politician Shailesh Macwana during both the preparatory and enactment phases of the Gujarat riots, which ranged from delivering "anti-Muslim speeches" inside the Dalit-dominated localities of the Isanpur neighborhood of Ahmedabad to "order[ing] people to burn Muslim hutments," respectively. Finally and most recently, BJP leader Kapil Mishra is known to have provoked his supporters to "hit the streets" in the run-up to the February 2020 Delhi riots (India Today 2020).

Despite the involvement of various parties in numerous severe riot incidents in India, the evidence is also clear that the Hindu nationalist BJP is the main beneficiary of such violence (Jaffrelot 2003; Dhattiwala and Biggs 2012; Ticku 2015; Iyer and Shrivastava 2018; Malik 2021). One study, for instance, has found that pre-election riots between 1980 and 2000 increased the BJP's vote share to the tune of 2.9% to 4.4% (Ticku 2015). Meanwhile, another analysis has demonstrated that for the period between 1981 and 2001, riot incidents that broke out in the twelve months prior to a Vidhan Sabha election led to "an average increase" in the party's "vote share [of] 5 percentage points or more" (Iyer and Shrivastava 2018: 105).

Recent work on newer forms of political conflict – including targeted low-level assaults against Muslims – has similarly highlighted the vital roles of elites in instrumentalizing, supporting, and justifying such violence, as well as the plum rewards that the BJP accrues from these attacks. For example, in investigations of the infamous 2015 assault on an ironworker and his son in Bisahda village, near Dadri, UP, researchers and journalists found that Vishal Rana, the son of BJP leader Sanjay Rana, was part of the mob that attacked and claimed the life of 52-year-old Mohammad Akhlaq (Jaffrelot 2021; Kumar 2017). Both Rana and his father were also known to be close to the leaders of a local cow protection group, known as the *Gau Raksha Dal* (Kumar 2017). In the wake of Akhlaq's murder, or in the postviolence interpretation phase, BJP MP Sakshi Maharaj further justified the events in Dadri stating, "We won't remain silent if somebody tries to kill our mother [the cow]. We are ready to kill or be killed" (Human Rights Watch 2019: 4).[3]

According to Pai and Kumar (2018: 4), much like the severe riots that India witnessed in prior decades, low-level clashes and targeted attacks against Muslims are also serving a political purpose for Hindu nationalists, as they are helping them to "gain power and establish majoritarian rule" in the country. Relatedly, the targeted, performative, and public nature of cow vigilante assaults are advancing prime cultural ends for Hindu nationalists by establishing "a permanent anti-Muslim bias" and legitimizing anti-minority violence as quotidian and normal (Pai and Kumar 2018: 5).

Taken together, the above transformations in party violence in India raise at least two important questions for scholars and researchers. First, what factors account for the significant declines in severe Hindu–Muslim riots, as shown in Figure 6.1? Second, how can we explain the rise of targeted anti-minority attacks, as seen in Dadri and elsewhere? In addressing these questions, I propose that important changes in the organization and stability of parties themselves ought to be taken into consideration. Extending the arguments developed in Chapter 3, I argue that the first few decades of India's postindependence period were marked by relative calm, as the dominant and well-institutionalized Congress party had strong reasons to steer clear of communal mobilization and violence. However, due to its weakening and the rise of new competitors, India began to witness rising levels of party instability from the late 1970s until the early 1990s. This period incentivized the instrumentalization of severe riots on the part of the declining Indian National Congress (INC) as well as other emerging parties, as politicians adopted short-term orientations to compete with one another at the polls. However, as party instability began to fall in

---

[3] Incidentally, even though Akhlaq and his son, Danish, were accused of "storing and consuming beef" in their home, a lab analysis of the recovered meat found that it was actually mutton, not beef (Ahuja 2019: 55).

New Modalities of Political Conflict in India

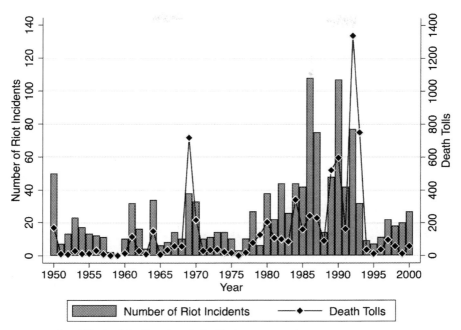

FIGURE 6.1 Hindu–Muslim riots in India (1950–2000)

the 1990s, leaders largely turned away from organizing and sponsoring major riots. I now proceed to discussing each of these periods in turn.

CONGRESS DOMINANCE, PARTY STABILITY, AND RELATIVE COMMUNAL CALM IN INDIA (1950s–LATE 1970s)

> The pre-Partition and Partition-era massacres had left the Muslims of India feeling thoroughly insecure. So, Nehru had to do something to win their confidence. And he tried to do it in various ways, including by promoting secularism. To some degree you can even say that he was successful: at least the violence against Muslims was limited during his time.[4]

The interview excerpt above suggests that under Nehru's stewardship, the postindependence Congress party had strong incentives to establish and maintain communal calm in India. Simply put, ruling elites could not afford a repeat of anything like the Partition. To ensure that the possibilities for renewed conflict were reined in, Nehru established a "new secular order" in the country (Pai and Kumar 2018: 48). This order was marked by a benevolent neutrality toward all religions (Staniland 2021).

[4] Interview with an academic, New Delhi, January 20, 2014.

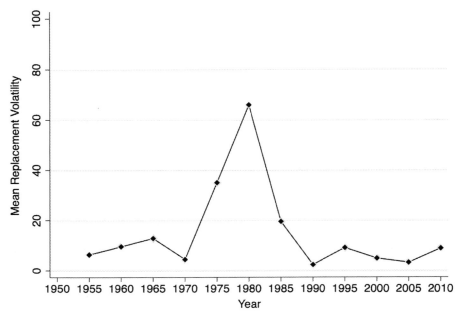

FIGURE 6.2 Mean replacement volatility in India (1951–2014)[5]

As one might expect, Nehru and his colleagues faced some challenges in this pursuit, particularly from communal elites in various states who held an uneasy relationship with this vision of secularism (Pai and Kumar 2018; Khosla 2020; Staniland 2021). It is also noteworthy that the PM sought to circumvent these voices not by giving into their demands but by wooing ethnic minorities instead. For instance, while his government passed various legislations to codify and reform Hindu personal laws in the 1950s, he stated in parliament in 1954 that the time for a uniform civil code – which would also extend to Muslims – was not "ripe" (Smith 2015: 290). This decision drew considerable criticism from Hindu nationalist leaders such as Syama Prasad Mukherjee as well as reformers such as Ambedkar who variously opposed it for being discriminatory and contrary to the spirit of secularism (Outlook 2022a, 2022b).

Nehru, however, was clearly playing the long game, and his decision to reach out to ethnic minorities made it possible to avoid major communal riots for much of the 1950s and 1960s. The dominance of the INC during this time – as depicted in Figure 6.2, which highlights the extremely to moderately stable levels of party volatility in the country – also helped to keep elites' incentives for violence in check.

[5] I calculated party replacement volatility for all Indian Lok Sabha elections between 1951 and 2014 using party seat share data from the ECI website. To aid with visual representation, I plot the mean figures in five-year intervals here.

Following Nehru's death in 1964, however, this period of "comparative peace and harmony" began to take a slow but steady turn for the worse (Pai and Kumar 2018: 13; Tudor and Slater 2016). To begin with, his demise increased disillusionment among Muslims who felt that the INC had not done enough to help their community (Pai and Kumar 2018). Organizationally, the Congress also began to display features of marked deterioration during these years and even faced "the danger of being reduced to a minority party" in the general elections of 1967 (Saxena 1996: 57). Given its weakening status, many INC elites became oriented toward the short term, and "winning elections [became their] prime concern" by any and all means necessary (Pai and Kumar 2018: 52). The Congress that was once known for its moderation thus began to use "populist slogans and radical rhetoric" to maintain its position as India's hegemonic party (Pai and Kumar 2018: 52). Added to this troubling mix was the emergence of the Hindu nationalist Bharatiya Jana Sangh (BJS) – a marginal entity during the 1950s (Weiner 1957) – as a key Congress competitor in the 1967 polls. Its rise crucially helped to mainstream the earlier claim that the INC stood for appeasing ethnic minorities as opposed to championing authentic secular principles (Pai and Kumar 2018; Staniland 2021).

Together, these important events culminated in a number of riot incidents after the end of the Nehruvian period when cities such as Ranchi in 1968, Ahmedabad in 1969, and Bhiwandi in 1970 – all places with favorable demographic profiles in terms of Hindu and Muslim populations – succumbed to violence. In each of these sites, the involvement of politicians in conflict was subsequently unearthed. In Ranchi, for example, leaders such as Jyoti Basu of West Bengal held that Chief Minister K. B. Sahay of the INC had played a part in the clashes (Wilkinson 2004). Meanwhile, in Gujarat, after Hindu priests and local Muslims clashed at a temple, Congress leaders are known to have declined to take an active role in "preventing and controlling the riots" in Ahmedabad apparently fearful that the use of force would result in a Jana Sangh government in 1972 (Shah 1970: 199). Finally, in Bhiwandi, a government-appointed investigatory commission pointed to "local BJS and Shiv Sena militants as the most likely culprits" for the violence, which claimed the lives of more than 70 individuals (Copland 2010: 138).

According to Pai and Kumar (2018: 51), many of these incidents of communal conflict during the 1960s reflected the "limitations of the [Nehruvian] secularization process." In order to correct this trajectory, recover from the 1967 elections in which the INC had seen its majority considerably weakened in the Lok Sabha, and bounce back from a split in the party that had emerged in 1969, Nehru's daughter Indira Gandhi adopted a pro-poor platform in the 1971 elections. This position enabled her to improve the party's performance and win votes in large numbers from both Hindus and Muslims. The years between 1971 and 1974 thus came to be marked by an absence of serious communal riots once again, as the survival of the Congress became linked to maintaining the support of Muslims and the party's leadership regained its confidence about the INC's crucial place in Indian politics. However, the party's electoral loss in 1977 not only ushered India into a new era of party politics but also set the stage for a significant period of communal violence that would follow.

CONGRESS DEFEAT, RISING PARTY INSTABILITY, AND ESCALATING HINDU–MUSLIM RIOTS IN INDIA (LATE 1970S–EARLY 1990S)

> In my estimation, from my political thinking, what happened is that after Sanjay Gandhi [Indira Gandhi's younger son] entered Congress politics ... after he became important in politics [in the mid-1970s], such individuals were admitted into the Congress who were neither invested in the future of the country nor were they invested in the future of the party. The Congress turned from being the party of Nehru and the other nationalists to the Congress of Sanjay Gandhi. And the people who entered politics at this time had no political thinking. If they got the chance, they fought with the government. If they got the chance, they attacked the Muslims. If they got the chance, they attacked the Dalits. They only worked for themselves and so the Congress became weaker and weaker. And as it became weaker, these communal disturbances kept increasing. The divisions increased, the rumors increased.... And the whole nation, across the nation we saw communal riots. Wherever they could occur, communal riots happened. There was no such city where communal riots could occur that was left untouched. And this entire situation continued for a long ten years. The years 1980 to 1990 were a very bad time for India. During this time, there was no city where riots did not occur. Entire cities were destroyed.[6]

The respondent quoted above describes a reality well-known to scholars of communal violence in India. Concretely, he suggests that the INC's relationship to secularism was fundamentally altered by its 1977 defeat to the Janata Party (JP). This defeat occurred after a period of slow economic growth, high poverty levels, famine, and the 1975–1977 state of emergency under Mrs. Gandhi. Even though Gandhi herself reclaimed the PM's post in 1980, her thinking about communal matters was changed considerably by three years in the opposition.

First, she seemed aware of the fact that Muslims had voted against the Congress in 1977, "angry over the misdeeds" of the government (Pai and Kumar 2018: 63, citing Engineer 1977: 458). Second, she was forced to reckon with ethnic mobilization, which had "moved from the margins of the political arena [to occupy] center-stage" (Chandra 2000: 27). Third, and finally, Gandhi now faced the BJP, which had formed in 1980 as the successor of the BJS, as a critical electoral rival on the national stage. Given these new dynamics, and

---

[6] Interview with an SP politician, Meerut, August 21, 2013.

New Modalities of Political Conflict in India

in a deliberate attempt to undercut Hindu nationalists, she began to "appeal more and more directly to Hindus" (Brass 2004: 4844). As one respondent from the Congress party admitted, "even those [who were once] call[ed] secular [did not] remain secular" after 1980.[7]

Data on party volatility help to corroborate these qualitative insights about changes in Congress leaders' strategies as they pertained to political violence. They show that the defeat of the INC caused a significant increase in party replacement rates from the extremely stable level of 4.44% in 1971 to the extremely unstable level of 35.01% in 1977. These numbers escalated further to 50.75% in 1980, as ethnic parties began to proliferate in many parts of the country (Chandra 2000).

Yet, importantly, it was not simply the new orientation of the Congress that was responsible for the escalation of communal violence in India during the 1980s. Rather, Hindu nationalist politicians also began to flirt with instrumentalizing conflict in various parts of the country. As one respondent from Meerut noted, they were able to make this choice because the risks of violence were strategically palatable at the time:

As you would know, they [Hindu nationalists] did not shy away from [using] the most divisive strategies [either]. They had little to lose at that time and their tactics wreaked havoc here during the 1980s.[8]

Such claims are supported by leading scholarly accounts of the Hindu nationalist movement in India. Jaffrelot (1996: 336), for example, documents that although the BJS/BJP had adopted a stance of "moderation" during the early 1980s, its leaders slowly but surely began to divide the electorate along religious lines thereafter.

Taken together, then, the evidence suggests that both INC strategies – under Indira Gandhi and her son Rajiv, who will receive greater attention in subsequent pages – and the tactics of the BJP unleashed a more "strident, open, and divisive" form of politics in India (Pai and Kumar 2018: 79; Staniland 2021). This atmosphere of competitive communal mobilization created conditions conducive to the emergence of severe riots in many parts of the country and especially in states such as Uttar Pradesh where the Hindu–Muslim divide could be easily exacerbated. To highlight these dynamics, I now turn to detailing two incidents: the 1980 Moradabad riots and clashes that exploded across UP around L. K. Advani's *rath yatra* or chariot journey in 1990. These events, which broadly bookend the period of escalating party instability in India, help to underline the roles of politicians from key parties in riot violence, as well as relevant local-level factors, such as socioeconomic changes and competition among subleaders over seats, which served to incentivize conflict.

---

[7] Interview with an INC politician, Meerut, August 21, 2013.
[8] Interview with an INC leader, Meerut, August 13, 2013.

The 1980 Moradabad Riots

According to the Varshney-Wilkinson (2004) dataset, the August 1980 riots in Moradabad claimed the lives of 112 individuals and caused injuries to 200 others. The violence emerged at the end of the holy month of Ramzan, and specifically on August 13, the day of Id, when it is alleged that a pig entered the town's *Idgah* where tens of thousands of Muslims had gathered to offer prayers (Brennan 1994; Graff and Galonnier 2013a).[9] When the police refused to intervene, arguing that removing the pig was not their job, an altercation broke out between local Muslims and law enforcement authorities (Brennan 1994). Senior police officers who were present at the scene reportedly faced attacks during this melee, and the Senior Superintendent of Police (SSP) was hit in the head by a stone after the crowd's anger devolved into stone throwing (Brennan 1994: 14).

As we might expect, the state did not respond kindly to these assaults, and police officers along with members of the Provincial Armed Constabulary (PAC) fired into the *Idgah*, creating a stampede (Brennan 1994).[10] From there, conflict ripped through Moradabad, and a mob of Muslims attacked and burned a police post on the night of August 13. The next day, the PAC reportedly beat 10 men to death in an infamous incident of excessive state force (Graff and Galonnier 2013a). The violence eventually continued for nearly three months until early November 1980.

Underlying this period of brutality were two key developments that incentivized and made conflict possible. First, the rising prosperity of the Muslim population employed in the local brassware industry had generated resentment among Hindu middlemen (Graff and Galonnier 2013a). Second, since the mid-1960s, Muslims across UP had been experimenting with supporting co-ethnic candidates not affiliated with the Congress party (Pai and Kumar 2018). In Moradabad, specifically, the Muslim League (ML) had emerged as "one of the main forces" in the city's politics (Gandhi 1980: 1507). As one of my interviewees described:

There were some significant changes that Muslims experienced beginning in the 1970s. Many of them became more prosperous. They went into trade and commerce, and there was increasing visibility and assertiveness on the part of the community. In places like Moradabad and Meerut, they started to move out of ghettos and formed their own colonies [neighborhoods]. They were no longer subdued, but they were also more easily targeted now. This targeting took off in a big way in the 1980s.[11]

Given its recent loss in 1977 and the fact that UP is India's largest state, the Congress was keen to ensure that it performed well in Uttar Pradesh in

---

[9] An *Idgah* is an open-air enclosure reserved for offering prayers during Id.
[10] The PAC is an armed police force in India. It was originally created as a dedicated entity for UP but now serves the Indian state across the length and breadth of the country.
[11] Interview with an academic, New Delhi, January 20, 2014.

1980. It pursued this goal through "dalliances with various kinds of religious symbols" as well as appeals to Hindu voters (Staniland 2021: 108). To a large extent, these strategies proved to be successful, as the party reclaimed the Chief Minister's office from the JP and also amassed 51 out of 80 Lok Sabha seats in the state in 1980. In Moradabad, specifically, INC(Indira) [INC(I)] candidate Hafed Ahmed Siddiqui delivered a jolt to the ML's Shamim Ahmed when he thoroughly defeated the Muslim League aspirant in the contest for the Vidhan Sabha seat (Gandhi 1980).

Despite these signs of hope, party instability and deterioration posed ongoing threats to the Congress's survival. Indeed, as per my data, replacement volatility rates from UP's Lok Sabha returns clocked in at a whopping 99.41% in 1980. Furthermore, "progressive de-institutionalization" of the INC continued apace throughout the 1980s (Rudolph and Rudolph 1981). As such, by the end of that decade, the Congress was reduced to "a deeply decayed party organization across India's states and districts" (Wilkinson 2015: 428; Kohli 1990).

Together, these challenges help to explain the behaviors and responses of key Congress leaders in the wake of the Moradabad riots. To begin with, Chief Minister V. P. Singh put up a veritable "smokescreen" and squarely placed the blame for violence at the doorstep of local Muslims (Brennan 1994: 26). He also justified the actions of his government as necessary measures to maintain law and order in Moradabad (Brennan 1994). Higher up in the party command, Prime Minister Gandhi echoed these sentiments and explicitly characterized the riots as "a major conspiracy 'to undermine the stability of the government'" (Noorani 1990: 2418). Moreover, the Working Committee of the Congress(I) party held that the Muslim community had displayed "a degree of preparedness to provoke confrontation with governmental authorit[ies]" in the town (Noorani 1990: 2418). All in all, the message was clear: amidst changing socioeconomic conditions of Muslims, rising rates of party instability, and a regime that no longer viewed ethnic minorities as crucial to its electoral calculus, the Congress leadership reframed the riots as events that had sought to undermine the government rather than a significant communal episode that had disproportionately claimed Muslims' lives and livelihoods.

Riots in Uttar Pradesh around Advani's 1990 Rath Yatra

Throughout the 1980s, Indira and then Rajiv Gandhi continued to operate with leniency toward Hindu revivalism, while the BJP adopted a deliberate and overt campaign of Hindutva politics (Pai and Kumar 2018). After Indira's assassination in 1984, her son Rajiv's "most pressing task" became realizing reconciliation between Hindus and Sikhs (Hardgrave 1985: 141). As such, his "policy toward Muslims" remained "as cynical" as that of his mother, further marking the retreat of the Congress from the secular position it had once vociferously championed (Noorani 1990: 2420). Meanwhile, in the aftermath of a "near wipeout" in the 1984 general elections, BJP leaders in the mid-1980s made the decision to turn to visibly divisive tactics such as organizing large religious processions (Staniland 2021: 108). Central to their strategic calculus was the creation of a "powerful religious symbol" – the *rath* or chariot – to mobilize Hindus nationwide across caste lines (Engineer 1991a: 1649).

In late September 1990, BJP leader L. K. Advani set off on his *rath* – actually a "swanky, air-conditioned vehicle" – from Somnath in Gujarat for Ayodhya in UP, over 10,000 kilometers away (India Today 2019). Along the way, he sought to marshal popular support for the demolition of the Babri Masjid in Ayodhya – a mosque dating back to the sixteenth century – and rally ordinary Hindus around the construction of a Ram temple in its place. This period of competitive communal mobilization resulted in a flurry of riot violence across India (Pai and Kumar 2018).

At every stage of Advani's journey, devotees flanked his procession in throngs. No less significant than such support was the "show of unprecedented aggressiveness by the cadres of the BJP, Vishva Hindu Parishad (VHP), Bajrang Dal, and Shiv Sena" who often accompanied the *rath* (Engineer 1991a: 1649; Panikkar 1993). A ticking time bomb had thus been cast, which exploded and generated communal conflict across numerous sites in Gujarat, Karnataka, Andhra Pradesh, Uttar Pradesh, and Bihar (Engineer 1991a). It is important in this respect to note that even though Advani reportedly wanted to "avoid any rioting along [his] route," he was far less bothered by the "shedding of blood in places [removed] from his [path]" (Engineer 1991c: 159).

Eventually, the BJP leader was arrested in Samastipur, Bihar, on October 23, 1990, for defying rules about the movement of his procession (Banerjee 1991). His arrest set off another wave of violence in cities such as Jaipur, Jodhpur, Ahmedabad, Baroda, and Hyderabad (Engineer 1991a; Panikkar 1993; Jaffrelot 1996). In fact, between September 1 and November 20, 1990, it is estimated that India experienced 116 Hindu–Muslim incidents – many of them linked to the *rath yatra* – in which 564 individuals lost their lives (Panikkar 1993).

Data on Type A volatility suggests that concerns about political survival may have informed the choices of many politicians, across different parties, to organize and support violence during this time. Specifically, even as the 1989 national election returns revealed a moderately stable party system with 19.51% of seats being replaced between entering and exiting parties, Type A levels from Uttar Pradesh's Lok Sabha and Vidhan Sabha returns clocked in at the extremely unstable levels of 41.48% and 36.94%, respectively. Importantly, UP was also the worst-affected state by riot violence during this time.

For the BJP, which was still carving out its place in national politics in India, the benefits from violence seemed to trump the potential costs. As one interviewee explained:

New Modalities of Political Conflict in India

The roots of the BJP of course go back a long way. But at the time of the [*rath yatra*], the party [as a successor of the BJS] was still relatively new. It hadn't done well in 1984. So, they needed to make an impact. Advani's whole campaign was about making an impact and building support among Hindus. It might have looked like a risky strategy, but the Congress was also more divisive at that time, so there was an overall atmosphere that made those things feasible.[12]

Meanwhile, in Uttar Pradesh, the response of Chief Minister Mulayam Singh Yadav of the Janata Dal (JD) was no less telling (Panikkar 1993). Even though he had collaborated with Jyoti Basu and Laloo Prasad Yadav of West Bengal and Bihar, respectively, to thwart Advani's procession early on, after the BJP leader's arrest, he appeared to give free rein to various coercive elements, including the PAC, to engage in anti-minority violence across Uttar Pradesh (Engineer 1991c). Furthermore, Mulayam Singh did nothing to stop the circulation of an inflammatory BJP-produced video cassette entitled, "We Shall Give Up Our Lives" in UP (Brosius 2004). The contents of the cassette – which called for the protection of Hindus "from attacks by 'Muslim infiltrators'" – were compiled at the studios of a BJP Rajya Sabha MP named Dr. J. K. Jain from the central state of Madhya Pradesh (Engineer 1991c: 157). It was subsequently disseminated through BJP party offices to countless Hindu activists, PAC members, and buyers across India (Jaffrelot 1999).

The fact that Yadav changed course in this manner from objecting to the *rath yatra* in one moment to becoming a "virtual bystander [to] anti-Muslim" riots in another is plausibly explained by the fact that his position as CM had only been realized through outside support from the BJP (Engineer 1991c: 155). As such, taking any action against Jain or other Hindu nationalists threatened Mulayam Singh's survival as well. Moreover, at the time of these developments, Yadav was himself affiliated with a relatively young Janata Dal, a party that had only been formed from the merger of various JP factions in October 1988. Taken together, then, it appears that in the period surrounding Advani's procession, politicians from several different parties were incentivized to favor, rather than oppose, party violence in India.

PARTY RE-EQUILIBRATION, DECLINING RIOTS, AND THE EMERGENCE OF EVERYDAY COMMUNALISM IN INDIA (EARLY 1990S–PRESENT)

> Riots used to cause a lot of damage. People don't want that anymore. [For example,] businesses suffered a lot after the 1987 riots. Workers who worked in the mills [in the local textile industry] – many of whom had come from Bihar – left. There was a massive labor shortage. People want, more than anything, to avoid to such circumstances.[13]

---

[12] Interview with a civil society leader, Meerut, March 1, 2013.
[13] Interview with a resident, Meerut, March 1, 2013.

The interview excerpt above offers one important reason for the decline of severe communal riots observed in India since the early 1990s: ordinary people's intolerance for such violence. Following a period of considerable conflict in the 1980s, voters in conflict-affected regions came to grasp that they had often had to live through riots due to the machinations of politicians. As they developed such knowledge, they slowly came to reject communal violence. This intolerance, coupled with the re-equilibration of Indian parties in the late 1980s, also began to turn politicians away from organizing severe Hindu–Muslim riots in the country.

This is not to say that the entire period since the early 1990s has been free of communal conflict. On the contrary, when a mob of 300,000 individuals led by VHP activists and members of affiliated Hindu nationalist organizations destroyed the Babri Masjid in Ayodhya on December 6, 1992, their actions ignited violence across many parts of the country (Pai and Kumar 2018: 42). These clashes claimed the lives of 1,700 citizens and injured at least 5,500 others (Pai and Kumar 2018: 42). Since then, however, India has witnessed a significant decline in severe Hindu–Muslim riots. As Asghar Ali Engineer (2002: 100) described in 2002, "the average riot in the post-Babri masjid demolition period [has] not [been] as worrying as previous ones." Yet, he also warned that this observation in and of itself "provide[d] little comfort" to those invested in maintaining communal harmony, as newer forms of conflict were slowly starting to emerge (Engineer 2002: 100).

In a similar vein, Pai and Kumar (2018) and Nath (2022) have more recently chronicled the everyday nature of low-intensity communal violence in India. Such violence is being fueled by parties – most notably the BJP – in rural areas of UP and other northern states where grievances about slow economic development and inequality are easily mobilizable (Pai and Kumar 2018). It is also being instrumentalized through a synchronized, grassroots campaign of Hindu nationalist organizations in states such as West Bengal – a place marked by a relative absence of riots – but where BJP elites are keen to carve out a subnational foothold (Nath 2022: 38–39).

My qualitative data reveal that Indian politicians are aware of voters' rejection of severe violence. Consequently, while they are keen to avoid major riots, they are nevertheless willing to engage in other forms of conflict. As one leader from leader from the INC admitted: "People are less likely to be incited into riots now because they [are the ones] who bear the brunt. The efforts at polarization continue even today, but the idea of curfew scares people."[14] In a similar vein, a politician from the BJP held:

It is ordinary people who die in riots.... The people always suffer. Ask the person who has lost a family member in such clashes. Will he ever think of voting for a violent party?[15]

---

[14] Interview with an INC leader, Meerut, August 13, 2013.
[15] Interview with a BJP MLA, Muzaffarnagar, December 18, 2015.

New Modalities of Political Conflict in India

Quantitative data on party volatility further help to support these claims. These data reveal that party replacement rates in parliamentary elections in India have stood at the extremely stable level of less than 10% since 1991. This has meant that for most parties – win or lose – enduring from election to election is no longer a major concern. As a result, politicians have begun to operate with relatively lengthy time horizons and have also taken stock of the fact that "organizing riots [is] not a paying proposition" anymore (Engineer 1997b: 326). Finally, this long-term orientation seems to be related to broader transformations in political conflict in India, such as rural riot incidents, like those seen in Muzaffarnagar and Shamli in 2013, and the rise of low-intensity assaults against Muslims. These newer forms of violence are not only tolerable to the BJP – as they are increasingly marked by the involvement of armed actors who are ideologically aligned with the party (Staniland 2021) – but they are also more "politically manageable" than the severe riots that afflicted India during the 1980s (Pai and Kumar 2018: 3).

SUMMARY AND CONCLUSION

Drawing on a host of quantitative and qualitative data, this chapter has chronicled the relationship between changes in party instability rates and elites' incentives for violence in India. It has traced major upticks in communal clashes observed between the early 1980s and early 1990s to prior escalations in party entry and exit levels, which first emerged in the late 1970s. The chapter has further shown that rising rates of party replacement enabled politicians from various organizations – including the eroding Congress and the relatively young BJP among others – to operate with short time horizons, discount the potential costs of violence including sanctioning from voters, and frequently instrumentalize or sponsor severe communal conflict. More recently, and since the early 1990s in particular, the re-equilibration of the party system has reoriented elites toward the future. This reorientation has contributed to significant declines in party-orchestrated Hindu–Muslim riots in the country. However, other forms of conflict – including targeted low-level attacks against Muslims as well as rural incidents of riots, which often come with fewer risks – have seen an uptick. Building upon this national-level analysis, Chapter 7 offers an accounting for the subnational trajectories of riot violence in Hyderabad and Meerut cities.

7

Party Politics and Subnational Trajectories of Riot Violence in India's Hyderabad and Meerut Cities

Hyderabad in Andhra Pradesh (AP) and Meerut in Uttar Pradesh (UP) are important subnational sites to investigate in a study of party violence. Through much of their postindependence period, and until the early 1990s, each of these places exhibited considerable vulnerabilities to Hindu–Muslim riots. Since then, however, they have both seen a notable decline in such clashes. In accounting for these subnational patterns, as in Chapter 6, I draw on a combination of event data, data on parliamentary party replacement, and in-depth qualitative interviews in the forthcoming pages. In addition, I also incorporate Type A volatility data from Vidhan Sabha returns in AP and UP.[1]

Vidhan Sabha volatility rates are important to include in this analysis because state-level assembly elections are often high-stakes contests in India (Deshpande 1993). In making choices about the utility of conflict, we might thus expect that subleaders will not simply take into account national-level party dynamics but that they will also pay heed to local or regional developments. Of course, insofar as my theory holds that party volatility *conditions* elites' incentives to instrumentalize violence, it does not rule out the possibility that major riots can occur amidst low levels of party instability. In turning to the empirical records of riot violence in Hyderabad and Meerut in the forthcoming pages, I thus also discuss key riots that broke out in stable party contexts.

This chapter proceeds as follows. I begin by detailing the association between party instability and riot violence in the cities of Hyderabad, and then trace the relationship between parties and communal riots in Meerut. In each of these sections, I marry discussions of key state-level and local-level factors

---

[1] These data extend until the 2014 and 2017 assembly elections in Andhra Pradesh and Uttar Pradesh, respectively. I have also calculated replacement volatility rates for the state of Telangana, which was carved out of Andhra Pradesh in 2014, for the 2014–2018 period.

Riot Violence in India's Hyderabad and Meerut Cities

with national-level developments that influenced elites' decisions about conflict. I also offer detailed accounts of several major riots to help elucidate the involvement of parties in these episodes. Within my discussion of communal violence in UP, I return to the rural Muzaffarnagar and Shamli clashes with which I opened this book. My findings about these riots reveal that they were deliberately mobilized in villages due to elites' incentives to avoid sanctioning from urban constituents and the stronger institutions that are present in cities. In addition, further expanding upon the insights presented in Chapter 6, I briefly discuss newer forms of party violence, particularly targeted attacks against Muslims, which are occurring more frequently in UP than in any other Indian state today (Krishnan 2018; D. Basu 2021; Engineer, Dabhade, and Nair 2020). The chapter concludes by addressing endogeneity concerns.

THE TRANSITION FROM PARTY VIOLENCE TO COMMUNAL QUIESCENCE IN HYDERABAD

> I remember that riot [of 1990]. It was terrible. I mean, I was coming down by air in the morning at about 8 o'clock [or] 9 o'clock when the curfew was on. Now to see such a big city with no movement, it's a very, very strange feeling. There's nothing moving on the roads. And friends have told me – Muslim friends – that even those who were not living in the Old City, who were living outside in big bungalows ... huge crowds were coming. So, people said that they couldn't sleep for days. Day and night, they had to be alert. There was so much tension, so much tension.[2]

The interview above encapsulates the memories of one Hyderabad resident about the December 1990 riots, the worst clashes ever seen in the city. It underscores the kind of devastation that major communal episodes can cause to citizens' lives. Importantly, however, the 1990 riot was merely one in a longer series of clashes that afflicted Hyderabad between the late 1970s and early 1990s. Indeed, according to the Varshney-Wilkinson (2004; also see Varshney 2002) dataset, which covers riot incidents between 1950 and 1995, Hyderabad is India's third-most riot-prone city. Over the period between 1950 and 2000, it fell prey to 22 separate riot incidents in which 330 individuals lost their lives (Varshney-Wilkinson 2004 dataset; Mitra-Ray 2007 dataset; author's extension). Several of the major riots that occurred during this period, including the December 1990 riot to which I will return, emerged from the direct and indirect involvement of various political elites. As one interviewee put it, "most of the riots [took] place because one political party or the other want[ed them] to happen."[3] Yet since the early 1990s, Hyderabad has only experienced mild communal episodes. This section offers an accounting of this trajectory.

---

[2] Interview with an academic, Hyderabad, August 1, 2013.
[3] Interview with a senior police officer, Hyderabad, August 7, 2013.

Beyond the many communal clashes seen in Hyderabad since 1947, it is worth noting that the city also succumbed to some violence prior to India's independence when it was administered as a princely state. The scale of such conflict was especially severe during a period known as "Police Action" in 1948. As with other princely states, much of Hyderabad's growth during this era was "propelled by the constant appropriation of revenue from the peasantry by the royalty and the nobility" (Naidu 1990: 65). The Muslim rulers of the state, known as the Nizams, established their seat of power in an area known as the Old City. This part of Hyderabad remains walled to the present day, and the official language of the Nizams' administration, Urdu, continues to be widely spoken in the region.

As per extant studies, peaceable relations between the city's Hindu and Muslim communities first started to weaken in the 1920s (Jairath and Kidwai n.d.). Over time, these cracks gave way to clashes of a patently "local nature" (Jairath and Kidwai n.d.: 1). Eventually, however, a deadly riot broke out in Hyderabad in 1938. Originating in the Dhoolpet area of the Old City, the incident claimed the lives of four individuals and left 170 others seriously injured (Times of India 1938).

Ten years later, in September 1948, "Police Action" brought severe communal violence to Hyderabad as the Indian government launched a "one-sided military campaign" to force the Nizam to accede to the Indian Union (Jairath and Kidwai n.d.: 1). Even though the campaign itself, known as "Operation Polo," concluded in a short five-and-a-half-day period, it unleashed a wave of conflict that lasted for several months.

Details from the Sunderlal Committee Report (Government of India 1949) – the most authoritative account of Police Action – establish the central facts about this period of violence (Purshotham 2015).[4] This committee was constituted by Prime Minister Nehru in November 1948 to investigate the massacres related to Operation Polo. It was led by nationalist leader Pandit Sunderlal, and members of the committee subsequently visited several violence-affected areas of the erstwhile princely state between November and December 1948.

In confidential notes attached to the main report, the Committee estimated that "the total number of deaths in the state could in no way have been less than 25,000" (Government of India 1949: 33). Consistent with patterns of communal riots and minority victimization observed throughout the postindependence era (Brass 2006; Wilkinson 2008), committee members also found that the unmistakable "sufferers" of the clashes in Hyderabad "were the Muslims, in a hopeless minority of nearly 1 to 10" (Government of India 1949: 3). Finally, they uncovered that constituents of "well-known, notorious"

---

[4] According to Sunil Purshotham (2015: 451), the Sunderlal Committee Report "was considered suppressed or destroyed until 1988" when the Indian scholar Omar Khalidi gained access to some of its key "fragments." The report only became available to the Indian public in 2013, 65 years after Operation Polo.

Hindu groups from the neighboring states of Maharashtra and Karnataka had supported a "number of armed and trained men" to carry out violence in Hyderabad (Government of India 1949: 4).

During fieldwork, several interviewees held that the legacies of "Police Action" live on in the city to this day. One respondent, for example, argued that the events of 1948 decidedly destroyed the city's historic "*Ganga-Jamuni Tehzeeb,*" or its intermingling of Hindu and Muslim cultures.[5] Meanwhile, another noted that Hyderabad's "two [major religious] communities are totally divided" even now, and further traced the roots of this division to Operation Polo.[6]

The 1978 Riots in Hyderabad City

Despite the devastation wrought by "Police Action," Hyderabad did not witness another major wave of Hindu–Muslim violence until March and April 1978. This incident, often referred to as the Rameeza Bee riots, broke out in the wake of the custodial rape of a young Muslim woman named Rameeza Bee. After her husband, a rickshaw-puller named Ahmed Hussain, found out about his wife's assault, he confronted police officers at the Nallakunta station where Bee had been raped. For raising the questions that he did, Hussain was badly beaten "on the head, neck, back, and stomach" and died as a result of his injuries (Reddy 2006: 93).

Bee's gang rape and her husband's subsequent killing spawned widespread anti-police agitations across Hyderabad.[7] According to Radha Kumar (1997: 128), following news of Hussain's death, some "twenty-two thousand Hyderabadis went to the [Nallakunta] police station, laid [his] dead body in the station verandah, set up road blocks, cut the telephone wires, stoned the building, and set fire to some bicycles in the compound."

At the time of these events, the city's demographic composition – with a 54% to 43% split between Hindus and Muslims (Graff and Galonnier 2013a) – was already conducive to instrumentalizing communal violence. Against this background, the sexual assault of a Muslim woman, the killing of her husband, and the resulting protests presented opportune triggers for politicians from both communities to escalate tensions.

According to the trade unionist and Communist Party of India (CPI) leader K. L. Mahendra (2006: 88) – who was friendly with the leadership of the Muslim political party, known as the All India Majlis-e-Ittehad'ul Muslimeen (AIMIM/MIM or Majlis) – the latter organization fueled the anti-government demonstrations. Mahendra (2006: 88) further held that Majlis leaders became involved in raising the communal temperature in Hyderabad at this time with

---

[5] Interview with a journalist, Hyderabad, July 29, 2013.
[6] Interview with a human rights activist, Hyderabad, July 26, 2013.
[7] Interview with a journalist, Hyderabad, July 25, 2013.

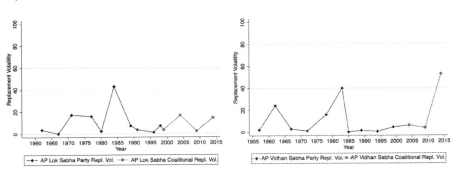

FIGURE 7.1 Party and coalitional replacement volatility in Andhra Pradesh's Lok Sabha (1957–2014) and Vidhan Sabha (1955–2014) elections[8]

the express intent of avenging Congress Chief Minister (CM) Chenna Reddy's decision to exclude MIM MLAs from key state-level sub-committees. The Majlis also reportedly appropriated Bee's custodial rape and Hussain's murder to instigate violence against Hindus.[9] As Neena Rao and Abdul Thaha (2012: 194) argue, in acting in this manner, the AIMIM positioned itself as coming "to the forefront in 'defending' Muslim life and property" in Hyderabad. Indeed, it is worth noting that the protests against Bee's rape did not emerge from the activities of women's groups but were instead led by Majlis politicians (Naqvi 2010). Not to be left behind, opposition leaders from parties such as the Bharatiya Jana Sangh (BJS) began to pressure Chenna Reddy to act swiftly against the agitators through any and all means necessary (Times of India 2003; Kumar 1997).

As shown in Figure 7.1, by the time the riots broke out in 1978, party instability in Andhra Pradesh was already on an upswing: replacement rates from Lok Sabha and Vidhan Sabha returns stood in the moderately stable range of 10% to 20%, compared to the extremely stable levels seen in the 1950s. These circumstances seem to have incentivized Hindu and Muslim politicians alike to provoke and gamble with riot violence. As one Congress leader recalled:

I was a student at that time and I have seen [the consequences of the 1978 riots]. This city was almost on fire for almost two weeks. That's not a small thing. The curfew was imposed in 28 police jurisdictions. The kind of incident [that] it was, it really moved the city.... This incident was definitely aggravated with the role of two elements. One is the Majlis party and the other was Narendra, a BJP strong goon of Hyderabad city. So, these two were the major players. They organized [it].[10]

---

[8] Since its formation as a state in 2014 and until the legislative assembly election of 2018, replacement rates in Telangana have stood at the quite stable level of 3.36%.
[9] Interview with an INC politician, Hyderabad, August 3, 2013; interview with a former bureaucrat, Hyderabad, August 5, 2013.
[10] Interview with an INC politician, Hyderabad, August 3, 2013.

Riot Violence in India's Hyderabad and Meerut Cities

Additional qualitative evidence reveals that these two groups had deliberately tilled the ground for communal violence for some time prior to the 1978 riots. According to one respondent, Sultan Salahuddin Owaisi – who served as the Majlis president between 1976 and 2008 – began to "build communal feelings among the Muslims of Hyderabad" soon after he clinched the Vidhan Sabha seat from Pathargatti as an independent candidate in 1962.[11] A few years later, Hindu nationalist forces also sought to intentionally carve out a sphere of influence in the region's politics. To quote an academic familiar with this era, even though Telangana as a whole and Hyderabad in particular had "always had a very, very strong identification and empathy [for] a politically resonant [form] of Hindu [politics]," this current grew considerably stronger from the 1970s onward.[12] Crucially, "the coming of the Jana Sangh and then the BJP" resulted in a noticeable uptick in communal provocations in the Old City area.[13] Finally, as in other parts of the country, a weakening Congress party, which was still ruling in AP, came to view communal discord as a means to advance its electoral interests in the state.[14] Beginning in the late 1970s, it thus granted both the AIMIM and Hindu nationalist organizations considerable latitude in planning their activities – especially large religious processions – in Hyderabad.

As one interviewee described, for Hindu nationalists in particular, the organization of these processions – and the related possibilities of communal violence – were viewed as acceptable risks to pursue their ambitions of establishing a subnational foothold in Andhra Pradesh:

Minorities [Muslims] who are politically organized exist in large measure in Hyderabad.... The Hindu majority was not so organized earlier [before the 1970s]. It was there ... strongly opposing some of the things. At that time, [the] BJP was not so strong also. The BJS was there [actually] ... Hardly any riots. Very rarely there used to be any riots.... The large-scale riots never took place in such a big way until 1978. Prior to '78 certain developments took place, like the processions for Bonalu, which is presently going on, and the processions for Ganesh [Chaturthi, which] were fully localized.... [But] then they [became] centralized.[15] [This] is a phenomenon post-77-78. And Ganesh [Chaturthi] ... if I remember right, around '77-78 when Chenna Reddy was Chief Minister, he was pressurized to permit this centralized Ganesh procession, which used to start from the other end of the city. [He received pressure] from the Hindu pressure groups mostly inspired by the [BJS/BJP]. Even though it was there, the BJP wasn't organized like that. But still they [Hindu nationalists] contributed, and they didn't seem to care much for the consequences. It was mostly a new force in Andhra politics, so they took this risk and it paid off.... Now it [processions] are huge [and they take place on] 20 ton, 30 ton

---

[11] Interview with a retired police officer, Hyderabad, July 29, 2013.
[12] Interview with an academic, Hyderabad, July 22, 2013.
[13] Ibid.
[14] Interview with a journalist, Hyderabad, July 23, 2013; interview with a TDP politician, Hyderabad, August 5, 2013.
[15] Bonalu and Ganesh Chaturthi are both Hindu festivals.

tractors, big floats nowadays, you know like what you see on Republic Day. This is a thing that became very organized from '78 onwards and now it is a major, major thing in Hyderabad. It is there every year [and] the police is on tenterhooks.[16]

Altogether, then, my data reveal that the Rameeza Bee riots broke out in a context where there was a growing appetite for violence among a number of different parties. While the Majlis seemed willing to gamble with riots in order to consolidate the support of the Muslim community, Hindu nationalists – who were still staking out their place in Andhra Pradesh's politics – viewed polarization and potential communal conflict as strategic risks that were worth undertaking. Finally, amidst a deteriorating party organization, the Congress turned a blind eye to communal provocations in Hyderabad city and a major riot thus emerged.

Party Violence as Riot Violence in 1980s Hyderabad

In the aftermath of the 1978 riots, many of these factors favorable to party violence remained firmly in place while others intensified during the 1980s. First, the AIMIM responded to the Bonalu and Ganesh Chaturthi processions by planning equally massive *Pankha* processions around the occasion of Muharram.[17] Notably, the reigning Congress not only allowed this, but it went further in the early 1980s by entering into a tacit agreement with the Majlis to split Lok Sabha and Vidhan Sabha seats. The goal of this agreement was clear: it was meant to undercut the BJP and prevent Hindu nationalists from making inroads in Andhra Pradesh's politics.[18] Second, in 1983, the regional Telugu Desam Party (TDP) – which had only formed the year prior – defeated the Congress and rose to power in the state. Owing to its birth and subsequent victory – the TDP went from holding no seats in 1978 to capturing 201 of 294 legislative seats a mere five years later – replacement volatility rates in both the 1983 Vidhan Sabha and in AP's 1984 returns from the Lok Sabha rose to extremely unstable levels of 39.80% and 42.86%, respectively.

Together, these developments influenced the fates of political parties in Andhra Pradesh as well as the trajectories of party violence in Hyderabad. From being a "marginal player in Hyderabad politics" in the 1960s, the Majlis witnessed a significant electoral rise during the 1980s, due in part to its leaders' willingness to take on an assertive role in advocating for Muslim interests (Rao and Thaha 2012: 193). Owing to this dispensation, the party won its first seats in AP's legislative assembly in 1989 (Rao and Thaha 2012: 193). In addition, its leader, Salahuddin Owaisi, ascended to the national parliament as an independent candidate from the Hyderabad Lok Sabha constituency in

---

[16] Interview with a TDP leader, August 2, 2013.
[17] Interview with a journalist, Hyderabad, July 23, 2013; also see Engineer 1991b; Agraharkar 2005.
[18] Interview with a journalist, Hyderabad, July 29, 2013.

1984. He subsequently held onto this seat as the Majlis candidate in every general election until his retirement from electoral politics in 2004. After this, his elder son, Asaduddin (Asad) Owaisi, became the MP from Hyderabad. At the time of this writing, Asad not only continues to serve in this position, but the MIM also holds power in seven Vidhan Sabha constituencies in the greater Hyderabad area.

During this era of widening electoral influence, AIMIM leaders engaged in what one respondent described as "continuous provocation of the communal issue."[19] These provocations led the BJP to dig in its heels further as well. As my interviewee recalled:

I was a friend of Salahuddin Owaisi [during that time] and everything was viewed through this one prism, which then led to a reaction from the other side. It was quite an undesirable way of doing politics.[20]

Unsurprisingly, then, between 1980 and the January 1983 victory of the TDP, Hyderabad fell prey to three separate riot incidents, as both Hindu nationalists and Majlis leaders sought to fan communal flames. However, the Telugu Desam Party appeared keen to control communal tensions, and its leader N. T. Rama Rao – a "judicious administrator"[21] – explicitly "laid stress on Hindu-Muslim unity" after coming to political power in Andhra Pradesh (Engineer 1983: 1969). As one interviewee suggested, even though it was clearly an ethnic party, the TDP viewed its role in politics in considerably broader terms:

Our party is founded on two main issues. One is Telugu unity, Telugu pride, and Telugu self-respect. Second, and on the economic side, our party is rooted in the concept of *roti, kapda, makaan* [food, clothing, and housing] for all. So, we believe in subsidizing food, clothing, and housing to create equal access.[22]

Despite these objectives, ultimately, the party did not prove successful in quelling riot violence in Hyderabad in the early-to-mid 1980s. In fact, the city succumbed to deadly clashes in 1983, 1984, and 1985. Beyond the previously described activities of the BJP and MIM, some of these violent events – including the riots of July 1984 – occurred due to intraparty rivalries *within* the TDP (Agraharkar 2005). In addition, one interviewee held that the many clashes of this time cannot be understood without reference to threat perception and the machinations of the Congress party:

N. T. Rama Rao founded the TDP to remove the Congress from power. He was a very popular leader. This was a real threat to the Congress. The party was already becoming weaker, and then in Andhra Pradesh he emerged and that was a big threat.[23]

---

[19] Interview with a former bureaucrat, Hyderabad, August 5, 2013.
[20] Ibid.
[21] Interview with an INC politician, Hyderabad, August 3, 2013.
[22] Interview with a TDP leader, Hyderabad, August 2, 2013.
[23] Interview with a journalist, Hyderabad, July 22, 2013.

Even in the face of all of these ingredients favorable to party violence, once party instability levels started to decline in Andhra Pradesh in the mid-to-late 1980s, communal riots also began to wane. As a result, the "city remained comparatively free of Hindu–Muslim violence for the remainder of N. T. [Rama Rao's] tenure," which came to an end in December 1989 (Agraharkar 2005: 44). But the worst communal violence for Hyderabad – the 1990 riots – was yet to come.

The December 1990 Riots in Hyderabad City

At the outset, it bears noting that the 1990 riots broke out during a period of extreme party stability. Specifically, in 1989, the AP Vidhan Sabha recorded a party replacement rate of 1.36%, while the state's Lok Sabha Type A return clocked in at 7.14%. As such, accounting for these riots requires looking beyond party instability to other major explanations for communal violence in India, including intraparty dynamics and competition over seats.

According to the Varshney-Wilkinson (2004) dataset, the clashes of December 1990 claimed the lives of 132 individuals. Other estimates, however, suggest that the death toll stood at more than 300.[24] There are also a number of different narratives about the events that triggered the riots. They range from the alleged stabbing of a young Hindu hawker[25] to the discovery of "the bodies of a woman and her child" in the Sabzimandi area of the Old City (Graff and Galonnier 2013b: 13).

Regardless of the actual precipitant, it is now well established that the violence was politically orchestrated – at least at the state level – to oust CM Chenna Reddy from power. As Varshney (2002: 209) writes, an adversarial faction of the ruling Congress organized the 1990 clashes with the express purpose of "embarrass[ing] the government." When Reddy eventually resigned, moreover, "the riots, which had been raging for weeks, immediately stopped" (Varshney 2002: 209).

During fieldwork, a number of respondents shared precisely the same account about the machinations behind the 1990 violence. One recounted:

Chenna Reddy resigned because he could not bring the violence under control. Once he resigned, the riots stopped. So, can we really now say that political engineering did not contribute to the carnage in Hyderabad?[26]

In a similar vein, another interviewee held:

We all, and [by that] I mean every single resident of Hyderabad who lived through that violence, knows that the 1990 riot was organized with the express intent of changing the Chief Minister of Andhra Pradesh. Chenna Reddy was the Chief Minister at the

---

[24] Interview with a journalist, Hyderabad, July 23, 2013.
[25] Interview with a journalist, Hyderabad, July 29, 2013; also see Engineer 2004.
[26] Interview with an academic, Hyderabad, August 1, 2013.

time. During that riot, more than 300 people were killed in Hyderabad. And when the Chief Minister was changed [and replaced by fellow Congress politician N. Janardhan Reddy], the next day there were no riots. So, you tell me, what was the purpose of the riot? Was it because the ordinary man spontaneously decided to go and attack people of the other community after the stabbing incident happened? No, the riot was purely and entirely strategic.[27]

Beyond these intrigues within the ruling Congress, micro-level evidence shows that the BJP and Majlis also took advantage of the disorder in Hyderabad to sponsor violence. These decisions were plausibly related to competition over Vidhan Sabha seats: even though the Majlis had claimed all three national parliamentary seats in the greater Hyderabad area in 1989, the seven seats in the legislative assembly were divided between the INC, MIM, BJP, and TDP (Government of India 2018). Existing research further reveals that leaders of both the Majlis and the BJP hired *pehlwans* or strongmen to spread communal violence in Hyderabad during the 1990 riots (Kakar 1996, 2000; Engineer 1991b). Recalling this period, an interviewee thus held that the clashes also owed a great deal to the "*goonda* element" or criminal component of Hyderabadi politics.[28]

As previously shown, the 1990 riots were ultimately devastating for the city. One interview summarized the consequences of the riot in the following words:

I have personally seen many riots taking place. The riots [of 1990] are best not described because they were truly terrible. The misery that you witnessed is something that you will never forget.[29]

Taken together, then, the 1990 riots emerge as a key case where intraparty rivalries within the incumbent regime and the desire of rival parties to carve out and strengthen their own electoral spheres – rather than rising levels of party replacement – incentivized communal violence on the part of political elites. Notably, these riots also proved to be a pivotal turning point in Hyderabad's larger trajectory of communal conflict, and they stand out today as the last case of severe Hindu–Muslim clashes in the city.

Quiescence in Hyderabad since 1991

Since the riots of December 1990, a number of important factors – many of them related to party stabilization – seem to have come together to dampen elites' incentives for violence in Hyderabad. The Majlis, for one, has established itself so firmly in the Old City that "it does not suit the [party] to start a riot now."[30] As one interviewee from the Congress described:

[27] Interview with a journalist, Hyderabad, July 29, 2013.
[28] Interview with a resident, Hyderabad, July 27, 2013.
[29] Interview with a TDP leader, Hyderabad, August 2, 2013.
[30] Interview with a senior police officer, Hyderabad, August 7, 2013.

Earlier, only the senior Owaisi was in office. Then he got another representative. After that, they have grown to such a strength, they are seven [MLAs] now. So, they are happy, their ranks are happy. So, that is another consideration not to go for this. The communal angle is there, but that need for violence is far less.[31]

During fieldwork, AIMIM leaders also consistently held that communal riots were squarely incompatible with their electoral craft.[32] One respondent implied that the tendency to steer clear of violence was motivated by the need to avoid voter sanctioning, as "Hyderabad's voters disfavor communal candidates."[33] A survivor of the September 1983 riots – which claimed the lives of 45 individuals (Varshney-Wilkinson dataset 2004) – provided greater insight into citizens' intolerance for violence-wielding candidates:

Those clashes were very intense.... People entered our homes and they didn't even spare our children. [Survivors] didn't know what happened to their family members. Sometimes, they found out the next day by reading the news. We were left hungry and thirsty for days. That's what we experienced. So of course, we never want to go back to that now. *And we also know that politicians do these things for their own [purposes]. So why should we vote for such parties? Now, the situation [in Hyderabad] is such that even if there is polarization, even if there is some division, no one – Hindu or Muslim – wants to support communal parties. We've seen such bad times that we refuse to go back.*[34]

Beyond the possibility of garnering punishment from voters, there is also evidence that sanctioning from other quarters may have contributed to the Majlis party's more restrained behavior over time. On January 8, 2013, Asaduddin Owaisi's younger brother, Akbaruddin (Akbar) Owaisi, was arrested by the AP police on charges of hate speech. The authorities alleged that Owaisi had made derogatory remarks about Hindus and Hindu deities in Adilabad district, approximately 300 kilometers from Hyderabad, on December 22, 2012. Journalists and scholars who reported on the incident further held that he declared that if the police were removed, Muslims would be able to kill 1 billion Hindus within a period of 15 minutes (*Times of India* 2012; Muralidharan 2014).

In March 2022, the courts acquitted Akbaruddin in the hate speech case, but at the time of fieldwork, the charges against him were still relatively new. In discussing this matter with me, a senior police officer noted that despite the speech, "the MIM never wanted a riot" because a major riot would lead "them [the party] to suffer very heavily."[35] A number of respondents unaffiliated with the AIMIM further held that Owaisi's example served as a powerful

---

[31] Interview with an INC politician, Hyderabad, August 3, 2013.
[32] Interview with an AIMIM leader, July 25, 2013; interview with an AIMIM politician, July 31, 2013.
[33] Interview with an AIMIM politician, Hyderabad, July 31, 2013.
[34] Interview with riot survivor, Hyderabad, July 26, 2013; emphasis added.
[35] Interview with a senior police officer, Hyderabad, August 7, 2013.

Riot Violence in India's Hyderabad and Meerut Cities

cautionary tale of how open calls for violence can result in the sanctioning of Indian politicians.[36] The future course for communalism was thus described as follows: "rather than provocation, there are attempts at polarization in Hyderabad."[37]

This broad understanding that violence can result in significant costs was also articulated by respondents with expertise on, and connections to, the BJP. One interviewee explicitly framed the matter in terms of the lengthy time horizons with which the party must operate:

> [This decline in major communal riots] is not only about Hyderabad. It is about all [of] India. There was this big exception in Gujarat.[38] Otherwise, overall, partly at least, because of some electoral results, it [the cost of violence] became clear. For example, with the BJP, what it did in UP with this Babri Masjid discourse – they came to power. Then, after the rioting and violence in the next election, the BJP was gone completely! Wiped out. So ... for some time now it has been seen or demonstrated that if you engage with this [fomenting communalism] the results will be terrible. So, one thing is that *there is a feeling that you can't get away. You can no longer get away because [you] have to continually look to the future. It was probably the 1980s and the early 1990s when it made sense to [deploy communal] aggression. But that has fizzled out now.*[39]

Meanwhile, and in keeping with its campaign strategy for the 2014 general elections, a politician from the Hindu nationalist party emphasized the BJP's developmental goals during an interview in Hyderabad:

> We are a party for the Indian people – that is what *Bharatiya Janata Party* means – and we want development for all. And let me tell you, it is only people like Mr. Modi who can solve our complex problems of development. You need leadership with determination and vision. And that is what the BJP can offer. That is what we want to bring to Andhra [Pradesh] – not riots that these other parties are interested in. You know, there has been no riot in Gujarat since 2002. There has only been development – development for Hindus and development for Muslims. That is our pledge to the people here too.[40]

Later on in our conversation, this respondent also noted that riots made little electoral sense for the party:

> Now, the general person is not prepared for communal riots ... be they Hindu or Muslim. Now, if you see, even when there are little triggers, the politicians know that

---

[36] Interview with an INC politician, August 3, 2013; interview with a CPI politician, Hyderabad, August 4, 2013.
[37] Interview with a journalist, Hyderabad, July 23, 2013.
[38] At the time of this interview, the Muzaffarnagar and Shamli clashes – another key exception in the wider pattern of declining riots in India (Varshney 2017) – had not yet broken out in UP.
[39] Interview with an academic, August 1, 2013; emphasis added.
[40] Interview with a BJP leader, Hyderabad, August 4, 2013.

all of Hyderabad can be affected. And they don't want that. So, things are now under control. The people will not tolerate violence and [so] the politicians also don't want the riots.[41]

Although there are good reasons to expect that politicians will emphasize goals such as development and underplay any involvement or benefits accrued from violence, it is nonetheless worth noting that varied forms of managed and calibrated everyday communal mobilization still persist in Hyderabad. As one respondent stated:

I perceive that they [political elites] would like the cauldron to be on the boil, but they would not like it to boil over. You know, they would like it to … always remain in a state of animation, but they would not like it to go beyond their control, no.[42]

As in other parts of the country, much of the work of everyday communalization is being carried out by key social movement partners of the BJP. These activities are fulfilling the cultural and revivalist goals of Hindu nationalists. Consider, for instance, the main activities of the Bajrang Dal in Hyderabad's Old City:

We are here to protect Hindu temples, to organize religious processions in Old City like the Muslims do, and we are also here to prevent "love jihad." The Muslims cannot just convert and take our daughters and sisters.[43]

On the whole, then, my findings from Hyderabad show that major riots have not reappeared in the city since the early 1990s because politicians across political parties have turned away from their instrumentalization and sponsorship; indeed, between 1995 and 2010, only six deadly riots broke out in the town, resulting in a cumulative death toll of 18 (Mitra-Ray 2007 dataset; author's extension). Lower rates of party instability seem to have partially contributed to this state of quiescence, but even amidst extremely high rates of party replacement – as seen around the 2014 Vidhan Sabha elections – as well as other conducive conditions such as the breakup of the MIM–Congress alliance over the decision to create the state of Telangana, the city's politicians have acted with restraint.

All the while, efforts at communal polarization have continued at a steady pace, and processions can still precipitate Hindu–Muslim skirmishes in Hyderabad, as seen in March 2010, when disputes over the hoisting of flags around the Hindu and Muslim festivals of Hanuman Jayanti and Milad-un-Nabi, respectively, devolved into deadly clashes that claimed two lives. However, as opposed to emanating from the activities of political elites themselves, research suggests that this particular incident was akin to a case of "collective vigilantism" through which Old City youths sought to uncover pathways for "navigating terrains of urban terror" in a communally tense city

---

[41] Ibid.
[42] Interview with a senior police officer, Hyderabad, August 7, 2013.
[43] Interview with a Bajrang Dal activist, Hyderabad, August 4, 2013.

(Sen 2012: 83). Altogether, then, Hyderabad seems to have settled into a state that as one interviewee described "is tense but under control."[44]

THE EVOLUTION FROM REGULAR COMMUNAL VIOLENCE TO RELATIVE CALM IN MEERUT

> The 1987 riot was so big and severe that countless people lost out on their livelihoods. But it was not just a matter of economics: entire families were destroyed. It took the city more than ten years to recover from that violence. It was truly an awful time.[45]

The interview above captures important facets of the widespread damage suffered by residents of Meerut during to the 1987 riots. These riots, known as the Hashimpura massacres, remain the most severe clashes to have occurred in the city. However, they also comprise a longer record of communal violence dating back to the early 1960s. In fact, following Hyderabad, the town of Meerut in UP is India's fourth most riot-prone city (Varshney 2002; Varshney-Wilkinson 2004 dataset). According to existing data, Meerut witnessed 17 separate communal riots between 1950 and 2010, which collectively claimed the lives of 273 individuals (Varshney-Wilkinson 2004 dataset; Mitra-Ray 2007 dataset; author's extension). Like Hyderabad, Meerut also succumbed to some Hindu–Muslim conflict prior to Indian independence, including clashes in October 1939 and November 1946, which culminated in eight and 29 fatalities, respectively (Brass 2004).

In the postindependence period, Paul Brass (2004) has documented the central place of the city's institutionalized riot system in enabling and mobilizing much of this violence. Specifically, Brass finds that this system was active from the early 1960s through the late 1980s, a period during which Meerut succumbed to several significant and deadly riots. Recalling this time of prolonged communal violence, one interviewee described some of the main actors in the city's riot network in the following words:

The politicians used to use gangs. The parties used to use the gangs for violence. That is how they could organize riots in these dense neighborhoods in the city where the people live close together. The gangs used to do the dirty work of lighting the flame and making people fight.[46]

The 1961 Riot in Meerut City

Against the backdrop of these connections between politicians and criminals, Meerut's first notable postindependence riot broke out in October 1961.

---

[44] Interview with a senior police officer, Hyderabad, August 7, 2013.
[45] Interview with a Meerut resident, New Delhi, March 3, 2013.
[46] Interview with an academic, Meerut, March 2, 2013.

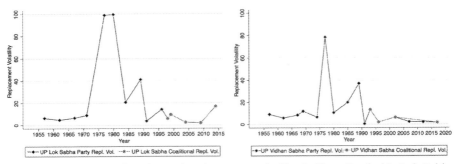

FIGURE 7.2 Party and coalitional replacement volatility in Uttar Pradesh's Lok Sabha (1951–2014) and Vidhan Sabha (1951–2017) elections

According to the historical record, the violence escalated due to the actions of some Congress subleaders and members of the Jana Sangh. The key events leading up to the riots were as follows: in early October, a group of Muslim students reportedly beat a Hindu youth named Iqbal Singh along with "two or three Hindu boys" at the campus of the Aligarh Muslim University, some 90 miles away (Brass 2004: 4840). Singh's father, an officer at the central police station in Meerut, then "led a procession of 150 supporters" through the city to condemn the assault on his son (Brass 2004: 4840). This event took place at some point between October 5 and 7, 1961, during which time those participating in the cavalcade "targeted an old Muslim college and some Muslim-owned shops" along their route (Graff and Galonnier 2013a).

Eyewitness accounts further allege that various unnamed Congressmen marched as a part of the angry mob while BJS leaders openly fanned the flames of communal discord in the city (Brass 2004). Yet other politicians – such as INC member Shaukat Hameed Khan, who was seeking the Congress party nomination for the upcoming legislative assembly elections from Meerut's rural Baghpat constituency – sought to quell communal tensions. Specifically, Khan reportedly traveled to one of the sensitive sites in the city and tried to appeal to civilians to maintain communal harmony (Brass 2004). His stance may have been motivated by the fact that politicians affiliated with the relatively secure Congress party, and especially those who were still seeking to build their careers, needed to look to the future at this time. As shown in Figure 7.2, the party system was extremely stable during this period, having recorded replacement rates in the 1957 Vidhan Sabha and UP's corresponding returns from the Lok Sabha at 6.24% and 9.07%, respectively. Thus, even though his calls for peace ultimately fell on deaf ears – after which Khan quickly "disappeared from the scene" – the evidence suggests that ambitious Congress leaders shared strong incentives against gambling with communal riots in the early 1960s (Brass 2004: 4842).

By contrast, the BJS was still a relatively marginal player (Weiner 1957) and thus had sound reasons to provoke Hindu–Muslim violence. Importantly, research has shown that the party also benefited from its involvement in the 1961 riots in Meerut and witnessed an approximate 20% increase in its vote share in the subsequent 1962 assembly polls (Brass 2004).

Party Violence as Riot Violence in 1980s Meerut

As opposed to the early 1960s when Congress politicians needed to avoid violence but Hindu nationalists could viably gamble with conflict, by the early 1980s, politicians across party lines shared strong incentives for driving and sponsoring communal riots in Meerut. This was not only because of the breakdown of Congress dominance on the national stage in the late 1970s, but also because of the "more strident, open, and at times violent form of communal mobilization" adopted by the newly formed BJP – in Uttar Pradesh and beyond – from the mid-1980s onward (Pai and Kumar 2018: 79). This set of tactics, as one might expect, slowly but surely began to threaten the position of the INC in India's largest state.

Under the stewardship of Indira Gandhi, and as previously discussed in Chapter 6, the Congress leadership started to operate with a short-term orientation during the 1980s. As one interviewee explained:

In 1980, Indira Gandhi came back to the Prime Minister's office again. But this time, rather than trying to appeal to Muslims, her government wanted to appeal to Hindus. It was a complete and major change, because now she was very uncertain.[47]

These developments – coupled with active connections between politicians and other constituents of Meerut's riot system, as well as a conducive 72.83% versus 25.30% district-level demographic divide between Hindus and Muslims (Government of Uttar Pradesh 1981) – facilitated two severe episodes of party violence in the city in September and October 1982[48] and April through July 1987.

Data on party replacement provide further support for the incentives of both the Congress and Hindu nationalists to contribute to communal violence in UP during this decade. At the time of the 1982 clashes in particular, party entry and exit rates in UP's returns from the Lok Sabha stood at a staggering 99.41%. The state assembly, admittedly, was significantly more stable with a replacement level of 10.47% in 1980. However, the CM Sripati Misra was known to be "one of the weakest in the state's history": not only was he at the helm of a government that was mired by several factional divisions, but he also had little to no latitude to "do anything of political importance" without

---

[47] Interview with an academic, Meerut, August 23, 2013.
[48] Varshney and Wilkinson (2004) list this incident as two separate events in their dataset, which began on September 6 and September 29, respectively. I follow Brass (2004), however, who has offered the most in-depth account of communal riots in Meerut, and who studied this episode as one lengthy Hindu–Muslim riot.

the express approval of "the Prime Minister or her son, Rajiv Gandhi, or other close associates of the ruling family in New Delhi" (Brass 2004: 4847). Thus, as a "communal mentality" virtually swept through the organization,[49] Misra found himself lacking in both "the will" and "the capacity to issue the necessary orders to bring the rioting to an end" (Brass 2004: 4847). This was despite the fact that he was in charge of the Home portfolio, which explicitly empowered him to maintain law and order in UP.

Whereas the Congress in Indira Gandhi's final years came to view communal riots as a strategy through which it could make vote gains in the short term, for the relatively new BJP, violence offered a pathway for carving out a key electoral domain. Given its lack of organizational heft, however, during the early 1980s, it was the Vishwa Hindu Parishad (VHP) and Rashtriya Swayamsevak Sangh (RSS) that took on much of the onus of pursuing political violence. In fact, not only did these groups step up their activities in various parts of India, but they even took to organizing a statewide agitation in UP to drive wedges between Hindus and Muslims for the BJP's electoral benefit (Engineer 1982).

Against this broader background, the violence in Meerut in 1982 originated as many such incidents do from patently local events: in this case, a dispute "over a piece of municipal land in the crowded area of Shahghasa" (Graff and Galonnier 2013a; Brass 2004). This site was competitively claimed as both a *mazar*, or the tomb of a Muslim saint, as well as the location of a Hindu temple (Graff and Galonnier 2013a; Brass 2004). Furthermore, according to a crucial government report (Government of Uttar Pradesh 1987), the alleged killing of a Hindu priest in Shahghasa in September 1982 also contributed to the riots.

Once these varied claims emerged, the constituents of Meerut's institutionalized riot network summarily latched onto them to advance their interests. On the one hand, Hindu nationalist politicians and religious leaders inflamed the passions of their local co-ethnics through incendiary speeches and various other incitements (Brass 2004). For example, Mohan Lal Kapoor, a former BJP MLA from the Meerut Vidhan Sabha constituency, mobilized a large group of angry demonstrators in a march against the administration's alleged anti-Hindu stance (Chawla 1982). On the other hand, "the Congress(I) incumbent MP, Mohsina Kidwai, and [former INC] MP, Shahnawaz Khan," both from the Meerut Lok Sabha constituency, sought to create their own "Muslim response to Hindu provocations" (Tatsumi 2009: 119; Engineer 1997a). All the while, the police and Provincial Armed Constabulary (PAC) "acted with impunity and deliberateness [and] slaughter[ed] Muslims of both sexes" (Brass 2004: 4847), even as local criminals ran amok throughout the city (Government of Uttar Pradesh 1987).

The worst violence during the 1982 riots occurred at the Feroze Building in the Bhumia ka Pul locality where anywhere from 29 to 42 lives were lost to countless PAC bullets on October 2 (Chisti 1982; Engineer 1982; Graff and

---

[49] Interview with an SP politician, Meerut, August 21, 2013.

Galonnier 2013a). Cumulatively, the riots claimed 42 (Varshney-Wilkinson dataset 2004) to 85 (Brass 2004) lives. Yet, Meerut's deadliest riot occurred a little over four years later between April and July 1987.

By this time, the Sangh Parivar had started to explicitly draw on the symbolic importance of the Babri Masjid to advance its electoral agenda in India (Pai and Kumar 2018). In Uttar Pradesh, specifically, this campaign – which emphasized the Ayodhya issue as well as "historical injustices done to Hindus" – slowly tapped into "antigovernment sentiment" against four decades of Congress rule (Hasan 1996: 84). At the same time, Hindu nationalists also benefited from tacit and active "cooperation from the state machinery" to pursue their political goals in UP (Hasan 1996: 83). For example, in January 1982, when RSS chief Balasaheb Deoras visited Meerut city mere months before the September riots, both the Superintendent of Police (SP) and Additional District Magistrate (ADM) saluted him in public (Engineer 1982).

The increasing strength of the BJP was mirrored by the dramatic erosion of the Congress base, and two challenges of the 1980s warrant particular consideration here. First, in UP, the April 1984 birth of the Bahujan Samaj Party (BSP) threatened the INC's long-standing projection of itself as "a party of the minorities" (Chandra 2000: 27). As shown earlier in Figure 7.2, the entry of such new parties contributed to an increase in party replacement levels – in both the state assembly and in returns from the national parliament – between the mid- and late 1980s. Second, the October 1984 assassination of Indira Gandhi led to grave concerns about the INC's ability to hold onto its "newly won gains" (Thompson 2012: 211).

In December 1984, the Congress successfully weathered these storms: Rajiv Gandhi rode a wave of sympathy in the wake of his mother's death and secured a "crushing victory" for the party in the national elections (Harriss 2010: 59). However, this was also the Lok Sabha contest around which party replacement in India reached an all-time high of 81.27%, and Rajiv's regime thus came to be marked by the same "strong communal overtones" as that of his mother (Pai and Kumar 2018: 70).

It was amidst these circumstances – wherein "political Hinduism [was] acquir[ing] unprecedented strength" and "the Congress as the principal actor in Uttar Pradesh politics" was declining and less committed to moderation – that the 1987 riots erupted across Meerut (Hasan 1996: 81, 84). The clashes escalated in two waves.[50] In the first phase, a fracas between two Muslim groups over the display of fireworks around Shab-e-Barat allegedly triggered violence in the month of April (Engineer 1987; Government of Uttar Pradesh 1987). This occasion is meant to commemorate the day on which the Prophet Muhammad entered the holy city of Mecca. During the melee, an on-duty police officer reportedly suffered some injuries (Engineer 1987). He angrily

---

[50] Interview with a civil society leader, Meerut, March 1, 2013; also see Engineer 1987; Government of Uttar Pradesh 1987; Schneider 2004.

responded by opening fire on the revelers, and in so doing, killed "two Muslims on the spot" (Engineer 1987: 969). According to existing accounts, this period of violence claimed the lives of 10 (Government of Uttar Pradesh 1987) to 12 individuals (Engineer 1987), and caused injuries to some 40 others (Varshney-Wilkinson 2004 dataset).

The second, and far more deadly, round of conflict in Meerut began on May 18, 1987.[51] Across several sources, the reported precipitant that unleashed the clashes in May has been variously described as an arson attack on a local Muslim weaver's stall (Engineer 1987: 970) or sports good store (Government of Uttar Pradesh 1987) to the destruction of a sweetmeat shop and the murder of its Hindu owner (Engineer 1987: 970; Government of Uttar Pradesh 1987; Schneider 2004: 64). According to one of my interviewees, who traced the riots to the last set of circumstances listed above, the confectioner in question was killed at 8pm on May 18, 1987.[52] At 6am the next morning, the violence in Meerut claimed the life of its second victim, a young doctor and the son of my respondent.[53]

Between these two events, an explosion also reportedly rocked the town (Engineer 1987; Schneider 2004). Violent Hindu mobs then quickly began to exert pressure on the district administration "to take immediate and firm action [against those] responsible for the [previous night's] arson and murder" (Government of Uttar Pradesh 1987). As this groundswell gained momentum across Meerut, the police and PAC stormed the Muslim-dominated Hashimpura area at some point between 11pm on May 18 (Engineer 1987: 970) and 2am and 3am on May 19 (Government of Uttar Pradesh 1987).

Once there, the authorities placed a large number of civilians under arrest (Engineer 1987; Government of Uttar Pradesh 1987; Schneider 2004). It is further reported that their actions resulted in the deaths of several Muslim residents, including a young girl (Engineer 1987; Government of Uttar Pradesh 1987; Schneider 2004). Meanwhile, messages blared through the nearby Imliyan mosque's loudspeakers, calling on citizens to resist the police and PAC (Engineer 1987; Government of Uttar Pradesh 1987). As Engineer (1987: 970) writes, these appeals only "added to the gravity of the situation" in Hashimpura on that fateful night.

The next morning, district officials put all of Meerut city under curfew. According to the Gian Prakash Committee report (Government of Uttar Pradesh 1987) – a group that was constituted under the leadership of bureaucrat Gian Prakash after the state government came under the "pressure of strong public opinion" (Engineer 1988: 30) to investigate the riots – "only some sporadic incidents [and] retaliatory [conflict] ensued" after 11am on May 19. However, expert accounts document that the curfew actually provided free rein to "the

---

[51] Interview with a civil society leader, Meerut, March 1, 2013; also see Schneider 2004.
[52] Interview with a civil society leader, Meerut, March 1, 2013.
[53] Ibid.

PAC and the Hindu mobs" to unleash conflict throughout the town (Engineer 1987: 970). Members of both the RSS and VHP thus operated without any restraints in the month of May, and their activities remained unchecked until May 23 (Government of Uttar Pradesh 1987; Engineer 1987; Tatsumi 2009).

Much like the 1982 Meerut riots, the Hashimpura massacres occurred with the express knowledge and complicity of the CM of Uttar Pradesh, Vir Bahadur Singh. After a Congress MP advised him to withdraw the PAC from Meerut, Singh casually "brushed aside" his colleague's suggestion (Engineer 1987: 969). Worse still, a number of documented attacks on Muslims' homes and shops took place when "the Chief Minister was present in the town" (Engineer 1987: 969). In fact, one of my respondents recalled that on May 19, Singh had ordered members of the district administration to take any and all actions necessary to keep local Muslims in line.[54]

In acting in this manner, the Chief Minister appeared to align with the expectations of party higher-ups in New Delhi, who reportedly "wanted to teach Muslims a lesson for not voting for the Congress" in the 1985 assembly elections and supporting rival organizations such as the Lok Dal (LKD) instead (Engineer 1987: 969; Balagopal 1988; Mander 2018). In this vein, it has also come to light that Singh's colleague and INC MP Mohsina Kidwai "abetted the ongoing violence" in a presumed reaction to the fact that non-Muslims, as opposed to Muslims, had voted in favor of her candidacy for the Meerut constituency seat in the 1984 Lok Sabha elections (Tatsumi 2009: 138).

Shortly after the events of May 18 and 19, the PAC returned to Hashimpura on May 22 and placed "more than 300 persons" under arrest (Engineer 1987: 970). It is further reported that the officers then killed "40–42 [of these] individuals" and dumped their bodies in a nearby canal (Times of India 2000). One of my interviewees, who was 17 years old at the time, recalled the day's events in chilling detail:

That day, May 22, 1987, was a day of Friday prayers, and it must have been around 2pm at the time. My father and I had been sitting in the courtyard of a neighbor's house. Suddenly, we heard a voice from outside and a banging on the door saying, "Open the door! We are police officers and we are conducting a search." So, we opened the door and the police entered. The military police, the PAC, [and] the women's police were all there. They brought all the men who were seated inside [their homes] to the outside and left the women where they were [inside their houses]. They searched everything: our boxes, our suitcases, whatever items we had. They searched it all and they kept us all seated away from our possessions. I think we must have been 100 to 150 men who were lined up in the lane. When they finished their search, they told us, "Okay, now we need to talk to all of you in front of Shahpeer Gate so put up your hands and stand up." So, we stood up in a line and from there we made our way to Hapur Road. There [was] a *peepal* tree there and we were made to sit underneath it.[55] And [it was] there

---

[54] Ibid.
[55] The *peepal* is a species of fig native to the South Asian region.

[that] I saw that whoever was young – let's say above 22 or 24 years of age – [those individuals] were made to sit on one side and the elderly and young children were made to sit separately. Then, I saw a PAC vehicle arrive and it looked like they were maybe sending the young people to jail. I think that there were approximately 400 or 500 people at that place, according to my estimation. I saw that some people from among them were being sent to jail. The others who were left were the elderly and the children. We were told, "You all can go home now. Walk back in a line." So, again, we formed a line. But [now,] if there was a healthy young person or [even] someone over 50 years of age who was healthy, [these individuals] were made to sit on one side. In that group, among us, there must have been 52 to 54 people. After that, when everyone else had been released and gone home, then one yellow colored PAC vehicle arrived and we were asked to sit in it. So, we all sat in it. And then, as we were being driven, we saw that there were some PAC officers sitting in the cabin of the vehicle and other PAC *jawans* who were sitting with us.[56] [There must have been] two dozen or so of them. And then, they took us near a canal and they stopped the vehicle near a bridge. They made one man alight and they shot him. A big commotion began. [We realized,] "Oh! They are shooting [us]!" So, what happened is that they then started shooting us in the truck itself. Lots of people died. I was also struck by a bullet in my side. 15 to 20 or 25 men were killed like that. After that, they turned the vehicle and stopped another car that was waiting at a red light. They told the driver that this was an encounter and that we were all miscreants. From there, we were taken to the Hindon river where we must have been 15-17 individuals. I was also among them. They held our arms to get us off the truck. Two of them held our arms and a third officer unflinchingly shot at us with a rifle. After shooting at us, they would dump us in the canal. Once they had shot all of us, they took the truck and left. For an hour or an hour and fifteen minutes, I just hid like that in the canal. Some 43 men were killed like this. Only five or six of us survived.[57]

A second respondent, who was eight to 10 years old in 1987, described his experiences as follows:

My father also died in that violence. It was the afternoon or the evening. They [the police and the PAC] came and banged on all our doors continuously. I was with my father at the time. When they banged on the door, they also yelled at us and abused us saying, "Come out or we will shoot you!" When I looked at him, I saw that my father had started to cry. He removed his watch and gave it to my mother. And then he left. We never saw him again after that day. We have not even recovered his body. We found out later from people in the neighborhood that he had been in that same vehicle that was taken to the canal. That is how we learned of his death.[58]

Eventually, anywhere from 117 (Engineer 1988: 30) to 329 (Brass 2004: 4840) civilian lives were lost in Meerut, and interviewees held that the short-term orientations of various political leaders crucially enabled the violence in Hashimpura. As one respondent explained:

---

[56] The term *jawan* here refers to a junior officer.
[57] Interview with a survivor of the Hashimpura massacres, Meerut, August 24, 2013.
[58] Interview with a witness to the Hashimpura arrests, Meerut, August 24, 2013.

Riot Violence in India's Hyderabad and Meerut Cities

On the one hand, you had the politicians who wanted to eliminate the Congress. They had only one goal: to eliminate the Congress. Some of them started to work on the plight of the Scheduled Castes and tried to mobilize them. And then, you had leaders who tried to mobilize Muslims telling them, "You aren't going to get anything. This Congress is only here to claim your votes. It does this and that to you." So, the Congress [as a result of all these strategies] was left with a very small vote base.... And then leaders turned to creating a communal frenzy because they were desperate.... The Congress did it to try and survive. But other issues that hadn't really been touched since 1947 – like issues about temples and mosques – from the 1980s onwards, they were animated [as well]. Action, then reaction.... They [the BJP] started the *Ramjanmabhoomi* movement in a big way at that time [as well].[59]

In addition to the considerable loss of human life, the riots caused record levels of damage to relations between the town's Hindu and Muslim communities. A leader of the local weavers' association, for example, held that the massacres left "the entire city divided and devastated."[60] Likewise, an academic recalled that the consequences of the riot were "not only economic, [as] Meerut was left ethnically segregated as well."[61]

But the staggering scale of the carnage also notably engendered a strong will among the town's residents not to succumb to communal provocations again. As one interviewee put it, "people do not want violence anymore. They have seen what the effects of such fighting can be."[62] Two others went into greater detail and contextualized the perspectives of ordinary citizens:

Hindus and Muslims both do not want riots now. They lost crores [many millions] everyday due to [violence]. No one wants riots here anymore.... Citizens have become smarter about the fact that leaders are the ones who entice them to participate in violence, but now they want peace.[63]

When riots occurred here in the past, especially in 1987, it was the ordinary people who suffered while the politicians benefited. So, we learned not to fall prey to these polarization efforts again3. Now, too, there are efforts at polarizing voters along Hindu–Muslim lines, but I believe that a large-scale riot is unlikely to occur here, and that's because ordinary people are not going to get riled up by these tactics.[64]

Finally, a politician from the Congress party summarized the main developments in the city:

The 1987 riot was the worst riot. Not only in Meerut, but probably in the nation's history, it remains the worst riot. We still get shivers even today when we hear the words "Hashimpura riots." In the 1987 violence, countless people lost their lives. Since then, too, small riots in Meerut continue to occur, but I am of the opinion that the people of

---

[59] Interview with an SP politician, Meerut, August 21, 2013.
[60] Interview with a leader of the Weavers' Welfare Association, Meerut, August 23, 2013.
[61] Interview with an academic, Meerut, February 27, 2013.
[62] Interview with a leader of the Boolean Jewelry Traders Association, Meerut, August 22, 2013.
[63] Interview with an academic, Meerut, March 1, 2013.
[64] Interview with a local businessman, Meerut, August 22, 2013.

Meerut took a lesson from that communal riot. And the people started to believe that "if we do this [engage in violence], all our work and businesses will come to a standstill. We will have to bear all kinds of costs." So, a [new] thinking [has] developed among the people.[65]

In the 1989 assembly elections that immediately followed these riots, Meerut's voters and citizens across UP roundly punished the INC, which not only lost 185 seats but also saw the Janata Dal (JD) rise to power in the state.[66] One respondent summarized this defeat in the following words: "the 1987 Meerut riots surely contributed to the [Congress] party's decline."[67] Meanwhile, there is also suggestive evidence that even though it didn't emerge victorious at this time, the decisions of the Congress "provided room" for the appeals of the BJP to gain traction in Uttar Pradesh (Pai and Kumar 2018: 18).

Quiescence in Meerut amidst Enduring Polarization since 1992

Since the Hashimpura massacres, Hindu–Muslim clashes in Meerut have decreased significantly in both their frequency and intensity. Apart from two riots in November 1990 and May 1991, which claimed the lives of 12 and 32 individuals, respectively, all of the city's remaining communal episodes have resulted in death tolls in the single digits (Brass 2004: 4840). Furthermore, as far as I am aware, the last lethal communal incident in Meerut occurred in the summer of 2004 and resulted in the relatively low fatality count of two lives lost (Engineer 2005). This diminution in violence is notable in light of the repeated appearance of "many precipitants" in Meerut city, and my work suggests that the comparatively high levels of party stability help in part to explain this development (Schneider 2004: 56). Indeed, since 1991, mean party birth and death rates in UP's returns from the Lok Sabha have stood at a low 7.74%, while those in its assembly have clocked in at 4%.

Owing to this re-equilibration, political elites have been compelled to recalibrate their strategies to win over and maintain the support of urban voters in a demographically mixed city. As one police officer explained:

[Small] communal incidents [may] take place from time to time, but big riots are now unlikely. A major reason for the reduction [in] communal riots [in Meerut] is there is a lot of awareness among the people. They [ordinary citizens] suffered a lot during previous riots. Political reasons are there [for communal violence]. People [politicians] bank upon their vote bank and they try to encash a particular section of the [citizenry]. For that also there is awareness among the people [now]. Earlier, [there were] those who were interested in [organizing] communal riots, [but] those groups can no longer encash

---

[65] Interview with an INC politician, Meerut, August 21, 2013.
[66] Interview with an academic, Meerut, August 23, 2013; interview with a BJP politician, Meerut, August 25, 2013.
[67] Interview with an SP politician, Meerut, August 21, 2013.

Riot Violence in India's Hyderabad and Meerut Cities

upon the common man. In fact, if a riot happens now, people are very clear: whosoever is responsible, they [citizens] are willing to turn against him or her and are [ready] to vote for someone else in the next election.[68]

These reassessments also seem to have resulted in important changes in the relationship between parties and criminal outfits. Specifically, even though "the gangs [of the 1980s] still exist, they are not affiliated with any parties [anymore]."[69] In a similar vein, Brass (2004: 483) argued in 2004 that Meerut's "institutionalized riot system" had entered a discernible state of "dormancy" during the prior decade.

Of course, none of this is to deny that many politicians continue to view and employ strategies of communal polarization to maintain and advance their political positions. Furthermore, a considerable body of work now shows that the BJP's rise to office in UP is both driven by and leading to anti-minority attacks across the state (Pai and Kumar 2018; D. Basu 2021). It shouldn't surprise us, then, that Meerut is still a "communally sensitive place," as one respondent described.[70] In fact, in the weeks prior to my arrival for fieldwork, the city witnessed a troubling, albeit increasingly familiar, example of ongoing efforts to polarize the electorate along religious lines.

These efforts unfolded around the festival of Ramzan in 2013. In the lead-up to this month, Muslims had appealed to the administration to permit them to pray out on the streets on Friday evenings, citing the overcrowding of local mosques in Meerut. While officials were still considering this request in July, Hindu politicians and religious leaders organized a prayer ceremony at a Shiva temple in the center of the city. They deliberately held this event on a Friday, allegedly to counter various *Jummah* congregations.[71] Devotional songs, known as *bhajans*, blared through the temple's loudspeakers, and BJP subleaders, such as MLA Satya Prakash Agarwal from the Meerut Cantonment constituency and Sangeet Som from Sardhana constituency, reportedly led their followers in prayer.[72]

When asked about these events, one Hindu nationalist politician who was present at the scene clarified his intentions:

We only went there to pray. If the Muslims have a right to pray in public, out on the streets and in such large numbers, then we Hindus should also be able to pray as we please and when we please. You must also ask, where did this Muslim demand come from? They have never asked to pray outside like this before. It has never happened. So,

---

[68] Interview with a senior police officer, Meerut, August 21, 2013.
[69] Interview with an academic, Meerut, March 2, 2013.
[70] Interview with an INC politician, Meerut, August 21, 2013; interview with a retired civil servant, Meerut, August 22, 2013.
[71] Interview with a journalist, Meerut, August 24, 2013.
[72] Ibid.; interview with a BJP politician, Meerut, August 25, 2013. Meerut Cantonment and Sardhana are two of seven Vidhan Sabha constituencies that fall within the broader Meerut district.

obviously, their leaders were involved in pushing for this cause. And if their leaders can ask like this, then we too must push for the causes and rights of the Hindus. But let me tell you that no one – neither their leaders nor us – no one wanted riots to happen that day. We don't want to see Hindu–Muslim violence in this city anymore. Things may have been tense on that day, but they were also entirely peaceful.[73]

As Pai and Kumar (2018: 205) write, however, even though major riots do not seem to be part of the agenda, events of this low-level and quotidian nature are certainly part of "a long, well-planned, competitive, and communally aggressive campaign" of the BJP to achieve grassroots support for its Hindu nationalist project. Other examples of such everyday mobilization in Meerut include vociferous objections to the construction of a mosque in the Shastri Nagar neighborhood, which ultimately prevailed and resulted in the cancellation of the project.[74] Taken together, then, it is now clear that even as Narendra Modi and his colleagues redefined Hindutva "ideology [to] include[e] rapid economic development" in 2014, the BJP "did not abandon" – but rather continues to expressly use – "its strategy of communal mobilization to secure the Hindu vote" (Pai and Kumar 2018: 206–207).

Everyday Communal Mobilization and Rising Party Violence in Rural Uttar Pradesh

The retention of this communal agenda is also marked by some important shifts in party violence, such as the rise of conflict in rural areas. In recent years, the Muzaffarnagar and Shamli riots have emerged as one of the most notorious examples of the changing landscape of conflict in India. However, it bears noting that targeted attacks against Muslims – as witnessed for example through cow vigilante assaults – are also on a dramatic upswing (Basu 2021; Basu 2021; Jaffrey 2021). Notably, these incidents seem to be escalating due to the same broader Sangh Parivar tactics as those responsible for rural riots.

As Pai and Kumar (2018: 182) document, Hindu nationalists are now deliberately pursuing communalism "in carefully selected new social and economic contexts ... which had not experienced large-scale and violent riots earlier." To break up prior alliances between Muslims and other Hindu castes – such as agricultural Jats – in western UP, the party has also used worsening agrarian decline since the 2000s to its benefit, as seen in the cases of Muzaffarnagar and Shamli (Pai and Kumar 2018). One respondent who had conducted research in this region drew on precisely these ground-level factors to account for the riots of 2013:

At the time that we went [to the region for fieldwork], the polarization was very sharp, especially vis-à-vis the Jats and the Muslims.... Inasmuch as the Jats dominate and the lower Hindu castes depend on the Jats for very many things, they also seemed to be

---

[73] Interview with a BJP politician, Meerut, August 25, 2013.
[74] Interview with a civil society leader, Meerut, March 1, 2013.

aligned with them, but not really on their own initiative, you know.... We did have reasons to believe that [this was instead because of] concerns regarding the issues of bread and butter, the agrarian concerns, the price of sugar, sugar mills not opening [etc].[75]

In a similar vein, a leader from the INC explained incidents of communal violence in villages as part of a far longer BJP calculus to make electoral gains in India's largest state:

The communal forces are making Uttar Pradesh a key domain where they want to carry out communal division. Look, there never used to be communal tensions in villages. The village was a strong example of brotherhood. One did not even know if a Muslim lived here or a Hindu lived here. One did not even know this. But today, the communal forces are turning Uttar Pradesh into their domain, and they want communal division. That's why every day, you are hearing about some small incident or the other. There is a boy walking by the stream, beat him up! Then both communities get aggravated. There is a new roundabout in the city, there are fights at roundabouts every day! There is a roundabout under construction, someone stops you at the roundabout, and that becomes a matter of communal tension: this community versus that community.... So, now what one does not understand is [communal incidents] are occurring in villages. One could never even have thought they would happen in villages! These circumstances are very grave circumstances, especially in a country like India where both communities must live together.... Earlier, these incidents used to happen in cities. Now if they are happening in villages, there must be some communal force behind them. And who that communal force is, everyone knows.... This is a pure campaign to divide society and they are being quite successful in that quest.[76]

Several years removed from the Muzaffarnagar and Shamli riots, the involvement of key BJP elites – such as Sangeet Som and Sanjeev Baliyan – in the clashes of 2013 is now well known. Both these leaders were not only present at the September *mahapanchayat* in Muzaffarnagar – previously discussed in Chapter 1 – but Som allegedly even shared a fake video in late August "of a Muslim mob lynching two Hindu youths" to prepare the ground for communal conflict (Pai and Kumar 2018: 233; Raghuvanshi 2015; Malik 2021). In addition to their direct involvement, BSP politician and former Muzaffarnagar MP Kadir Rana reportedly also contributed to the riots by delivering incendiary speeches in Muzaffarnagar (Raghuvanshi 2015).

For each of these parties, the macro-level goal in the run-up to the 2014 general elections was clearly an electoral one. However, the particular groups that party leaders hoped to win over through violence differed considerably. Specifically, whereas the BJP sought to use communal conflict to bring Jats into its broader Hindu voting bloc, BSP leaders organized their *mahapanchayat* around injustices that Muslims had faced under the regime of the Samajwadi Party, so as to woo community members away from the SP. Despite these efforts, the party failed to capture a single seat in the general elections, as

---

[75] Interview with an academic, New Delhi, December 15, 2015.
[76] Interview with an INC leader, Meerut, August 21, 2013.

communal rather than caste-based identities occupied center stage in 2014 (Pai 2014). Finally, Chief Minister Akhilesh Yadav's government hedged its bets on coming in at the eleventh hour and positioning itself as the "best guarantor of [Muslims'] security," a calculation that ultimately failed.[77]

Despite the involvement – both active and tacit – of all these parties, only the BJP benefited electorally from the clashes in Muzaffarnagar and Shamli. In addition to the considerable increase in its seat share as previously described in Chapter 1, individual politicians also drew rich electoral dividends from the riots. According to Vaishnav (2017: 285), Lok Sabha candidate Sanjeev Baliyan won the Muzaffarnagar constituency seat "in spite – indeed, perhaps *because* – of his [role in] inciting the violent riots." Meanwhile, even though Som was arrested by the state police for his role in the clashes in September 2013, he was subsequently released on bail, and in 2021, a special court in Muzaffarnagar accepted the report of a special investigation team (SIT) of the UP police – in a now BJP-ruled state – to close the case against him. He also retained the Sardhana constituency MLA seat in UP's 2017 state elections.

Qualitative data further show that the BJP organized the Muzaffarnagar and Shamli riots carefully and mindfully with an eye toward the future. The targeting of villages was central to this long-term orientation. As one interviewee explained:

This riot was a contribution of the BJP.... Some political people ... they are MPs and MLAs today ... they started by inciting small fights and then it [the tension] kept increasing. From there, it took the form of the *panchayat*. First, there was the small *panchayat* meeting. Then, there was the *mahapanchayat*.... [So,] this riot was manufactured! And, this is the first time that the riot began in villages. Earlier, riots used to move from cities to villages, but this time it was organized in the villages. It was done very deliberately to peel off Jats and get them towards the party [BJP] as voters. It was a long-term strategy.[78]

In addition to pursuing strategies to swing Jats to their side, BJP elites also wagered on the idea that rural citizens' lower exposure to riots would make them less likely to engage in sanctioning. Owing to these calibrated tactics of everyday communalization as well as the lower likelihood of sanctioning around rural riots, villages in UP now face acute risks of witnessing party violence. As two interviewees noted:

We already know that Indian cities are polarized. In Meerut, the Hindu–Muslim divide is still deep, but parties know that they will suffer losses if they organize a riot. So, now everything is turning on what happens in the villages. The voting patterns are more or less predictable in cities. It's the rural areas that matter and elites can easily organize riots there.[79]

---

[77] Interview with a village leader, Kakhda village, Muzaffarnagar, December 21, 2015; interview with a Muslim religious leader, Muzaffarnagar, December 21, 2015.
[78] Interview with an SP politician, Muzaffarnagar, December 18, 2015.
[79] Interview with an academic, New Delhi, December 17, 2013.

They [rural voters] don't understand the costs and benefits of riots for politicians [just yet]. They only look at one thing: which party is saying that it will take care of me. So, they are very easily instigated. [I]t can be done in a second, and this instigation is what causes trouble. Until now, riots have affected cities. But these riots [Muzaffarnagar and Shamli] started in the villages and they impacted the villages. And I expect that this trend will continue into the future.[80]

Along with such incidents, and also due to their relatively risk-free nature (A. Basu 2021; D. Basu 2021), recent trends suggest that targeted and individual attacks against Muslims are likely to further escalate in the future. As Varshney (2017) writes, major riots in cities today stand to "upset those who voted for the BJP for economics, governance, and Modi's leadership [and] not for its Hindu nationalist ideology." But other forms of conflict, including the "murder, coercion, and harassment" of minorities as well as "the destruction of homes, businesses, and places of worship" do not come with the same dangers (A. Basu 2021: 277). Overall, then, it bears restating that even as party stabilization has disincentivized the instrumentalization and sponsorship of severe riots, the possibilities and opportunities for other forms of party violence have actually widened in India in recent years.

ENDOGENEITY CONCERNS

As in Kenya, this book finds that rates of party replacement in India have informed elites' incentives to orchestrate or sponsor communal violence rather than the other way around. The multi-method approach adopted herein helps to establish the direction of this relationship in three key ways. First, and at the national level, I find that strong party organization and INC hegemony prevented rapid party birth and death prior to the late 1970s and mid-1980s. Moreover, it was only *after* the precipitous escalation of party instability after this time that major riots became a recurring phenomenon in the country.

Second, and at the subnational level, data from Hyderabad in Andhra Pradesh and Meerut in Uttar Pradesh also provide support for this claim. Concretely, these data reveal that replacement volatility in AP's Lok Sabha returns increased from 15.82% in 1977 to 42.86% in 1984. Meanwhile, party birth and death in the Vidhan Sabha grew from 15.83% in 1978 to 39.8% in 1983. As previously discussed, it was precisely during this period that politically-orchestrated communal riots, such as the Rameeza Bee clashes, dramatically surged in Hyderabad. Likewise, Lok Sabha replacement rates in UP rose from less than 10% in 1971 to over 99% in 1980. Nearly a decade later in 1989, these levels remained extremely high at 41.18%. Similarly, Type A volatility in the state assembly increased from 6.48% in 1974 to 78.17% in 1977. In 1989, the Vidhan Sabha recorded a party replacement level of 36.94%. As discussed in prior pages of this book, it was during this time of

[80] Interview with a journalist, Muzaffarnagar, December 19, 2015.

extreme levels of party instability in Uttar Pradesh that towns such as Meerut and Moradabad fell prey to severe communal clashes in the 1980s.

Third and finally, qualitative interviews substantiate the link between party instability and political violence in India. These data show that riots have become costly for elites since the stabilization of the party system three decades ago. As an activist affiliated with the Bajrang Dal – a group that is actively involved in everyday communalization – in Hyderabad explained:

People [politicians] can do all sorts of things for politics. What the political leaders want to do for their own interests, what is it that they want to do, when to do what, these are [the] elite-level decisions that can lead to riots. So, if they want, they can make riots happen again. But now they won't do it, because riots in Hyderabad are costly to them. The riots can break the parties. In those years [between the late 1970s and early 1990s], the riots could make the parties because there were so many small parties everywhere. But not today. Things are very different now.[81]

Likewise, an academic from Meerut noted:

The calculations of politicians have changed. Political leaders depend on voters, and voters do not want any more riots. So, the politicians also cannot take the risk because it can cost their parties. [As a result,] the police are also under pressure to keep communal violence under check.[82]

There is also considerable qualitative evidence that ordinary individuals have learned about elites' involvement in large-scale communal episodes in India over the course of time. According to a respondent from Meerut, for example, following the 1987 Hashimpura massacres, residents became "more aware of the root causes of riots."[83] Specifically, they recognized that such clashes had "occurred so that [some] political parties could come to power."[84] Voters further developed an intolerance for parties responsible for violence as a result of these experiences. As one interviewee put it, citizens arrived at a consensus that "no good [can] come from riots [breaking out again]."[85]

Nevertheless, it is important to acknowledge that as per public opinion data, issues pertaining to corruption, economic growth, and inflation far outrank matters relating to communalism in the minds of Indian voters today (Vaishnav 2015; CSDS 2014, 2019). Subnational data from states such as UP likewise showed that ordinary citizens viewed development, price rise, corruption, unemployment, and the condition of roads as their most pressing concerns in 2014 (Ahmed 2014). These data perhaps help to explain the BJP's explicitly development-oriented campaign around that contest. The fact that the party has increasingly turned to mobilizing low-level communal events, as

---

[81] Interview with a Bajrang Dal activist, Hyderabad, August 4, 2013.
[82] Interview with an academic, Meerut, February 28, 2013.
[83] Interview with a religious leader, Meerut, March 1, 2013.
[84] Interview with a Rashtriya Lok Dal (RLD) leader, Meerut, August 23, 2013.
[85] Interview with a police officer, Meerut, August 21, 2013.

opposed to major riots, also points to its sensitivity as a stable organization to steer clear of instrumentalizing or sponsoring severe episodes of party violence. Finally, even though Hindu nationalists have consistently benefited from communal conflict in India, the punishment suffered by other parties such as the BSP and SP helps to underscore that politicians across the board share strong incentives against driving major episodes of Hindu–Muslim violence in the country today.

Taken together, then, the totality of the data demonstrates that rising rates of party replacement have preceded rather than followed high-intensity waves of communal clashes in India. Moreover, due to the stabilization of the country's political parties over the last three decades, elites' incentives for organizing or supporting severe riots have accordingly declined.

SUMMARY AND CONCLUSION

Expanding upon the national-level insights previously provided in Chapter 6, this chapter has proffered a subnational accounting of trajectories of party violence in Hyderabad and Meerut cities. It has shown that many severe riots in both places broke out amidst rising rates of party instability and the short-term orientations of politicians. These orientations not only encumbered the decisions of leaders from a declining Congress, but also became observable among elites affiliated with the INC's national and regional rivals in Andhra Pradesh and Uttar Pradesh. The chapter has further argued that the communal quiescence seen in these cities from the early 1990s onward can be attributed to the stabilization of many of their parties since the late 1980s. This stabilization has dampened the willingness of politicians to gamble with organizing large-scale violence. Finally, my qualitative interviews reveal that voters in Hyderabad and Meerut display an acute displeasure about major past riots as well as an intolerance toward the escalation of severe clashes in the future. Competing on the backs of relatively stable parties, many politicians in India have little choice but to pay attention to these attitudes.

At the same time, however, it is vital to note that the reduction in severe riots is countered by a marked increase in lower-level clashes, targeted attacks against Muslims, and rural incidents of conflict. Drawing on evidence from Uttar Pradesh, this chapter has argued that episodes of this nature are now escalating for several reasons: they are easier to manage than major riots, present lower risks to Hindu nationalist politicians, and still offer pathways to the BJP to further consolidate and extend its majoritarian mandate (Pai and Kumar 2018; D. Basu 2021; Jaffrey 2021). Thus, where the Kenyan case provides crucial insights about the possible risks of party violence in unstable party settings, evidence from India shows how conflict can take new shapes and forms in places populated by stable parties. A party instability framework in which levels of party fragility exert a *conditioning*, rather than causal, effect on elites' decisions about violence thus helps us to account for locations and modalities of conflict that might seem otherwise surprising to researchers. Concretely, in the Indian context, this framework reveals that as party instability levels have dropped, politicians have not entirely abandoned conflict. Instead, they have carefully revised their choices about where and how to orchestrate violence. Adjustments of this nature have allowed them to sidestep the intolerance of voters for destabilizing episodes of political conflict, an attitude that has developed over some time in cities like Hyderabad and Meerut.

In Chapter 8, I evaluate the explanatory power of my argument about the conditioning effect of party instability on elites' choices about conflict by turning to cases beyond Kenya and India and investigating party violence in Ghana and Turkey. The selection of these cases also helps me to assess the alternative explanation about the influence of democratic age on politicians' decisions about conflict.

8

Party Instability and Political Violence
Comparative Insights from Ghana and Turkey

To what extent does the central claim of this book – that party instability incentivizes political violence – extend beyond the main cases of Kenya and India? Furthermore, how might differences in democratic age serve to explain variations in party violence within and across countries? In addressing these important questions, this chapter leverages a cross-regional comparison of patterns of political conflict in Ghana and Turkey. Together, these cases help to show how party instability – beyond democratic longevity – can independently condition elites' incentives to organize or sponsor party violence.

The first case examined in this chapter – Ghana – is a relatively young democracy. It has succumbed to mild party-sponsored electoral clashes since the restoration of multiparty competition in the early 1990s (Bob-Milliar 2014; Asunka et al. 2019). By contrast, Turkey fell prey to a severe wave of conflict, known as the *anarşi* (i.e., anarchy), between 1976 and 1980. This period of violence claimed the lives of more than 5,000 individuals (Sayari 2010: 198). At the time of the crisis, Turkey had been holding multiparty elections for more than two decades.

In the coming pages, I show that the stability of political parties in Ghana has helped to keep major events of party violence at bay. Contrariwise, I demonstrate that the *anarşi* exploded across urban areas of Turkey during a time when leftist and ultranationalist groups and parties faced acute insecurities about their future survival (Sayari 2010). These comparative insights underscore that scholars should treat democratic age and party stability as distinct and separate attributes. Even though party institutionalization can occur as democracies mature, in places where parties remain unstable, I argue that democratic maturity alone will not necessarily serve to disincentivize violence.[1]

---

[1] Beyond enabling conflict, unstable parties can contribute to attenuated party-voter linkages, as seen in contexts like Brazil (Novaes 2018).

Recent work on party strength and electoral violence has come to similar conclusions. In writing about the African experience, for example, Staffan Lindberg (2007: 216) has observed that the institutionalization of "party systems has *not* occurred over an extended period of time." Meanwhile, other scholars have explicitly pointed to the weakness of African parties as a key factor in several countries' vulnerabilities to electoral violence (Mehler 2007; Mueller 2008; Wanyama and Elkit 2018). Furthermore, cross-national studies have found that "party strength cannot simply be reduced" to other variables such as levels of democracy, democratic longevity, or indicators of good governance and state capacity (Fjelde 2020: 147–148).

In addressing external validity concerns and evaluating democratic longevity as a potential confounder, I selected Ghana and Turkey as my main cases in this chapter to further the cross-regional scope of this book. Given the recent reinstatement of multiparty competition in the region, many democracies in Africa are relatively young. I thus focused on Africa in choosing a young democracy for further analysis, and the availability of robust data on both party strength and electoral violence led to my selection of the Ghanaian case. There are also relatively few older democracies in the Global South. These countries, often talked about as "deviant democracies," include places such as Botswana, Costa Rica, and until recently Turkey and India (Seeberg 2014; Klingemann 1999). The presence of party violence in Turkey – both historically and in the contemporary period – combined with its democratic age prior to recent autocratization, led to the selection of this case. Finally, to the extent that there have also been vigorous debates in Turkey about secularism versus the place of religion in public life, this case offers important parallels with India and an opportunity for better understanding how religion can become a key cleavage in elites' decisions about conflict.

Collectively, then, as shown in Figure 8.1, the country cases of Kenya, India, Ghana, and Turkey provide critical variation in the stability of political

	Unstable Political Parties	Stable Political Parties
Younger Democracies	**Kenya** High-intensity ethnic clashes (1992–2013)	**Ghana** Low-intensity electoral violence (1992–Present)
Older Democracies	**Turkey** High-intensity party-sponsored violence (1976–1980)	**India** Low-intensity ethnic riots (1991–Present)

FIGURE 8.1 Democratic longevity, party instability, and political violence in comparative perspective

parties, democratic longevity, and vulnerabilities to party violence. To begin with, both Kenya and Turkey experienced major episodes of party violence amidst highly unstable party systems. But the ages of their democracies differ considerably. Meanwhile, since the early 1990s, India and Ghana have chiefly exhibited susceptibilities to low levels of party violence despite significant differences in democratic longevity. As such, these four countries offer a fruitful selection of cases to tease out the impact of party instability versus democratic age on elites' incentives to drive or sponsor party violence.

The remainder of this chapter proceeds as follows. I begin by discussing the case of Ghana to illustrate the relationship between stable political parties and low levels of electoral violence in the West African nation. Much like in India, I show that although party conflicts do occur in Ghana from time to time, in order to minimize the possibilities of backlash, the country's elites generally make careful decisions about where and how to sponsor such violence. The second section then shifts to an examination of the Turkish case where I trace the link between party instability, which began to increase in the 1960s, and the 1976–1980 *anarşi* violence. As in Kenya, I find that politicians in Turkey were willing to gamble with political conflict due to the short time horizons with which they were operating. I develop and illustrate these arguments by drawing on data from the Social Conflict Analysis Database (SCAD version 3.3; Salehyan and Hendrix 2018) and the Varieties of Democracy project (V-Dem Institute version 9; Coppedge et al. 2019) to operationalize my dependent and independent variables, respectively. In particular, I use the V-Dem measure of political party institutionalization to capture party instability in this chapter.[2]

STABLE PARTIES AND LOW-INTENSITY ELECTORAL VIOLENCE IN GHANA (1992–PRESENT)

Ghana is an important case of a young democracy with stable political parties. According to Riedl and Dickovick (2014: 33), the nation stands out as Africa's

---

[2] The political party institutionalization variable measures the extent to which the party system of a country is institutionalized. The attributes used to build this composite measure include the "level and depth of [party] organization, links to civil society, cadres of party activists, party supporters within the electorate, coherence of party platforms and ideologies, party-line voting among representatives within the legislature" (Coppedge et al. 2019: 281). The political party institutionalization variable can take on values from 0 to 1, with higher scores reflecting higher levels of party system institutionalization. Although this measure is not identical to replacement volatility, I use it in this chapter because it captures important facets of party instability. For instance, the coherence of party platforms measures the extent to which political parties in a country develop, maintain, and publicly disseminate distinct platforms or manifestos to voters (Coppedge et al. 2019: 90). It is reasonable to expect that well-established parties will usually be more coherent than their newer and fledgling counterparts, and I argue that we should thus see a positive relationship between political party institutionalization and party replacement.

"clearest example of a competitive and coherent party system." Not only do Ghanaian parties form and compete in discernible and identifiable blocks, but members of parties across the party system also hold reasoned perceptions of the structure of political competition (Riedl 2014).

Several factors have helped Ghana to achieve this enviable degree of party coherence. Key among them are the restrictive registration requirements for individual parties (Riedl 2014). These requirements have established crucial barriers to entry and thus helped to contain new party birth, one of the main processes associated with party replacement. Consequently, it is unsurprising that breakaway or splinter factions of Ghana's two dominant parties – the National Democratic Congress (NDC) and the National People's Party (NPP) – have repeatedly failed to secure electoral influence. Indeed, as Lindsay Whitfield (2009: 630) puts it, these smaller entities have fallen short precisely due to their inabilities to "reproduce the institutional networks and loyalties" of the two major party organizations.

The 2008 elections offer a vivid illustration of such difficulties. In the run-up to those elections, both Emmanuel Ansah-Antwi and Dr. Kwabena Adjei parted ways with the NDC and formed their own parties. However, neither candidate secured more than 0.5% of the total vote in the presidential polls (Whitfield 2009). Taken together, Ghana thus exemplifies a case where key system-level measures have helped to keep party birth rates in check.

At the same time, individual parties have also devised strategies to keep new candidate entry at bay. Specifically, and in contrast to Kenya, where leaders of "briefcase parties" (Holmquist and Githinji 2009; Wanyama 2010) hand out party tickets at will, aspirants for legislative seats in Ghana are required to demonstrate that they have "nurture[ed] the constituenc[ies]" from which they seek to stand for consideration (Bob-Milliar 2019: 482). These efforts can take many different shapes and forms, including paying constituents' medical bills, sponsoring infrastructure, and championing local development (Bob-Milliar 2019). It is also worth noting that party leaders and officers in Ghana try to select candidates with a credible record of past performance and robust patronage networks to compete at the polls.

Micro-level observations of party activities corroborate these larger insights about Ghana's robust party structures. As Ichino and Nathan (2016: 7) highlight, "for nearly every one of [the nation's] 26,000 polling stations," there is a dedicated committee of NDC and NPP branch executives in place. The decentralization of party structures helps Ghanaian subleaders to "maintain accurate membership registers [at] the polling station, branch, [and] constituency levels" alike (Bob-Milliar 2019: 482). In a similar vein, George Bob-Milliar (2019) shows that the nation's parties go to great lengths to make themselves legible to constituents at the local level. Not only do their leaders seek to establish formal party headquarters across all of the country's regions, but subleaders also try to ensure that these offices are painted in party colors so as to make them visible to voters (Bob-Milliar 2019).

Beyond party coherence, Ghana boasts high degrees of competition in a well-institutionalized two-party system. As per a recent study, since the restoration of multipartyism in the early 1990s, the NDC and NPP have captured more than 95% of the total vote in presidential contests (Bob-Milliar 2019: 482). Importantly, Ghana has also witnessed multiple alternations in power during the multiparty era, pointing to its successful achievement of a democratic transition after decades of authoritarianism.

In addition to the rich body of work on Ghanaian parties and party organizations, recent scholarship has shed important light on the opportunities for and constraints around organizing and sponsoring election-related violence in the country. This body of work has shown that Ghana has witnessed electoral conflict both within and across party lines (Bob-Milliar 2019). In the northern areas of the country, for example, violence has sometimes taken the form of arson attacks as well as assaults against candidates and party members. However, election-related violence has most commonly entailed the harassment and intimidation of voters and ordinary citizens (Bob-Milliar 2014; Asunka et al. 2019).

Much of this violence in Ghana has occurred at a low intensity, "inflamed by party competition after democratization in 1992" (Nathan 2023: 250). In the episodes of conflict witnessed since that time, two kinds of actors – "party foot soldiers" (Bob-Milliar 2014; Asunka et al. 2019) and "macho men" (Amankwaah 2013) – have been prime contributors. As seen in Kenya and India, these violence specialists have engaged in violence in Ghana at the behest of individual politicians and political parties who have often relied on them due to "the manpower and sheer physicality" that they can bring to the enterprise of mounting election-related conflict (Driscoll 2018: 409). Scholars further note that "foot soldiers" have been known to attack political elites either when these individuals have failed to share the "spoils of [their] office" with party activists or when they have gone against their preferences in installing outside candidates in crucial party branch posts (Bob-Milliar 2014: 135; Driscoll 2018; Lamptey and Sahilu 2012). Meanwhile, voters have typically become victims of violence during registration exercises (Bob-Milliar 2014).

Public opinion data from Ghana shows that ordinary citizens are aware of parties and elites' roles in instrumentalizing electoral conflict. In the seventh round of Afrobarometer (2017: 21) surveys, for example, 37% of respondents held that competition between political parties often led to violence while another 17% indicated that this was always the case. Yet, like their counterparts in Kenya and India, Ghanaians also did not view political conflict as one of the most urgent issues affecting their lives. In fact, when surveyed in 2017, 55% of respondents held that the government's handling of violence during election campaigns was fairly good or very good (Afrobarometer 2017: 40). However, 22% expressed dissatisfaction with the authorities' performance on this matter (Afrobarometer 2017: 40).

Nevertheless, based on the central claims of this book as well as data on party institutionalization, we might expect that elites will be motivated to steer clear of organizing major episodes of violence. Existing studies provide some support for these claims. Consider findings about the country's 2012 parliamentary and presidential elections as an illustrative example. These elections were noteworthy for two reasons. First, the scale of electoral manipulation – which involved both the extreme bloating of electoral registers and even the bussing in of foreigners – was considerably higher than what was seen in prior elections (Bob-Milliar and Paller 2018). Second, beyond electoral fraud, Ghana also witnessed significant episodes of violence during this period (Asunka et al. 2019).

In reacting to these troubling developments, opposition politicians filed a petition at the Supreme Court in which they asked for a thorough review of the election results. As tensions around these events mounted, those competing for political positions made distinctly measured decisions about the organization of election-related conflict. Specifically, parties used their local political networks and grassroots partnerships with activists to shift violence away from competitive constituencies where domestic observers were present on the ground to competitive constituencies and polling stations where these observers were not stationed (Asunka et al. 2019). Extant studies further reveal that they deliberately carried out such redirections to avoid attention and sanctioning from legal and security officials (Asunka et al. 2019).

This strategic displacement of election-related conflict in Ghana in 2012 is comparable to the manner in which Indian politicians have recently started to instrumentalize Hindu–Muslim riots in villages as well as sponsor nonriot forms of conflict to advance their political goals. In both places, it bears noting that political elites have not completely abandoned violence. Rather, they have sought to manage its risks and possible negative consequences by adjusting the sites and scales at which conflict is mobilized.

In the Ghanaian case, beyond simply seeking to avoid sanctioning from legal and security institutions, there is also some evidence that politicians might be mounting low-level episodes of conflict with an eye toward minimizing backlash from voters. In October 2016, for example, a pre-election poll found that 54% of Ghanaians feared that the upcoming presidential contest would turn violent at some point (CDD 2016: 78). They also displayed high levels of awareness about the parties and politicians responsible for the country's major socioeconomic problems, including corruption and a declining economy (News24 2016). Even though blame attribution for economic concerns and violence are not identical, voters' overall levels of awareness might suggest that they would have been capable of punishing elites for violence if conflict had occurred around the 2016 election. In addition, insofar as civil society groups in Ghana were training and planning to deploy over 26,000 observers to polling stations across the country, voters plausibly stood to learn about incidents of intimidation and conflict in quick order (Brierley and Ofosu 2016).

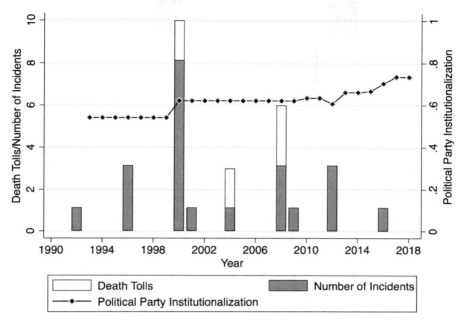

FIGURE 8.2 Political party institutionalization and electoral violence in Ghana (1992–2018)

In addition to political elites, research also suggests that "party foot soldiers" and "macho men" are keen to avoid major events of violence. This is because many of these violence specialists nurture ambitions of attaining high positions within political parties or standing for elected office in the future (Bob-Milliar 2012; Driscoll 2018). Owing to their embeddedness in local communities, mounting high-intensity conflict could hurt their electoral prospects. As such, it is unsurprising that violence and intimidation against voters have been found to be the "exception rather than the norm" in Ghana (Owusu Kyei and Berckmoes 2020: 331). Moreover, qualitative interviews with violence specialists have uncovered that these actors often talk about their core activities in terms of protecting, rather than attacking, citizens (Owusu Kyei and Berckmoes 2020).

Quantitative data on levels of political party institutionalization and election-related conflict, as operationalized in V-Dem and SCAD, respectively, further reveal that as levels of party institutionalization have improved, Ghana has successfully avoided severe outbreaks of electoral conflict. Indeed, as shown in Figure 8.2 above, the most intense period of electoral violence in the country occurred around the 2000 elections when clashes between government and opposition supporters claimed the lives of 10 individuals (Salehyan and Hendrix 2018). As Nathan describes, these clashes were mainly concentrated in Bawku in the Upper East region of northern Ghana. In this area, overlapping partisan and ethnic cleavages – coupled with the triumph of the NPP – led to a "violent riot between political party activists" over a vote-counting dispute (Nathan 2023: 266). This episode was followed by a second riot in 2001. However, beyond such incidents, recent events of electoral conflict in the country have resulted in fatalities in the single digits (Salehyan and Hendrix 2018).

Overall, then, Ghana typifies a case of a young democracy where the scale of party violence has been relatively mild amidst stable and durable political parties. So long as the country's parties continue to endure from election to election, I posit that politicians as well as violence specialists will have strong reasons to steer clear of organizing high-intensity episodes of party conflict. In this regard, Ghana's projected trajectory mirrors that of contemporary India, where party stability has played a crucial part in disincentivizing political leaders from instrumentalizing major episodes of conflict. Ghana also shares another similarity with India as a place marked by extensive patron–client connections (Paller 2014; Driscoll 2018), including linkages between politicians and armed actors (Amankwaah 2013). Driscoll (2018: 409, citing Democracy Watch 2007: 6), for example, writes that foot soldiers constitute the "soft underbelly of democratic politics" in Ghana and urgently need to be restrained. Likewise, Vaishnav (2017: 8, 311) notes that the "dalliance between crime and politics" in India is symptomatic of a "deeper malaise."

Yet, scholars of patron–client relations also agree that both Ghana and India are home to a form of party-centered patronage, wherein "incumbent part[ies] rel[y] on state resources and distribute [these resources] through iterative exchanges [with] locally rooted party networks" (Berenschot and Aspinall 2020: 10–11; also see Auerbach et al. 2022). This mode of clientelism is distinctive, as it involves "longer-term [and] ongoing relationships [between] politicians, their agents, and voters" (Berenschot and Aspinall 2020: 5). Such connections, in turn, offer real advantages to ruling parties and their associated intermediaries – including violence specialists – as they enable them to maintain political power and influence over considerable periods of time. It thus follows that both politicians and their brokers share strong incentives to avoid upsetting the status quo in party-centered patronage settings such as Ghana and India. Taken in this light, the addition of the Ghanaian case to the broader comparative terrain of this book helps to show that party stability is not only at the heart of strategic elite decisions about violence but is also linked with a form of clientelism that appears to be incompatible with the repeated instrumentalization of severe conflict.

UNSTABLE PARTIES AND THE *ANARŞI* CRISIS IN TURKEY (1976–1980)

In a manner comparable to Ghana in Africa, Turkey enjoyed a reputation for some time as a successful democracy in the Middle East. In a study of "anomalous democracies" during the Cold War era, for example, the nation was found to have notably maintained her democratic status despite patently "inauspicious structures" (Seeberg 2014: 108). Public opinion data collected through the World Values Surveys in the 1990s further revealed that at least part of this retention may have been due to the fact that the vast majority of Turkish citizens – an estimated 89% – were highly supportive of democracy (Klingemann 1999).

Despite these achievements, Turkey has not been immune to challenges in transitioning to and maintaining a democratic regime. The same World Values Surveys that uncovered high levels of support for democracy in the 1990s, for instance, also found that only 25% of respondents felt that the system of government was performing well at the time (Klingemann 1999). Prior to this, and between the 1960s and 1980s, moreover, Turkey had fallen prey to three separate coups. These interruptions to elected regimes had vital implications for the development of political parties: indeed, by the time that the *anarşi* clashes erupted in the late 1970s, the nation was already riddled by high levels of "volatility, fragmentation, and ideological polarization" as well as patently transient and vulnerable party organizations (Özbudun 1996: 128).

Even today, a somber degree of "existential insecurity" marks many of Turkey's political actors, and some analysts hold that these anxieties provide a partial explanation for the country's rapid and recent "exit from democracy" under the Adalet ve Kalkınma Partisi (AKP or Justice and Development Party) (Akkoyunlu and Öktem 2016: 507). Specifically, scholars argue that due to real struggles for political survival, an "'all or nothing' logic" has been operating in Turkish politics since at least the 2000s (Akkoyunlu and Öktem 2016: 508). This logic has not only opened up space for elite-level power struggles, but it has also motivated a fundamental reshaping of the country's institutions, including by replacing parliamentary democracy with an executive presidency in 2017 (Akkoyunlu and Öktem 2016; Esen and Gümüşçü 2017).

As in other contexts examined in this book, the instability of parties in modern Turkey – a factor core to the current analysis – was a long-run upshot of the decisions of her founding leaders and their early successors. Beginning with the statesman and country's first president, Mustafa Kemal Atatürk, and in a style similar to many postcolonial African elites including those in Kenya, Turkish politicians strongly opposed the introduction of multiparty competition in the initial decades of the Republic. Thus, even as the Kemalist system championed nationalism, populism, republicanism, revolutionism, and secularism on the one hand, it advocated for a fusion between the party and the state on the other (Cooper 2002: 116; Bayar 1996). In fact, in 1922, on the verge of establishing Turkey's Cumhuriyet Halk Partisi (CHP or Republican People's Party), Atatürk himself warned against the dangers of multiparty politics, stating that there could "be no greater sin than pushing the nation that [was] still suffering from political organizations based on personal rather than national aims ... to engage in activities of a similar nature" (Özbudun 2012: 75).

During his subsequent reign as president from 1923 to 1938, Atatürk established and consolidated a single-party regime in Turkey with the CHP at its helm (Özbudun 2012). Following his demise, his successor Ismet İnönü followed in these footsteps. In fact, it wasn't until the end of World War II that Turkish leaders started to slowly open up the political system to rival entities. Adopting a piecemeal approach to this transition, they first "allowed the social and political opposition to form parties" and then introduced "limited democracy" in the form of free elections in May 1950 (Erdogan 1999: 34–35).

One of the first parties to emerge on the scene during this time was the Demokrat Parti (DP or Democratic Party) (Erdogan 1999). Formed in 1946, it championed free enterprise and heavily criticized the "confines of statism" as practiced by the CHP (Bayar 1996: 776). In 1949, the DP devised a campaign squarely focused on the "betterment of the [country's] peasants" (Ellis 1950: 283). It then ran with these ideas in the May 1950 elections and pulled off an "astounding victory" in the parliamentary polls (Ellis 1950: 284).

In the aftermath of this unexpected result, the CHP made its intentions about meaningful democratization amply clear. Not only did the party leadership refuse to transfer power to the DP, but it also severely limited the ability of the new government to implement its promised economic and political reforms (Erdogan 1999). In addition, CHP elites predetermined the "boundaries of acceptable political discussion" in Turkey – which were restricted to expressing ideas compatible with the Kemalist program – and stressed "the centrality of state power [for] achiev[ing] development and progress" (VanderLippe 2005: 138).

Beyond the CHP, the military also emerged as a key player in modern Turkish politics, and members of the Türk Silahlı Kuvvetleri (TSK or Turkish Armed Forces) mounted three separate coups in 1960, 1971, and 1980. As a result, the country's "nascent democracy [remained] under the tutelage of the army" – the only institution with any internal unity – for a significant part of the late twentieth century (Erdeniz 2016: 86; Özbudun 1994). Meanwhile, within the party system, frequent party birth and death became a defining feature of politics. Take the contrasting cases of the Adalet Partisi (AP or Justice Party or JP) and the DP as illustrative examples. Whereas the former emerged in February 1961, the latter collapsed in the face of considerable state suppression in September of that same year. Approximately two decades later, in August 1981, the JP also fell apart. A central figure from the organization, Süleyman Demiral, then went on to form the Doğru Yol Partisi (DYP or Truth Power Party) in June 1983. These processes of party emergence and disintegration contributed to overall rates of party volatility in the country, which clocked in at a minimum figure of approximately 15% and a maximum figure of 30% between 1960 and 1977 (Çarkoğlu's 1998: 548).

Predictably, unstable parties also made for extremely unstable and divided governments, and significant internal bickering within incoherent alliances led to the downfall of several coalition governments throughout the 1970s

(Gunter 1989; Rubin 2002). In addition, this decade came to be marked by the rise of extremist parties and groups on both ends of the political spectrum. On the one hand were left-wing entities such as the Turkish People's Liberation Army (THKO) and the Turkish People's Liberation Party-Front (THKO-C), both of which formed in 1971. These groups drew considerable inspiration from the radical student movements of the 1960s, whose members had agitated against the Vietnam War, the Turkish government's ties with the United States, and the regime of the center-right JP (Sayari and Hoffman 1994; Sayari 2010). The protests of the 1960s had also led to violent clashes between leftist "revolutionaries" and right-wing and ultranationalist "idealists." On the other hand was the Millî Nizam Partisi (MNP or National Order Party or NOP), which entered the electoral arena in 1970, and emerged as the first political party to propagate an Islamic orientation in Turkey (Dagi 2008). After being banned in May 1971, the MNP was succeeded by the Millî Selâmet Partisi (MSP or National Salvation Party) in October 1972, which bore the same Islamist stripes.

Amidst this period of frequent party birth and death, several left-wing organizations – with their roots in the THKO and THKO-C movements – became involved in the *anarşi* in the late 1970s. These entities included the Revolutionary Way (DEV-YOL), the Marxist-Leninist Armed Propaganda Union (MLSPB), and the Turkish Worker Peasant Liberation Army (TIKKO) (Sayari 2010). Indeed, during the height of the crisis from December 1978 to September 1980, it is estimated that left-wing groups were responsible for approximately "33% of [all violent] incidents" recorded in the country (Sayari 2010: 202). But there were also numerous right-wing groups, including the Idealist Club Association, the Idealist Path Association, and the Idealist Youth Organization or Association of Idealist Youth, whose activities contributed to this crisis.

As in the Kenyan case, qualitative research from Turkey has uncovered manifold links between political parties and militant groups both prior to and during the *anarşi*. Some right-wing parties, for instance, allegedly set up camps to train student militants during the late 1960s (Sayari 2010). In addition, the far-right Milliyetçi Hareket Partisi (MHP or Nationalist Movement Party or NAP) is known to have informally supported members of the Association of Idealist Youth for many years, a task for which it received backing from the JP (Landau 1982; Sayari 2010; Özbudun 1981). Finally, supplying violence during the *anarşi* became possible due to the presence of key enabling factors, such as rapid rural to urban migration, the rise of overcrowded cities, and increases in underemployment and unemployment, all of which offered up a "large recruitment pool" of young people to conflict-sponsoring elites (Karpat 1988: 18, cited in Sayari and Hoffman 1994: 170).

For at least some of the political organizations present on the ground during this period, supporting violence was also plausibly related to insecurities about future survival. Consider, for instance, the developments that unfolded in the wake of the 1977 general elections. Even though the CHP emerged as the top performer in that parliamentary contest, it fell short of achieving the absolute majority required to form the government. While Republican leaders scrambled to find coalition partners to overcome this electoral hurdle, the second-place JP managed to cobble together a three-way alliance with the National Salvation Party and the MHP (Gunter 1989). However, the Adalet Partisi's grasp on political power did not last long either and defections from the organization culminated in the collapse of the JP-led government in 1978 (Gunter 1989). In the wake of this fall, CHP politician Bülvent Ecevit secured his third term as the nation's Prime Minister, but he too resigned in November 1979 due to the crumbling economy and the scale of the *anarşi* violence.

Ultimately, then, rather than coming to an end due to the actions of elected representatives, it was the September 1980 military coup that brought the crisis to a close. Three years later, when Turkey held her next elections, the TSK only allowed three parties – the Motherland Party (ANAP), the Populist Party (HP), and the National Democratic Party (NDP) – to compete. Notably, each of these organizations was an entirely new entrant to the electoral arena. Even after the violence came to an end, in other words, Turkey continued to be marked by frequent party birth and death.

Another major upshot of the *anarşi* was the normalization and routinization of party violence more broadly. This was first seen during the 1979–1980 rule of Süleyman Demiral of the JP, who briefly succeeded Ecevit after his resignation. Demiral's administration notably appropriated progovernment militias (PGMs) to deal with regime threats, and in doing so, laid the foundation for the creation of the Provisional Village Guards (GKK) system (Kinzer 1996; Gurcan 2015; Biberman 2018). Formally launched in 1985, village guards have since emerged as a vital prong of the Turkish state's efforts to deal with the thorny "Kurdish question" (Aydinli and Ozcan 2011; Davis et al. 2012; Ünal 2012). In their current incarnation, these armed actors are meant to combat the activities of the Kurdistan Workers' Party (PKK) and quash the separatist demands of ethnic Kurds (Kinzer 1996; Biberman 2018). For carrying out this work, members of the GKK receive an average monthly salary of $300 "along with clothing expenses and social security benefits" (Gurcan 2015: 1). As of 2015, moreover, it was estimated that there were "more than 60,000 village guards" operating in the nation, largely in the southeastern areas (Gurcan 2015: 2).

In addition to village guards, Turkish politicians also began to use "death squads" for political purposes in the post-*anarşi* years. These violence specialists were primarily deployed to attack and assassinate supporters of the Kurdish cause, and it is estimated that death squad-led assaults claimed the lives of at least 64 Kurdish political leaders and more than 500 civilians – including several journalists and human rights activists – between 1990 and 1994.

Twenty-two years after the end of the *anarşi*, party system volatility peaked in Turkey, reaching 50.2% (Sayari 2007: 2002). Simultaneously, interbloc volatility also rose to its zenith, as an estimated 15.5% of voters crossed over from

Comparative Insights from Ghana and Turkey

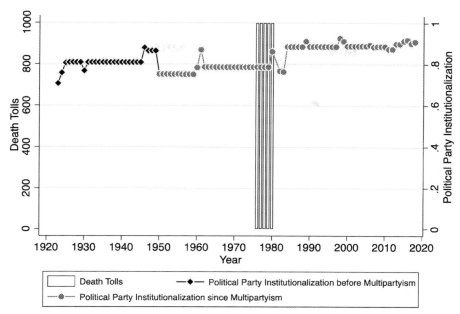

FIGURE 8.3 Political party institutionalization and the *anarşi* crisis in Turkey (1950–2018)[3]

supporting left-wing to right-wing parties between 1999 and 2002 (Sayari 2007: 2002). Finally, in the broader trajectory of Turkish politics, the election constituted a significant moment, as it brought the AKP to power.

Taken as a whole, then, there is now a considerable body of evidence establishing relatively high levels of party volatility in Turkey, with party replacement being core to this process (Çarkoğlu 1998; Başlevent, Kirmanoğlu, and Şenatalar 2004). As Figure 8.3 above shows, the *anarşi* escalated in 1976 when the country's political party institutionalization score stood at 0.786, well below its mean level of 0.836.[4] By contrast, the massive scale of death squad killings recorded from 1990 to 1994 occurred during a time when

---

[3] Unlike the Ghanaian case, for which the SCAD (Salehyan and Hendrix 2018) dataset provides disaggregated yearly event data on incidents of party violence, I am not aware of any comparable data for the entirety of Turkey's *anarşi*. Sayari and Hoffman (1994) offer perhaps the most detailed and disaggregated account of conflict during this period, but their data are also limited, as they only include the timeframe between November 1979 and July 1980. In developing Figure 8.3, I have thus evenly split Sayari's (2010) estimate of 5,000 total fatalities incurred over the 1976–1980 period. Although this is a crude approximation, it does help us to think about the scale of the *anarşi* violence.

[4] In the V-Dem dataset (Coppedge et al. 2019), Turkey recorded its lowest score of party institutionalization – 0.75 – between 1956 and 1959 and its highest party institutionalization level – 0.927 – in 1998.

party institutionalization clocked in at 0.886. The timing of these killings thus suggests that the logic of state-sponsored repression against a restive ethnic minority could hinge on factors other than levels of party instability.[5]

Finally, as per newer research on Turkish politics, the country has once again started to experience significant party deinstitutionalization (Toros and Birch 2019; Yardımcı-Geyikçi and Yavuzyilmaz 2020) and "protracted processes of institutional decay" in recent years (Özbudun 2002: 238). These processes have not only generated concerns about the quality of the country's elections, but they have also been tied to increasing levels of electoral violence (Toros and Birch 2021) and practices of familial electoral coercion, especially among weak partisans of the ruling AKP and less educated sectors of the electorate (Toros and Birch 2019). Indeed, according to one study, one in five Turkish voters were victims of familial or kin-based coercion in the run-up to the 2018 election (Toros and Birch 2019).

Overall, then, Turkey emerges as a key case where a significant period of party violence – the *anarşi* – occurred in a relatively mature multiparty system marked by unstable and transient political parties. It is also worth noting that party violence has not disappeared from Turkey since the end of the 1976–1980 crisis. Instead, it persists in various forms and through various actors – including familial and kin networks of coercion – so as to benefit the reigning AKP. In this sense, Turkey also provides a useful counterpoint to the Indian case: both countries have witnessed democratic weakening in recent years and are sites of enduring party violence. However, whereas politicians and agents affiliated with the ruling BJP in India seem to be trying to carefully manage the risks of conflict, the AKP and its supporters appear to be wielding and sponsoring violence more broadly. Should party deinstitutionalization continue to occur in Turkey in the future, this book holds that significant events of party violence could thus remain a risk in the country.

SUMMARY AND CONCLUSION

Through a cross-regional comparison of patterns of political conflict in Ghana and Turkey, this chapter has demonstrated that party instability can exert an independent impact – separate from democratic longevity – on elites' incentives to organize and sponsor violence. On the one hand, my exploration of the Ghanaian case has shown that young democracies are not necessarily doomed to violence if political parties are stable and coherent. On the other hand, evidence from Turkey has highlighted that even party systems with relative degrees of maturity can fall prey to severe conflict when their parties are

---

[5] Staniland's (2021) recent work on armed orders in South Asia proffers one potential explanation for a case of this nature. Applied to the Turkish case, this framework would suggest that the incompatibility between supporters of the Kurdish cause and successive Turkish governments' ideological projects could plausibly account for the 1990–1994 killings.

unstable and fleeting. Taken together, these insights underscore a central claim of the book: stabilizing parties can offer a viable means of orienting political leaders away from organizing major episodes of conflict. In some contexts, such as India, durable parties might help to quell elites' appetites for high-level violence by sensitizing them to the potential of garnering sanctioning from voters. In other cases, such as Ghana, stable parties may help to avert major conflict by compelling elites to also consider the possibilities of incurring punishment from legal and security officials. Beyond institutions such as courts, then, which have already received attention in studies of violence prevention, this book finds that party structures themselves might play a part in dampening elites' incentives for conflict.

9

Conclusion

This book opens with the cases of Tana River County in Kenya and Muzaffarnagar and Shamli districts in Uttar Pradesh, India. The former is a setting in which Orma and Wardei pastoralists, as well as their political leaders who were responsible for initiating lethal and destructive violence in 2012-2013, benefited significantly from its mobilization: in the 2013 county-level and parliamentary elections, all elected positions from Tana River fell to the members of these two groups. By contrast, the fates of parties and politicians with a hand in the 2013 riots in Muzaffarnagar and Shamli were far more variable: whereas the Hindu nationalist BJP benefited immensely from the worst communal episode to have occurred in India in over a decade, voters sanctioned the Bahujan Samaj Party (BSP) and Samajwadi Party (SP) in the 2014 general elections. How do we account for these differing outcomes across and within the two cases?

To address this question, I ask an additional set of questions in this book, going beyond the elite-level benefits of violence and taking into account its potential political costs. I show that politicians are likely to be attuned to these costs – particularly the possibilities of incurring sanctioning from voters – in some contexts more than others. I further demonstrate that varying levels of party instability can condition political leaders' incentives to organize or sponsor party violence. In places where parties are unstable, politicians can afford to operate with short time horizons and discount the possibilities of garnering punishment for conflict in the future. By contrast, in places where parties are stable and durable, the lengthier time horizons of political elites can turn them away from fomenting violence, especially at a severe scale, via political parties.

These arguments fit comfortably within the larger instrumentalist literature on political violence (Wilkinson 2004; Kalyvas 2006; Birch 2020). However, compared to some recent work in this vein – which has focused on the importance of electoral institutions (Burchard 2015; Fjelde and Höglund 2016;

Conclusion

Müller-Crepon 2022) and election type (Daxecker and Rauschenbach 2023) – I draw on both quantitative and qualitative data to open up the black box of political parties. In so doing, I show how politicians can make choices about conflict based on key *party* attributes. Whereas some scholars argue that weak or weakly institutionalized parties (Mehler 2007; Mueller 2008; Höglund 2009; Wanyama and Elkit 2018; Fjelde 2020) can create conditions conducive for conflict, my work demonstrates that the weakness attributable to *party instability* ought to receive greater attention due to the particular ways in which it can influence the size of elites' shadows of the future.

Much of my attention in this book is thus focused on unpacking elite-level decision-making about violence. Nevertheless, in centering voter sanctioning as a potential cost of violence, I also join a growing body of work on voters' responses to conflict (Rosenzweig 2021, 2023; Gutiérrez-Romero and LeBas 2020; Horowitz and Klaus 2020; Daxecker and Fjelde 2022). Like many other scholars of this topic, I find that ordinary citizens are not doomed to becoming participants in or victims of violence alone, but are capable of holding conflict-wielding leaders to account. In fact, I argue that given the devastating costs of severe episodes of conflict, there are strong reasons to expect that voters will try to punish violent politicians in circumstances where broader institutional conditions allow them to do so.

Recent developments in Kenya suggest that one institutional context in which we might see elites' incentives for violence weaken is in places where organizations beyond political parties exert some weight on these proclivities. The 2022 elections in particular show us that greater faith in the Supreme Court and lower stakes around the presidency – which were in turn brought about through devolution in part – as well as the prominence of class-based considerations rendered ethnicity less relevant than has been true of prior contests. Yet, we also know that the creation of the county system has generated incentives for violence in some subnational sites in Kenya where they did not exist before. Furthermore, because the salience of "political ethnicity is always contingent," it is too early at this stage to say that ethnic considerations will be entirely irrelevant to Kenyan politics going forward (Opalo 2022: 9). Thus, if we are to further dampen the possibilities for party violence in the future, we might need to look beyond institutions such as the Supreme Court and seek to strengthen political parties themselves. Barring this, I argue that conflict at the subnational level could remain a recurring phenomenon in Kenya.

Evidence from India similarly reveals that there are enduring motivations for politicians – particularly those affiliated with the BJP – to instrumentalize or sponsor violence in the country. However, I also find that owing to healthy expectations about party longevity, the scale at which they are likely to do so going forward is mild. As we have observed over the last decade, low-intensity conflict in India can take the shape of relatively minor riots or targeted attacks against minorities, which are supported by Hindu nationalists. The mild scale of such violence does not mean that it is insignificant by any means. Indeed, as Pai and Kumar (2018: 4) show, "everyday communalism" is helping the Bharatiya Janata Party to carry out important political and cultural work by advancing a Hindu state and society in India. However, where institutions beyond political parties seem to be responsible for recent developments around party violence in Kenya, this book finds that it is in fact party stability levels that have largely kept politicians from organizing or sponsoring severe riots in the Indian context over the last three decades.

AREAS FOR FUTURE RESEARCH

The arguments developed and evaluated in this book apply to contexts where the rule of law is weak enough that politicians could conceivably get away with organizing or sponsoring violence via political parties. Put differently, it is in places where accountability institutions are generally feeble that I expect unstable parties to shorten elites' time horizons and incentivize conflict. Settings marked by extensive patron-client relations – a factor known to have weakened accountability in several contexts (Weitz-Shapiro 2014; Berenschot and Mulder 2019; Auerbach 2022), including in Kenya, India, and Ghana – thus fit well within the scope conditions of my work.

Beyond clientelism, however, I propose that scholars might also consider other factors – perhaps most importantly the rise of populism – that can attenuate accountability institutions and thereby enable elite-driven violence. We now know that populism poses threats not only to democracy broadly conceived but to democratic accountability in particular. These threats include "weaken[ing] checks and balances, [the hollowing out of] institutional safeguards (minority protection), [and] facilitat[ing] the centralization of power" (Guasti 2020: 48; Ruth-Lovell et al. 2019). Insofar as populism is on the rise globally, moreover, it follows that an increasing number of countries around the world might find themselves within the scope of this book.

In this regard, the United States stands out as a key case, and much of the evidence about the events that preceded the January 6 siege on the U.S. Capitol suggests that President Trump resorted to violence owing to short time horizons in a context where many institutional checks on the executive had already been damaged. Writing in June 2019, for instance – more than eighteen months before January 6 – Kaufman and Haggard (2019: 427) observed that Trump's "takeover" of the Republican Party had already "pushed it increasingly towards positions of intolerance and extremism." They further highlighted the declining credibility of the press as well as the deteriorating "legitimacy and integrity of the judicial system" – both institutions crucial to maintaining accountability in democracies – and warned presciently that the latter posed serious implications for the "integrity of the electoral system" (Kaufman and Haggard 2019: 427). Similarly, Adam Schiff (2021: 85) has argued that the die for an event such as the attack on the Capitol was cast in advance and must be understood against the backdrop of earlier developments, including

Conclusion

Trump's acquittal during his first impeachment trial and "his recognition that the Republicans in Congress would never confront him, never constrain him, and had been fully and successfully cowed." While these dynamics do not perfectly map onto party instability, they do provide important insights about how broader institutional deterioration – including party deterioration – can enable elites to resort to violence.

By mid-December 2020, the evidence about Trump's desperation to hold onto power was clear. "Irritated" by his electoral defeat, he seemed to know that "his time [was] up" (Holland and Mason 2020). Yet, his broader belief system – that he was beyond accountability – prevailed. Days before the Capitol siege, Trump thus pressured Georgia's Secretary of State, Brad Raffensberger, to "find" him enough votes to overturn the election results (Balz 2021; Shear and Saul 2021). In a one-hour phone call that alternated between begging, berating, flattering, and threatening Raffensberger, he acted in a manner bereft of any limits (Balz 2021; Gardner 2021). When even this last-ditch effort did not work, Trump took to the Ellipse on January 6 and urged his supporters to march on the Capitol.

This infamous, albeit predictable, event of major party violence under a populist politician in the United States highlights the importance of considering populism as an enabling factor for political conflict in the twenty-first century. Our collective knowledge about party violence would thus benefit from the careful examination of other countries, beyond the United States, where populism might render party-based and party-sponsored violence viable. In addition, the burgeoning literature on this topic could be further developed by studying forms of party violence that I have not considered in this book. One form that appears ripe for further investigation is *intra-party* violence, which has been recently observed in places such as Malawi (Seeberg and Wahman 2019) and Uganda (Reeder and Seeberg 2018). Another modality – which may not be tied strictly to elections but is clearly related to parties more broadly – is elite-level assassinations. This form of conflict is worthy of our consideration in part because it does not seem to engender the same kinds of backlash from voters (Pierson 2021) as the ethnic party-based conflicts that I have studied in this book.

POLICY IMPLICATIONS

Beyond opening up these new avenues for inquiry and making key theoretical and empirical contributions to the study of political violence, this book also offers important lessons to practitioners and policymakers. For some time now, global and comparative evidence has shown us that parties play key roles in many different forms of conflict – from election-related violence to political assassinations to targeted attacks against minorities. While several studies have engaged with ideas about how different institutions – from electoral rules (Horowitz 1991; Burchard 2015; Fjelde and Höglund 2016;

Müller-Crepon 2022) to subnational governments (Brancati 2006, 2009) – might best be designed to reduce the possibilities for conflict, there have been relatively few concrete recommendations proffered with respect to party organization itself.

The arguments of this book, which are developed through the comparison of two countries in different world regions, suggest that parties ought to receive dedicated and close attention within these broader debates. Specifically, I argue that strengthening and *stabilizing* political parties could go a long way toward lessening political violence. This is because consolidating parties – and reducing party instability – can help to orient leaders toward the future and thereby deter politicians from resorting to conflict as a political strategy. If we are to tackle party violence, in other words, we ought to take political parties and their longevity seriously.

Appendix A

National and Subnational Correlations between Replacement Volatility and Alternative Measures of Party Instability

This appendix offers descriptive statistics and summarizes bivariate relationships between replacement volatility and alternative measures of party instability, including Pedersen volatility, Party Strength (PS), and Party Organization (PO). It first discusses the relationship between replacement volatility and Pedersen volatility based on my computations of these measures from national parliamentary election results in Kenya and India, as well as the association between Type A volatility and national-level PS scores in both countries, drawing on Fjelde's (2020) data on Party Strength. It then provides a subnational accounting of the association between replacement volatility and Pedersen volatility in Andhra Pradesh (AP) and Uttar Pradesh (UP) based on my computations from Vidhan Sabha election results, as well as the association between party replacement and PO scores for these states, drawing on Chhibber, Jensenius, and Suryanarayan (2014).

CONCEPTS, DESCRIPTIVE STATISTICS, AND BIVARIATE RELATIONSHIPS AT THE NATIONAL LEVEL IN KENYA AND INDIA

As previously described in Chapter 2, Type A volatility is one subtype of Pedersen volatility. In places where total party system volatility is driven by entry and exit volatility, as is the case in many Latin American countries (Cohen, Kobilanski, and Zechmeister 2018), we should expect to see a strong and positive relationship between Pedersen and replacement volatility. By contrast, in places where vote-switching volatility lies at the heart of total party system volatility, we should find a weak association or no discernible relationship between Pedersen and replacement volatility.

Another measure that might help to capture party instability – the concept core to this book's arguments – is Fjelde's new measure of PS. This measure uses five components to operationalize the strength of parties: the number of parties with permanent national party organizations, the number of parties with permanent regional and local party branches, the extent to which parties rely on programmatic versus clientelistic links with voters, the degree to which candidate selection procedures are centralized, and the level of internal party discipline (Fjelde 2020: 146). The earliest country-year entries for PS in Fjelde's dataset date back to 1946, and the dataset provides information on party strength for 164 countries. The values for PS in the dataset "range from −1.95 to 1.45, with a mean of 0.132" (Fjelde 2020: 147). Given the attention that PS gives to incorporating information on the *permanence* of national, regional, and local party branches – features that we should more commonly expect to find among durable as opposed to fleeting parties – replacement volatility and PS should be negatively correlated.

Table A.1 presents descriptive statistics for Pedersen volatility, PS, and replacement volatility in Kenya and India. It also summarizes bivariate relationships between replacement volatility and these alternative measures of party instability.

Three key findings from these data warrant further discussion. First, in both Kenya and India, there is a statistically significant and positive relationship between replacement volatility and Pedersen volatility. Thus, party entry and exit is the central driver of total party system volatility in both countries. Second, the data show that Kenya's mean and minimum replacement and Pedersen volatility scores are higher than those of India, while India's maximum values for these two measures are higher than those of Kenya.[1] These higher maximum values in the Indian case, however – which were attained in 1984 – are attributable to the death of a previously splintered wing of the Congress party, namely the Congress(U), and the birth of new parties such as the Telugu Desam Party (TDP), which finished in second place in the general elections held that year. Third, PS is negatively correlated with replacement volatility in both Kenya and India. The statistical significance of this association, however, is mixed: whereas the relationship is statistically significant at the 5% level in the Kenyan case, it does not attain any significance in India. Kenya also exhibits a lower mean score of PS than the mean value of 0.132 in Fjelde's global dataset, while India attains a mean value higher than this figure. Taken together, then, regardless of the measure that one chooses, the evidence shows that Kenyan parties are more unstable and weaker than their Indian counterparts.

---

[1] Drilling down into recent country-level data on replacement volatility further reveals important differences between Kenyan and Indian parties. Replacement volatility scores for Kenya for parliamentary and presidential elections clocked in at 58.1% and 54.9% in 2017, respectively, indicating extreme levels of party instability. By contrast, in 2014 – the last parliamentary election for which I computed party replacement – India recorded a Type A score of 8.84%, rendering her party system quite stable.

TABLE A.1 *Descriptive statistics and correlations between Pedersen volatility, party strength, and replacement volatility in Kenya and India*

	Kenya				India			
	Mean (Standard Deviation)	Minimum Score	Maximum Score	Correlation with Replacement Volatility	Mean (Standard Deviation)	Minimum Score	Maximum Score	Correlation with Replacement Volatility
Pedersen Index(n=21 for Kenya; n=58 for India)	51.59% (18.48)	27.29%	71.19%	0.9909***	33.93% (26.69)	9.97%	89.63%	0.9240***
Party Strength(n=45 for Kenya; n=62 for India)	−0.0726 (0.1687)	−0.2869	0.1700	−0.6568**	0.5396 (0.0774)	0.4189	0.7055	−0.07
Replacement Volatility(n=21 for Kenya; n=58 for India)	37.34% (19.70)	11.25%	58.29%	N/A	18.01% (23.44)	2.35%	81.27%	N/A

*** indicates statistical significance at the 1% level;
** indicates statistical significance at the 5% level

CONCEPTS, DESCRIPTIVE STATISTICS, AND BIVARIATE RELATIONSHIPS AT THE SUBNATIONAL LEVEL IN INDIA

Chhibber, Jensenius, and Suryanarayan's (2014) measure of Party Organization (PO) provides another reasonable proxy for party instability. PO refers to "a collection of organizational characteristics that provide clarity to politicians about their role in the organization ... the process for upward mobility in the party, the rules of succession planning, the organization's tolerance for intra-party factionalism, and ... the extent to which party decisions are taken based on clearly understood institutional norms as opposed to the whims of leaders" (Chhibber, Jensenius, and Suryanarayan 2014: 492). Less organized parties are those in which clear succession plans are lacking, the roles of party functionaries are "fluid or election-focused," opportunities for upward mobility are either limited or determined by the impulses of a few leaders, internal decision-making is generally unpredictable, and "the charisma of a single leader" affects the overall functioning of the organization (Chhibber, Jensenius, and Suryanarayan 2014: 493). By contrast, more organized parties are governed by "transparent and routinized" procedures for adjudicating functionaries' career trajectories and leaders' succession plans (Chhibber, Jensenius, and Suryanarayan 2014: 493). Furthermore, these entities exhibit "organizational continuity" that endures beyond elections (Chhibber, Jensenius, and Suryanarayan 2014: 493).

In their subnational dataset, which includes information on election returns from 15 Indian states from 1967 to 2004, Chhibber, Jensenius, and Suryanarayan also include a variable for the proportion of organized parties. This variable is "calculated as the number of organized parties in [the] dataset divided by the number of parties with more than 5% of the vote share in the state in each state election" (Chhibber, Jensenius, and Suryanarayan 2014: 500). In light of the fact that PO uses levels of *organizational continuity* – which should be higher among stable parties – to distinguish between more and less organized party entities, we should expect to see a negative relationship between replacement volatility and the proportion of organized parties.

Table A.2 presents descriptive statistics for Pedersen volatility, the proportion of organized parties, and replacement volatility in Andhra Pradesh and Uttar Pradesh, India.[2] It also summarizes bivariate relationships between replacement volatility and these alternative measures of party instability at the state level.

---

[2] Because Chhibber, Jensenius, and Suryanarayan's dataset begins in 1967, their first entries for Pedersen volatility in Andhra Pradesh and Uttar Pradesh are for the years 1972 and 1969, respectively. In performing the calculations presented in Table A.2, I rely on my own computations of Pedersen volatility for these states, which include information on total party system volatility for 1967. Bivariate correlations reveal that our scores for Pedersen volatility (based on seat shares) for AP and UP are highly correlated, at 0.994 and 0.9959, respectively. One possible explanation for the marginal differences in our figures is that Chhibber, Jensenius, and

TABLE A.2 *Descriptive statistics and correlations between party organization, Pedersen volatility, and replacement volatility in Andhra Pradesh and Uttar Pradesh*

	Andhra Pradesh				Uttar Pradesh			
	Mean (Standard Deviation)	Minimum Score	Maximum Score	Correlation with Replacement Volatility	Mean (Standard Deviation)	Minimum Score	Maximum Score	Correlation with Replacement Volatility
Pedersen Volatility (n=9 for AP; n=11 for UP)	33.98% (21.97)	5.27%	70.24%	0.5764	39.29% (26.86)	6.09%	84.12%	0.6658**
Proportion of Organized Parties (n=9 for AP; n=11 for UP)	0.0555 (0.1666)	0	0.5	−0.1517	0.2196 (0.1873)	0	0.6666	−0.3514
Replacement Volatility (n=9 for AP; n=11 for UP)	7.98% (12.88)	0	39.80%	N/A	17.63% (22.41)	0.47%	78.17%	N/A

** indicates statistical significance at the 5% level

Three findings merit emphasis from these data. First, in both Andhra Pradesh and Uttar Pradesh, there is a positive relationship between replacement volatility and Pedersen volatility. However, this relationship only achieves statistical significance at the 5% level in UP, which suggests that it is in this state – but not in AP – that party entry and exit significantly drive total party system volatility. Second, the data show that the minimum, maximum, and mean levels of both Pedersen and replacement volatility are higher in UP than in AP. Combined with the first finding discussed above, this pattern suggests that Uttar Pradesh is home to a more unstable subnational party system than Andhra Pradesh. Third, the proportion of organized parties is negatively associated with replacement volatility in both AP and UP, but this association does not attain statistical significance at any level in either state. The lack of statistical significance is possibly attributable to the fact that the proportion of organized parties is derived from PO, and PO in turn includes some information that is unrelated to party instability.

Suryanarayan's dataset only includes parties that gained more than 5% of the vote share in state assembly elections. As such, it follows that they would have excluded parties with very marginal seat shares. By contrast, since I am fundamentally interested in studying *party* instability, I only exclude independents from my computations of Pedersen volatility but include all parties, regardless of their seat share size.

Appendix B

Elite Interviews

This appendix discusses the interview methods that I adopted during fieldwork in Kenya and India, as well as the methods that I used to interpret my qualitative data. As several studies have shown, interviews can provide vital insights about periods of political violence. From helping to identify the narratives that are used to frame and mobilize various conflicts (Klaus 2020) to uncovering survivors' memories and recollections (Butalia 2000; Wood 2003), many scholars of conflict now regularly rely on interviews to better understand violent events in different parts of the world. At the same time, ethically implementing interview techniques in conflict and postconflict settings and accurately interpreting the information gathered from these conversations is not without its challenges. As such, this appendix also details some key difficulties that I experienced while conducting interviews in Kenya and India and puts forth suggestions for navigating such fieldwork-based challenges.

In her seminal account of peasant support for the leftist insurgency in El Salvador, Elisabeth Wood (2003) has discussed a number of difficulties that interview-based researchers of political violence can encounter. Her work finds that "violence and terror often leave behind a legacy of silence, fear, and uncertainty that can be deeply corrosive of self-confidence, trust, and hope" (Wood 2003: 40). These after-effects can make it difficult for respondents to engage in open and frank conversations about violence. In a related vein, Noam Lupu and Leonid Peisakhin (2017: 848) show that the effects of conflict on the "political attitudes and behaviors" of survivors sometimes endure for generations to come.

Given these lasting impacts, many political violence scholars have sought to shed light on the potential benefits, costs, and risks – to both the research participants and the researcher herself – of conducting work on these contentious topics (Arjona, Mampilly, and Pearlman 2021). In addition, experts have offered valuable insights on navigating the terrain of interview-based work in conflict and postconflict settings. Wood, for example, has emphasized the need for implementing safeguards such as informed consent procedures. More recently, Lee Ann Fujii (2010: 231) has called for paying attention to both the data and *meta-data* – that is, the "spoken and unspoken thoughts and feelings" – that respondents can communicate during interview sessions. Her research among survivors and perpetrators of the Rwandan genocide has further illuminated five different kinds of meta-data – rumors, inventions, denials, evasions, and silences – that can emerge from these conversations (Fujii 2010).

Given the emphasis of my research on better understanding elites' incentives for violence, and especially in light of the many interviews that I conducted with politicians, party leaders, and party functionaries, there are sound reasons to expect that these respondents might have relied on inventions, denials, and other evasive tactics to answer some of my questions. Indeed, given the vested interests of politicians to deny engaging in or encouraging political violence, it could even be argued that conducting interviews with respondents from this category might offer little insight into the core questions of this book.

Yet, insofar as party violence hinges critically on the choices and actions of politicians and political party leaders, I made the deliberate decision to interview these respondents in both Kenya and India. As shown in Table B.1, I met with 69 politicians and party leaders in total, including current and former Members of Parliament (MPs), representatives elected to various subnational bodies, and political candidates and party functionaries. As discussed in Chapter 1, I supplemented these interviews with conversations with various nonpolitical respondents, including policy and security sector experts, human rights activists and civil society leaders, ethnic and religious elites, academics, journalists, and police officers.

Whereas the main goal of my interviews with political elites was to better understand their decision-making around orchestrating, or steering clear of, political violence, the purpose of my conversations with actors outside the party realm was to confirm the veracity of politicians' statements or uncover discrepancies or evasions in their accounts, as appropriate. I also used the latter group of interviews to evaluate various alternative explanations for party violence. In addition, following Fujii's (2010) advice, I kept an eye out for spoken and unspoken cues that might point to strategies of invention, denial, or evasion during my conversations with political elites. Finally, in each of my research sites, I met with local residents to understand their experiences of, and responses to, episodes of party violence.[1]

---

[1] Since some local residents in these sites also worked for civil society or human rights organizations, I have only classified those individuals as residents or survivors in Table B.1 who I could not place in any other category. The total number of residents or civilians interviewed for this project is thus greater than the five specifically enumerated here.

Appendix B: Elite Interviews

TABLE B.1 *Breakdown of elite interviews in Kenya and India*

Country Case: Kenya

Category	Nairobi	Mombasa	Nakuru	Eldoret	Total
Politicians/political party leaders/party members and functionaries	19	8	6	3	36
Policy and security sector experts	9	2	1	0	12
Human rights activists and civil society leaders	5	9	4	4	22
Ethnic and religious elites	2	2	4	9	17
Academics	9	1	1	0	11
Journalists	0	1	0	0	1
Police and retired police officers	0	1	0	1	2
Civil servants	0	1	1	0	2
IDP camp residents	0	0	2	0	2
Total	44	25	19	17	105

Country Case: India

Category	Hyderabad	Meerut	Muzaffarnagar and Shamli	New Delhi	Total
Politicians/political party leaders/party members and functionaries	15	10	8	0	33
Human rights activists and civil society leaders	3	11	1	3	18
Ethnic and religious elites, including village leaders	5	4	4	0	13
Academics	4	4	0	3	11
Journalists	5	2	1	1	9
Police and retired police officers	4	5	3	0	12
Civil servants and retired civil servants	1	0	3	0	4
Residents/survivors	1	2	0	0	3
Total	38	38	20	7	103

Given the sensitive nature of this research, I offered all respondents, including all politicians and party leaders, confidentiality as part of the informed consent process. Following Wood (2003), I also informed all of my interviewees that I would be speaking with politicians and political party leaders from across the political spectrum. I deemed it important to share such information so that respondents could make informed decisions about what they wanted to share and disclose to me.

INTERVIEWEE RECRUITMENT AND DATA COLLECTION STRATEGIES

During fieldwork, I made contact with political elites in one of three main ways. First, I visited the offices of several political parties, oftentimes repeatedly, to secure interviews with politicians and party functionaries. I started to use this strategy in the initial days of fieldwork, after I quickly learned that contacting party offices through their publicly listed phone numbers would not help me to meet with their members or representatives.[2] Second, I relied on academics and local journalists in the places where I was conducting research to refer me to leaders of various political parties. I especially relied on such references when visits to party offices did not yield meetings or interviews with political elites. Third, insofar as references from journalists and academics occasionally provided me with a crucial entry point to political parties, I found that once I spoke to a few party leaders and functionaries at one organization, they usually connected me with politicians and officials in other organizations. This was especially the case if these entities were part of the same alliance or coalition.

I did not attempt to construct representative samples of respondents as a part of this research. Instead, drawing on Wood's work, I sought to interview members of a wide range of organizations, including political parties. Put differently, in each of the places where I conducted fieldwork, I met with politicians and political party leaders from as many parties as possible, as well as nonpolitical elites from the groups mentioned above. For instance, in Nairobi, I met with representatives and functionaries of 12 different parties. Likewise, in Mombasa, Nakuru, and Eldoret, I interviewed individuals affiliated with six, six, and two different parties, respectively. Finally, in Hyderabad, Meerut, and Muzaffarnagar and Shamli, I interviewed respondents affiliated with seven, five, and five distinct party organizations.

---

[2] In Hyderabad, for example, I spent numerous days at the AIMIM party headquarters, Darussalam, in the Old City. In addition to offering me a chance to observe various Majlis leaders and their daily routines, these recurring visits also provided me with an opportunity to interact with ordinary citizens and supporters of the party. Similarly, in Nairobi, I made several visits to the offices of the Orange Democratic Movement (ODM) and Wiper Democratic Movement-Kenya (WDM-K) parties. These visits ultimately yielded face-to-face meetings with leaders and functionaries at both organizations.

Appendix B: Elite Interviews

While I was ultimately successful in interviewing politicians and political party leaders from many major parties in my research sites, I did face challenges in gaining access to other key respondent groups. For instance, despite my best efforts, I struggled to secure interviews with police officers in Kenya. At the time of my first round of research in early 2013, Kenyan authorities were implementing an ambitious police reform program, and the nation was also rapidly hurtling toward presidential, parliamentary, and county elections. These realities all made police officers hesitant to meet with me. A few months later, during my second round of fieldwork, I further learned that several incidents of political conflict around the 2013 elections had rendered the police cautious about meeting with researchers. For these reasons, I largely relied on interviews with policy and security sector experts to better understand how politicians' incentives for violence might affect the actions of the police during conflict-ridden periods in Kenya.

Prior to each interview, and in trying to secure various meetings, I introduced myself as a doctoral student, and later a postdoctoral scholar based in the United States.[3] I devised two separate questionnaires for my interviews with political elites and respondents unaffiliated with political parties, respectively. Although I did pose some common questions to members of these groups, I ensured that the majority of items remained specific to the respondent group with which I was engaging.

I asked politicians, political party leaders, and political party functionaries three kinds of questions during interview sessions. First, I sought to collect background information on the history of the party organization and party branch, the main goals and objectives of the political party, as well as information on my respondents' involvement with the party in question. This set of questions helped me to better understand the ways in which party leaders and members of various party organizations understood their work on their own terms and in their own words. In addition, posing questions to interviewees about organizational background and their political careers helped me to build some rapport with respondents. This rapport often enabled me to ask interviewees more difficult questions about topics such as party violence in subsequent portions of our conversations.

Second, I asked Kenyan and Indian political elites a set of open-ended questions about the history of ethnic and communal conflict in their nations. I crafted these questions to gather information on the trajectories of party violence at both the national and sub-national levels. For instance, in meeting with politicians and party leaders in Mombasa, I asked respondents some broad questions about the history of political conflict in Kenya, as well as more specific questions about ethnic clashes in Mombasa and the Coast region. Similarly, in meeting with elites in Meerut, I posed questions to respondents about Hindu–Muslim riots in India, Uttar Pradesh (UP), and Meerut city. Finally, I included

[3] I conducted fieldwork in Muzaffarnagar and Shamli after the conclusion of my PhD.

items about particular episodes and periods of political violence during this stage of interviews. For example, I asked respondents in the Rift Valley specific questions about the ethnic clashes that had accompanied the 1992, 1997, and 2007 presidential elections. Similarly, in Hyderabad, I asked elites about the city's 1978 and 1990 communal riots in considerable detail.

Third, I asked politicians and political party leaders a set of questions about the actors responsible for various episodes of conflict. My initial questions about these topics were broad in scope and sought to solicit responses from interviewees about the key players that they deemed relevant to such events. In responding to questions about these topics, many respondents spoke about the roles of criminal gangs and armed groups.[4] On several occasions, however, political elites also openly acknowledged the activities of parties as protagonists in party violence.[5] For instance, in accounting for the clashes in Kenya's Rift Valley around the 1992 presidential elections, one party official held, "Moi and KANU party elites had divided the people along ethnic lines [so as] to remain in power."[6] Likewise, in recounting the 1978 and 1990 riots in Hyderabad city, a Congress spokesperson stated, "both the Congress and the MIM had incited these riots."[7]

Even though leaders sometimes acknowledged the activities of various political entities in instrumentalizing party violence in these ways, over time, I found that their accounts chiefly underscored the actions of rival parties as key provocateurs of conflict. In other words, party elites rarely volunteered information about the roles of their own organizations in contributing to political violence.

In order to tackle these omissions, I introduced specific questions and cited extant evidence about the party in question's involvement in political violence during interview sessions. Following Fujii (2010), I further treated the reactions and responses to such questions *as data* when interpreting my interviews. While some respondents flatly denied any involvement in violence on the part of their organizations, others evaded the matter by stating that they were personally unaware of such activities. Finally, a small group of respondents attributed party violence to various systemic forces. One MIM politician in Hyderabad, for example, simply held that the city's communal riots were related to "the roughness of Indian politics."[8]

My second questionnaire for interviews with policy and security sector experts, human rights activists and civil society leaders, ethnic and religious elites, academics, journalists, police officers, and local residents included two

---

[4] Interview with an AIMIM politician, Hyderabad, July 31, 2013; interview with a WDM-K politician, Mombasa, October 5, 2013.
[5] Interview with an INC politician, Hyderabad, August 3, 2013; interview with a KANU party official, Nakuru, October 24, 2013.
[6] Interview with an ODM party official, Eldoret, November 4, 2013.
[7] Interview with an INC party official, Hyderabad, August 2, 2013.
[8] Interview with an AIMIM politician, Hyderabad, July 31, 2013.

Appendix B: Elite Interviews

kinds of questions. The first sought to understand the roles of political parties in organizing or sponsoring party conflicts as well as the reactions of local residents to major episodes of party violence in their communities. The purpose of these questions was to verify or invalidate the claims of political elites, as appropriate. The second set of questions sought to uncover additional factors and evaluate alternative explanations that might account for episodes of party violence in Kenya and India.

INTERVIEW LOCATIONS AND TRANSCRIPTION STRATEGIES

I conducted the majority of my interviews with political elites at party offices or at their homes. In Kenya, a number of these conversations also occurred at restaurants or coffee shops. Mirroring Kanchan Chandra's (2004: 293) experiences, and especially in instances where interviews took place at party offices or politicians' residences, I found that there were usually "other people present or within calling distance, including family members, political associates, and favor seekers." Throughout my fieldwork, I sought to record as many interviews as possible, and most politicians and political party functionaries consented to this request. When my proposed use of a recorder made respondents uncomfortable, I took detailed notes during and after each interview instead.

I conducted most of my interviews in Kenya in English. Although I have elementary listening, speaking, and writing knowledge of Swahili, I was not proficient enough to conduct entire interviews in the language. In the small handful of cases in which my Kenyan respondents did not have a working knowledge of English, family members typically stepped in as interpreters. In India, I conducted all of my interviews in English, Hindi, or in some combination of the two languages, as I am fluent in both.

During and after various rounds of fieldwork, I personally transcribed and translated most of my recorded and handwritten interviews. For those interviews that I did not have enough time to transcribe, I hired qualified undergraduate students to help me with this work. In the end, my student Research Assistants (RAs) transcribed a handful of English-language interviews from Kenya. I only supplied them with the necessary recordings after erasing any and all identifying information from the tapes. In addition, all of the transcribers completed the relevant human subjects training programs as required by the Institutional Review Board (IRB) before beginning their work on this project.

INTERVIEW INTERPRETATION AND ANALYSIS

As Wood has detailed, interview data on political violence must be interpreted with caution. More recently, Ana Arjona, Zachariah Mampilly, and Wendy Pearlman (2021: 201) have further advised that conflict scholars should pay particular attention to a "researcher's positionality" – that is, her "race, gender, class, sexuality, nationality, and institutional support, among other aspects" – since these social factors can impact and shape the research process in important ways.

For this study, I deemed it especially important to carefully interpret the interview data that I had gathered from conversations with political elites. This is because I expected various vested interests to keep political leaders from openly discussing or admitting to their involvement in episodes of party violence, particularly if these events had taken place recently. To ensure the reliability of the interview data that I collected, I sought to cross-check political leaders' claims with the claims of interviewees who were unaffiliated with political parties. Where possible, I also tried to verify the information that politicians had shared with me with the data presented in extant written sources. These sources included newspaper reports, existing academic studies, and descriptive information as provided in the Varshney-Wilkinson (2004), Mitra-Ray (2007), and Kenya Violent Elections Dataset (KVED) (Malik 2023) datasets. Thus, to the extent possible, I sought to triangulate the information that political leaders presented to me across various sources of data.

I also made note of instances wherein leaders or functionaries of the same party accounted for specific instances of violence in the same way. I deemed such overlaps important insofar as they could potentially help to corroborate key aspects of a conflict episode or point to strategies of invention, denial, or evasion. I checked these shared accounts of party violence against other data sources in interpreting political leaders' responses. Following Chandra (2004: 296), furthermore, "if I could [observe a tendency] to lie or obfuscate," I did not use claims from political elites as part of my evidence "unless I could cross-check [them] with a second source." Employing this rule not only allowed me to weed out those claims that were likely to be false, but it also helped me to arrive at compelling evidence about the involvement of political elites in particular events of conflict.

Take, for example, the following instances of invalidation and corroboration that emerged from my interviews with politicians in Hyderabad. After several interviews with Bharatiya Janata Party (BJP) elites, I found that the leaders and functionaries of this party were exhibiting a tendency to displace blame for the city's riots onto the Indian National Congress (INC) and All India Majlis-e-Ittehad'ul Muslimeen (AIMIM).[9] In so doing, they usually also minimized the contributions of Hindu nationalism in creating tense and often combustible circumstances in Hyderabad. Had I taken these claims at face value, I would have missed a crucial element of the city's riot production process, which has involved various deliberate and divisive activities on the part of the BJP and its social movement affiliates.[10] However, by conducting interviews

---

[9] Interview with a BJP leader, Hyderabad, July 23, 2013; interview with a BJP leader, August 4, 2013.
[10] Interview with an academic, Hyderabad, July 22, 2013; interview with an academic, Hyderabad, August 1, 2013.

Appendix B: Elite Interviews

with individuals *beyond* the BJP apparatus and by paying close attention to the scholarly literature and journalistic accounts on these topics, I was able to develop a clear understanding of the ways in which Hindu nationalist pursuits have contributed to divides between local Hindus and Muslims. One interviewee, for example, detailed the growing momentum around Hindu processions in Hyderabad city as follows:

They [Hindu nationalists] started with Ganesh Puja and then recently they introduced Durga Puja, which is a Bengali affair. And the latest that I hear is that they are going to encourage Hanuman Puja. If they do this, then from the Muslim side, it is the Prophet's birthday, you know? These celebrations are increasing ... something which was not done earlier.[11]

At the same time, I also came across some instances in which party elites willingly provided damning evidence about the involvement of their organizations and colleagues in major events of party violence. Most of these episodes had occurred quite some time ago, and I surmised that respondents were willing to discuss their parties' roles in such events because they did not expect to be sanctioned for these actions either legally or electorally. A politician affiliated with the INC, for instance, admitted that the 1990 riots in Hyderabad had been instrumentalized by a rival Congress faction to remove the Chief Minister, Chenna Reddy, from power.[12] Given the extensive documentation of this riot in various extant studies (Engineer 1991b; Varshney 2002), corroborating the above account was a relatively straightforward task. Likewise, a KANU leader granted that ruling party elites had played a key part in the ethnic clashes that had broken out across the Rift Valley around the 1992 elections.[13] Leaders and functionaries affiliated with other political parties, several nonpolitical interviewees, and the existing scholarship on political violence in Kenya all helped to confirm these claims.[14] Overall, then, I found that when combined with and compared against other sources of data, interviews with political elites generated some critical insights for better understanding party violence in both my country cases.

POSITIONALITY AND RESEARCHER IDENTITY

A final insight gleaned from my fieldwork was the impact of my positionality on the data collection phase of this project. Simply put, I found that I faced greater challenges in securing interviews, especially with politicians and political party leaders and functionaries, in India – which also happens to be

---

[11] Interview with an academic, Hyderabad, August 1, 2013.
[12] Interview with an INC politician, Hyderabad, August 3, 2013.
[13] Interview with a KANU party leader, Nakuru, October 24, 2013.
[14] Interview with a PNU party leader, Nakuru, October 29, 2013; interview with a policy expert, Nairobi, December 3, 2013; also see Klopp 2001; Kahl 2006.

the country of my birth – than in Kenya. These experiences mirror those of other social scientists who have convincingly argued against assuming that "doing research at 'home' or in a familiar place is somehow easier" than doing research "abroad" (Godbole 2014: 86; Dam and Lunn 2014).

In my case, the group that treated me with the greatest suspicion were BJP politicians. On the whole, I also found that as opposed to Kenya, where my repeated visits to party offices usually facilitated some kind of face-to-face meeting, this strategy only yielded interview sessions with AIMIM leaders among politicians in India. Learning from these initial experiences, I ultimately came to rely on references from academics and journalists to secure interviews with party officials in Hyderabad, Meerut, and Muzaffarnagar and Shamli.

The relative ease of securing interviews with politicians and political party leaders in Kenya, however, did not mean that I was always successful in recruiting respondents, as a number of potential interviewees declined to speak with me after I introduced the research to them. Nevertheless, two individuals also explained their decision and told me that they were uncomfortable speaking with someone who held an affiliation with a university in the United States. They further stated that their discomfort stemmed from the fact that the trials pertaining to the 2007–2008 post-election crisis were still ongoing at the Hague, and that they viewed these proceedings as an unjust Western intervention into a domestic political matter.

On the whole, however, I found that I faced fewer challenges in securing meetings with Kenyan party officials or functionaries than their Indian counterparts. In fact, when these individuals learned that I originally hailed from India and not the United States, they often appeared to become more comfortable with our proposed conversation. Over time, I even found that disclosing my background early led to some lively discussions about the status of Kenyan Asians. While this subject was not directly related to the core concerns of my work, speaking with respondents about the Kenyan Asian community usually helped me to develop a healthy rapport with them.

By contrast, upon first meeting me, many Indian political leaders, particularly those from the BJP, questioned me about my decision to study riots as opposed to other topics such as development.[15] In fact, one politician in Meerut went so far as to state that I was "imposing [my] views [about the decline of communal riots in cities], like a journalist would."[16] Following Fujii, I did not treat such statements as irrelevant to the main concerns of my work, but used them as meta-data to piece together the ways in which various parties publicly articulated their views and relationship to communalism in India.

Beyond my national background, my gender also affected my prospects for data collection. Although I had received some clues about this matter

---

[15] Interview with a BJP leader, Hyderabad, August 4, 2013; interview with a BJP politician, Meerut, August 13, 2013.
[16] Interview with a BJP politician, Meerut, August 13, 2013.

Appendix B: Elite Interviews

throughout the lengthier stints of my fieldwork in 2013, the reality became most apparent to me during research in Muzaffarnagar in 2015. This is because it was at this stage that my central concerns about political parties' involvement in riot violence most directly intersected with issues of gender: indeed, it was in Muzaffarnagar that BJP politicians had used the alleged harassment of a young Hindu woman – by her Muslim classmate – to mobilize Hindu men in violence (Berenschot 2014; Pai and Kumar 2018; Malik 2021). One of the Hindu leaders who had planned and organized the September *mahapanchayat* described in Chapters 1 and 7 had also shared a fraudulent video online to escalate communal tensions in the run-up to the riots.

By the time that I met with this politician in late December 2015, authorities had charged him under various sections of the Indian Penal Code (IPC) for disseminating the fake video. As with all of my other interviews with political elites, my goal for this meeting was to better understand the BJP's calculus around instrumentalizing the riots under consideration. To ease into these topics, however, I did not ask this respondent about the video or the allegations against him. Instead, we first talked about the BJP's 61-seat increase in its Lok Sabha performance in UP. Furthermore, once I eventually probed the issue of the Muzaffarnagar and Shamli riots, I began by asking my interviewee questions about how and why a case of alleged harassment had given way to one of the worst instances of communal violence in the country's recent history. When faced with these questions, my respondent posed a counter-question in Hindi and followed it up by declaring:

Anyone, whether he is Hindu or Muslim ... If someone molests his sister, would he tolerate it? Absolutely not! Think about it. You too are a woman.[17]

By this round of fieldwork, I had grown accustomed to BJP elites' pointed questions about my interest in riot violence and their various tests of my political commitments. However, this exchange was one of the clearest instances in which I learned that in addition to the topic itself, my gender was also shaping the manner in which politicians and political leaders were reading me.

Taken together, my experiences conducting interviews among Kenyan and Indian political elites reveal that such conversations, while challenging, can proffer useful sources of information about political violence. First, when combined with other kinds of data, interviews with politicians can help to uncover important descriptive information about parties' involvement in key episodes of conflict. Rather than assuming that such conversations will mainly yield untrue claims, violence researchers would thus be well served by developing innovative strategies to secure interviews with political elites and carefully interpreting these data as part of their work. Second, compared to the use of quantitative proxies (Wilkinson 2004) or interviews conducted with violence

---

[17] Interview with a BJP MLA, Muzaffarnagar, December 18, 2015.

specialists (Brass 1997; Cleven 2013) or members of conflict-affected communities (Klaus 2020), conversations with politicians stand to proffer more direct insights into elite decision-making about violent conflict. Third, the meta-data engendered from these conversations can be just as informative as what respondents directly share with researchers. Of course, as with all interview-based research, scholars should carefully think about how their positionality can condition their knowledge about political violence and plan ahead about potential challenges that they might face in the field. In short, then, while researchers should operate with a healthy dose of skepticism about politicians' willingness to openly admit to organizing conflict, my research reveals that thoughtful and intentional interview-based fieldwork can elicit rich information about elites' involvement in violent episodes.

Appendix C

The Development of Civil Society in Kenya and India

This appendix provides a historiography of the development of civic associations in Kenya and India. In addition, it uses qualitative interview data marshalled from subnational research sites to assess the alternative claim that the composition and activities of civic associations – as opposed to party instability – might better help us to account for patterns of party violence. The forthcoming pages reveal two central insights. First, they show that as in many parts of the Global South, civil society in both Kenya and India remains subordinate to "political society," or the realm in which "actors compete for ... the right to exercise legitimate political authority" (Heller 2009: 124; Chatterjee 1998, 2004, 2011). As a result, civil society organizations (CSOs) and nongovernmental organizations (NGOs) are less powerful than state actors and face significant limitations in challenging the state, including in its deployment and uses of violence.

Second, and on an empirical note, I find that larger ethnic communities in Kenya, such as the Kikuyu and Luo, tend to dominate nongovernmental organizations. As a result, these entities do not offer much potential for bridging divides across multiple groups, as Varshney's argument encourages, or avoiding elite-initiated violence. Likewise, my data from Hyderabad and Meerut, India, reveal an abundance of intraethnic, rather than interethnic, associations. Among the few interethnic associations that populate these cities – and even among those that are dedicated to maintaining communal peace – most are found to be temporary organizations. Rather than consistently working toward quelling violence, they seem to form around managing sensitive events, such as elections and religious processions, and dissolve quickly thereafter.[1] For all these reasons, I argue that party instability

---

[1] Focus group discussion with peace committee members of the *Balmiki Samaj Pragiti Sangh* or Balmiki Society Progress Union, Hyderabad, July 28, 2013.

warrants primacy over the ethnic composition of civil society in accounting for elites' incentives to mobilize or sponsor party violence in Kenya and India.

THE EVOLUTION OF CIVIL SOCIETY IN KENYA AND INDIA IN COMPARATIVE AND HISTORICAL PERSPECTIVE

Compared to the development of party systems – which took on drastically different paths in Kenya and India, as shown in Chapter 3 – it is important at the outset to note that the contours of associational life in these countries unfolded in largely similar ways. This is because after independence, ruling elites from dominant parties constrained meaningful engagement on the part of CSOs and NGOs. In so doing, these politicians built on a longer colonial-era history of limiting and exploiting civil society to maintain the state.

Although the term "civil society" is relatively new in the study of these regions, it is worth emphasizing that organizations resembling civic associations were present in precolonial East Africa and South Asia. In East Africa, these groups typically took the form of "horizontal social networks" organized around kin relations (Nasong'o 2007: 25). There were also several *"harambee'* (a Swahili term meaning, 'let's pull it together') ... groups that originated in [the region's] pre-colonial cooperative work parties" (Brass 2016: 63). Meanwhile, associational life in precolonial South Asia usually occurred within "village republics" (Prakash 2002: 29). The primary purpose of many of these groups – across the two regions – was to provide security against external threats, such as rival ethnic groups or princely rulers, although *harambee* self-help organizations also played a vital part in service provision.

The Evolution of Civil Society in Kenya and India during the Colonial Period

Following the arrival of the British, civic associations in East Africa witnessed a deliberate undermining, as colonial administrators bypassed or co-opted existing kinship-based or self-help systems to extend and consolidate their power. In the short term, these decisions transformed civil society into an "an array of formal and informal institutions," which were oriented to advancing the interests of European settlers (Maina 1998: 41). As Bruce Berman (1998: 340) describes, the new entities also completely "ignored the dense networks of indigenous institutions" in the area.

Of course, some reformist and radical movements – such as the Young Kavirondo Association (YKA), the Kikuyu Central Association (KCA), the Kikuyu Karing'a Education, and the *Dini ya Msambwa* or Religion of the Ancestral Customs – did form to challenge the colonial state in Kenya (Rosberg and Nottingham 1966; de Wolf 1983; Anderson 2005; Nasong'o 2007). However, most of these groups were either "co-opted ... into collaboration" with the British or swallowed by political parties (Nasong'o 2007: 26).

Appendix C: The Development of Civil Society in Kenya and India

As previously discussed in Chapter 3, furthermore, many political elites in the Kenya Colony were deliberately propped up to "protect [the] strategic and economic interests" of London after independence (Branch 2006: 28). The co-optation of civil society groups by the colonial regime or Kenyan political parties thus meant that the country entered the postcolonial period with a thin and weak associational arena.

Across the Indian Ocean, colonial authorities in India likewise showed little interest in developing civil society. Among the few organizations that they tolerated were a handful of social and religious reform movements, such as the Brahmo Samaj and the Arya Samaj. Both organizations openly "opposed the caste [hierarchies], ritualism, and idolatry" practiced within Hinduism and advocated for women's education and widow remarriage (Chandhoke 2011: 173). However, their membership base was narrow from the very beginning, comprised largely of the Indian bourgeoisie and English-speaking urbanites (Rudolph and Rudolph 2015). The Arya Samaj was known to be divisive as well, as its prominent members – many of whom owned "important publishing houses and newspapers" published in the United Provinces or present-day Uttar Pradesh (UP) – "carried out a massive campaign against Muslims and Islam" in the preindependence years (Pai and Kumar 2018: 12).

In the 1920s, the transformation of the Indian nationalist movement into a "popular agitation" led to some important expansions in the nature and reach of civic associations (Rudolph and Rudolph 2015: 161). First, under the leadership of Gandhi, groups affiliated with the anti-colonial struggle "began to reach significant publics" across the country (Rudolph and Rudolph 2015: 161; Varshney 2001). Second, Congress leaders' vociferous campaigns against untouchability helped to spawn entities such as the *Harijan Sevak Sangh* or Dalit Service Syndicate (Chhibber 1999; Rudolph and Rudolph 2015). Indeed, INC elites themselves established "a number of affiliated groups" – particularly around women's rights and the youth – during the nationalist phase (Chandhoke 2011: 173). Third, owing to the "ideological alternative" that Hindu nationalism offered, entities such as the RSS and Hindu Mahasabha also emerged in India in the early decades of the twentieth century (Staniland 2021: 108; Chandhoke 2011). In sum, even though colonial administrators were equally disinterested in supporting associational life in Kenya and India, the mass nature of the anti-colonial struggle in the Indian case led to the rise of more far-reaching civic groups in the country.

The Evolution of Civil Society in Kenya and India in the Initial Decades after Independence

Following these nations' respective attainment of independence, however, the differences between their associational domains shrank significantly, as "more privileged and influential groups [such as] government functionaries [and] political parties and leaders" became the main conduits through which citizens could reach the state (Chatterjee 2004: 40). Amidst these developments, Kenya's *harambee* groups found themselves in a somewhat exceptional position. Contrary to most other civil society groups whose "range of maneuverability" was severely constrained during the Kenyatta years, the country's first president "called on local *harambee* groups to pull together to achieve what they could on their own, promising that the government would supplement local efforts" (Nasong'o 2007: 30; Brass 2016: 63). In the subsequent years, *harambee* organizations impacted the lives of many Kenyans, particularly those living in rural areas, through the provision of schools and clinics. However, most other civic associations were left with little choice but to mimic KANU's tactics. As a result, they either started to back "specific group values" or leveraged patron-client connections to reach ordinary citizens (Nasong'o 2007: 30). Much like parties themselves, then, many civil society groups became "highly ethnicized" during the Kenyatta years and emerged as subordinate to political society (Nasong'o 2007: 30).

Following Kenyatta's demise, the Moi years came to be marked by what Jennifer Brass (2016: 66) has described as both "conflict and control" between the Kenyan state and NGOs. On the one hand, domestic and international human rights groups that raised a voice against the president's policies – such as the Kenya Human Rights Commission (KHRC), the Law Society of Kenya (LSK), the National Council of Churches of Kenya (NCCK), Africa Watch, Amnesty International, and Article 19 – met with swift action from the regime. These actions included cumbersome requirements of registration to ensure that their operations were in keeping with "the national interest" as well as prohibitions on publications and the dissemination of information about the excesses of the ruling party (VonDoepp 1996: 36). On the other hand, it is also true that the number of "NGOs grew nearly fifteen-fold" during the Moi presidency (Brass 2016: 66). In tandem with NGO growth, leadership within this sector "shifted from a missionary and voluntary orientation to a professional, educated middle class" (Brass 2016: 68; Kanyinga 1996).

Owing to these developments, ruling politicians became increasingly concerned that they had no way to track what NGOs were doing. In addition, they worried that the central role of nongovernmental organizations in the provision of basic services would weaken citizens' opinions of the state. Consequently, from 1986 onward, the Moi regime began to heavily regulate NGO activity in Kenya, including by requiring staff to "submit their plans and budgets to the government for approval" (Brass 2016: 68). At the same time, however, the state also purposively nurtured a number of entities as "security organ[s]" to protect its longevity (Kanyinga and Njoka 2002: 90; Wanyade 2009). These groups included Youth for KANU or YK '92, the youth wing of the party, and *Jeshi la Mzee* or "The Old Man's Army." Both organizations received financial backing from the state and were directed toward carrying out violence against KANU's political opponents in the multiparty era.

Appendix C: The Development of Civil Society in Kenya and India

Between these two poles of conflict and control on the one hand and state sponsorship and support on the other lay a handful of churches – namely the Anglican Church of Kenya (ACK), the Catholic Church, and the Presbyterian Church of East Africa (PCEA) – that the Moi regime was forced to tolerate. Expressly using violence against these organizations was a risky proposition because, along with *harambee* groups, churches had emerged as important "providers of health and education services" in rural areas (Nasong'o 2007: 27). At the same time, and because these churches had marked out the "political sphere as [their] primary target for social action," they presented a clear threat to KANU elites (Chacha 2010: 108). Where it could, therefore, the regime tried to pressure church leaders to limit their activities, and only rarely turned to violence to achieve this end. Nevertheless, in August 1990, Anglican Bishop of Eldoret Alexander Kipsang Muge perished in a mysterious automobile accident, three days after receiving a threat from Moi's Minister of Labor (Fredland 1989). Even so, contrary to human rights organizations, KANU leaders were unable to entirely silence churches in Kenya and were instead left to begrudgingly let them continue their activities, including their campaigns for democratization.

As previously discussed, India marched into its postcolonial phase on the flank of a strong and stable political party – the Congress – which held a core commitment to democracy. Despite this advantage, India's associational arena in the initial decades after independence developed in a manner similar to that of post-1963 Kenya. As Pradeep Chhibber (1999: 53; also see Rudolph and Rudolph 1987) writes, with the INC as the "key link between state and society," civic associations moved to the background of Indian political life and largely took on the role of operating as narrow "demand groups".

During the 1970s, Indira Gandhi's attempts to centralize and personalize authority brought new momentum to the country's associational domain, as activists organized countless "strikes, marches, fasts, and sit-ins" to challenge her regime (Sahoo 2013: 261). Gandhi responded to these campaigns by prohibiting the "involvement of voluntary organizations in politics" and only allowed "apolitical NGOs" to operate (Sahoo 2013: 261). To mark a break from the past, the national governments that formed in the post-Emergency years actively sought to encourage volunteerism on the part of ordinary citizens and funneled in considerable "funding and bureaucratic support" to such groups (Sahoo 2013: 261). However, associational life remained strikingly weak in India until the early 1990s. Indeed, according to data from 1991, "most Indians [did] not belong to formal associations" at the time (Chhibber 1999: 13). Furthermore, in keeping with arguments about the dominance of political society over civil society (Chatterjee 1998, 2004, 2011; Heller 2009), India's associations were "either tied to political parties" or found to be "transitory or ineffective politically, if autonomous" (Chhibber 1999: 13).

Structural Adjustment and the Evolution of Civil Society in Kenya and India since the 1980s

Structural adjustment reforms and the turn to neoliberalism marked the next major stage in the evolution of civic life in my two country cases. As Shadrack Nasong'o (2007: 34) describes, once foreign donors began to channel funding away from the state and toward civic organizations, Kenya witnessed a "process of implosion" in associational life from the mid-1980s onward. Similarly, Brass (2016: 66) argues that the significant growth in NGOs witnessed during the Moi years was engendered by both "the neoliberal swing in development thinking" and the erosion of the Kenyan economy. Owing to these neoliberal origins, the associations that emerged reflected – at least in an outward sense – the "new policy agenda" of "advocacy and good governance," broadly construed (Nasgong'o 2007: 34–35).

Following Moi's departure from the presidency in 2002, the Kibaki regime "moved from conflict toward cooperation" with NGOs (Brass 2016: 72). Such cooperation took many forms, including bringing civil society elites into government positions. Between 2005 and 2011, for example, the Kibaki "administration invited a number of prominent civil society leaders to direct government departments" (Brass 2016: 73). Yet, it is also true that successive Kenyan regimes – even in this era of cooperation – provided little funding to NGOs. Instead, the majority of total funding came and continues to come from international donors. Consequently, even as the language of democracy and good governance is frequently used in the Kenyan NGO sector – and "human rights, democratization, and governance organizations in Nairobi are visible both nationally and internationally" – nearly 40% of the country's NGOs in 2006 were involved in "general development" activities (Brass 2016: 82–83). In other words, it is the priorities of donors that continue to inform the work of many civic associations in Kenya today.

One observable implication of these dynamics is seen in the kinds of spaces that Kenyan NGOs and CSOs create. As one interviewee described, the country's countless religious organizations, local community-based groups, and online and digital collectives mainly offer opportunities for practicing "fragmented citizenship."[2] This individual stated:

> There are few formal spaces to practice citizenship in this country. What we have now are "spaces of belonging." These are civic spaces: many of them are ethnic and religious, many of them are technocratic. But they are not spaces where everyone can practice citizenship. These are narrow groups.[3]

Taken together, the evidence suggests that civic associations in Kenya are neither programmatically dedicated nor compositionally broad enough to credibly bridge divides between ethnic communities. In fact, my data indicate that, if

---

[2] Interview with an academic, Nairobi, February 4, 2013.
[3] Ibid.

Appendix C: The Development of Civil Society in Kenya and India

anything, politicians' attempts to instrumentalize conflict will trump the efforts of civic leaders to prevent such violence. As one church leader from Uasin Gishu County summarized, "we can open up our churches to the people who are being attacked, but if the politicians want to make people fight, then there [will be] clashes."[4]

Mirroring the Kenyan case, India's embrace of "neoliberal conditions for aid" also led to a rapid proliferation of NGOs in the country (Sahoo 2013: 263). This growth in nongovernmental organizations occurred slightly later than witnessed in the Kenyan case and mainly took off from the early 1990s onward. Nevertheless, today, NGOs in India run the gamut from "non-profit service providers" to "advocacy and policy research organizations" to "local territorial and identity-based groups" (Harriss 2007: 2718). As John Harriss (2007: 2718) suggests, it is not uncommon to find "an NGO on every [street] corner" in large Indian cities. However, as in Kenya, many of these entities remain tied to the priorities of their external donors. Meanwhile, occupation-specific groups – such as Press Clubs and Business Associations – are often narrow in their membership and dominated by upper-caste Hindus.[5] This renders them quite different in their ethnic composition from the interethnic groups that Varshney privileges in his work. Finally, even where there are groups with mixed membership and express agendas for promoting "communal harmony, peace, and social justice" – such as the Confederation of Voluntary Associations (COVA) in Hyderabad, a network of hundreds of NGOs and community-based organizations (COVA Website 2018) – their leaders admit that associational attempts to maintain peace often fail in the face of incitement by politicians and party leaders.[6] In sum, a historiography of associationalism in Kenya and India highlights that despite marked deviations in party organization and postcolonial regime-type, the rise of dominant party systems in both countries rendered political society stronger than civil society. This arrangement, in turn, undermined in a path-dependent fashion the ability of associational groups to withstand and counteract elites' provocations and sponsorship of party violence. In the remaining pages of this appendix, I provide further evidence for this latter claim by drawing on interviews with civil society leaders in the two countries.

EVALUATING THE CIVIC ASSOCIATIONS CLAIM IN KENYA: EVIDENCE FROM THE RIFT VALLEY

In the Kenyan context, I study the potential for civic associations to ameliorate ethnic divides by focusing on the activities of church leaders in the Rift Valley. This emphasis on churches is appropriate for three key reasons. First, given

---

[4] Skype interview with a church leader in Eldoret from the Uasin Gishu County Gospel Ministers, March 12, 2017.
[5] Interview with a leader of the *Sanyukt Vyapar Sangh* or Joint Business Association, Meerut, August 21, 2013.
[6] Interview with a civil society leader, Hyderabad, July 23, 2013.

the country's high levels of religiosity, churches touch the lives of millions of ordinary Kenyans (McClendon and Riedl 2015). Second, church groups have a long history of advocating for political change in Kenya. In addition to their strident campaigns for democratization during the autocratic Moi years and their efforts to unite the opposition in a bid to oust KANU from power in 1992 (Sabar-Friedman 1995), church leaders have also pushed for reforms in the post-2002 era at various critical junctures. For example, after voters rejected the draft constitution in the country's 2005 referendum, leaders of the Catholic Church reasserted their demands for institutional reforms in mid-February 2007 (Chacha 2010: 117). Third, church groups are widely viewed as the most trusted grassroots organizations in the nation today: not only do their leaders hold enviable reputations as problem-solvers, but aspiring politicians also regard church groups as their chief points of entry into local communities (Maina 1998).[7]

For all of these reasons, we might expect that of all civil society groups in Kenya, churches are in the best position to bridge ethnic divisions and prevent major episodes of party violence. However, the empirical evidence reveals two significant challenges in church leaders' efforts to ensure peace. First, as with other CSOs, "the Church" in Kenya "is itself divided by the cleavages of class and tribe" (Maina 1998: 144). As a result, many churches remain narrow in their make-up and offer spaces for practicing fragmented forms of citizenship, as previously discussed (Ernstorfer 2018). Second, church appeals – or indeed the appeals of any non-state actors – for peace stand to be overpowered if Kenyan politicians are oriented toward organizing violence.

In laying out the narrow ethnic composition of many churches, a leader from the Uasin Gishu County Gospel Ministers shared the following information with me:

Our city [Eldoret] is cosmopolitan. And when it is cosmopolitan, you find that there are different ethnic groups coming within the community area.... We try to bring in all types of tribes because most of the children go to school together.... We preach forgiveness, we preach coming together, they also do business together. And so, you find that [there are efforts] of bringing different tribes and ethnic groups together. But most of the people in the church that I lead, they are Kalenjin. Then, there are other churches that are mostly Kikuyu and some for the Luos and the Luhyas, so it is like that for many of the big ones.[8]

Despite such challenges, it is important to note that religious leaders of various faiths have intentionally sought to overcome the above problems in recent years. In the run-up to the 2022 elections, for example, Uasin Gishu clergy and politicians signed a peace accord to ensure calm during the August elections

---

[7] Skype interview with a church leader from the Bethel Family Church in Eldoret, March 18, 2017.
[8] Skype interview with a church leader from the Uasin Gishu County Gospel Ministers in Eldoret, March 12, 2017.

Appendix C: The Development of Civil Society in Kenya and India

(Cherono 2022). Meanwhile, members of the Inter-Religious Council of Kenya carried out youth training programs to help young people avoid falling prey to elites' calls for violence, should they be deployed (The Monitor 2022). But the evidence suggests that even these efforts are unlikely to withstand politicians' appeals for conflict. As a respondent affiliated with the Logos Revival Ministries explained:

> During the four years after [an] election, everything looks okay and calm. But once [we reach the] the beginning of the election year, like this year, then certain things begin to crop up on a tribal basis. People begin recruiting in tribes, and that brings a bit of animosity.... The past begins to come forth.... I can say that ... when [some] people stand for elected posts, they definitely believe that they will win. When they don't [win], then they believe in their mind that the election was stolen.... So that brings a lot of conflicts and the past injustices begin to come to the surface. And we [church leaders] can try to keep [things] calm, but it is very difficult for us to do so when the political leaders are inciting the people.... In 2007-2008, there was no way that we could control [the clashes]. The only contribution that we had [was] that we opened our churches [to] the people who were fleeing their homes. We let them take our church compounds and set up temporary homes and [fed] them and collect[ed] food and clothing. But stopping violence ... you can't stop violence when you are not armed. Ours was just to give them shelter, food, and a place to sleep. Of course, there was mediation much, much later, but during the actual violence, the churches were helpless.[9]

Since the post-election crisis, Kenyan policymakers have admittedly designed some important instruments to overcome such long-standing ethnic and communal divides. In 2008, for example, legislators passed the National Cohesion and Integration Act through which they authorized the creation of the National Cohesion and Integration Commission (NCIC). Today, this organization is tasked with "facilitat[ing] and promot[ing] equality of opportunity, good relations, harmony, and peaceful coexistence between persons of the different ethnic and racial communities of Kenya" (Nderitũ 2018: 104). In order to foster ethnic dialogue and understanding, NCIC Commissioners and Officers also serve as advisers to the government. Since its inception in 2010, the commission has routinely liaised with faith-based organizations to counter hate speech, preach peace, and promote national cohesion (Nderitũ 2018: 154). However, at least as of 2017, church leaders held that these programs were largely geared toward reducing tensions during electoral periods.[10] As such, they did not view them as long-term solutions for preventing violence in the country.

---

[9] Skype interview with a church leader in Eldoret from the Logos Revival Ministries, March 27, 2017.

[10] Skype interview with a church leader in Eldoret from the Global Empowerment Christian Center, March 24, 2017; Skype interview with a church leader in Eldoret from the Logos Revival Ministries, March 27, 2017.

To the extent that donors have made significant investments in local Kenyan peace programs in recent years, we might expect that these initiatives will offer viable pathways for deterring conflict in the future. Such efforts might be particularly helpful in making up for the lack of regular funding for peacebuilding that several church leaders brought up during interviews.[11] These individuals further held that this dearth in resources presents a key challenge in pursuing conflict prevention and mitigation over sustained periods of time.[12] At the time of this writing, it is still too early to make conclusive claims about the possibility of stemming conflict through donor-funded peace programs. Nevertheless, it is true that several factors conducive to the organization and sponsorship of violence – including unstable parties, fragile coalitional arrangements, subnational grievances, and the ongoing dominance of political society over civil society – persist in Kenya.

Beyond the churches that are closely studied in this work, I also find that nonreligious CSOs and NGOs appear to have limited scope for controlling political violence in the country. As Wachira Maina (1998: 148) suggests, part of this is because "inward-looking" associational development has long marked the country's civil society groups. In the 1980s and 1990s, for example, communities aligned with the political opposition dominated Kenya's civic education organizations (Maina 1998). Despite Moi's efforts to neutralize their influence, Arriola (2013) found that Kikuyu elites continued to dominate occupational groups such as business associations in the multiparty era, which precluded their potential to contribute to peace. Recent evidence from the post-2007–2008 context further reveals that efforts aimed at bridging divides between different ethnic groups – through *barazas* (public meetings) and District Peace Committees (DPCs) – have proven insufficient due to their focus on *individual*, rather than community, contributions to conflict mitigation and prevention (Lynch 2018: 36). Indeed, Lynch (2018: 36) writes that many of these forums are top-down enterprises through which citizens receive little more than "one-way lectures" about their duties. Taken together, then, while it is theoretically plausible that some CSOs, such as local peace programs, could credibly dampen the risks of political violence in Kenya, the evidence suggests that recent instances in which the country avoided conflict were primarily attributable to conducive coalitional and institutional arrangements and strong incentives among political leaders against organizing violence, as opposed to the activities of peace-oriented non-state actors.

---

[11] Skype interview with a church leader in Eldoret from the Overcomers Christian Church, March 22, 2017; Skype interview with a church leader in Eldoret from the Global Empowerment Christian Center, March 24, 2017; Skype interview with a church leader in Eldoret from the Logos Revival Ministries, March 27, 2017.

[12] Skype interview with a church leader from the Uasin Gishu County Gospel Ministers, March 12, 2017; Skype interview with a church leader in Eldoret from the Overcomers Christian Church, March 22, 2017; Skype interview with a church leader in Eldoret from the Global Empowerment Christian Center, March 24, 2017.

Appendix C: The Development of Civil Society in Kenya and India

EVALUATING THE CIVIC ASSOCIATIONS CLAIM IN INDIA: EVIDENCE FROM HYDERABAD AND MEERUT

Much like in the Kenyan context, I also do not find empirical evidence to support the notion that fluctuations in the activities of civic associations in India lie at the crux of vicissitudes in communal riots. On the contrary, I uncover three central reasons that cut against this logic. First, and as previously discussed, there is now a plethora of evidence to demonstrate that CSOs remain subordinate to political society in India (Chatterjee 1998, 2004, 2011; Heller 2009). Brass (2003a), for example, holds that the limitations of CSOs as autonomous actors in the Indian context are so significant that many arguments that privilege these groups amount to little more than "artificial transplant[s]" of claims "from the American social science literature." A recent study of the *Zila Shanti Samiti* or District Peace Committee in Bhagalpur, Bihar, further illuminates the ongoing dominance of Indian political society. This research finds that it is state authorities who have "carefully selected locally-embedded non-state actors to calm tensions between Hindus and Muslims" since the 1989 riots (Malik and Prasad 2022: 206). Put differently, the impetus for peace or conflict appears to first emerge from the activities of political elites themselves, and then from the actions of administrators and police officers who are answerable to Indian politicians. In circumstances where political incentives favor the orchestration or sponsorship of violence, civil society leaders are scarcely in a position to control such conflict. As an interviewee from COVA admitted:

The reality is that there can't be riots without political incitement. The BJP and MIM have both incited riots for their own reasons in Hyderabad, and the Congress has done the same for its reasons. So, what does one do in this situation? If the state sees some advantage in making people fight, then it is [incumbent upon] us—as civil society [actors]—to step in and show people that rioting is costly. But it is also very difficult for us to do so effectively if the political leaders don't want us to succeed.[13]

Second, in places where civil society leaders collaborate with the state to respond to constituents' needs, it is not uncommon that they run into challenges in building trust with residents. This trust deficit can further undermine efforts to maintain communal harmony. As one member of the *Balmiki Samaj Pragiti Sangh* or Balmiki Society Progress Union – a group that constitutes neighborhood-level peace committees in Hyderabad's Old City – noted:

Mohalla samiti activists in Hyderabad face considerable challenges in our work. Our biggest challenge [pertains] to building trust with the residents. The main problem is that many times, they [local residents] stop seeing us as their neighbors and start to think of us as police informants with vested interests. So, in this context, bringing [about] communal harmony becomes very difficult.[14]

---

[13] Interview with a civil society leader, Hyderabad, July 23, 2013.
[14] Interview with a civil society leader from *Balmiki Samaj Pragiti Sangh* or Balmiki Society Progress Union, Hyderabad, July 28, 2013.

Likewise, a respondent from Meerut described the limitations of that town's *mohalla samitis* or local peace committees in the following words:

> These *samitis* in Meerut are installed by the administration. They don't really work for peace. They only work for the people who create them. When you create a committee [like this], you strip people of their agency. So, I would [go so far as to] say that the decline in violence in the city has nothing at all do to with the peace committees.[15]

In addition to the above problems, and as previously noted, *mohalla samitis* in India are oftentimes temporary entities rather than permanent structures. In Hyderabad, for example, state authorities routinely create such organizations around sensitive events such as religious festivals or elections.[16] But because these groups rarely endure past such events, they lack the longevity necessary to achieve sustained periods of quiescence, as witnessed in Hyderabad over the last three decades.

Third, numerous CSOs in India remain highly skewed toward one ethnic group or another. In Meerut, for example, an interviewee estimated that 95% of the members of the *Sanyukt Vyapar Sangh* or Joint Business Association are Hindu Baniyas, members of the traditional caste group of traders and merchants.[17] Likewise, an officer from the Boolean Jewelry Traders Association held that approximately 75% of his organization is composed of Hindus.[18] Meanwhile, respondents revealed that Muslims hold a monopoly in the city's scissor and meat industries.[19] Indeed, it is only in Meerut's famous textile trade that Hindus and Muslims regularly interact as traders and weavers, respectively.[20] For all these reasons, it appears that rather than being attributable to the activities of civil society groups, the decrease in severe Hindu–Muslim riots observed across Indian cities over the last thirty years is more directly related to the recalculations and attendant choices of the country's politicians.

SUMMARY AND CONCLUSION

This appendix has presented a comparative and historical analysis of the development of civil society in Kenya and India, as well as original interview evidence to assess the alternative claim that the ethnic composition of civic associations more proximately accounts for variations in party violence than

---

[15] Interview with an SP politician, Meerut, August 21, 2013.
[16] Focus group discussion with members of the *Balmiki Samaj Pragiti Sangh* or Balmiki Society Progress Union, Hyderabad, July 28, 2013.
[17] Interview with a leader of the *Sanyukt Vyapar Sangh* or Joint Business Association, Meerut, August 21, 2013.
[18] Interview with a leader of the Boolean Jewelry Traders Association, Meerut, August 22, 2013.
[19] Interview with a BSP political leader, Meerut, August 23, 2013; interview with a journalist, Meerut, August 24, 2013.
[20] Interview with a leader of the Weavers' Welfare Association, Meerut, August 23, 2013; also see Engineer 1982.

Appendix C: The Development of Civil Society in Kenya and India

levels of party instability in these two countries. Broadly, the appendix has put forth two key findings. First, due to the dominance of political society over civil society, most CSOs and NGOs are far less powerful than the state. As a result, even if they are engaged in peacebuilding, conflict prevention, and conflict mitigation activities broadly conceived, their efforts to contain violence typically stand to be overpowered by elites' exhortations to citizens to participate in conflict. Second, there is a dearth of interethnic CSOs – of the kind that Varshney argues are necessary to keep violence from escalating – in the subnational research sites investigated in this book. In short, and as previously discussed in Chapter 2, while the composition of civil society can certainly shape *where* elites might direct their efforts to instrumentalize violence – as well as the sites where these campaigns might find success – a party instability framework offers greater insight into the conditions under which politicians might turn to violence as a political strategy in the first place.

References

Abdulai, Abdul-Gafaru and Sam Hickey. 2016. "The Politics of Development under Competitive Clientelism: Insights from Ghana's Education Sector," *African Affairs* 115(458): 44–72.

Adar, Korwa G. 2000. "Assessing Democratization Trends in Kenya: A Post-mortem of the Moi Regime," *Commonwealth and Comparative Politics* 38(3): 103–130.

Adeagbo, Oluwafemi and John-Mark Iyi. 2011. "Post-Election Crisis in Kenya and Internally Displaced Persons: A Critical Appraisal," *Journal of Politics and Law* 4(2): 174–179.

Africa Watch/Human Rights Watch. 1993. *Divide and Rule: State-Sponsored Ethnic Violence in Kenya*. New York, NY: Human Rights Watch.

Afrobarometer. 2017. "*Summary of Results – Afrobarometer Round 7 Survey in Ghana*," Accra, Ghana: Center for Democratic Development.

Agraharkar, Vishal. 2005. "Political Incentives and Hindu-Muslim Violence: A Study of Hyderabad, India," Undergraduate Thesis (Department of Political Science), Williams College. Unpublished Manuscript.

Ahmed, Hilal. 2014. "Muslims in Uttar Pradesh: Caste, Class, and Electoral Politics," *Economic & Political Weekly* 49(18): 1–5.

Ahram, Ariel. 2011. "The Theory and Method of Comparative Area Studies," *Qualitative Research* 11(1): 69–90.

Ahram, Ariel. 2016. "Pro-Government Militias and the Repertoires of Illicit State Violence," *Studies in Conflict & Terrorism* 39(2): 207–226.

Ahram, Ariel, Patrick Köllner, and Rudra Sil. 2018. *Comparative Area Studies: Methodological Rationales and Cross-Regional Applications*. New York, NY: Oxford University Press.

Ahuja, Juhi. 2019. "Protecting Holy Cows: Hindu Vigilantism against Muslims in India," in Tore Bjørgo and Miroslav Mareš (eds.) *Vigilantism against Migrants and Minorities*. Abingdon, UK: Routledge, pp. 55–68.

Aiyar, Sana. 2011. "Anticolonial Homelands across the Indian Ocean: The Politics of the Indian Diaspora in Kenya, ca. 1930–1950," *The American Historical Review* 116(4): 987–1013.

Aiyar, Sana. 2015. *Indians in Kenya: The Politics of Diaspora*. Cambridge, MA: Harvard University Press.

Akkoyunlu, Karabekir and Kerem Öktem. 2016. "Existential Insecurity and the Making of a Weak Authoritarian Regime in Turkey," *Southeast European and Black Sea Studies* 16(4): 505–527.

Akwiri, Joseph. 2014. "Kenya Arrests Governor over Attacks that Killed 65," *The Star*, June 26.

Alabi, Mojeed. 2009. "The Legislatures in Africa: A Trajectory of Weakness," *African Journal of Political Science and International Relations* 3(5): 233–241.

Alizada, Nafiza, Rowan Cole, Lisa Gastaldi, Sandra Grahn, Sebastian Hellmeier, Palina Kolvani, Jean Lachapelle, Anna Lührmann, Seraphine F. Maerz, Shreeya Pillai, and Staffan Lindberg. 2021. *Autocratization Turns Viral: Democracy Report 2021*. Gothenburg, Sweden: Varieties of Democracy (V-Dem) Institute.

Al Jazeera. 2004. "Who Is Behind the Maluku Violence?" *Al Jazeera*, May 13.

Al Jazeera. 2013. "Violence and Impunity," *Al Jazeera*, February 23.

Al Jazeera. 2022. "Kenya's President Kenyatta Backs His Former Rival Odinga in Polls," *Al Jazeera*, March 13.

All India Congress Committee. 1954. *Building New India: Selections from M.K. Gandhi, Rabindranath Tagore, Jawaharlal Nehru, S. Radhakrishnan, and Vinoba Bhave*. New Delhi, India: All India Congress Committee.

Aluaigba, Moses. 2016. "Democracy Deferred: The Effects of Electoral Malpractice on Nigeria's Path to Democratic Consolidation," *Journal of African Elections* 15(2): 136–158.

Amankwaah, Clementina. 2013. "Election-Related Violence: The Case of Ghana," *Current African Issues* 56: 5–37. Uppsala, Sweden: Nordiska Afrikainstitutet.

Ambedkar, Bhimrao. 1946. *What Congress and Gandhi Have Done to the Untouchables*. Delhi, India: Gautam Book Centre.

Anderson, Christopher. 1998. "Political Satisfaction in Old and New Democracies," Institute for European Studies, Working Paper # 98.4, Cornell University.

Anderson, David. 2005. *Histories of the Hanged: The Dirty War in Kenya and the End of Empire*. New York, NY: W.W. Norton & Company.

Angar, Jane and Kathleen Klaus. 2022. "Three Things to Know about Kenya's Elections Tomorrow," *The Washington Post*, August 8.

Angelo, Anaïs. 2020. *Power and the Presidency in Kenya: The Jomo Kenyatta Years*. New York, NY: Cambridge University Press.

Anyadike, Obi. 2014. "Conflict Dynamics on Kenya's Coast," *The New Humanitarian*, July 23.

Arjona, Ana, Zachariah Mampilly, and Wendy Pearlman. 2021. "Research in Violent or Post Conflict Political Settings (Working Group IV.2)" in "The Qualitative Transparency Deliberations: Insights and Implications," *Perspectives on Politics* 19(1): 200–202.

Arriola, Leonardo. 2013. *Multiethnic Coalitions in Africa: Business Financing of Opposition Election Campaigns*. New York, NY: Cambridge University Press.

Assies, William and Ton Salman. 2005. "Ethnicity and Politics in Bolivia," *Ethnopolitics* 4(3): 269–297.

Asunka, Joseph, Sarah Brierley, Mariam Golden, Eric Kramon, and George Ofosu. 2019. "Electoral Fraud or Violence: The Effect of Observers on Party Manipulation Strategies," *British Journal of Political Science* 49(1): 129–151.

References

Atieno-Odhiambo, Elisha. 2004. "Hegemonic Enterprises and Instrumentalities of Survival: Ethnicity and Democracy in Kenya," in Bruce Berman, Dickson Eyoh, and Will Kymlicka (eds.) *Ethnicity and Democracy in Africa*. Athens: Ohio University Press, pp. 167–182.

Auerbach, Adam, Jennifer Bussell, Simon Chauchard, Francesca Jensenius, Gareth Nellis, Mark Schneider, Neelanjan Sircar, Pavithra Suryanarayan, Tariq Thachil, Milan Vaishnav, Rahul Verma, and Adam Ziegfeld. 2022. "Rethinking the Study of Electoral Politics in the Developing World: Reflections on the Indian Case," *Perspectives on Politics* 20(1): 250–264.

Auerbach, Kiran. 2022. "Accountable to Whom? How Strong Parties Subvert Local Democratic Institutions," *Party Politics* 28(5): 865–878.

Axelrod, Robert. 1984. *The Evolution of Cooperation*. New York, NY: Basic Books.

Aydinli, Ersel and Nihat Ozcan. 2011. "The Conflict Resolution and Counterterrorism Dilemma: Turkey Faces Its Kurdish Question," *Terrorism and Political Violence* 23(3): 438–457.

Baah, Belinda. 2014. "Insecurity Intensifies in Kenya," *Africa Conflict Monthly Monitor* 2014(9): 37–40.

Bajpai, Rochana. 2000. "Constituent Assembly Debates and Minority Rights," *Economic and Political Weekly* 35(21/22): 1837–1845.

Balagopal, K. 1988. "Meerut 1987: Reflections on an Inquiry," *Economic and Political Weekly* 23(16): 768–771.

Balaton-Chrimes, Samantha. 2021. "Who are Kenya's 42(+) Tribes? The Census and the Political Utility of Magical Uncertainty," *Journal of Eastern African Studies* 15(1): 43–62.

Balz, Dan. 2021. "Trump Knows No Limits as He Tries to Overturn the Election," The Washington Post, January 3.

Banerjee, Abhijit, Donald P. Green, Jeffrey McManus, and Rohini Pande. 2011. "Are Poor Voters Indifferent to Whether Elected Leaders are Criminal or Corrupt? A Vignette Experiment in Rural India," *Political Communication* 31(3): 391–407.

Banerjee, Sumanta. 1991. "'Hindutva' – Ideology and Social Psychology," *Economic & Political Weekly* 26(3): 97–101.

Banerjee, Vasabjit. 2019. *Undoing the Revolution: Comparing Elite Subversion of Peasant Rebellions*. Philadelphia, PA: Temple University Press.

Banerji, Annie. 2012. "Indian Lawmaker Gets 28 Years for 2002 Massacre," Reuters, August 31.

Barkan, Joel. 2004. "Kenya after Moi," *Foreign Affairs* 83(1): 87–100.

Barkan, Joel. 2009. "African Legislatures and the 'Third Wave of Democratization,'" in Joel Barkan (ed.) *Legislative Power in Emerging African Democracies*. Boulder, CO: Lynne Rienner Publishers, pp. 1–32.

Barkan, Joel and John Okumu. 1978. "'Semi-Competitive' Elections, Clientelism, and Political Recruitment in a No-Party State: The Kenyan Experience," in Guy Hermet, Richard Rose, and Alain Rouquié (eds.) *Elections without Choice*. New York, NY: Palgrave Macmillan, pp. 88–107.

Barlas, Asma. 2019. *Democracy, Nationalism, and Communalism: The Colonial Legacy in South Asia*. Abingdon, UK: Routledge.

Barma, Naazneen. 2012. "Peace-building and the Predatory Political Economy of Insecurity: Evidence from Cambodia, East Timor, and Afghanistan," *Conflict, Security, & Development* 12(3): 273–298.

Barma, Naazneen. 2014. "The Rentier State at Work: Comparative Experiences of the Resource Curse in East Asia and the Pacific," *Asia & the Pacific Policy Studies* 1(2): 257–272.

Barma, Naazneen. 2016. *The Peacebuilding Puzzle: Political Order in Post-conflict States*. New York, NY: Cambridge University Press.

Barron, Patrick. 2019. *When Violence Works: Postconflict Violence and Peace in Indonesia*. Ithaca, NY: Cornell University Press.

Barron, Patrick, Kai Kaiser, and Menno Pradhan. 2004. *Local Conflict in Indonesia: Measuring Incidence and Identifying Patterns*. World Bank Policy Research Paper # 3384.

Başlevent, Cem, Hasan Kirmanoğlu, and Burhan Şenatalar. 2004. "Voter Profiles and Fragmentation in the Turkish Party System," *Party Politics* 10(3): 307–324.

Basu, Amrita. 2021. "Changing Modalities of Violence: Lessons from Hindu Nationalist India," in Karen Barkey, Sudipta Kaviraj, and Vatsal Naresh (eds.) *Negotiating Democracy and Religious Pluralism: India, Pakistan, and Turkey*. New York, NY: Oxford University Press, pp. 277–300.

Basu, Deepankar. 2021. "Majoritarian Politics and Hate Crimes against Religious Minorities: Evidence from India 2009–2018," *World Development* 146: 1–15.

Bates, Robert. 2008. *When Things Fell Apart: State Failure in Late-century Africa*. New York, NY: Cambridge University Press.

Bayar, Ali. 1996. "The Developmental State and Economic Policy in Turkey," *Third World Quarterly* 17(4): 773–786.

Bekoe, Dorina and Stephanie Burchard. 2017. "The Contradictions of Pre-election Violence: The Effects of Violence on Voter Turnout in Sub-Saharan Africa," *African Studies Review* 60(2): 73–92.

Berenschot, Ward. 2009. "Rioting as Maintaining Relations: Hindu-Muslim Violence and Political Mediation in Gujarat, India," *Civil Wars* 11(4): 414–433.

Berenschot, Ward. 2011a. "On the Usefulness of *Goonda* in Indian Politics: 'Moneypower' and 'Musclepower' in a Gujarati Community," *South Asia: The Journal of South Asian Studies* 34(2): 255–275.

Berenschot, Ward. 2011b. *Riot Politics: Hindu-Muslim Violence and the Indian State*. New York, NY: Columbia University Press.

Berenschot, Ward. 2011c. "The Spatial Distribution of Riots: Patronage and the Instigation of Communal Violence in Gujarat, India," *World Development* 39(2): 221–230.

Berenschot, Ward. 2014. "Muzaffarnagar Riots: Perils of a Patronage Democracy," *Economic & Political Weekly* 49(12): 15–18.

Berenschot, Ward. 2020. "Patterned Pogroms: Patronage Networks as Infrastructure for Electoral Violence in India and Indonesia," *Journal of Peace Research* 57(1): 171–184.

Berenschot, Ward and Edward Aspinall. 2020. "How Clientelism Varies: Comparing Patronage Democracies," *Democratization* 27(1): 1–19.

Berenschot, Ward and Peter Mulder. 2019. "Explaining Regional Variation in Local Governance: Clientelism and State-dependency in Indonesia," *World Development* 122: 233–244.

Berman, Bruce. 1998. "Ethnicity, Patronage, and the African State: The Politics of Uncivil Nationalism" *African Affairs* 97(388): 305–341.

References

Berman, Bruce and John Lonsdale. 1980. "Crises of Accumulation, Coercion and the Colonial State: The Development of the Labor Control System in Kenya, 1919–1929," *Canadian Journal of African Studies* 14(1): 55–81.

Berry, Marie. 2018. *War, Women, and Power: From Violence to Mobilization in Rwanda and Bosnia-Herzegovina*. New York, NY: Cambridge University Press.

Bhavnani, Rikhil and Bethany Lacina. 2015. "The Effects of Weather-induced Migration on Sons of the Soil Riots in India," *World Politics* 67(4): 760–794.

Biberman, Yelena. 2018. "Self-Defense Militias, Death Squads, and State Outsourcing of Violence in India and Turkey," *Journal of Strategic Studies* 41(5): 751–781.

Birch, Sarah. 2001. "Electoral System and Party System Stability in Post-communist Europe." Paper presented at the 2001 Annual Conference of the American Political Science Association, San Francisco, CA, 26–29 August.

Birch, Sarah. 2003. *Electoral Systems and Political Transformation in Post-communist Europe*. London, UK: Palgrave Macmillan.

Birch, Sarah. 2020. *Electoral Violence, Corruption, and Political Order*. Princeton, NJ: Princeton University Press.

Birch, Sarah, Ursula Daxecker, and Kristine Höglund. 2020. "Electoral Violence: An Introduction," *Journal of Peace Research* 57(1): 126–139.

Biswas, Soutik. 2021. "'Electoral Autocracy': The Downgrading of India's Democracy." *BBC News*, March 16.

Bob-Milliar, George. 2012. "Political Party Activism in Ghana: Factors Influencing the Decision of the Politically Active to Join a Political Party," *Democratization* 19(4): 668–689.

Bob-Milliar, George. 2014. "Party Youth Activists and Low-intensity Electoral Violence in Ghana: A Qualitative Study of Party Foot Soldiers' Activism," *African Studies Quarterly* 15(1): 125–152.

Bob-Milliar, George. 2019. "Place and Party Organizations: Party Activism Inside Party-branded Sheds at the Grassroots in Northern Ghana," *Territory, Politics, and Governance* 7(4): 474–493.

Bob-Milliar, George and Jeffrey Paller. 2018. "Democratic Ruptures and Electoral Outcomes in Africa: Ghana's 2016 Election," *Africa Spectrum* 53(1): 5–35.

Boone, Catherine. 2011. "Politically Allocated Land Rights and the Geography of Electoral Violence: The Case of Kenya in the 1990s," *Comparative Political Studies* 44(10): 1311–1342.

Boone, Catherine. 2012. "Land Conflict and Distributive Politics in Kenya," *African Studies Review* 55(1): 75–103.

Brancati, Dawn. 2006. "Decentralization: Fueling the Fire or Dampening the Flames of Ethnic Conflict and Secessionism?" *International Organization* 60(3): 651–685.

Brancati, Dawn. 2009. *Peace by Design: Managing Intrastate Conflict through Decentralization*. New York, NY: Cambridge University Press.

Branch, Daniel. 2006. "Loyalists, Mau May, and Elections in Kenya: The First Triumph of the System, 1957–1958," *Africa Today* 53(2): 27–50.

Branch, Daniel. 2009. *Defeating Mau Mau, Creating Kenya: Counterinsurgency, Civil War, and Decolonization*. New York, NY: Cambridge University Press.

Branch, Daniel and Nic Cheeseman. 2006. "The Politics of Control in Kenya: Understanding the Bureaucratic-Executive State, 1952–78," *Review of African Political Economy* 33(107): 11–31.

Branch, Daniel and Nic Cheeseman. 2008. "Democratization, Sequencing, and State Failure in Africa: Lessons from Kenya," *African Affairs* 108(430): 1–26.

Branch, Daniel and Nic Cheeseman. 2010. "Introduction: Our Turn to Eat," in Daniel Branch, Nic Cheeseman, and Leigh Gardner (eds.) *Our Turn to Eat: Politics in Kenya Since 1950*. Münster, Germany: Lit Verlag, pp. 1–22.

Brass, Jennifer. 2016. *Allies or Adversaries: NGOs and the State in Africa*. New York, NY: Cambridge University Press.

Brass, Paul. 1990. *The Politics of India since Independence*. New York, NY: Cambridge University Press.

Brass, Paul. 1997. *Theft of an Idol: Text and Context in the Representation of Collective Violence*. Princeton, NJ: Princeton University Press.

Brass, Paul. 2003a. "An Open Letter in Response to Ashutosh Varshney," *H-Net*, December 4.

Brass, Paul. 2003b. *The Production of Hindu-Muslim Violence in Contemporary India*. Seattle: University of Washington Press.

Brass, Paul. 2004. "Development of an Institutionalised Riot System in Meerut City, 1961 to 1982," *Economic & Political Weekly* 39(44): 4839–4848.

Brass, Paul. 2006. *Forms of Collective Violence: Riots, Pogroms, and Genocide in Modern India*. New Delhi, India: Three Essays Collective.

Bratton, Michael and Mwangi S. Kimenyi. 2008. "Voting in Kenya: Putting Ethnicity in Perspective," *Journal of Eastern African Studies* 2(2): 272–289.

Brender, Adi and Allan Drazen. 2007. "Why Is Economic Policy Different in New Democracies? Affecting Attitudes about Democracy," Paper # w13457, National Bureau of Economic Research (NBER), Cambridge, MA.

Brennan, Lance. 1994. "The State and Communal Violence in UP: 1947–1992," *South Asia: Journal of South Asian Studies* 17(s1): 19–34.

Brierley Sarah and George Ofosu. 2016. "9 Things You Should Know about Ghana's Election," *The Washington Post*, December 7.

Brosius, Christiane. 2004. *Empowering Visions: The Politics of Representation in Hindu Nationalism*. New York, NY: Anthem Press.

Brown, Stephen. 2001. "Authoritarian Leaders and Multiparty Elections in Africa: How Foreign Donors Help to Keep Kenya's Daniel arap Moi in Power," *Third World Quarterly* 22(5): 725–739.

Buijtenhuijs, Robert. 1974–1975. "The Kenya African National Union," *International Journal of Politics* 4(4): 58–76.

Bulutgil, Zeynep and Neeraj Prasad. 2023. "Inequality, Elections, and Communal Riots in India," *Journal of Peace Research* 60(4): 619–633. https://doi.org/10.1177/00223433221091307.

Burbidge, Dominic. 2015. "Democracy versus Diversity: Ethnic Representation in a Devolved Kenya," Working Paper, University of Oxford.

Burchard, Stephanie. 2015. *Electoral Violence in Sub-Saharan Africa*. Boulder, CO: Lynne Rienner Publishers.

Butalia, Urvashi. 2000. *The Other Side of Silence: Voices for the Partition of India*. Durham, NC: Duke University Press.

Campante, Filipe, Davin Chor, and Quoc-Anh Do. 2009. "Instability and Incentives for Corruption," *Economics & Politics* 21(1): 42–92.

Caramani, Danielle. 2000. *Elections in Western Europe since 1815: Electoral Results by Constituencies*. Oxford, UK: Macmillan Reference.

References

Çarkoğlu, Ali. 1998. "The Turkish Party System in Transition: Party Performance and Agenda Change," *Political Studies* 46(3): 544–571.
Center for Democratic Development (CDD). 2016. *Ghana's 2016 Elections: Prospects for Credibility and Peacefulness*. Accra, Ghana: CDD.
Centre for the Study of Developing Societies (CSDS). 2014. *National Election Study 2014*. New Delhi, India: CSDS/Lokniti.
Centre for the Study of Developing Societies (CSDS). 2019. *National Election Study 2019 Pre-poll Survey Findings*. New Delhi, India: CSDS/Lokniti.
Ceron, Andrea. 2017. "Intra-party Politics in 140 Characters," *Party Politics* 23(1): 7–17.
Chacha, Babere. 2010. "Pastors or Bastards? The Dynamics of Religion and Politics in the 2007 General Elections in Kenya," in Karuti Kanyinga and Duncan Okello (eds.) *Tensions and Reversals in Democratic Transitions: The Kenya 2007 General Elections*. Nairobi, Kenya: Society for International Development (SID) and the Institute for Development Studies (IDS), University of Nairobi, pp. 101–134.
Chandhoke, Neera. 2011. "Civil Society in India," in Michael Edwards (ed.) *The Oxford Handbook of Civil Society*. New York, NY: Oxford University Press, pp. 171–182.
Chandra, Kanchan. 1999. "The Ethnificiation of the Party System in Uttar Pradesh and its Consequences," in Ramashray Roy and Paul Wallace (eds.) *Indian Politics and the 1998 Election*. New Delhi, India: Sage Publications, pp. 55–104.
Chandra, Kanchan. 2000. "The Transformation of Ethnic Politics in India: The Decline of Congress and the Rise of the Bahujan Samaj Party in Hoshiarpur," *The Journal of Asian Studies* 59(1): 26–61.
Chandra, Kanchan. 2004. *Why Ethnic Parties Succeed: Patronage and Ethnic Head Counts in India*. New York, NY: Cambridge University Press.
Chandra, Kanchan. 2005. "Ethnic Parties and Democratic Stability," *Perspectives on Politics* 3(2): 235–252.
Chatterjee, Partha. 1998. "Beyond the Nation? Or Within?" *Social Text* 56(1/2): 57–69.
Chatterjee, Partha. 2004. *The Politics of the Governed: Reflections on Popular Politics in Most of the World*. New York, NY: Columbia University Press.
Chatterjee, Partha. 2011. *Lineages of Political Society*. New York, NY: Columbia University Press.
Chauchard, Simon, Marko Klašnja, and S. P. Harish. 2019. "Getting Rich Too Fast? Voters' Reactions to Politicians' Wealth Accumulation," *Journal of Politics* 81(4): 1197–1209.
Chawla, Prabhu. 1982. "Meerut Burns in Communal Fire Ignited by Squabble for 200 Sq. Foot Property," India Today, October 31.
Cheeseman, Nic. 2006. *The Rise and Fall of Civilian-Authoritarianism in Africa: Patronage, Participation, and Political Parties in Kenya and Zambia Government*, DPhil Dissertation (Department of Politics), University of Oxford, Unpublished Manuscript.
Cheeseman, Nic. 2008. "The Kenyan Elections of 2007: An Introduction," *Journal of Eastern African Studies* 2(2): 166–184.
Cheeseman, Nic, Gabrielle Lynch, and Justin Willis. 2016. "Decentralization in Kenya: The Governance of Governors," *Journal of Modern African Studies* 51(1): 1–35.
Chege, Michael. 2008. "Kenya: Back from the Brink?" *Journal of Democracy* 19(4): 125–139.

Cherono, Kiptanui. 2022. "Religious Approaches to Peacebuilding in Uasin Gishu," *Kenya News Agency*, June 23.

Chhibber, Pradeep. 1999. *Democracy without Associations: Transformation of the Party System and Social Cleavages in India*. Ann Arbor: University of Michigan Press.

Chhibber, Pradeep, Francesca Jensenius, and Pavithra Suryanarayan. 2014. "Party Organization and Party Proliferation in India," *Party Politics* 20(4): 489–505.

Chisti, Anees. 1982. "Meerut: Anatomy of a Riot," *Economic & Political Weekly* 17(44): 1765–1768.

Cleven, Erik. 2013. *Elites, Youth, and Informal Networks: Explaining Ethnic Violence in Kenya and Kosovo*, PhD Dissertation (Department of Political Science), Purdue University. Unpublished Manuscript.

Cohen, Mollie, Facundo Salles Kobilanski, and Elizabeth Zechmeister. 2018. "Electoral Volatility in Latin America," *Journal of Politics* 80(3): 1017–1022.

Collier, Paul. 2009. "Post-conflict Recovery: How Should Strategies Be Distinctive?" *Journal of African Economies* 18(suppl_1): i99–i131.

Collier, Ruth. 1999. *Paths toward Democracy: The Working Class and Elites in Western Europe and South America*. New York, NY: Cambridge University Press.

Conboy, Kevin. 1978. "Detention Without Trial in Kenya," *Georgia Journal of International and Comparative Law* 8: 444–461.

Confederation of Voluntary Associations (COVA). 2018. "About Us – Overview," www. covanetwork.org/about-us/overview/.

Coppedge, Michael. 1993. "Party and Society in Mexico and Venezuela: Why Competition Matters," *Comparative Politics* 25(3): 253–274.

Coppedge, Michael, John Gerring, Carl Henrik Knutsen, Staffan I. Lindberg, Jan Teorell, David Altman, Michael Bernhard, M. Steven Fish, Adam Glynn, Allen Hicken, Anna Lührmann, Kyle Marquardt, Kelly McMann, Pamela Paxton, Daniel Pemstein, Brigitte Seim, Rachel Sigman, Svend-Erik Skaaning, Jeffrey Staton, Agnes Cornell, Lisa Gastaldi, Haakon Gjerløw, Valeriya Mechkova, Johannes von Römer, Aksel Sundtröm, Eitan Tzelgov, Luca Uberti, Yi-ting Wang, Tore Wig, and Daniel Ziblatt. 2019. "V-Dem Codebook v9," Varieties of Democracy (V-Dem) Project. University of Gothenburg, Sweden.

Copland, Ian. 2010. "The Production and Containment of Communal Violence: Scenarios from Modern India," *South Asia: Journal of South Asian Studies* 33(1): 122–150.

Cooper, Malcolm. 2002. "The Legacy of Atatürk: Turkish Political Structures and Policy Making," *International Affairs* 78(1): 115–128.

Cyr, Jennifer. 2016. "Between Adaptation and Breakdown: Conceptualizing Party Survival," *Comparative Politics* 49(1): 125–145.

Cyr, Jennifer. 2017. *The Fates of Political Parties: Institutional Crisis, Continuity, and Change in Latin America*. New York, NY: Cambridge University Press.

Dagi, Ihsan. 2008. "Islamist Parties and Democracy: Turkey's AKP in Power," *Journal of Democracy* 19(3): 25–30.

Dam, Rinita and Jenny Lunn. 2014. "First Impressions Count: The Ethics of Choosing to Be A 'Native' or a 'Foreign' Researcher – Two Tales from Fieldwork in India," in Jenny Lunn (ed.) *Fieldwork in the Global South: Ethical Challenges and Dilemmas*. Abingdon, UK: Routledge, pp. 96–108.

Damary, Rita. 2011. "Stand Firm and Shun Tribal Alliances, Misoi tells Kalenjin," *The Star*, September 20.

References

Dasgupta, Adi. 2011. "India," in Nic Cheeseman (ed.) *Programmatic Parties in Comparative Perspective*. Stockholm, Sweden: Institute for Democracy and Electoral Assistance (IDEA), pp. 63–82.

Davis, Paul, Eric Larson, Zachary Haldeman, Mustafa Oguz, and Yashodhara Rana. 2012. "Public Support of the Kurdistan Workers' Party (PKK) in Turkey," in Paul Davis, Eric Larson, Zachary Haldeman, Mustafa Oguz, and Yashodhara Rana (eds.) *Understanding and Influencing Public Support for Insurgency and Terrorism*. Santa Monica, CA: RAND Corporation, pp. 99–118.

Daxecker, Ursula. 2020. "Unequal Votes, Unequal Violence: Malapportionment and Election Violence in India," *Journal of Peace Research* 57(1): 156–170.

Daxecker, Ursula and Hanne Fjelde. 2022. "Electoral Violence, Partisan Identity, and Perceptions of Election Quality: A Survey Experiment in West Bengal, India," *Comparative Politics* 55(1): 47–69.

Daxecker, Ursula and Mascha Rauschenbach. 2023. "Election Type and the Logic of Pre-election Violence: Evidence from Zimbabwe," *Electoral Studies*. https://doi.org/10.1016/j.electstud.2023.102583.

de Kadt, Daniel and Evan Lieberman. 2020. "Nuanced Accountability: Voter Responses to Service Delivery in Southern Africa," *British Journal of Political Science* 50(1): 185–215.

de Kadt, Daniel, Ada Johnson-Kanu, and Melissa Sands. 2023. "State Violence, Party Formation, and Electoral Accountability: The Political Legacy of the Marikana Massacre," *American Political Science Review*. https://doi.org/10.1017/S0003055423000448.

de Wolf, Jan. 1983. "*Dini ya Msambwa*: Militant Protest or Millenarian Promise?" *Canadian Journal of African Studies* 17(2): 265–276.

de Zeeuw, Jeroen (ed.) 2008. *From Soldiers to Politicians: The Transformation of Rebel Movements after War*. Boulder, CO: Lynne Rienner Publishers.

Democracy Watch. 2007. "The Party Foot Soldier Phenomenon and Ghanaian Democracy," *Center for Democratic Development* 7(3): 4–6.

Dercon, Stefan and Roxana Gutiérrez-Romero. 2012. "Triggers and Characteristics of the 2007 Kenyan Electoral Violence," *World Development* 40(4): 731–744.

Deshpande, J. V. 1993. "Assembly Elections: Winnability Is All," *Economic & Political Weekly* 28(46–47): 2505.

Devasher, Madhavi and Elena Gadjanova. 2021. "Cross-ethnic Appeals in Plural Democracies," *Nations and Nationalism*. https://doi.org/10.1111/nana.12686: 1–17.

Dhattiwala, Raheel and Michael Biggs. 2012. "The Political Logic of Ethnic Violence: The Anti-Muslim Pogrom in Gujarat, 2002," *Politics and Society* 40(4): 483–516.

Dietz, Henry and David Myers. 2007. "From Thaw to Deluge: Party System Collapse in Venezuela and Peru," *Latin American Politics and Society* 49(2): 59–86.

Dionne, Kim. 2011. "The Role of Executive Time Horizons in State Response to AIDS in Africa," *Comparative Political Studies* 44(1): 55–77.

Doctor, Austin and Stephen Bagwell. 2020. "Risky Business: Foreign Direct Investment and the Economic Consequences of Electoral Violence," *Journal of Global Security Studies* 5(2): 339–360.

Driscoll, Barry. 2018. "Why Political Competition Can Increase Patronage," *Studies in Comparative International Development* 53(4): 404–427.

Dupas, Pascaline and Jonathan Robinson. 2010. "Coping with Political Instability: Micro Evidence from Kenya's 2007 Election Crisis," *American Economic Review* 100(2): 120–124.

Dupas, Pascaline and Jonathan Robinson. 2012. "The (Hidden) Costs of Political Instability: Evidence from Kenya's 2007 Election Crisis," *Journal of Development Economics* 99(2):314–329.

Dutta, Bhaskar and Poonam Gupta. 2014. "How Indian Voters Respond to Candidates with Criminal Charges: Evidence from the 2009 Lok Sabha Elections," *Economic & Political Weekly* 49(4): 43–51.

Dyzenhaus, Alex. 2021. "Patronage or Policy? The Politics of Property Rights Formalization in Kenya," *World Development*. https://doi.org/10.1016/j.worlddev.2021.105580.

Eisenstadt, Todd. 2003. *Courting Democracy in Mexico: Party Strategies and Electoral Institutions*. New York, NY: Cambridge University Press.

Elder, Claire, Susan Stigant, and Jonas Claes. 2014. *Elections and Violent Conflict in Kenya: Making Prevention Stick*. Washington, DC: United States Institute of Peace.

Elischer, Sebastian. 2010. "Political Parties, Elections and Ethnicity in Kenya," in D. Branch, N. Cheeseman, and L. Gardner (eds.) *Our Turn to Eat: Politics in Kenya since 1950*. Münster, Germany: Lit Verlag, pp. 199–220.

Elischer, Sebastian. 2013. *Political Parties in Africa: Ethnicity and Party Formation*. New York, NY: Cambridge University Press.

Ellis, Ellen. 1950. "Turkey Looks Toward the West," *Current History* 19(111): 282–286.

Engholm, G. M. 1956. "Kenya's First Direct Election for Africans, March 1957," *Parliamentary Affairs* 10(4): 424–433.

Engineer, Asghar Ali. 1977. "Do Muslims Vote as A Block?" *Economic & Political Weekly* 12(11): 458–459.

Engineer, Asghar Ali. 1982. "The Guilty Men of Meerut," *Economic & Political Weekly* 17(45):1803–1805.

Engineer, Asghar Ali. 1983. "Communal Killings in Hyderabad," *Economic & Political Weekly* 18(40): 1688–1690.

Engineer, Asghar Ali. 1987. "Meerut: The Nation's Shame," *Economic & Political Weekly*, 22(25): 969–971.

Engineer, Asghar Ali. 1988. "Gian Prakash Committee Report on Meerut Riots," *Economic & Political Weekly*, 23(1/2): 30–31, 33.

Engineer, Asghar Ali. 1991a. "Lok Sabha Elections and Communalization of Politics," *Economic & Political Weekly* 26(27–28): 1649, 1651–1652.

Engineer, Asghar. 1991b. "Making of the Hyderabad Riots," *Economic & Political Weekly* 26(6): 271–274.

Engineer, Asghar Ali. 1991c. "The Bloody Trail: Ramjanmabhoomi and Communal Violence in UP," *Economic & Political Weekly* 26(4): 155, 157–159.

Engineer, Ashgar Ali. 1993. "Bombay Riots: Second Phase," *Economic & Political Weekly* 28(12/13): 505–508.

Engineer, Asghar Ali. 1997a. "An Analytical Study of the Meerut Riot," in Asghar Ali Engineer (ed.) *Communal Riots in Post-Independence India* (2nd edition). Hyderabad, India: Sangam Books, pp. 271–280.

Engineer, Asghar Ali. 1997b. "Communalism and Communal Violence, 1996," *Economic & Political Weekly* 32(7): 323–326.

Engineer, Asghar Ali. 2002. "Communal Riots: Review of 2001," *Economic & Political Weekly* 37(2): 100–104.

References

Engineer, Asghar Ali. 2004. *Communal Riots after Independence: A Comprehensive Account*. New Delhi, India: Shipra Publications.

Engineer, Asghar Ali. 2005. "Communal Riots, 2004," *Economic and Political Weekly* 40(6):517–520.

Engineer, Irfan, Neha Dabhade, and Suraj Nair. 2020. "India and Communal Violence: Mob Lynching in 2019," Center for the Study of Society and Secularism, Mumbai, India.

Erdeniz, Gözde. 2016. "Challenges to the Religious-Political Establishment: The Cases of Anti-capitalist Muslims in Turkey and Women of the Wall in Israel," in Aviad Rubin and Yusuf Sarfati (eds.) *The Jarring Road to Democratic Inclusion: A Comparative Assessment of State-Society Engagements in Turkey and Israel*. Lanham, MD: Lexington Books, pp. 83–112.

Erdogan, Mustafa. 1999. "Islam in Turkish Politics: Turkey's Quest for Democracy without Islam," *Middle East Critique* 8(15): 25–49.

Ernstorfer, Anita. 2018. *Peacebuilding Networks and Alliance in Kenya: A Retrospective Look at Collective Peacebuilding Effectiveness*. Cambridge, MA: CDA Collaborative Learning Projects.

Esen, Berk and Gümüşçü, Şebnem. 2017. "A Small Yes for Presidentialism: The Turkish Constitutional Referendum of April 2017," *South European Society and Politic* 22(3): 303–326.

Ezeibe, Christian and Okey Ikeanyibe. 2017. "Ethnic Politics, Hate Speech, and Access to Political Power in Nigeria," *Africa Today* 63(4): 64–83.

Farooqui, Adnan and E. Sridharan. 2016. "Can Umbrella Parties Survive?" *Commonwealth & Comparative Politics* 54(3): 331–361.

Feldmann, Linda. 1983. "High Kenyan Official Resigns Under Cloud," *The Christian Science Monitor*, July 1.

Ferree, Karen. 2010. "The Social Origins of Electoral Volatility in Africa," *British Journal of Political Science* 40(4): 759–779.

Fjelde, Hanne. 2020. "Political Party Strength and Electoral Violence," *Journal of Peace Research* 57(1): 140–155.

Fjelde, Hanne and Kristine Höglund. 2016. "Electoral Institutions and Electoral Violence in Sub-Saharan Africa," *British Journal of Political Science* 46(2): 297–320.

Fjelde, Hanne and Kristine Höglund. 2018. "Ethnic Politics and Elite Competition: The Roots of Electoral Violence in Kenya," in Mimmi Söderberg Kovacs and Jasper Bjarnesen (eds.) *Violence in African Elections: Between Democracy and Big Man Politics*. London, UK: Zed Books, pp. 27–46.

Franda, Marcus. 1962. "The Organizational Development of India's Congress Party," *Pacific Affairs* 35(3): 248–260.

Fredland, Richard A. 1989. "Kenyan Government Cracks Down on Dissent," Salem Press Encyclopedia.

Frenz, Margret. 2013. "Swaraj for Kenya, 1949–1965: The Ambiguities of Transnational Politics," *Past & Present* 218(supplement 8): 151–177.

Frye, Timothy, Ora John Reuter, and David Szakonyi. 2019. "Hitting Them with Carrots: Voter Intimidation and Vote Buying in Russia," *British Journal of Political Science* 49(3): 857–881.

Fujii, Lee Ann. 2010. "Shades of Truth and Lies: Interpreting Testimonies of War and Violence," *Journal of Peace Research* 47(2): 231–241.

Gaitho, Macharia. 2020. "Hold Uhuru, Raila, and Ruto to Account if Politics Breeds Violence," *The Daily Nation*, June 15.

Gandhi, Krishna. 1980. "Anatomy of the Moradabad Riots," *Economic & Political Weekly* 15(36): 1505–1507.

Gardner, Amy. 2021. "'I just Want to Find 11,780 Votes': In Extraordinary Hour-Long Call, Trump Pressures Georgia Secretary of State to Recalculate the Vote in his Favor," *The Washington Post*, January 3.

Gautam, Kul. 2005. "Mistakes, Miscalculations, and the Search for Middle Ground: An Exit Strategy for Nepal," *Liberal Democracy Nepal Bulletin* 1(1): 1–9.

Gherghina, Sergiu. 2013. "One-Shot Party Primaries: The Case of the Romanian Social Democrats," *Politics* 33(3): 185–195.

Godbole, Girija. 2014. "Revealing and Concealing: Ethical Dilemmas of Maneuvering Identity in the Field – Experiences from Researching the Relationship between Land and Rural Women in Western India," in Jenny Lunn (ed.) *Fieldwork in the Global South: Ethical Challenges and Dilemmas*. Abingdon, UK: Routledge, pp. 85–95.

Goldsworthy, David. 1982a. "Kenyan Politics since Kenyatta," *Australian Journal of International Affairs* 38(1): 27–31.

Goldsworthy, David. 1982b. *Tom Mboya: The Man Kenya Wanted to Forget*. Nairobi, Kenya: East African Publishers.

Good, Kenneth. 1968. "Kenyatta and the Organization of KANU," *Canadian Journal of African Studies* 2(2): 115–136.

Gottschalk, Keith. 2016. "Political Violence in South Africa Points to Rising Tensions in the ANC," *The Conversation*, June 22.

Government of India. 1949. *Sunderlal Committee Report on Police Action in Hyderabad*. New Delhi, India: Government Printer.

Government of India. 2014. *Dr. Babasaheb Ambedkar: Writings and Speeches* (Volume 2). New Delhi, India: Ministry of Social Justice and Empowerment.

Government of India. 2018. *Statistical Report on General Election, 1989 to the Legislative Assembly of Andhra Pradesh*. New Delhi, India: Election Commission of India.

Government of Kenya. 1965. "Annual District Report." Nyeri, Kenya: Government Printer.

Government of Uttar Pradesh. 1981. *Census of India 1981—Uttar Pradesh*. Lucknow, India: Director of Census Operations.

Government of Uttar Pradesh. 1987. *Gian Prakash Committee Report on the 1987 Meerut Riots*, published in installments in *The Telegraph* (Calcutta), November 22–30, 1987.

Graff, Violette and Juliette Galonnier. 2013a. "Hindu-Muslim Communal Riots in India I (1947–1986)," Mass Violence and Resistance Research Network. Paris: SciencesPo.

Graff, Violette and Juliette Galonnier. 2013b. "Hindu-Muslim Communal Riots in India II (1986–2011)," Online Encyclopedia of Mass Violence, Mass Violence Resistance Research Network. Paris: SciencesPo.

Graham, Carol. 1992. *Peru's APRA: Parties, Politics, and the Elusive Quest for Democracy*. Boulder, CO: Lynne Rienner Publishers.

Guasti, Petra. 2020. "The Impact of the COVID-19 Pandemic in Central and Eastern Europe: The Rise of Autocracy and Democratic Resilience," *Democratic Theory* 7(2): 47–60.

Guha, Ramachandra. 2019. *India After Gandhi: The History of the World's Largest Democracy*. New York, NY: HarperCollins Publishers.

Gunter, Michael. 1989. "Political Instability in Turkey during the 1970s," *Journal of Conflict Studies* 9(1): 63–77.

Gurcan, Metin. 2015. "Arming Civilians as a Counterterror Strategy: The Case of the Village Guard System in Turkey," *Dynamics of Asymmetric Conflict* 8(1): 1–22.

Gutiérrez-Romero, Roxana and Adrienne LeBas. 2020. "Does Electoral Violence Affect Vote Choice and Willingness to Vote? Conjoint Analysis of a Vignette Experiment," *Journal of Peace Research* 57(1): 77–92.

Hafner-Burton, Emilie, Susan Hyde, and Ryan Jablonski. 2014. "When do Governments Resort to Election Violence?" *British Journal of Political Science* 44(1): 149–179.

Hardgrave, Robert. 1985. "India in 1984: Confrontation, Assassination, and Succession," *Asian Survey* 25(2): 131–144.

Harmel, Robert and John D. Robertson. 1985. "Formation and Success of New Parties: A Cross National Analysis," *International Political Science Review* 6(4): 501–523.

Harriss, John. 2007. "Antinomies of Empowerment: Observations on Civil Society, Politics, and Urban Governance in India," *Economic & Political Weekly* 42(26): 2716–2724.

Harriss, John. 2010. "Political Change, Political Structure, and the Indian State since Independence," in Paul Brass (ed.) *Routledge Handbook of South Asian Politics: India, Pakistan, Bangladesh, Sri Lanka, Nepal*. Abingdon, UK: Routledge, pp. 55–66.

Hasan, Mushirul. 2019. *Legacy of a Divided Nation: India's Muslims from Independence to Ayodhya*. Abingdon, UK: Routledge.

Hasan, Zoya. 1979. "Review: On Indian Politics," *Social Scientist* 8(2): 62–65.

Hasan, Zoya. 1996. "Communal Mobilization and Changing Majority in Uttar Pradesh," David Ludden (ed.) *Contesting the Nation: Religion, Community, and the Politics of Democracy in India*. Philadelphia: University of Pennsylvania Press, pp. 81–97.

Hassan, Mai. 2017. "The Strategic Shuffle: Ethnic Geography, the Internal Security Apparatus, and Elections in Kenya," *American Journal of Political Science* 61(2): 382–395.

Hassan, Mai. 2020. *Regime Threats and State Solutions: Bureaucratic Loyalty and Embeddedness in Kenya*. New York, NY: Cambridge University Press.

Heath, Oliver and Adam Ziegfeld. 2018. "Electoral Volatility and Turnout: Party Entry and Exit in Indian Elections," *Journal of Politics* 80(2): 570–584.

Heller, Patrick. 2000. "Degrees of Democracy: Some Comparative Lessons from India," *World Politics* 52(4): 484–519.

Heller, Patrick. 2009. "Democratic Deepening in India and South Africa," *Journal of Asian and African Studies* 44(1): 123–149.

Hickman, John. 2009. "Is Electoral Violence Effective? Evidence from Sri Lanka's 2005 Presidential Election." *Contemporary South Asia* 17(4): 429–435.

Höglund, Kristine. 2009. "Electoral Violence in Conflict-ridden Societies: Concepts, Causes, and Consequences," *Terrorism and Political Violence* 21(3): 412–427.

Holland, Steve and Jeff Mason. 2020. "Irritated by Loss, Trump Hunkers Down at the White House and Avoids Talk of Future," *Reuters*, December 18.

Holmquist, Frank and Mwangi wa Githinji. 2009. "The Default Politics of Kenya," *The Brown Journal of World Affairs* 16(1): 101–117.

Holmquist, Frank, Frederick S. Weaver, and Michael D. Ford. 1994. "The Structural Development of Kenya's Political Economy," *African Studies Review* 37(1): 69–105.

Horowitz, Donald. 1985. *Ethnic Groups in Conflict*. Berkeley: University of California Press.

Horowitz, Donald. 1991. *A Democratic South Africa? Constitutional Engineering in a Divided Society*. Berkeley: University of California Press.

Horowitz, Donald. 2001. *The Deadly Ethnic Riot*. Berkeley: University of California Press.

Horowitz, Jeremy and Kathleen Klaus. 2020. "Can Politicians Exploit Ethnic Grievances? An Experimental Study of Land Appeals in Kenya," *Political Behavior* 42(1): 35–58.

Horowitz, Michael, Rose McDermott, and Allan Stam. 2005. "Leader Age, Regime Type, and Violent International Relations," *Journal of Conflict Resolution* 49(5): 661–685.

Huber, Evelyne, Dietrich Rueschemeyer, and John Stephens. 1997. "The Paradoxes of Contemporary Democracy: Formal, Participatory, and Social Dimensions," *Comparative Politics* 29(3): 323–342.

Hughes, Barry, Mohammod Irfan, Haider Khan, Krishna Kumar, Dale Rothman, and José Roberto Solórzano. 2015. *Reducing Global Poverty*. Abingdon, UK: Routledge.

Human Rights Watch. 2002. *Playing with Fire: Weapons Proliferation, Political Violence, and Human Rights in Kenya*. New York, NY: Human Rights Watch.

Human Rights Watch. 2008. *Ballots to Bullets: Organized Political Violence and Kenya's Crisis of Governance*. New York, NY: Human Rights Watch.

Human Rights Watch. 2013a. *High Stakes: Political Violence and the 2013 Elections in Kenya*. New York, NY: Human Rights Watch.

Human Rights Watch. 2013b. "Kenya: Discrimination against Rift Valley Displaced," *Human Rights Watch*, January 17.

Human Rights Watch. 2014. "Kenya: Third Imam Killed in 2 Years," Human Rights Watch, April 4.

Human Rights Watch. 2015. *Insult to Injury: The 2014 Lamu and Tana River Attacks and Kenya's Abusive Response*. New York, NY: Human Rights Watch.

Human Rights Watch. 2019. *Vigilante Cow Protection in India: Vigilante Groups Attack Minorities*, New York, NY: Human Rights Watch.

Ichino, Nahomi and Noah Nathan. 2016. "Democratizing the Party: The Effects of Primary Election Reforms in Ghana," *Working Paper*, University of Michigan, Ann Arbor.

India Today. 2013. "Police Foil Telangana March, Hundreds Arrested in Hyderabad," India Today, June 14.

India Today. 2019. "Arrest of L.K. Advani: The Incident that Bled India but Gave BJP Political Heft," India Today, November 9.

India Today. 2020. "Won't Listen After 3 Days: Kapil Mishra's Ultimatum to Delhi Police to Vacate Jaffrabad Roads," February 23.

International Criminal Court. 2011. *Situation in the Republic of Kenya in the Case of the Prosecutor v. William Samoei Ruto, Henry Kiprono Kosgey, and Joshua Arap Sang*. Pre-Trial Chamber. The Hague, Netherlands.

International Crisis Group. 2004. "Indonesia: Violence Erupts Again in Ambon," Asia Briefing, Brussels, Belgium: International Crisis Group, May 17.

International Crisis Group. 2022. "Kenya's 2022 Election: High Stakes," Brussels, Belgium: International Crisis Group, June 9.

References

Ishiyama, John and Michael Widmeier. 2013. "Territorial Control, Levels of Violence, and the Electoral Performance of Former Rebel Political Parties after Civil Wars," *Civil Wars* 15(4): 531–550.
Iyer, Sriya and Anand Shrivastava. 2018. "Religious Riots and Electoral Politics in India," *Journal of Development Economics* 131: 104–122.
Jackson, Karl and Lucian Pye. 1978. *Political Power and Communications in Indonesia*. Berkeley: University of California Press.
Jaffrelot, Christophe. 1996. *The Hindu Nationalist Movement in India*. New York, NY: Columbia University Press.
Jaffrelot, Christophe. 1999. *The Hindu Nationalist Movement and Indian Politics, 1925 to the 1990s: Strategies of Identity-building, Implantation, and Mobilization (with Special Reference to Central India)*. New Delhi, India: Penguin Books India.
Jaffrelot, Christophe. 2003. "Communal Riots in Gujarat: The State at Risk?" Working Paper No. 17, University of Heidelberg.
Jaffrelot, Christophe. 2019. "A De-Facto Ethnic Democracy? Obliterating and Targeting the Other, Hindu Vigilantes, and the Ethnic State," in Angana Chatterji, Thomas Blom Hansen, and Christophe Jaffrelot (eds.) *Majoritarian State: How Hindu Nationalism is Changing India*. New York, NY: Oxford University Press, pp. 41–68.
Jaffrelot, Christophe. 2021. *Modi's India: Hindu Nationalism and the Rise of Ethnic Democracy*. Princeton, NJ: Princeton University Press.
Jaffrey, Sana. 2021. "Right-wing Populism and Vigilante Violence in Asia," *Studies in Comparative International Development* 56(2): 223–249.
Jain, Bharti. 2013. "Government Releases Data of Riot Victims Identifying Religion," Times of India, September 24.
Jairath, Vinod and Huma Kidwai. n.d. "Violence of Silence: 'Police Action' in Hyderabad and its Aftermath," Working Paper, University of Hyderabad.
Jalal, Ayesha. 1995. *Democracy and Authoritarianism in South Asia: A Comparative and Historical Perspective (No. 1)*. New York, NY: Cambridge University Press.
Jensenius, Francesca. 2011. "Review Essay – Power and Influence in India: Bosses, Lords, and Captains," *Forum for Development Studies* 38(3): 391–398.
Johnson, Gordon. 2005. *Provincial Politics and Indian Nationalism: Bombay and the Indian National Congress, 1880–1915*. New York, NY: Cambridge University Press.
Kagwanja, Peter. 2009. "Courting Genocide: Populism, Ethno-nationalism, and the Informalization of Violence in Kenya's 2008 Post-Election Crisis," *Journal of Contemporary African Studies* 27(3): 365–387.
Kahl, Colin. 2006. *States, Scarcity, and Civil Strife in the Developing World*. Princeton, NJ: Princeton University Press.
Kakar, Sudhir. 1996. *The Colors of Violence: Cultural Identities, Religion, and Conflict*. Chicago, IL: University of Chicago Press.
Kakar, Sudhir. 2000. "The Time of Kali: Violence between Religious Groups in India," *Social Research* 67(3): 877–899.
Kalyvas, Stathis. 2006. *The Logic of Violence in Civil War*. New York, NY: Cambridge University Press.
Kanogo, Tabatha. 1987. *Squatters and the Roots of May Mau, 1905–63*. Athens: Ohio University Press.
Kanyinga, Karuti. 1996. "The Politics of Development Space in India," in Joseph Semnoda and Ole Therkildsen (eds.) *Service Provision Under Stress in East Africa:*

State, NGOs, and People's Organizations in Kenya, Tanzania, and Uganda. Copenhagen, Denmark: Centre for Development Research, pp. 70–86.

Kanyinga, Karuti. 2009. "The Legacy of the White Highlands: Land Rights, Ethnicity, and the Post-2007 Election Violence in Kenya," *Journal of Contemporary African Studies* 27(3): 325–344.

Kanyinga, Karuti and John Njoka. 2002. "The Role of Youth in Politics: The Social Praxis of Party Politics among the Urban Lumpen in Kenya," *African Journal of Sociology* 4(2): 89–111.

Karpat, Kemal. 1988. "Turkish Democracy at Impasse: Ideology, Party Politics, and the Third Military Intervention," *International Journal of Turkish Studies* 2(1): 27–29.

Kasara, Kimuli. 2017. "Does Local Ethnic Segregation Lead to Violence? Evidence from Kenya," *Quarterly Journal of Political Science* 11(4): 441–470.

Kaufman, Robert and Stephan Haggard 2019. "Democratic Decline in the United States: What Can We Learn from Middle-Income Countries," *Perspectives on Politics* 17(2): 417–432.

Keer, Dhananjay. 1971. *Dr. Ambedkar: Life and Mission*. Mumbai, India: Popular Prakashan.

Kemboi, Weldon. 2017. "Likoni Residents Vow to Form Vigilante Groups to Fight Criminal Gangs," *Baraka FM*, March 3.

Kenny, Paul. 2017a. *Populism and Patronage: Why Populists Win Elections in India, Asia, and Beyond*. New York, NY: Oxford University Press.

Kenny, Paul. 2017b. "The Origins of Patronage Politics: State Building, Centrifugalism, and Decolonization," *British Journal of Political Science* 45(1): 141–171.

Kenny, Paul. 2020. "'The Enemy of the People': Populists and Press Freedom," *Political Research Quarterly* 73(2): 261–275.

Kenya Human Rights Commission. 2011. *Lest We Forget: The Faces of Impunity in Kenya*. Nairobi, Kenya: Kenya Human Rights Commission.

Kenya National Commission on Human Rights. 2008. *On the Brink of the Precipice: A Human Rights Account of Kenya's Post-2007 Election Violence*. Nairobi, Kenya: Kenya National Commission on Human Rights.

Kenya National Commission on Human Rights. 2012. *29 Days of Terror in the Delta: KNCHR Account into the Atrocities at Tana Delta*. Nairobi, Kenya: Kenya National Commission on Human Rights.

Kenyatta, Jomo. 1968. *Suffering without Bitterness: The Founding of the Kenya Nation*. Nairobi, Kenya: East African Publishing House.

Khalid, Hussein. 2021. "Hustlers versus Dynasties Rhetoric Getting Out of Hand," *The Star*, February 5.

Khamisi, Joe. 2011. *The Politics of Betrayal: Diary of a Kenyan Legislator*. Bloomington, IN: Trafford Publishing.

Khosla, Madhav. 2020. *India's Founding Moment: The Constitution of a Most Surprising Democracy*. Cambridge, MA: Harvard University Press.

Kimenyi, Mwangi and Njuguna Ndung'u. 2005. "Sporadic Ethnic Violence: Why Has Kenya Not Experienced a Full-Blown Civil War?" in Paul Collier and Nicholas Sambanis (eds.) *Understanding Civil War*. Washington, DC: The World Bank, pp. 123–156.

Kinzer, Stephen. 1996. "In Turkey, New Accusations of Links between Police, Politicians, and Criminals," *The New York Times*, December 31.

Kirchner, Katja. 2013. "Conflicts and Politics in the Tana Delta, Kenya: An Analysis of the 2012 2013 Clashes and the General and Presidential Elections 2013," M.A. Thesis (African Studies Centre), University of Leiden. Unpublished Manuscript.

Kirpal, Raman. 2013. "Muzaffarnagar Riots: How the BJP, SP, and BSP Fanned the Flames," *Firstpost*, September 16.

Kiruga, Morris. 2020. "Fallout with Kenyatta: Door Closed on Succession for Ruto," *The Africa Report*, June 10.

Klašnja, Marko. 2017. "Uninformed Voters and Corrupt Politicians," *American Politics Research* 45(2): 256–279.

Klašnja, Marko and Joshua Tucker. 2013. "The Economy, Corruption, and the Vote: Evidence from Experiments in Sweden and Moldova," *Electoral Studies* 32(2): 536–543.

Klašnja, Marko, Noam Lupu, and Joshua Tucker. 2020. "When Do Voters Sanction Corrupt Politicians?" *Journal of Experimental Political Science*. https://doi.org/10.1017/XPS.2020.13, 1–11.

Klaus, Kathleen. 2017. "Contentious Land Narratives and the Nonescalation of Election Violence: Evidence from Kenya's Coast Region," *African Studies Review* 60(2): 51–72.

Klaus, Kathleen. 2020. *Political Violence in Kenya: Land, Elections, and Claim-Making*. New York, NY: Cambridge University Press.

Klingemann, Hans-Dieter. 1999. "Mapping Political Support in the 1990s: A Global Analysis," in Pippa Norris (ed.) *Critical Citizens: Global Support for Democratic Government*. New York, NY: Oxford University Press, pp. 31–56.

Klopp, Jacqueline. 2001. "'Ethnic Clashes' and Winning Elections: The Case of Kenya's Electoral Despotism," *Canadian Journal of African Studies* 35(3): 473–517.

Klopp, Jacqueline. 2009. "The NCCK and the Struggle against 'Ethnic' Clashes in Kenya," in Ben Knighton (ed.) *Religion and Politics in Kenya: Essays in Honor of a Meddlesome Priest*. New York, NY: Palgrave Macmillan, pp. 183–200.

Kochanek, Stanley. 1967a. "Political Recruitment in the Indian National Congress: The Fourth General Election," *Asian Survey* 7(5): 292–304.

Kochanek, Stanley. 1967b. *The Congress Party of India: The Dynamics of a One-party Democracy*. Princeton, NJ: Princeton University Press.

Kochanek, Stanley. 1987. "Briefcase Politics in India: The Congress Party and the Business Elite," *Asian Survey* 27(12): 1278–1301.

Kohli, Atul. 1990. *Democracy and Discontent: India's Growing Crisis of Governability*. New York, NY: Cambridge University Press.

Kohli, Atul. 1994. "Centralization and Powerlessness: India's Democracy in a Comparative Perspective" in Joel Migdal, Atul Kohli, and Vivienne Shue (eds.) *State Power and Social Forces: Domination and Transformation in the Third World*. New York, NY: Cambridge University Press, pp. 89–107.

Kohli, Atul. 2004. *State-directed Development: Political Power and Industrialization in the Global Periphery*. New York, NY: Cambridge University Press.

Kolarova, Rumyana and Maria Spirova. 2019. "Bulgaria: Stable Coalitions of Unstable Parties," in Torbjörn Bergman, Gabriella Ilonszki, and Wolfgang C. Müller (eds.) *Coalition Governance in Central Eastern Europe*. New York, NY: Oxford University Press, pp. 86–128.

Köllner, Patrick, Rudra Sil, and Ariel Ahram. 2018. "Comparative Area Studies: What It Is, What It Can Do," in Ariel Ahram, Patrick Köllner, and Rudra Sil (eds.) *Comparative Area Studies: Methodological Rationales and Cross-Regional Applications*. New York, NY: Oxford University Press, pp. 3–28.

Kothari, Rajni. 1964. "The Congress 'System' in India," *Asian Survey* 4(12): 1161–1173.

Krause, Jana. 2018. *Resilient Communities: Non-violence and Civilian Agency in Communal War*. New York, NY: Cambridge University Press.

Kriger, Norma. 2005. "ZANU(PF) Strategies in General Elections, 1980–2000; Discourse and Coercion," *African Affairs* 104(414): 1–34.

Krishna, Anirudh. 2007. "Politics in the Middle: Mediating Relationships between the Citizens and the State in Rural North India," in Herbert Kitschelt and Steven Wilkinson (eds.) *Patrons, Clients, and Policies: Patterns of Democratic Accountability and Political Competition*. New York, NY: Cambridge University Press, pp. 141–158.

Krishna, Gopal. 1966. "The Development of the Indian National Congress as a Mass Organization, 1918–1923," *The Journal of Asian Studies* 25(3): 413–430.

Krishnan, Varun. 2018. "The Cow Vigilante Menace: UP Records Highest Number of Incidents," *The Hindu*, December 5.

Kuenzi, Michelle and Gina Lambright. 2001. "Party System Institutionalization in 30 African Countries," *Party Politics* 7(4): 437–468.

Kumar, Abhimanyu. 2017. "The Lynching that Changed India," *Al Jazeera*, October 5.

Kumar, Radha. 1997. *The History of Doing: An Illustrated Account of Movements for Women's Rights in India, 1800–1990*. New Delhi, India: Zubaan.

Lamptey, Afua and Naila Salihu. 2012. "Interrogating the Relationship between the Politics of Patronage and Electoral Violence in Ghana," in Kwesi Aning and Kwaku Danso (eds.) *Managing Election-Related Violence for Democratic Stability in Ghana*. Accra, Ghana: Friedrich-Ebert-Stifung.

Landau, Jacob. 1982. "The Nationalist Action Party in Turkey," *Journal of Contemporary History* 17(4): 587–606.

Lang'at, Patrick and Daniel Nyassy. 2020. "Former Minister's Appointment at Kenya Petroleum Refineries Revoked in Mysterious Circumstances," *The Nation*, July 2.

LeBas, Adrienne. 2011. *From Protest to Parties: Party-building and Democratization in Africa*. New York, NY: Oxford University Press.

LeBas, Adrienne. 2013. "Violence and Urban Order in Nairobi, Kenya and Lagos, Nigeria," *Studies in Comparative International Development* 48(3): 240–262.

Levitsky, Steven. 2018. "Peru: The Institutionalization of Politics without Parties," in Scott Mainwaring (ed.) *Party Systems in Latin America: Institutionalization, Decay, and Collapse*. New York, NY: Cambridge University Press, pp. 326–358.

Levitsky, Steven, James Loxton, and Brandon Van Dyck. 2016. "Introduction: Challenges of Party-building in Latin America," in Steven Levitsky, James Loxton, Brandon Van Dyck, and Jorge I. Dominguez (eds.) *Challenges of Party-building in Latin America*. New York, NY: Cambridge University Press, pp. 1–48.

Lieberman, Evan and Prerna Singh. 2012. "The Institutional Origins of Ethnic Violence," *Comparative Politics* 45(1): 1–24.

Lieberman, Evan and Prerna Singh. 2017. "Census Enumeration and Group Conflict: A Global Analysis of the Consequences of Counting," *World Politics* 69(1): 1–53.

Lindberg, Staffan. 2007. "Institutionalization of Party Systems? Stability and Fluidity among Legislative Parties in Africa's Democracies," *Government & Opposition* 42(2): 215–241.

Linke, Andrew. 2022. "Post-election Violence in Kenya: Leadership Legacies, Demography, and Motivations," *Territory, Politics, Governance* 10(2): 180–199.
Lupu, Noam. 2016. *Party Brands in Crisis: Partisanship, Brand Dilution, and the Breakdown of Political Parties in Latin America*. New York, NY: Cambridge University Press.
Lupu, Noam. 2018. "Party Brands, Party Erosion, and Party Breakdown," in Scott Mainwaring (ed.) *Party Systems in Latin America: Institutionalization, Decay, and Collapse*. New York, NY: Cambridge University Press, pp. 359–379.
Lupu, Noam and Rachel Riedl. 2013. "Political Parties and Uncertainty in Developing Democracies," *Comparative Political Studies* 46(110): 1339–1365.
Lupu, Noam and Leonid Peisakhin. 2017. "The Legacy of Political Violence across Generations," *American Journal of Political Science* 61(4): 836–851.
Lynch, Gabrielle. 2008. "Courting the Kalenjin: The Failure of Dynasticism and the Strength of the ODM Wave in Kenya's Rift Valley Province," *African Affairs* 107(429): 541–568.
Lynch, Gabrielle. 2014. "Electing the 'Alliance of the Accused': The Success of the Jubilee Alliance in Kenya's Rift Valley," *Journal of Eastern African Studies* 8(1): 93–114.
Lynch, Gabrielle. 2011. *I Say to You: Ethnic Politics and the Kalenjin in Kenya*. Chicago, IL: University of Chicago Press.
Lynch, Gabrielle. 2018. *Performances of Injustice: The Politics of Truth, Justice, and Reconciliation in Kenya*. New York, NY: Cambridge University Press.
Lynch, Gabrielle and David Anderson. 2015. "Democratization and Ethnic Violence in Kenya: Electoral Cycles and Shifting Identities," in Jacques Bertrand and Oded Haklai (eds.) *Democratization and Ethnic Minorities: Conflict or Compromise?* Abingdon, UK: Routledge, pp. 83–102.
Magu, Stephen. 2018. *The Socio-cultural, Ethnic, and Historic Foundations of Kenya's Electoral Violence: Democracy on Fire*. Abingdon, UK: Routledge.
Mahendra, K.L. 2006. *Recollections and Reflections*. Hyderabad, India: Prachee Publications.
Mahoney, James and Dietrich Rueschemeyer. 2003. *Comparative Historical Analysis in the Social Sciences*. New York, NY: Cambridge University Press.
Maina, Wachira. 1998. "Kenya: The State, Donors, and the Politics of Democratization," in Alison Van Rooy (ed.) *Civil Society and the Aid Industry: The Politics and Promise*. London, UK: Earthscan Publications, pp. 134–167.
Mainwaring, Scott. 2018. "Party System Institutionalization, Predictability, and Democracy," in Scott Mainwaring (ed.) *Party Systems in Latin America: Institutionalization, Decay, and Collapse*. New York, NY: Cambridge University Press, pp. 71–101.
Mainwaring, Scott and Timothy Scully. 1995. *Building Democratic Institutions: Party Systems in Latin America*. Palo Alto, CA: Stanford University Press.
Mainwaring, Scott and Edurne Zoco. 2007. "Political Sequences and the Stabilization of Inter Party Competition: Electoral Volatility in New and Old Democracies," *Party Politics* 13(2): 155–178.
Makali, David. 2002. "Shakombo Shot Himself in the Foot," *The Nation*, May 11.
Maksiç, Adis. 2015. "Priming the Nation for War: Ana Analysis of Organizational Origins and Discursive Machinations of the Serb Democratic Party in Pre-war Bosnia-Herzegovina," *Journal of Muslim Minority Affairs* 35(3): 334–343.
Malik, Aditi. 2016. "Mobilizing a Defensive Kikuyu-Kalenjin Alliance: The Politicization of the International Criminal Court in Kenya's 2013 Presidential Election," *African Conflict & Peacebuilding Review* 6(2): 48–73.

Malik, Aditi. 2018. "Constitutional Reform and New Patterns of Electoral Violence: Evidence from Kenya's 2013 Elections," *Commonwealth & Comparative Politics* 56(3): 340–359.

Malik, Aditi. 2020. "Devolution and Electoral Violence in Kenya," in Abu Bakarrr Bah (ed.) *Post Conflict Institutional Design: Peacebuilding and Democracy in Africa*. London, UK: Zed Books, pp. 164–196.

Malik, Aditi. 2021. "Hindu-Muslim Violence in Unexpected Places: Theory and Evidence from Rural India," *Politics, Groups, & Identities* 9(1): 40–58.

Malik, Aditi and Philip Onguny. 2020. "Elite Strategies, Emphasis Frames, and Mass Perspectives on Electoral Violence in Kenya," *Journal of Contemporary African Studies* 38(4): 560–578.

Malik, Aditi and Monica Prasad. 2022. "Peace by Committee: State, Society, and the Control of Communal Violence in Bhagalpur, Bihar," *India Review* 21(2): 181–215.

Maloba, Wunyamari O. 2017. *The Anatomy of Neo-Colonialism in Kenya: British Imperialism and Kenyatta, 1963–1978*. New York, NY: Palgrave Macmillan.

Mander, Harsh. 2018. "Hashimpura: 31 Years after Custodial Massacre of Muslims by Men in Uniform, Justice is Incomplete," *Scroll Media*, November 2.

Manning, Carrie. 2007. "Revolutionaries to Politicians: The Case of Mozambique," in Kalowatie Deonandan, David Close, and Gary Prevost (eds.) *From Revolutionary Movements to Political Parties: Cases from Latin America and Africa*. New York, NY: Palgrave Macmillan, pp. 181–210.

Mares, Isabella and Lauren Young. 2016. "Do Voters Punish Electoral Malfeasance?" Working Paper. Columbia University.

Martin, Pilly. 2012. "Conflicts between Pastoralists and Farmers in Tana River District," in Karen Witsenburg and Fred Zaal (eds.) *Spaces of Insecurity: Human Agency in Violent Conflicts in Kenya*. Leiden, The Netherlands: African Studies Centre, pp. 167–193.

Martz, John. 1999. "Political Parties and Candidate Selection in Venezuela and Colombia," *Political Science Quarterly* 114(4): 639–659.

Matanock, Aila. 2017a. "Bullets for Ballots: Electoral Participation Provisions and Enduring Peace after Civil Conflict," *International Security* 41(4): 93–132.

Matanock, Aila. 2017b. *Electing Peace: From Civil Conflict to Political Participation*. New York, NY: Cambridge University Press.

Maupeu, Hervé. 2008. "Revisiting Post-election Violence," *Les Cahiers d'Afrique d l'Est/The East African Review* 38: 193–230.

McClendon, Gwyneth and Rachel Beatty Riedl. 2015. "Religion as a Stimulant of Political Participation: Experimental Evidence from Nairobi, Kenya," *Journal of Politics* 77(4): 1045–1057.

McLane, John. 1988. "The Early Congress, Hindu Populism, and the Wider Society" in Richard Sisson and Stanley Wolpert (eds.) *Congress and Indian Nationalism: The Pre-Independence Phase*. Berkeley, CA: University of California Press, pp. 47–61.

McMillan, Alistair. 2008. "Deviant Democratization in India," *Democratization* 15(4): 733–749.

Mehler, Andreas. 2007. "Political Parties and Violence in Africa: Systematic Reflections against Empirical Background," in Matthias Basedau, Gero Erdmann, and Andreas Mehler (eds.) *Votes, Money, and Violence: Political Parties and Elections in Sub-Saharan Africa*. Uppsala, Sweden: Elanders Gotab, pp. 194–223.

References

Mghanga, Mwandawiro. 2010. *Usipoziba ufa utajenga ukuta: Land, Elections, and Conflicts in Kenya's Coast province*. Nairobi, Kenya: Heinrich Böll Stifung East and Horn of Africa.

Miguel, Edward. 2004. "Tribe or Nation? Nation Building and Public Goods in Kenya versus Tanzania," *World Politics* 56(3): 327–362.

Morgan, Jana. 2011. *Bankrupt Representation and Party System Collapse*. University Park, PA: Pennsylvania State University Press.

Morris-Jones. W. H. 1966. "Dominance and Dissent: Their Inter-relations in the Indian Party System," *Government & Opposition* 1(4): 451–466.

Morris-Jones, W. H. 1967. "The Indian Congress Party: A Dilemma of Dominance," *Modern Asian Studies* 1(2): 109–132.

Morse, Yonatan. 2019. *How Autocrats Compete: Parties, Patrons, and Unfair Elections in Africa*. New York, NY: Cambridge University Press.

Mudi, Maureen. 2011. "Ex-Minister Shakombo Declares Candidature," *The Star*, July 25.

Mueller, Susanne. 2008. "The Political Economy of Kenya's Crisis," *Journal of Eastern African Studies* 2(2): 185–210.

Mueller, Susanne. 2011. "Dying to Win: Elections, Political Violence, and Institutional Decay in Kenya," *Journal of Contemporary African Studies* 29(1): 99–117.

Mueller, Susanne. 2014b. "The Resilience of the Past: Government and Opposition in Kenya," *Canadian Journal of African Studies* 48(2): 333–352.

Müller-Crepon, Carl. 2022. "Local Ethno-political Polarization and Election Violence in Majoritarian vs. Proportional Systems," *Journal of Peace Research* 59(2): 242–258.

Mumo, Michael and Patrick Mayoyo. 1998. "Aspirant 'was to be Killed,'" *The Nation*, September 30.

Mungai, Allan. 2022. "Presidential Candidates Pledge to Uphold Peace in Polls," *The Standard*.

Muralidharan, Sukumar. 2014. "Alternate Histories: Hyderabad 1948 Compels a Fresh Evaluation of the Theology of India's Independence and Partition," *History and Sociology of South Asia* 8(2): 119–138.

Mutahi, Patrick. 2005. "Political Violence in the Elections," in Hervé Maupeu, Musambayi Katumanga, and Winnie Mitullah (eds.) *The Moi Succession: Elections 2002*. Nairobi, Kenya: Transafrica Press, pp. 69–96.

Mutua, Makau Wa. 1992. "The Troubled Transition," *Africa Report* 37(5): 34–38.

Mwakwaya, Mwakwaya. 2017. "Tana River Politics Takes Shape as Communities Rush for 'Negotiated Democracy' Ahead of Polls," *The Coast*, June 22.

Naidu, Ratna. 1990. *Old Cities, New Predicaments: A Study of Hyderabad*. New Delhi, Delhi: Sage Publications.

Nath, Suman. 2022. *Democracy and Social Cleavage in India: Ethnography of Riots, Everyday Politics, and Communalism in West Bengal, c. 2012–2021*. Abingdon, UK: Routledge.

Naqvi, Farah. 2010. "This Thing Called Justice: Engaging with Laws on Violence against Women in India," in Bishakha Datta (ed.) *Nine Degrees of Justice: New Perspectives on Violence against Women in India*. New Delhi, India: Zubaan Books, pp. 13–51.

Naqvi, Saba. 2013. "Masjid is Far: Why Banking on Hindu-Muslim Polarization is a Folly," *Outlook*, August 19.

Nasong'o, Shadrack. 2007. "Negotiating New Rules of the Game: Social Movements, Civil Society, and the Kenyan Transition," in Godwin Murunga and Shadrack Nasong'o (eds.) *Kenya: The Struggle for Democracy*. Dakar, Senegal and London, UK: Codesria and Zed Books, pp. 19–57.

Nathan, Noah. 2023. *The Scarce State: Inequality and Political Power in the Hinterland*. New York, NY: Cambridge University Press.

Nderitū, Alice Wairumū. 2018. *Kenya: Bridging Ethnic Divides, A Commissioner's Experience on Cohesion and Integration*. Nairobi, Kenya: Mdahalo Bridging Divides Limited.

Ndonga, Simon. 2012. "Dhadho Godhana Sacked over Tana Killings." *Capital News*, September 13.

Nehru, Jawaharlal. 1954. *Jawaharlal Nehru's Speeches, 1949–1953*. New Delhi, India: Government Printer.

News24. 2016. "Ghana 'at the Brink of Deadly Political Violence' as it Heads to the Polls," *News24*, December 7.

Noorani, A.G. 1990. "Indira Gandhi and Indian Muslims," *Economic & Political Weekly* 25(44): 2417–2420.

Novaes, Lucas. 2018. "Disloyal Brokers and Weak Parties," *American Journal of Political Science* 62(1): 84–98.

Ochami, David. 2012. "How Years of Impunity Bred Tana Conflict," *The Standard*, August 26.

Oded, Arye. 1996. "Islamic Extremism in Kenya: The Rise and Fall of Sheikh Khalid Balala," *Journal of Religion in Africa* 26(4): 406–415.

Odinga, Oginga. 1968. *Not Yet Uhuru: The Autobiography of Oginga Odinga*. Nairobi, Kenya: Heinmann.

O'Donnell, Guillermo. 1998. "Horizontal Accountability in New Democracies," *Journal of Democracy* 9(3): 112–126.

Okoth-Ogendo, H.W.O. 1972. "The Politics of Constitutional Change in Kenya since Independence, 1963–1969," *African Affairs* 71(282): 9–34.

Okoth-Ogendo, H.W.O. 1991. *Tenants of the Crown: Evolution of Agrarian Law and Institutions in Kenya*. Nairobi, Kenya: African Centre for Technology Studies Press.

Okpu, Ugbana. 1985. "Inter-Party Political Relations in Nigeria, 1979–1983," *Africa Spectrum* 30(2): 191–209.

Olzak, Susan, Suzanne Shanahan, and Elizabeth McEneaney. 1996. "Poverty, Segregation, and Race Riots: 1960–1993," *American Sociological Review* 61(4): 590–613.

Omolo, Ken. 2002. "Political Ethnicity in the Democratization Process in Kenya," *African Studies* 61(2): 209–221.

Opalo, Ken. 2019. *Legislative Development in Africa: Politics and Postcolonial Legacies*. New York, NY: Cambridge University Press.

Opalo, Ken. 2022. "Hustlers versus Dynasties? The Elusive Quest for Issue-based Politics in Kenya," *Working Paper*. Georgetown University.

Oucho, John. 2002. *Undercurrents of Ethnic Conflicts in Kenya*. Leiden, The Netherlands: Brill Publishers.

Outlook. 2022a. "Ambedkar and the Uniform Civil Code," *Outlook Magazine*, February 3.

Outlook. 2022b. "Nehru and the Hindu Code Bill," *Outlook Magazine*, February 3.

References

Otzen, Ellen. 2015. "Kenyan MP's Murder Unsolved 40 Years On," *BBC News*, March 11.
Owusu Kyei, Justice and Lidewyde Berckmoes. 2020. "Political Vigilante Groups in Ghana: Violence or Democracy?" *Africa Spectrum* 55(3): 321–338.
Özbudun, Ergun. 1981. "The Turkish Party System: Institutionalization, Polarization, and Fragmentation," *Middle Eastern Studies* 17(2): 228–240.
Özbudun, Ergun. 1994. "State Elites and Democratic Political Culture in Turkey," in Larry Diamond (ed.) *Political Culture and Democracy in Developing Countries*. Boulder, CO: Lynne Rienner Publishers, pp. 247–268.
Özbudun, Ergun. 1996. "Democratization in the Middle East: Turkey – How Far from Consolidation?" *Journal of Democracy* 7(3): 123–138.
Özbudun, Ergun. 2002. "The Institutional Decline of Parties in Turkey," in Larry Diamond and Richard Gunther (eds.) *Political Parties and Democracy*, Baltimore, MD: John Hopkins University Press, pp. 238–265.
Özbudun, Ergun. 2012. "Turkey – Plural Society and Monolithic State," in Ahmed T. Kuru and Alfred Stepan (eds.) *Democracy, Islam, and Secularism in Turkey*. New York, NY: Columbia University Press, pp. 61–94.
Pai, Sudha. 2014. "Understanding the Defeat of the BSP in Uttar Pradesh: National Election 2014," *Studies in Indian Politics* 2(2): 153–167.
Pai, Sudha and Sajjan Kumar. 2018. *Everyday Communalism: Riots in Contemporary Uttar Pradesh*. New Delhi, India: Oxford University Press.
Paller, Jeffrey. 2014. "Informal Institutions and Personal Rule in Urban Ghana," *African Studies Review* 57(3): 123–142.
Pande, Rohini. 2011. "Can Informed Voters Enforce Better Governance? Evidence from Low Income Democracies," *Annual Review of Economics* 3(1): 215–237.
Panikkar, K.N. 1993. "Religious Symbols and Political Mobilization: The Agitation for a Mandir at Ayodhya," *Social Scientist* 21(7): 63–78.
Parsons, Timothy. 2012. "Being Kikuyu in Meru: Challenging the Tribal Geography of Colonial Kenya," *Journal of African History* 53(1): 65–86.
Pattison, James. 2011. Orma Livelihoods in Tana River District, Kenya: A Study of Constraints, Adaptation, and Innovation, PhD Dissertation, University of Edinburgh. Unpublished Manuscript.
Pedersen, Mogens N. 1979. "The Dynamics of Party Systems: Changing Patterns of Electoral Volatility," *European Journal of Political Research* 7(1): 1–26.
Peic, Goran. 2014. "Civilian Defense Forces, State Capacity, and Government Victory in Counterinsurgency Wars," *Studies in Conflict & Terrorism* 37(2): 162–184.
Pelletier, Alexandre and Jessica Soedirgo. 2017. "The De-escalation of Violence and the Political Economy of Peace-Mongering," *South East Asia Research* 25(4): 325–341.
Pierson, Paul. 2000. "Increasing Returns, Path Dependence, and the Study of Politics," *American Political Science Review* 94(2): 251–267.
Pierson, Patrick. 2021. "Political Assassinations and Voter Behavior: Evidence from South Africa," Working Paper. Emory University.
Posner, Daniel. 2007. "Regime Change and Ethnic Cleavages in Africa," *Comparative Political Studies* 40(11): 1302–1327.
Powell, Bingham G. 2000. *Elections as Instruments of Democracy: Majoritarian and Proportional Visions*. New Haven, CT: Yale University Press.

Powell, Eleanor and Joshua Tucker. 2014. "Revisiting Electoral Volatility in Post-Communist Countries: New Data, New Results and New Approaches," *British Journal of Political Science* 44(1): 123–147.

Prakash, Gyan. 2002. "Civil Society, Community, and the Nation in India," *Etnográfica* 6(1): 27–39.

Purshotham, Sunil. 2015. "Internal Violence: The 'Police Action' in Hyderabad," *Comparative Studies in History and Society* 57(2): 435–466.

Pyne-Mercier, Lee, Grace John-Stewart, Barbara Richardson, Njeri Kagondu, Joan Thiga, Haidy Noshy, Nadia Kist, and Michael Chung. 2011. "The Consequences of Post-election Violence on Antiretroviral HIV Therapy in Kenya," *Aids Care* 23(5): 562–568.

Raghuvanshi, Umesh. 2015. "Speeches, Video by Sangeet Som, Rana Fueled Muzaffarnagar Riots." *Hindustan Times*, October 14.

Rakner, Lise and Nicolas van de Walle. 2009. "Democratization by Elections? Opposition Weakness in Africa," *Journal of Democracy* 20(3): 108–121.

Raleigh, Clionadh. 2022. "Kenya's Political Violence Landscape in the Lead-up to the 2022 Elections," Armed Conflict Location and Event Data Project, August 9.

Rao, Neena Ambre and S. Abdul Thaha. 2012. "Muslims of Hyderabad—Landlocked in the Walled City," in Laurent Gayer and Christophe Jaffrelot (eds.) *Muslims in Indian Cities: Trajectories of Marginalization*. Noida, India: HarperCollins Publishers, pp. 189–212.

Rauschenbach, Mascha and Katrin Paula. 2019. "Intimidating Voters with Violence and Mobilizing them with Clientelism," *Journal of Peace Research* 56(5): 682–696.

Reddy, Thiven. 2005. "The Congress Party Model: South Africa's African National Congress (ANC) and India's Indian National Congress (INC) as Dominant Parties," *African & Asian Studies* 4(3): 271–300.

Reddy, Deepa. 2006. *Religious Identity and Political Destiny: Hindutva in the Culture of Ethnicism*. Walnut Creek, CA: AltaMira Press.

Reeder, Bryce and Merete Bech Seeberg. 2018. "Fighting for your Friends? A Study of Intra Party Violence in Sub-Saharan Africa," *Democratization* 25(6): 1033–1051.

Reilly, Ben, Per Norlund, and Edward Newman. 2008. *Political Parties in Conflict-prone Societies: Regulation, Engineering and Democratic Development*. Tokyo, Japan: United Nations University Press.

Reno, William. 2011. *Warfare in Independent Africa*. New York, NY: Cambridge University Press.

Republic of Kenya. 1999. *Report of the Judicial Commission Appointed to Inquire into Tribal Clashes in Kenya*. Nairobi, Kenya: Government Printer.

Republic of Kenya. 2008. *Commission of Inquiry on Post-election Violence*. Nairobi, Kenya: Government Printer.

Republic of Kenya. 2013. *Judicial Commission of Inquiry into the Ethnic Violence in Tana River, Tana North, and Tana Delta Districts*. Nairobi, Kenya: Government Printer.

Republic of Kenya. 2017a. *End of Assignment Report (Dr. Roselyn Akombe)*. Nairobi, Kenya: Government Printer.

Republic of Kenya. 2017b. "Annex 2: Status of Preparations for the Fresh Presidential Election," Independent Electoral and Boundaries Commission, Nairobi, Kenya. 16 October.

Republic of Kenya. 2019. *Kenya Population and Housing Census: Distribution of Population by Socio-Economic Characteristics*. Nairobi Kenya: Kenya National Bureau of Statistics.

Reuters. 2017. "Three Dead in Machete Attack on Kenya Vote Tallying Center on Coast," *Reuters News*, August 9.

Richburg, Keith. 1991. "Tribalism Still Shapes Kenyan Political Life," *The Washington Post*, December 5.

Riedl, Rachel. 2014. *Authoritarian Origins of Democratic Party Systems in Africa*. New York, NY: Cambridge University Press.

Riedl, Rachel and J. Tyler Dickovick. 2014. "Party Systems and Decentralization in Africa," *Studies in Comparative International Development* 49(3): 321–342.

Robinson, Amanda. 2014. "National versus Ethnic Identification in Africa: Modernization, Colonial Legacy, and the Origins of Territorial Nationalism," *World Politics* 66(4): 709–746.

Rosberg, Carl. 1963. "Independent Kenya: Problems and Prospects," *The Africa Report* 8(11): 3–7.

Rosberg, Carl and John Nottingham. 1966. *The Myth of "Mau Mau": Nationalism in Kenya*. New York, NY: Praeger Publishers.

Rosenthal, A.M. 1964. "His Life was India's; Nehru's Aim to Salve Nation's Wounds Exemplifies a Garland of his Legacies," *New York Times*, May 28.

Rosenzweig, Steven. 2021. "Dangerous Disconnect: Voter Backlash, Elite Misperception, and the Costs of Violence as an Electoral Tactic," *Political Behavior* 43(4): 1731–1754.

Rosenzweig, Steven. 2023. *Voter Backlash and Elite Misperception: The Logic of Violence in Electoral Competition*. New York, NY: Cambridge University Press.

Rubin, Barry. 2002. "Turkey's Political Parties: A Remarkably Important Issue," in Barry Rubin and Metin Heper (eds.) *Political Parties in Turkey*. Abingdon, UK: Routledge, pp. 12–15.

Rudolph, Lloyd and Susanne Rudolph. 1981. "Transformation of the Congress Party: Why 1980 Was not a Restoration," *Economic & Political Weekly* 16(18): 811–813, 815–818.

Rudolph, Lloyd and Susanne Rudolph. 1987. *In Pursuit of Lakshmi: The Political Economy of the Indian State*. Chicago, IL: University of Chicago Press.

Rudolph, Lloyd and Susanne Rudolph. 2010. "The Coffee House and the Ashram Revisited: How Gandhi Democratized Habermas' Public Sphere," in Lloyd Rudolph and Susanne Rudolph (eds.) *Postmodern Gandhi and Other Essays: Gandhi in the World and at Home*. Chicago, IL: University of Chicago Press, pp. 140–176.

Rudolph, Susanne and Lloyd Rudolph. 1980. "The Centrist Future of Indian Politics," *Asian Survey* 20(6): 575–594.

Rudolph, Susanne and Lloyd Rudolph. 2015. "The Coffee House and the Ashram: Gandhi, Civil Society and Public Spheres," in Siegfried O. Wolf, Jivanta Schöttli, Dominik Frommherz, Kai Fürstenberg, Marian Gallenkamp, Lion König, and Markus Pauli (eds.) in *Politics in South Asia: Culture, Rationality, and Conceptual Flow*. New York, NY: Springer, pp. 157–168.

Ruth-Lovell, Saskia, Anna Lührmann, and Sandra Grahn. 2019. "Democracy and Populism: Testing a Contentious Relationship," Working Paper #91, Varieties of Democracy (V-Dem) Institute.

Rutten, Marcel. 2001. "'Fresh Killings': The Njoro and Laikipia Violence in the 1997 Kenyan Election Aftermath" in Marinus MEM Rutten, Alamin M. Mazrui, and François Grignon (eds.) *Out for the Count: The 1997 General Elections and Prospects for Democracy in Africa*. Kampala, Uganda: Fountain Publishers Limited. pp. 536–582.

Rutten, Marcel and Sam Owuor. 2009. "Weapons of Mass Destruction: Land, Ethnicity, and the 2007 Elections in Kenya," *Journal of Contemporary African Studies* 27(3): 305–324.

Sabar-Friedman, Galia. 1995. "'Politics' and 'Power' in the Kenyan Discourse and Recent Events: The Church of the Province of Kenya (CPK)," *Canadian Journal of African Studies* 29(3): 429–453.

Sahoo, Sarbeswar. 2013. "Doing Development or Creating Dependency? NGOs and Civil Society in India," *South Asia: Journal of South Asian Studies* 36(2): 258–272.

Sarkar, Sumit. 2002. *Modern India, 1885–1947*. New Delhi, India: Macmillan India.

Savkova, Lyubka. 2005. "Election Briefing No. 21: Europe and the Parliamentary Election in Bulgaria, 25 June 2005," *European Parties Elections and Referendums Network*. Brighton, United Kingdom, pp. 1–12.

Saxena, Rekha. 1996. "Party System in Transition," in Mahendra Prasad Singh and Rekha Saxena (eds.) *India's Political Agenda: Perspectives on the Party System*. New Delhi, India: Kalinga Publications, pp. 49–81.

Sayari, Sabri. 2007. "Towards A New Turkish Party System?" *Turkish Studies* 8(2): 197–210.

Sayari, Sabri. 2010. "Political Violence and Terrorism in Turkey, 1976–1980: A Retrospective Analysis," *Terrorism and Political Violence* 22(2): 198–215.

Sayari, Sabri and Bruce Hoffman. 1994. "Urbanization and Insurgency: The Turkish Case, 1976–1980," *Small Wars & Insurgencies* 5(2): 162–179.

Schedler, Andreas. 2002. "Elections without Democracy: The Menu of Manipulation," *Journal of Democracy* 13(2): 36–50.

Schedler, Andrea and Javier Santiso. 1998. "Democracy and Time: An Invitation," *International Political Science Review* 19(1): 5–18.

Schedler, Andreas, Larry Diamond, and Marc Plattner. 1999. *The Self-restraining State; Power and Accountability in New Democracies*. Boulder, CO: Lynne Rienner Publishers.

Schiff, Adam. 2021. *Midnight in Washington: How We Lost Our Democracy*. New York, NY: Random House.

Schneider, Mark. 2004. "Breaking the Wave: Explaining the Emergence of Ethnic Peace in a City of Historic Ethnic Violence," Undergraduate Thesis (Department of Political Science), University of Michigan-Ann Arbor. Unpublished Manuscript.

Schuberth, Moritz. 2015. "A Transformation from Political to Criminal Violence? Politics, Organized Crime, and the Shifting Functions of Haiti's Armed Groups," *Conflict, Security, and Development* 15(2): 169–196.

Scott-Villiers, Patta. 2017. "Small Wars in Marsabit County: Devolution and Political Violence in Northern Kenya," *Conflict, Security, & Development* 17(3): 247–264.

Seeberg, Merete Bech and Michael Wahman. 2019. "Why does Malawi have 1,331 Candidates Running for 193 Seats in Parliament," *The Monkey Cage Blog, The Washington Post*, March 11.

Seeberg, Michael. 2014. "Mapping Anomalous Democracies during the Cold War," *Australian Journal of Political Science* 49(1): 102–110.

References

Seawright, Jason. 2012. *Party-system Collapse: The Roots of Crisis in Peru and Bolivia.* Palo Alto, CA: Stanford University Press.

Sen, Atreyee. 2012. "'Exist, endure, erase the city' (*Sheher mein jiye, is ko sahe, ya ise mitaye?*): Child Vigilantes and Micro-cultures of Urban Violence in a Riot-affected Hyderabad Slum," *Ethnography* 13(1): 71–86.

Serra, Gilles. 2016. "Vote Buying with Illegal Resources: Manifestation of a Weak Rule of Law in Mexico," *Journal of Politics in Latin America* 8(1): 129–150.

Shah, Ghanshyam. 1970. "Communal Riots in Gujarat: Report of a Preliminary Investigation," *Economic & Political Weekly* 5(3/5): 187–189, 191, 193, 195, 197–200.

Shah, Seema. 2012. *Intra-ethnic Electoral Violence in War-torn, Divided Societies: The Case of Sri Lanka*, PhD Dissertation (Department of Political Science), University of California Los Angeles. Unpublished Manuscript.

Shani, Ornit. 2018. *How India Became Democratic: Citizenship and the Making of Universal Franchise.* New York, NY: Cambridge University Press.

Sharma, Nagendar. 2009. "Gujarat Disowns Kodnani Affidavit," *Hindustan Times*, February 24.

Shear, Michael and Stephanie Saul. 2021. "Trump, in Taped Call, Pressured Georgia Official to 'Find' Votes to Overturn Election," *New York Times*, January 5.

Shiundu, Alphonce. 2014. "Boy Juma Boy Relives Glorious Past, Opens Up on His Fury with State," *The Standard*.

Siddiqui, Niloufer. 2022. *Under the Gun: Political Parties and Violence in Pakistan.* New York, NY: Cambridge University Press.

Singh, Mahendra Pratap. 1981. *Split in a Predominant Party: The Indian National Congress in 1981.* New Delhi, India: Abhinav Publications.

Skocpol, Theda. 1979. *States and Social Revolutions: A Comparative Analysis of France, Russia, and China.* New York, NY: Cambridge University Press.

Skocpol, Theda and Margaret Somers. 1980. "The Uses of Comparative History in Macrosocial Inquiry," *Comparative Studies in Society and History* 22(2): 174–197.

Smith, David. 2015. *India as a Secular State.* Princeton, NJ: Princeton University Press.

Smith, Donald. 1958. *Nehru and Democracy: The Political Thought of an Asian Democrat.* London, UK: Orient Longmans.

Söderberg-Kovacs, Mimmi. 2007. *From Rebellion to Politics: The Transformation of Rebel Groups to Political Parties in Civil War Peace Processes*, PhD Dissertation (Department of Peace and Conflict Research), Uppsala University. Unpublished Manuscript.

Speight, Jeremy and Katrin Wittig. 2018. "Pathways from Rebellion: Rebel-party Configurations in Côte d'Ivoire and Burundi," *African Affairs* 117(446): 21–43.

Sridharan, E. 1991. "Leadership Time Horizons in India: The Impact of Economic Restructuring," *Asian Survey* 31(12): 1200–1213.

Staniland, Paul. 2014. "Violence and Democracy," *Comparative Politics* 47(1): 99–118.

Staniland, Paul. 2021. *Ordering Violence: Explaining Armed Group-state Relations from Conflict to Cooperation.* Ithaca, NY: Cornell University Press.

Steeves, Jeffrey. 1999. "The Political Evolution of Kenya: The 1997 Elections and Succession in Politics," *Commonwealth & Comparative Politics* 37(1): 71–94.

Steeves, Jeffrey. 2006. "Presidential Succession in Kenya: The Transition from Moi to Kibaki," *Commonwealth & Comparative Politics* 44(2): 211–233.

Stokes, Susan. 2001. *Mandates and Democracy: Neoliberalism by Surprise in Latin America*. New York, NY: Cambridge University Press.

Straus, Scott. 2012. "Retreating from the Brink: Theorizing Mass Violence and the Dynamics of Restraint," *Perspectives on Politics* 10(2): 343–362.

Straus, Scott and Charlie Taylor. 2012. "Democratization and Electoral Violence in Sub-Saharan Africa, 1990–2008," in Dorina Bekoe (ed.) *Voting in Fear: Electoral Violence in Sub Saharan Africa*. Washington, DC: United States Institute of Peace, pp. 15–38.

Strohm, Rachel. 2019. "What Do We Learn from Cross-regional Comparisons in Political Science?" Working Paper, University of California-Berkeley.

Stuligross, David and Ashutosh Varshney. 2002. "Ethnic Diversities, Constitutional Designs, and Public Policies in India," in Andrew Reynolds (ed.) *The Architecture of Democracy: Constitutional Design, Conflict Management, and Democracy*. Oxford, UK: Oxford University Press, pp. 429–458.

Subrahmanyam, Gita. 2006. "Ruling Continuities: Colonial Rule, Social Forces, and Path Dependence in British India and Africa," *Commonwealth & Comparative Politics* 44(1):84–117.

Suhas, Prashant and Vasabjit Banerjee. 2021. "The Association of Electoral Volatility and Religious Riots in India," *Politics & Religion* 14(4): 787–808.

Susewind, Raphael, and Raheel Dhattiwala. 2014. "Spatial Variation in the 'Muslim Vote' in Gujarat and Uttar Pradesh, 2014," *Internationales Asien Forum/International Quarterly for Asian Studies* 45(3–4): 353–381.

Tajima, Yuhki. 2018. "Political Development and the Fragmentation of Protection Markets: Politically Affiliated Gangs in Indonesia," *Journal of Conflict Resolution* 62(5): 1100–1126.

Tamarkin, Mordechai. 1978. "The Roots of Political Stability in Kenya," *African Affairs* 77(208): 297–320.

Tatsumi, Kayoko. 2009. *Coalition Politics, Ethnic Violence, and Citizenship: Muslim Political Agency in Meerut, India, 1950–2004*, PhD Dissertation (Institute of Development Studies), London School of Economics and Political Science. Unpublished Manuscript.

Taylor, Charles, Jon Pevehouse, and Scott Straus. 2017. "Perils of Pluralism: Electoral Violence and Incumbency in sub-Saharan Africa," *Journal of Peace Research* 54(3): 397–411.

Thaler, Kai. 2017. "Mixed Methods Research in the Study of Political and Social Violence and Conflict," *Journal of Mixed Methods Research* 11(1): 59–76.

Tharoor, Shashi. 2003. *Nehru: The Invention of India*. New York, NY: Arcade Publishing.

The Monitor. 2022. "Blissful are Kenya's Peacemakers," *The Monitor*, August 16.

The New Humanitarian. 2012. "Several Thousand Displaced after Fresh Clashes in Isiolo," *The New Humanitarian*, April 2.

Thomas, Lynn. 2003. *Politics of the Womb: Women, Reproduction, and the State in Kenya*. Berkeley, CA: University of California Press.

Thomson, Henry, Halvard Buhaug, Henrik Urdal, and Elisabeth Rosvold. 2021. "Group Organization, Elections and Urban Political Mobilization in the Developing World," *Democratization* 28(8): 1525–1544.

Thompson, Mark. 2012. "Asia's Hybrid Dynasties," *Asian Affairs* 43(2): 204–220.

References

Throup, David. 2020. "Daniel arap Moi and One-Party Rule," in Nic Cheeseman, Karuti Kanyinga, and Gabrielle Lynch (eds.) *The Oxford Handbook of Kenyan Politics*. New York, NY: Oxford University Press, pp. 56–68.

Throup, David and Charles Hornsby. 1998. *Multi-Party Politics in Kenya: The Kenyatta and Moi States and the Triumph of the System in the 1992 Election*. Athens, OH: Ohio University Press.

Ticku, Rohit. 2015. "Riot Rewards? Study of BJP's Electoral Performance and Hindu-Muslim Riots." Working Paper No. 19/2015. Graduate Institute of International and Development Studies.

Times of India. 1938. "Hyderabad Riot Casualties: No Women Injured," *The Times of India*, May 13.

Times of India. 2000. "Government Shield's UP's Most Wanted Policemen," *The Times of India*, May 17.

Times of India. 2003. "Clashes between Communities, A Recent History," *The Times of India*, December 15.

Times of India. 2012. "Akbaruddin is in Trouble for Hate Speech," *The Times of India*, December 29.

Tilly, Charles. 1984. *Big Structures, Large Processes, Huge Comparisons*. New York, NY: Russell Sage Foundation.

Tordoff, William. 2002. *Government and Politics in Africa*. Bloomington, IN: Indiana University Press.

Toros, Emre and Sarah Birch. 2019. "Who are the Targets of Familial Electoral Coercion? Evidence from Turkey," *Democratization* 26(8): 1342–1361.

Toros, Emre and Sarah Birch. 2021. "How Citizens Attribute Blame for Electoral Violence: Regional Differences and Party Identification in Turkey," *Southeast European & Black Sea Studies* 21(2): 251–271.

Travaglianti, Manuela. 2014. *Threatening Your Own: Electoral Violence within Ethnic Groups in Burundi and Beyond*, PhD Dissertation (Department of Politics), New York University. Unpublished Manuscript.

Tudor, Maya. 2013a. "Explaining Democracy's Origins: Lessons from South Asia," *Comparative Politics* 45(3): 253–272.

Tudor, Maya. 2013b. *The Promise of Power: The Origins of Democracy in India and Autocracy in Pakistan*. New York, NY: Cambridge University Press.

Tudor, Maya and Dan Slater. 2016. "The Content of Democracy: Nationalist Parties and Inclusive Ideologies in India and Indonesia," in Nancy Bermeo and Deborah Yashar (eds.) *Parties, Democracy, and Movements in the Developing World*. New York, NY: Cambridge University Press, pp. 28–60.

Turnbull, Megan. 2020. "Elite Competition, Social Movements, and Election Violence in Nigeria," *International Security* 45(3): 40–78.

Tyce, Mathew. 2019. "The Politics of Industrial Policy in a Context of Competitive Clientelism," *African Affairs* 118(472): 553–579.

Un, Kheang. 2019. *Cambodia: Return to Authoritarianism*. New York, NY: Cambridge University Press.

Ünal, Mustafa Coşar. 2012. *Counterterrorism in Turkey: Policy Choices and Policy Effects toward the Kurdistan People's Party*. Abingdon, UK: Routledge.

UNDP. 2011. *Understanding Electoral Violence in Asia*. New York, NY: United Nations Development Programme.

Unnithan, Sandeep. 2013. "Muzaffarnagar Communal Violence: The Three Crucial Akhilesh Failures," *India Today*, September 10.
Vaishnav, Milan. 2015. *Understanding the Indian Voter*. Washington, DC: Carnegie Endowment for International Peace.
Vaishnav, Milan. 2017. *When Crime Pays: Money and Muscle in Indian Politics*. New Haven, CT: Yale University Press.
van Bruinessen, Martin. 1996. "Turkey's Death Squads," *Middle East Report* 199: 20–23.
VanderLippe, John. 2005. *The Politics of Turkish Democracy: İsmet İnönü and the Formation of the Multi-Party System, 1938–1950*. Albany, NY: State University of New York Press.
van de Walle, Nicolas. 2003. "Presidentialism and Clientelism in Africa's Emerging Party Systems," *The Journal of Modern African Studies* 41(2): 297–321.
van Klinken, Gerry and Su Mon Thanzin Aung. 2017. "The Contentious Politics of Anti-Muslim Scapegoating in Myanmar," *Journal of Contemporary Asia* 47(3): 353–375.
Varkey, Ouseph. 1979. "The CPI-Congress Alliance in India," *Asian Survey* 19(9): 881–895.
Varshney, Ashutosh. 1998. "Why Democracy Survives: India Defies the Odds," *Journal of Democracy* 9(3): 36–50.
Varshney, Ashutosh. 2001. "Ethnic Conflict and Civil Society: India and Beyond," *World Politics* 53(3): 362–398.
Varshney, Ashutosh. 2002. *Ethnic Conflict and Civic Life: Hindus and Muslims in India* (2nd edition). New Haven, CT: Yale University Press.
Varshney, Ashutosh. 2017. "Crime and Context," *Indian Express*, July 7.
Varshney, Ashutosh. 2019. "Modi Consolidates Power: Electoral Vibrancy, Mounting Liberal Deficits," *Journal of Democracy* 30(4): 63–77.
Varshney, Ashutosh. 2022. "India's Democratic Longevity and Its Troubled Trajectory," in Scott Mainwaring and Tarek Masoud (eds.) *Democracy in Hard Places*. New York, NY: Oxford University Press, pp. 34–72.
Volisi, Victor. 2019. "Agro-Pastoral Conflicts and Cooperation in Kenya: The Case of Orma and Pokomo in Tana Delta, 1992–2017," M.A. Thesis (Department of Armed Conflict and Peace Studies), University of Nairobi, Unpublished Manuscript.
von Borzyskowski, Inken and Patrick Kuhn. 2020. "Dangerously Informed: Voter Information and Pre-Electoral Violence in Africa," *Journal of Peace Research* 57(1): 15–29.
VonDoepp, Peter. 1996. "Political Transition and Civil Society: The Cases of Kenya and Zambia," *Studies in Comparative International Development* 31(1): 24–47.
Vyakweli, Mbaruku. 2005. "Civic Elections at the Coast," in Hervé Maupeu, Musambayi Katumanga, and Winnie Mitullah (eds.) *The Moi Succession: Elections 2002*. Nairobi, Kenya: Transafrica Press, pp. 349–374.
Wachanga, D. Ndirangu. 2011. "Kenya's Indigenous Radio Stations and Their Use of Metaphors in the 2007 Election Violence," *Journal of African Media Studies* 3(1): 109–125.
Wadekar, Neha. 2022. "Tensions Simmer in Kenya as Candidate Who Lost Presidential Election Contests Vote," *PBC News*, August 17.
Wahman, Michael. 2023. *Controlling Territory, Controlling Voters: The Electoral Geography of African Campaign Violence*. New York, NY: Oxford University Press.

References

Wahman, Michael and Edward Goldring. 2020. "Pre-Election Violence and Territorial Control: Political Dominance and Subnational Election Violence in Polarized African Electoral Systems," *Journal of Peace Research* 51(1): 93–110.

Wanyade, Peter. 2009. "Civil Society and Transition Politics in Kenya: Historical and Contemporary Perspectives," in Michael Chege (ed.) *Discourses on Civil Society in Kenya*. Nairobi, Kenya: African Research and Resource Forum (ARRF), pp. 8–19.

Wanyama, Fredrick. 2010. "Voting without Institutionalized Political Parties: Primaries, Manifestos, and the 2007 General Elections in Kenya," in Karuti Kanyinga and Duncan Okello (eds.) *Tensions and Reversals in Democratic Transitions: The Kenya 2007 General Elections*. Nairobi, Kenya: Society for International Development (SID) and the Institute for Development Studies (IDS), University of Nairobi, pp. 61–100.

Wanyama, Frederick and Jørgen Elklit. 2018. "Electoral Violence during Party Primaries in Kenya," *Democratization* 25(6): 1016–1032.

wa Wamwere, Koigi. 2003. *Towards Genocide in Kenya: The Curse of Negative Ethnicity*. New York, NY: Seven Stories Press.

Weiner, Myron. 1957. *Party Politics in India: The Development of a Multi-Party System*. Princeton, NJ: Princeton University Press.

Weiner, Myron. 1967. *Party Building in a New Nation: The Indian National Congress*. Chicago, IL: University of Chicago Press.

Weitz-Shapiro, Rebecca. 2014. *Curbing Clientelism in Argentina: Politics, Poverty, and Social Policy*. New York, NY: Cambridge University Press.

Welsh, David. 1996. "Ethnicity in sub-Saharan Africa," *International Affairs* 72(3): 477–491.

Whitfield, Lindsay. 2009. "'Chand for a Better Ghana': Party Competition, Institutionalization, and Alternation in Ghana's 2008 Elections," *African Affairs* 108(433): 621–641.

Widner, Jennifer. 1992. *The Rise of a Party-State in Kenya: From "Harambee!" to "Nyayo!"* Berkeley, CA: University of California Press.

Wilkinson, Steven. 2000. "India, Consociational Theory, and Ethnic Violence," *Asian Survey* 40(5):767–791.

Wilkinson, Steven. 2004. *Votes and Violence: Electoral Competition and Ethnic Riots in India*. New York, NY: Cambridge University Press.

Wilkinson, Steven. 2008. "Which Group Identities Lead to Most Violence? Evidence from India," in Stathis Kalyvas, Ian Shapiro, and Tarek Masoud (eds.) *Order, Conflict, and Violence*. New York, NY: Cambridge University Press, pp. 271–300.

Wilkinson, Steven. 2015. "Where's the Party? The Decline of Party Institutionalization and What (if Anything) that Means for Democracy," *Government & Opposition* 50(3): 420–445.

Willis, Justin and Ngala Chome. 2014. "Marginalization and Political Participation on the Kenyan Coast: The 2013 Elections," *Journal of Eastern African Studies* 8(1): 115–134.

Wood, Elisabeth. 2000. *Forging Democracy from Below: Insurgent Transitions in South Africa and El Salvador*. New York, NY: Cambridge University Press.

Wood, Elisabeth. 2003. *Insurgent Collective Action and Civil War in El Salvador*. New York, NY: Cambridge University Press.

Wolf, Thomas. 2009. "'Poll Poison?' Politicians and Polling in the 2007 Kenya Election" *Journal of Contemporary African Studies* 27(3): 279–304.

Wright, Joseph. 2008. "To Invest or Insure? How Authoritarian Time Horizons Impact Foreign Aid Effectiveness," *Comparative Political Studies* 41(7): 971–1000.

Yardımcı-Geyikçi, Şebnem and Hajan Yavuzyilmaz. 2020. "Party (De)Institutionalization in Times of Political Uncertainty: The Case of the Justice and Development Party in Turkey," *Party Politics* https://doi.org/10.1177/1354068820960010.

Ziegfeld, Adam. 2012. "Coalition Government and Party System Change: Explaining the Rise of Regional Political Parties in India," *Comparative Politics* 45(1): 69–87.

Ziegfeld, Adam. 2016. *Why Regional Parties? Clientelism, Elites, and the Indian Party System*. New York, NY: Cambridge University Press.

Datasets

Afrobarometer. 2018. "The Quality of Democracy and Governance in Kenya: Afrobarometer Round 7."
African Elections Database. 2021. "Elections in Kenya, 1992–2007."
Chhibber, Pradeep, Francesca Jensenius, and Pavithra Suryanarayan. 2014. "Dataset for 'Party Organization and Party Proliferation in India,'" *Party Politics* 20(4): 489–505.
Coppedge, Michael, John Gerring, Carl Henrik Knutsen, Staffan I. Lindberg, Jan Teorell, David Altman, Michael Bernhard, M. Steven Fish, Adam Glynn, Allen Hicken, Anna Lührmann, Kyle Marquardt, Kelly McMann, Pamela Paxton, Daniel Pemstein, Brigitte Seim, Rachel Sigman, Svend-Erik Skaaning, Jeffrey Staton, Steven Wilson, Agnes Cornell, Lisa Gastaldi, Haakon Gjerløw, Nina Ilchenko, Joshua Krusell, Laura Maxwell, Valeriya Mechkova, Juraj Medzihorsky, Josefine Pernes, Johannes von Römer, Natalia Stepanova, Aksel Sundstr̈om, Eitan Tzelgov, Yiting Wang, Tore Wig, and Daniel Ziblatt. 2019. "VDem [Turkey-1950/Turkey-2018] Dataset v9," Varieties of Democracy (V-Dem) Project. https://doi.org/10.23696/vdemcy19.
Fjelde, Hanne. 2020. "Dataset for 'Political Party Strength and Electoral Violence,'" *Journal of Peace Research* 57(1): 140–155.
Kenya Election Database. 2021. "Constituency Election Results."
Malik, Aditi. 2023. "Kenya Violent Elections Dataset (KVED), 1991-2015."
Mitra, Anirban and Debraj Ray. 2007. "Hindu-Muslim Violence in India, 1996–2000."
Salehyan, Idean and Cullen Hendrix. 2018. "Social Conflict Analysis Database (SCAD), Version 3.3."
Varshney, Ashutosh and Steven Wilkinson. 2004. "Hindu-Muslim Violence in India, 1950–1995."

Index

accommodationist alliances, 104
accountability
  and clientelism, 33
  defiance of, 191
  democratic, 30, 190
  political, 17
accountability institutions, 7, 190
Adalet Partisi (AP), 182–184
Adalet ve Kalkınma Partisi (AKP), 181, 185–186
Adjei, Kwabena, 176
Advani, L. K., 128, 135, 138–139
Africa Watch, 103, 214
Afrobarometer, 122, 177
Agarwal, Satya Prakash, 165
agency, 10, 18, 56, 222
agriculture, 1, 110, 118–120, 166
Ahmed, Shamim, 137
Ahmedabad
  1969 violence, 133
  1990 violence, 138
  fomenting conflict, 129
  interview data, 8
aid
  conditions for, 217
  disbursement, 32
Akali Dal, 73
Akhlaq, Mohammad, 130
Akiwumi Commission, 23, 102, 113
Aligarh Muslim University, 156
All India Majlis-e-Ittehad'ul Muslimeen (AIMIM/MIM)
  alliances, 154
  benefits of weakening INC, 147–148
  blame for riots, 206
  communal conflict, 149
  defense of Muslims, 146, 148
  elites, 145–149
  exclusion from Hyderabad government, 146
  interview data, 152, 204, 208
  parliamentary seats, 149, 151
  party stability, 151
  relationship to other parties, 145
  utilization of disorder, 151
  utilization of religious processions, 148
  utilization of violence, 146, 148, 149, 151, 204, 221
  voter sanctioning, 152
Ambedkar, B. R., 58, 63, 132
American Popular Revolutionary Alliance (APRA), 36. See also Peru
Amnesty International, 214
Anderson, David, 68, 78
Andhra Pradesh
  communal conflict, 138
  Hindu nationalism, 147–148
  INC in, 147
  party instability, 150
  party replacement, 146, 149–150
  party violence, 142, 148, 150
  patterns of riot violence, 29
  police, 152
  replacement volatility, 142
  subnational research site, 193–198
  trajectories of Hindu–Muslim violence, 21, 124
  volatility trajectories, 124
Anglican Church of Kenya (ACK), 215
Annan, Kofi, 92

259

Ansah-Antwi, Emmanuel, 176
anti-colonialism, 53, 58, 69, 74, 213
anti-minority violence, 6, 75, 125–130, 139, 165
anti-Muslim bias, 130
Arabs, 110
Argentina, 35
Aristide, Jean Bertrand, 4
Arjona, Ana, 205
Armed Conflict Location and Event Dataset (ACLED), 97, 109
armed groups, 4, 10, 30, 106, 204
Arriola, Leonardo, 220
arson, 103, 160, 177
Article 19, 214
Arya Samaj, 213
Aspinall, Edward, 33
assassination
  elite-level, 191
  political, 4, 114, 191
Atatürk, Mustafa Kemal, 181–182
authoritarianism, 13, 26, 47, 50, 52, 71, 74, 79, 177
autocracy, 17, 52, 70, 79, 81, 174, 218
Ayodhya, 138, 140, 159

backlash
  consideration, 27, 38, 42
  electoral, 17
  from voters, 13
  lack of, 191
  magnitude of, 19
  minimization, 19, 175, 178
  mitigation, 16
Baghpat constituency, 156
Bahujan Samaj Party (BSP)
  appeal, 67
  communal conflict, 3
  electoral goals, 167
  electoral losses, 3, 4, 14, 188
  elites, 3
  fomenting conflict, 167
  party birth, 159
  voter punishment, 171
Bajrang Dal, 138, 154, 170
Balala, Najib, 89
Balala, Sheikh, 113
Balaton-Chrimes, Samantha, 64
Baliyan, Sanjeev, 167, 168
Balmiki Samaj Pragiti Sangh (Balmiki Society Progress Union), 221
Banerjee, Vasabjit, 14, 15, 20
Baniyas, 222

Barma, Naazneen, 32
Baroda, 138
Basu, Amrita, 127
Basu, Deepankar, 16, 20, 21, 127, 143, 165, 166, 169, 171
Basu, Jyoti, 133, 139
Bates, Robert, 81
benefits
  attention to, 13
  calculation, 6, 8, 12, 25, 30, 38, 75
  concerns, 13
  of conflict, 124
  electoral, 121
  maximization, 13, 40
  of research, 199
  of violence, 92, 122, 138, 154, 169, 188
  to violence specialists, 184
Berenschot, Ward, 8, 11, 18, 33, 40, 129
Berman, Bruce, 54, 62, 212
between-group inequality, 5, 11
Bhagalpur
  1989 riots, 9
  interview data, 18
  peace committees, 221
Bharatiya Jana Sangh (BJS), 133
  benefits of violence, 157
  emergence, 133
  fomenting violence, 156
  incentives to organize violence, 156
  militants, 133
  moderation, 135
  as opposition, 146
  predecessor to BJP, 134
  utilization of violence, 147
Bharatiya Janata Party (BJP)
  aggressiveness, 138
  appeals to voters, 164
  attacks against Muslims, 28
  beneficiaries of violence, 168
  benefits of violence, 3, 4, 129, 130, 188, 190
  calculus around violence, 209
  candidates, 139
  coercion, 139
  comparison to AKP, 186
  costs of violence, 153
  divisive tactics, 138
  electoral calculus, 167
  electoral defeat, 153
  electoral goals, 167, 168
  elites, 3, 128–130, 138–141, 158, 165, 167, 168
  emergence, 128, 134

Index

fomenting conflict, 158, 167
goals, 153, 169
grassroots support, 166
growth, 138, 165
Hindu nationalism, 3, 67, 166
Hindutva politics, 137
incentives for violence, 158
interview data, 140, 206–209
leaders, 138
mahapanchayat, 168
mandate, 171
moderation, 135
narratives, 170
opposition, 148, 149
opposition to INC, 159
panchayat, 168
parliamentary seats, 151
partners, 154
party development, 127
party organization, 147
party strength, 127
party tactics, 135
protection of Hindu women, 3
Ramjanmabhoomi movement, 163
rural violence, 141
subleaders, 165
subnational influence, 140
utilization of conflict, 128
utilization of disorder, 151
utilization of media, 139
utilization of violence, 3, 16, 140, 146, 147, 149, 151, 157, 168, 189, 209, 221
Uttar Pradesh, 165, 168
vote share, 129
Bhavnani, Rikhil, 40
Bhiwandi, 133
Bihar
1989 riots, 9, 18
BJP religious processions, 138, 139
communal conflict, 138
interview data, 18
migration from, 139
peace committees, 221
Birch, Sarah, 5, 7, 16, 17, 23, 186
Birla, G. D., 70
Biwott, Nicholas, 84, 102, 107
Bob-Milliar, George, 176
Bolivia, 36, 37, 45
Boone, Catherine, 39, 101, 103
Botswana, 174
Brahmo Samaj, 213
Branch, Daniel, 55, 59, 69, 81

Brass, Jennifer, 214, 216
Brass, Paul, 8, 9, 18, 71, 155, 156, 165, 214, 216, 221
British India. *See* British Raj
British Raj, 52, 53, 58
Buijtenhuijs, Robert, 61
Bulgaria, 37
Bulutgil, Zeynep, 5
Bungoma County, 83, 93, 95
Burchard, Stephanie, 10
bureaucracy, 30, 65, 70, 74
Burundi, 5, 16, 46
Busia County, 93

Cambio 90, 36. *See also* Peru
Cambodia, 4
Cameroon, 13
candidate selection, 62, 194
Cantonment constituency, 165
caste system
  Hindu nationalism, 138
  opposition to, 57
  politics within, 166
Catholic Church (Kenya), 215, 218
census
  colonial, 57
  ethnic (Kenya), 66
  Indian, 64
Central Province, 54
Central Province (Kenya)
  European settlement, 105
  Kikuyu migration from, 101, 111
  Nairobi, 55
  political importance, 65
  violence, 78, 91
  voters, 55
Ceron, Andrea, 12
Chandra, Kanchan, 48, 64, 205, 206
Cheeseman, Nic, 55, 59, 69, 81
Chepkok, Paul, 84, 107
Chhibber, Pradeep, 193, 196, 215
Christians (India), 57
Christians (Indonesia), 40
churches (Kenya)
  amelioration of ethnic conflict, 218, 219
  community service, 215
  ethnic make-up, 218
  leaders, 26, 215, 217, 219, 220
  opposition to violence, 215
  political action, 215, 218
  relative weakness, 218
  trust for, 218

city dwellers, 127
civic associations. *See also* civil society organizations (CSOs)
  amelioration of ethnic conflict, 217
  colonial undermining, 212
  colonial-era expansion, 213
  donor priorities, 216
  ethnic composition, 222
  fluctuations, 221
  framework, 49, 211
  historiography, 211
  interethnic, 9
  precolonial, 212
  relationship to INC, 215
  relationship to KANU, 214
  weakness, 216
civil society
  colonial co-optation (Kenya), 213
  colonial disinterest, 213
  colonial exploitation, 212
  colonial transformation, 212
  development, 222
  effects on violence, 221
  election observers, 178
  elites, 216, 221
  ethnic composition, 212, 214
  historiography, 212
  interview data, 77, 85, 128, 200, 204, 217
  KANU repression, 214
  leaders, 9, 18, 26, 43, 72
  mohalla samitis (peace committees), 222
  political dominance over, 215
  relationship to party violence, 45
  relationship to political violence, 48
  revitalization (Kenya), 85
  subordination to political society, 211, 217, 220, 222
civil society organizations (CSOs)
  Boolean Jewelry Traders Association (India), 222
  churches, 218
  composition, 48
  constrained by colonial government, 212
  effects on political violence, 220
  ethnic composition, 223
  ethnic membership, 222
  impact on citizenship, 216
  limitations, 221
  nonreligious, 220
  relative weakness, 211
  subordination to political society, 221, 223
civil war, 6, 46

civilians
  agency, 10
  arrests, 160
  deaths, 40, 103
  interview data, 26
  Kurdish, 184
  participation in violence, 11, 97
  peacebuilding, 93, 156
  prevention of violence, 40
  reactions to violence, 125
  responses to conflict, 20
  role in de-escalating violence, 9
  vulnerability, 9
clientelism
  competitive, 33, 82
  connections, 180
  differences between Kenya and India, 64, 68
  effects on conflict, 180
  emergence, 33
  impact, 33
  INC dependence, 66
  KANU use, 79
  logics, 74
  Moi, Daniel Arap, 65, 66, 72
  multiethnic coalitions, 67
  networks, 176
  party, 180
  predatory, 81
  scholarship, 180
  short-term orientation, 33
  truncated time horizons, 33
  weakening, 67
clientelistic parties, 33, 194
Coalition for Reforms and Democracy (CORD), 116
coalitional politics
  changes in Kenya, 121
  competitive party system, 9
  cross-ethnic, 5, 10
  effect on elite incentives for violence, 77
  emergence in Kenya, 1, 87, 99
  fleeting, 98, 106
  multiethnic, 67
  party instability, 77, 105
  persistence in Kenya, 94, 116
  replacement volatility, 82
  short-lived (Kenya), 88
  urban and rural, 63
  volatility, 93, 107
  voter sanctioning, 43
  within-group inequality, 11

Index

Coast Province
  1997 violence, 18
  2007 elections, 116
  2007 violence, 91, 92
  2013 conflict, 93, 95
  challenges, 18
  coalitional politics, 115
  communal harmony, 2
  death tolls, 115
  electoral violence, 115
  elites, 65, 98
  ethnic leaders, 89
  indigeneity, 122
  instrumentalization of conflict, 117
  instrumentalization of violence, 111
  interview data, 85, 97, 111, 203
  KANU campaigns, 114
  KANU defeat, 112, 113
  KANU losses, 110
  KANU-sponsored conflict, 85
  Kikuyu settlers, 111
  land disputes, 86, 97, 111
  marginalization, 97, 110
  Mijikenda leaders, 18
  NaRC support, 118
  Odinga support, 116
  ODM support, 116, 117
  opposition stronghold, 116
  parliamentary elections, 98, 113
  party competition, 98
  party emergence, 113
  party instability, 124
  party violence, 110, 117
  patterns of violence, 100
  political conflict, 110
  purpose of election violence, 122
  relationship to state, 111
  resistance to violence, 112
  subnational research site, 21, 28, 99, 100
  utilization of violence, 85
  violence targeting Kikuyu, 116
  voters, 111, 116
Cold War, 181
collaborators, 54
Colombia, 35
colonialism, 20, 52, 53, 59, 61, 74, 118, 213
Commission of Inquiry on Post-Election Violence (CIPEV) (Kenya), 23, 103
Commission on Revenue Allocation (CRA), 119
communal conflict
  alternative forms, 128
  BJP instrumentalization, 141, 167
  causes, 167
  civilian responses, 20
  Hindu nationalist, 148, 171
  Hindu–Muslim conflict, 138
  limits of secularization, 133
  ongoing, 140
  political elites, 203
  severe, 125
  trajectories, 151
communal elites, 132
communal harmony, 2, 140, 156, 217, 221
communal peace, 211
communal polarization, 3, 154, 165
communal provocations, 147, 148, 163
communal violence, 157
  absence, 133
  avoidance, 132
  between Hindus and Muslims, 24
  BJP instrumentalization, 128
  civic networks, 48
  controlling, 170
  deaths from, 155
  decline, 28, 140, 150, 153, 164, 208
  distinct from ethnic violence, 20
  escalation, 135
  explanations, 150
  frequency, 124, 128
  high-intensity, 171
  Hindu nationalism, 157
  Hindu–Muslim, 145, 147
  history, 155
  Hyderabad Police Action (1948), 144
  INC instrumentalization, 158
  incentivizing, 151
  increase in, 141
  instances, 23
  intensification, 150
  interview data, 134, 152, 155, 167, 204
  intolerance toward, 153, 156
  low-intensity, 140
  participation, 127
  party instability, 170
  party system volatility, 14, 134
  patterns, 144
  political motivations, 164
  politically-orchestrated, 169
  possibilities, 147
  proliferation, 151
  rejection, 140
  relationship to civic associations, 221
  relationship to parties, 142
  rural, 143

communal violence (cont.)
  segregation, 39
  shifts, 127
  sponsorship of, 169
  targeting Muslims, 5
  terminology, 23
  triggers for, 209
  urban, 127
  widespread, 134
communalism, 57, 127, 153, 154, 166, 168, 170, 190, 208
Communist Party of India (CPI), 73, 145
comparative area studies, 15, 19, 20
comparative politics, 7, 15, 32
confidence, 2, 13, 131, 134
Congress (United States), 191
Congress Socialist Party (CSP), 70
Constituent Assembly (India), 63
corruption, 32, 68, 70, 81, 122, 170, 178
Costa Rica, 35, 174
costs, 16
  attention to, 13
  calculation, 6, 8, 12, 38, 75
  concerns, 13
  correlation to election type, 13
  devastating, 189
  discounting, 16, 34, 45, 49, 77, 97, 99, 141
  efforts to reduce, 38
  electoral, 4
  low, 12, 13
  minimization, 13, 14, 31, 40
  miscalculation of, 46
  misunderstanding, 169
  potential, 14, 15, 38, 40, 138
  relative to incentives, 12, 25, 124, 188
  to research participants, 199
  severity, 46
  significant, 153
  subnational, 12
  underestimation, 31
  to voters, 43
Côte d'Ivoire, 17
counterinsurgency, 6
COVID-19, 122
credibility
  civic associations, 216
  civil society organizations (CSOs), 220
  declining, 190
  elites, 32
  parties, 14, 17, 32, 81
  patrons, 107, 176
  relationship to programmaticity, 33
  threats to ruling elites, 33
  time horizons, 13
cross-national comparison, 8, 10, 13, 16, 21, 41, 174
cross-regional comparisons, 14, 15, 20, 21, 29, 35, 49, 173, 174, 186
Cumhuriyet Halk Partisi (CHP), 181, 182, 184
curfews, 17, 140, 143, 146, 160

Dado, Hussein, 2
Daily Nation (Kenya), 56
Dalits
  attacks against, 134
  Harijan Sevak Sangh (Dalit Service Syndicate), 213
  party appeals to, 67, 129
Daxecker, Ursula, 5, 13–15
decision-making
  about party violence, 12
  complexity, 16
  consideration of costs, 15
  effects of time horizons, 32
  elite, 15, 35, 52, 53, 189, 200
  factors in, 38, 77, 98
  historical, 74
  internal, 196
  interview insights, 210
  model, 31
  regarding violence, 27
  religion as factor, 174
  role of grievances, 104
  role of party insecurity, 35
  role of party instability, 32, 180
decolonization, 52
Demiral, Süleyman, 182, 184
democracy maturation, 173
democratic age
  associations, 47
  cross-national comparison, 173, 174
  distinct from party stability, 173, 175
  elite incentives for violence, 47
  influence of, 172
  limitations as explanatory factor, 48
  maturation, 47
  mature, 48
  older, 47, 174
  vulnerability to party violence, 47
  young, 47, 48, 173–175, 180
democratic consolidation, 52
democratic longevity, 29, 32, 45, 47, 173–175, 186
Democratic Party (DP), 103, 111

Index

democratic quality, 32
Demokrat Parti (DP), 182
Deoras, Balasaheb, 159
development policies, 20
deviant democracies, 174
Dhebar, U. N., 62
Dickovick, J. Tyler, 175
Dini ya Msambwa (Religion of the Ancestral Customs), 212
disintegrating parties, 34, 36
District Commissioner (DC), 60
Doğru Yol Partisi (DYP), 182
domestic courts, 17
domestic migration, 40
dominant party systems, 5, 16, 217
donors, 216, 217, 220
Driscoll, Barry, 180
durable party contexts, 25, 34
Dyzenhaus, Alexander, 81

Eastern Province, 81
Ecevit, Bülvent, 184
economic growth, 134, 170
Ecuador, 35
efficacy of violence, 13, 14
Egypt, 17
El Salvador, 199
Eldoret
  Anglican Church, 215
  effects of violence, 108
  interview data, 83, 109, 202
  subnational research site, 21
Eldoret South constituency. *See* Kapseret
election type, 13, 189
election-related violence
  analyses, 13
  attributed to political elites, 6
  avoidance, 179
  backlash, 13
  commonality, 13
  constraints, 177
  displacement, 178
  emergence, 6
  ethnic, 5, 10
  Ghana, 177
  high level, 87
  incentivizing, 6
  increase, 186
  instrumentalization, 177
  intense, 179
  intraethnic, 5
  likelihood, 5
  limits, 15
  low levels, 175
  mobilization, 10
  organization, 178
  organized groups, 8
  participants, 8
  party violence, 191
  relationship to land disputes, 105
  relationship to party stability, 48
  relationship to party strength, 174
  relationship to party violence, 4, 6
  role of party violence, 15
  urban, 8
  varieties of, 5
  violence specialists, 177
  weak parties, 6
electoral autocrats, 15
electoral coercion, 186
electoral competition, 10, 12, 14, 16, 33
electoral dynamics, 13
electoral fraud, 89–91, 178
electoral institutions, 10, 188
electoral politics, 20, 30, 67, 114, 149
Elgeyo-Marakwet, 102
Elischer, Sebastian, 62
elite calculations, 52
elite provocations, 7, 11
elite success, 19
elite-driven violence, 128, 190
Emergency (India), 215
endogeneity concerns, 27–29, 32, 45, 143
Engineer, Asghar Ali, 140, 160
ethnic cleavages, 14, 19, 35, 39, 90, 180
ethnic conditions
  transient parties, 122
ethnic conflict, 11, 27, 49, 63, 72
  civic associations and, 217
  data, 104
  devolution, 28, 121
  electoral benefits, 84
  elite involvement, 207
  interethnic clashes, 2
  interview data, 21, 97, 203
  opportunity for elites, 19, 40, 41
  party violence, 20, 99
  scale, 103
  targets, 83
ethnic demography, 10, 39, 41, 49, 100, 101
ethnic minorities, 4, 20, 38, 127, 132, 133, 137
ethnic parties, 20, 62, 135
ethnic party violence, 6, 14, 23, 28, 82

ethnic politics
  comparison between Kenya and India, 68, 71, 74
  elite approaches to, 60
  negative, 62
ethnic segregation, 39, 48, 49, 91, 163
ethnic violence
  as electoral violence, 10
  effects, 18
  elite involvement, 79
  elite-driven, 7
  lethal, 79
  outbreak, 5
  pre-election, 39
  prevention, 9
  recurring, 21
  relationship to multiparty system, 84
  as threat, 84
ethnic wedges, 53, 63
ethno-linguistic groups, 53
ethnonationalism, 5, 10
extremist parties, 183

factionalism, 71, 196
farmer-herder conflict. *See* pastoralism
Fjelde, Hanne, 10, 12–16, 193, 194
food insecurity, 18, 96, 122
FORD-Asili, 103, 111
Forty Brothers. *See* vigilantism
Frente de Unidad Nacional (NUF), 36. *See also* Bolivia
Frente Democrático (FREDEMO), 36. *See also* Peru
Frenz, Margaret, 53, 69
Fujii, Lee Ann, 200, 208
Fujimori, Alberto, 36
Funga Five. *See* vigilantism

Gaitho, Macharia, 96
Galole constituency, 120, 121
Gandhi, Indira
  appeal to Hindus, 157
  assassination, 137, 159
  centralization of power, 215
  challenges of Hindu revivalism, 137
  Congress leadership, 157, 158
  consensus governance model, 71
  electoral platform, 133
  Emergency (1975–1977), 47, 134
  opposition to, 134
  re-election, 134
  regulation of NGOs, 215
  response to Moradabad riots (1980), 137

Gandhi, Mahatma, 57–60, 213
Gandhi, Rajiv
  challenges of Hindu revivalism, 137
  Congress leadership, 135, 158
  electoral success, 159
  Hindu–Sikh relations, 137
Gandhi, Sanjay, 134
gangs. *See also* vigilantism
  decline in importance, 165
  local, 114
  party funded, 78
  political utilization, 4, 30, 92, 129, 155, 204
Garissa County, 2, 93
Garsen constituency
  2013 violence, 118
  avoidance of violence, 118
  party replacement, 120
  pastoralist violence, 118
  patterns of violence, 101
  subnational research site, 100, 110
  Tana River clashes, 118
Gatundu South constituency, 78
Gau Raksha Dal, 130
Gbagbo, Laurent, 17
Ghana
  case study, 29, 48, 172–177, 180, 186
  civil society organizations (CSOs), 178
  comparison to India, 175, 177, 178, 180
  comparison to Kenya, 176, 177
  comparison to Turkey, 180
  competitive constituencies, 178
  election-related violence, 177
  electoral law, 176
  opposition politicians, 178
  parliamentary elections, 178
  party coherence, 176
  party stability, 173
  party structure, 176
  party system, 177
  presidential elections, 178
  public opinion, 177
  Supreme Court, 178
  Upper East, 180
  young democracy, 173, 175, 180, 186
Goan, 69
Godhana, Dhadho, 2, 120, 121
good governance, 174, 216
Good, Kenneth, 65
Grand Coalition, 92
grassroots politicians, 13
grievances
  demographic, 39, 40, 42
  electoral, 91, 101

Index

elite utilization, 39
ethnic, 89, 91
historical, 106
impact of devolution (Kenya), 120
indigenous, 117
intercommunal, 40, 41
land, 39, 83–85, 104, 108, 109
local, 27, 49, 60, 100, 107, 109, 110, 124
manipulable, 39
party utilization, 19, 35
state neglect, 110
utilization, 140
utilization through media, 11
Guatemala, 4, 35
Gujarat
communal conflict, 138
decline in violence, 153
Hindu–Muslim clashes, 133
interview data, 8
pogrom (2002), 3, 129
riots, 40, 153
subnational research site, 11

Haggard, Stephen, 190
Haiti, 4
Haji, Yusuf, 2, 120
harambee groups, 212, 214, 215
Harriss, John, 217
Hasan, Zoya, 68
Hassan, Mai, 48, 52, 65, 70
hegemonic party settings, 16, 74, 133, 169
Heller, Patrick, 48, 211, 215, 221
high-intensity conflict, 39, 44, 179, 180
Hindu nationalism
accountability for conflict, 206
attacks against minorities, 189
attacks against Muslims, 130, 147
benefits of violence, 171, 188
BJP ideology, 3, 129, 153, 166, 169
BJS ideology, 133
civil society organizations (CSOs), 147
communalism, 149
Congress attempts to undercut, 135
cow protection, 130
cross-caste appeal, 138
destruction of Babri Masjid, 140
fomenting conflict, 158, 207
goals, 28, 154
grassroots, 140
Hindu Mahasabha, 73, 213
Hyderabad, 147
ideological alternative, 213
incentives to use violence, 157

increase, 51
Jana Sangh, 73
leaders, 129, 132, 171
mahapanchayat, 209
marginalization of Muslims, 166
opposition to, 148
political influence, 139
political narratives, 39
provocation of Muslims, 165
resiliency in Indian politics, 73
rise, 67
risk analysis, 148
state approval, 159
survival under Congress hegemony, 64
threat to Congress ideology, 73
utilization of communalism, 127, 157, 166
utilization of conflict, 135
utilization of media, 139
utilization of religious processions, 147, 148, 154, 207
Hindu personal laws, 132
Hindu–Muslim conflict
BSP organized, 156
colonial-era, 155
salience in Indian politics, 64
Hindu–Muslim violence
datasets, 24, 128
decline, 48, 130, 140, 141, 164, 222
disincentivized, 171
elite instrumentalization, 126, 129
Hindu nationalism, 166
Hyderabad, 145, 151
institutionalized riot system, 8
interview data, 203
Muzaffarnagar and Shamli, 3
party replacement, 128
party stability, 20, 150
party system volatility, 14
party utilization, 127
postindependence analysis, 127
relationship to religious holidays, 138, 154
rural instrumentalization, 178
state incentives to quell, 9
trajectories, 21, 124
urban, 127
vulnerabilities, 142
Hindus
attacks against, 156, 158, 160
attacks against Muslims, 145
deities, 152
demonstrations against attacks, 156
economic specialization, 222
hate speech against, 152

Hindus (cont.)
  holy sites, 158, 165
  importance to INC, 157
  religious festivals, 154
  threats of violence against, 152
  threats to, 159
  violence against, 150
Hindustan Times (India), 129
Hindutva, 73, 74, 127, 137, 166
Höglund, Kristine, 5, 10, 17
Homa Bay County, 95
Hornsby, 65, 72
human rights activists
  government (Kenya), 2
  interview data, 26, 77, 108, 128, 200, 204
human rights organizations, 214–216
Human Rights Watch, 24, 103, 113
Hussein, Saddam, 17
Hyderabad
  1938 riot, 144
  1980s riots, 149
  1983 riots, 152
  1990 riots, 138, 143, 150, 151, 207
  attacks against Muslims, 144
  communal mobilization, 154
  comparison to Meerut, 155
  Confederation of Voluntary Associations (COVA), 217
  cost of riots, 170
  decline in violence, 143, 151, 153–155
  demographics, 145
  escalation of conflict, 148
  frequency of violence, 169
  Ganga-Jamuni Tehzeeb, 145
  Hindu–Muslim conflict, 152
  Hindu–Muslim violence, 154
  interview data, 63, 126, 150, 170, 202, 204, 206, 208, 221
  mohalla samitis (peace committees), 222
  Muslim community, 147
  Muslim politics, 148
  Muslim rulers, 144
  Nizams, 144
  nongovernmental organizations (NGOs), 217
  Old City, 143, 144, 147, 150, 151, 154, 221
  Operation Polo, 144, 145
  party instability, 142
  party replacement, 169
  party violence, 142
  patterns of riot violence, 29
  peace committees, 221
  polarization, 153

  Police Action (1948), 144, 145
  Rameeza Bee riots (1978), 145–148, 169
  rape, 145, 146
  research data, 211
  subnational research site, 141, 142
  Sunderlal Committee Report (1949), 144
  trajectories of Hindu–Muslim violence, 21, 124
  voters, 152
  vulnerability to violence, 143

Ichino, Nahomi, 176
identities
  caste-based, 168
  census, 57
  communal, 168
  depolarization, 10
  ethnic, 17, 39, 64
incumbent politicians
  electoral manipulation, 13
  incumbent-driven violence, 42
  likelihood of electoral violence, 5
  targeting opposition areas, 13
India constitution (1950)
  democratization, 74
  emphasis on equality, 63
  minority protections, 64, 67
  promulgation, 63
Indian Councils Act (1909), 58
Indian National Congress (INC), 149
  alliances, 154
  appeals to Hindus, 161
  attempts to stem violence, 161
  attitude toward violence, 140
  avoiding violence, 130
  blame for riots, 206
  candidates, 156
  charges of anti-Hindu stance, 158
  colonial elites, 213
  colonial-era, 58
  commitment to universal suffrage, 74
  comparison to KANU, 16, 27, 28, 51–53, 59–61, 64, 68, 71, 73, 74
  Congress system, 51, 67, 71
  constitution (1920), 58
  criticism, 58
  debates over postcolonial role, 59
  decline, 130, 134, 137, 147, 159, 163, 164
  democracy promotion, 73
  democratization, 48, 50
  deterioration, 133
  divisive, 139

Index

effects on opposition parties, 164
efforts to stem ethnic conflict, 57
egalitarianism, 57
electoral defeat, 128, 135, 148
electoral reforms, 58
electoral strategy, 136
electoral success, 159
elites, 133, 134, 171
ethnic politics, 64
extra-organizational threats, 73, 74, 149, 157
factionalism, 71
fundraising, 58
hegemonic party status, 59
hegemony, 132, 169
Hindu nationalism, 73
Hindu nationalist opposition, 133
Hindu–Muslim conflict, 57, 63
ideological project, 64
incentives against violence, 156, 157
incentives for peace, 131
incentives for violence, 157, 158
insecurity, 128
intraparty divisions, 70
leaders, 167
link to civil society, 215
Mandal Congress Committees (MCCs), 62
minority support, 159
mitigation of caste differences, 57
moderation, 64, 133, 159
multi-level apparatus, 58
Muslim disillusionment, 133
Muslim opposition, 134
Muslim support, 133, 136, 148
Muslim voters, 161
narratives, 137
nationalist-era, 48, 52, 53, 57, 61, 63, 70, 74, 213
nation-building, 59
opposition, 163
opposition to communalism, 57
orientation, 135
parliamentary elections, 133, 156
parliamentary seats, 151
participants in violence, 156
party competition, 73
party death, 194
party finances, 60, 61
party organization, 52, 58, 61–63, 70, 148, 169
party stability, 156
party strength, 58
patronage system, 65–67, 71

prioritizing consensus, 68, 70, 71
relationship to voters, 62
response to Hindu–Muslim conflict, 158
role in independence movement, 60
role in Indian nationalism, 57
secularism, 134, 135, 137
short-term orientation, 157
strategies of rule, 135
subleaders, 156
transformation into political party, 59
utilization of violence, 57, 204, 207, 221
voters, 67
weakening, 28
Working Committee, 58, 71, 137
Indian National Congress (Indira), 137
Indian National Congress (Urs), 194
Indian Penal Code (IPC), 209
Indonesia, 4, 10, 11, 39, 40
informed voters, 49
initiation of violence, 37, 40
İnönü, Ismet, 182
institutional deterioration, 191
institutional sanctions, 178
internally displaced persons (IDPs), 98
International Criminal Court (ICC), 78, 92, 94
International SOS, 24
international tribunals, 17
Inter-Religious Council of Kenya, 219
Iraq, 17
Islamic Party of Kenya (IPK), 113

Jackson, Karl, 33
Jaffrelot, Christophe, 135
Jain, J. K., 139
Jaipur, 138
Jana Sangh, 133, 147, 156
Janata Dal (JD), 139, 164
Janata Party (JP), 95, 134, 137, 139
Jats, 166–168
Jensenius, Francesca, 193, 196
Jharkhand Party, 73
Jodhpur, 138
Jubilee Alliance, 93–96, 104, 105, 109, 123
Judicial Commission of Inquiry into Inter-Communal Violence in the Tana Delta, 2
Juma Boy, Boy, 113–115
Justice and Development Party. *See* Adalet ve Kalkınma Partisi (AKP)
Justice Party (JP). *See* Adalet Partisi (AP)

Kaggia, Bildad, 68
Kagwanja, Peter, 120

Index

Kalenjin
  alliance with Kikuyu, 93
  blame for violence, 92
  churches, 218
  claims to indigeneity, 106
  conflict with Kikuyu, 90, 94, 101, 103, 105, 106, 108, 109
  elites, 123
  IDP camp, 43
  intraethnic conflict, 105
  KADU membership, 56
  land acquisition, 105
  militias, 104
  Moi coalition, 65
  ODM participants, 89, 98
  Ruto violence network, 78
Kamba
  coalitional politics, 86, 89
  demographics, 110
  land politics, 81
Kamole, Suleiman, 114
Kapoor, Mohan Lal, 158
Kapseret constituency, 107
  2007 election-related violence, 107
  ethnic massacres, 106
  interview data, 106
  KANU, 107
  parliamentary representation, 106
  party instability, 107
  party replacement, 107, 109
  subnational research site, 100
Kariuki, J. M., 65, 69
Karnataka
  communal conflict, 138
  Hindu groups, 145
Kasara, Kimuli, 39, 91
Kaufman, Robert, 190
Keen, John, 60, 61
Keiyo North constituency, 84
Keiyo South constituency, 84, 102
Kenny, Paul, 32, 33
Kenya African Democratic Union (KADU), 56, 72
Kenya African National Union (KANU)
  assassinations, 69, 70
  attempts to silence churches, 215
  benefits of ethnic violence, 84
  British loyalists, 54, 56, 65, 68
  candidates, 103, 112–114
  church opposition, 218
  coalitions, 114
  comparison to INC, 16, 27, 51, 52, 59–61, 64, 71, 74

confusion over postcolonial role, 59
contested future, 81
corruption, 81
defections to ODM, 107
District Commissioners, 65
divisions, 69
effects on civil society, 214
electoral defeat, 47, 86, 88, 110, 113, 115
electoral success, 107, 112
electoral victories, 86
elites, 48, 52, 101, 105, 111, 113, 114, 204
emergence, 55
ethnic divisions, 56
ethnic party violence, 83
ethnic politics, 62, 65, 68
failed utilization of violence, 87
failure of mass appeal, 59
fracture, 84
instrumentalization of grievances, 84
internal threats, 56
interview data, 82, 207
Jeshi la Mzee (The Old Man's Army), 214
Jomo Kenyatta leadership, 55, 56, 61, 65, 68
Kikuyu dominance, 69
land distribution, 117
leaders, 56
loss of leaders, 83
Moi leadership, 18, 65, 69, 111
National Assembly, 69
nation-building, 62
one-party state, 27, 70, 101
opponents, 214
opposition, 103
opposition from Moi, 81
organizational capacity, 69
party branches, 81
party discipline, 56
party finances, 60, 81
party insecurity, 50
party instability, 103
party narrative, 55
party organization, 27, 53, 56, 61, 64, 80, 82, 84, 115
party organizing, 62
party strength, 80
patronage system, 68, 81
postcolonial regime threats, 56
prosecution of opponents, 71
Provincial Administration (PA), 48, 52, 55, 56, 65, 70, 72, 80
  patronage system, 66
Provincial Commissioners, 65
relationship to rivals, 79

Index

relationship to voters, 61
Rift Valley zone, 78
support, 69, 111, 113
threats, 122, 215
Uhuru Kenyatta leadership, 87
use of coercion, 81
utilization of violence, 77, 99, 103, 107, 109, 110, 113, 122
voter opposition to, 81
weak institutionalization, 50
Youth for KANU (YK '92), 106, 214
Kenya African National Union A (KANU A), 85
Kenya African National Union B (KANU B), 85
Kenya African Union (KAU), 55
Kenya Colony, 52–55, 58, 212, 213
Kenya constitution (1963)
  detention without trial, 71
  presidential system, 71
Kenya constitution (1969)
  efforts to reform, 85
  elimination of judicial independence, 72
  opposition parties, 72, 79
  political constraints, 67
  term limits, 87
Kenya constitution (2010)
  2013 reform, 77, 93
  citizen priorities, 122
  development, 119
  devolution, 1, 99
  electoral reform, 74
  promulgation, 1, 28, 51, 93
  term limits, 109
Kenya constitutional referendum (2005), 218
Kenya Human Rights Commission (KHRC), 24, 106, 107, 214
Kenya National Commission on Human Rights (KNCHR), 24
Kenya People's Union (KPU), 69, 72
Kenya Supreme Court, 189
Kenya Violent Elections Dataset (KVED), 23, 24, 77, 79, 104, 112, 118, 206
Kenyan Asians, 66, 208
Kenyatta, Jomo
  alienation of allies, 68, 69
  autocratic regime, 70
  comparison to Moi, 72
  comparison to Nehru, 73
  death, 214
  ethnic patronage system, 65, 69
  imprisonment, 55
  KANU leadership, 65, 69, 71, 80
  KANU party discipline, 56
  KANU party organization, 61

KANU party weakness, 48
Kikuyu prominence in KANU, 65
Kikuyu resettlement schemes, 111
legacy, 65
Mau Mau legacy, 57, 68
move to authoritarianism, 71
Muigwathania, 68
neglect of Coast Province, 111
one-party state, 71, 72, 111
opposition repression, 69
patronage system, 65
relationship to civil society organizations (CSOs), 214
relationship to voters, 111
symbolism, 59
utilization of Provincial Administration (PA), 56
Kenyatta, Uhuru
  2017 elections, 95, 96
  advocacy for Kikuyu, 117
  failure on material concerns, 111
  ICC indictments, 92, 94
  ineffectiveness of ethnic conflict, 87, 93
  Jubilee Alliance, 93, 95, 96
  pact with Ruto, 95, 96
  support for Odinga, 96
  utilization of violence, 78
Khan, Shahnawaz, 158
Khan, Shaukat Hameed, 156
Kiano, Julius, 65
Kibaki, Mwai, 86–89, 91, 92, 111, 216
Kidwai, Mohsina, 158, 161
Kikuyu
  anxieties about power, 111
  attacks against, 103, 106, 117
  churches, 218
  coalitional politics, 86
  colonial laborers, 54
  colonial land ownership, 54
  colonial reserves, 54
  conflict in Tana River, 118
  conflict with Kalenjin, 90, 105, 108, 109
  conflict with Luo, 89
  deaths, 115
  demographics, 110
  displaced, 102
  elites, 123, 220
  ethnic coalition, 90
  fomenting violence against, 84
  gangs, 78
  IDP camp, 43
  intraethnic conflict, 105
  Jomo Kenyatta patronage, 65, 70

Kikuyu (cont.)
    KANU domination, 56
    land acquisition, 101, 105
    majority areas, 101
    marginalization, 66, 101
    Mau Mau, 54
    migration from Central Province, 101
    migration to Coast, 86
    negative perception, 90
    nongovernmental organizations (NGOs), 211
    opposition to KANU, 83
    rejection of KANU, 111
    resettlement in Uasin Gishu, 106
    resettlement to Coast Province, 111
    Ruto violence coalition, 94
    state dominance, 69
    targets of violence, 116
    threats of violence, 102
    voters, 92
Kikuyu Central Association (KCA), 212
Kikuyu Karing'a Education, 212
Kikuyu-Kalenjin alliance, 94, 98
Kimani, Dickson, 103
Kimenyi, Mwangi, 102
Kisiero, Wilberforce, 78
Kisii
    conflict with Kikuyu, 101
    threats of violence, 102
Kisumu County, 83, 93, 95
Klaus, Kathleen, 6, 10, 11, 15, 39, 89, 104, 108, 110
Kochanek, Stanley, 60
Kodnani, Mayaben, 129
Koros, David Kiptanui, 107
Kothari, Rajni
    Congress system, 66, 71
Krause, Jana, 10, 20, 40
Kuenzi, Michelle, 25
Kumar, Radha, 145
Kumar, Sajjan, 127, 130, 133, 140, 166, 190
Kurdistan Workers' Party (PKK), 184

Lacina, Bethany, 40
Lambright, Gina, 25
land politics
    colonial, 54
    disputes, 158
    land distribution, 84, 85, 105, 110
    land insecurity, 104
    land reclamation, 86, 108
    land rights, 39, 81

land security, 104
land tenure, 11, 39, 110
land-related grievances. *See* grievances
    narratives, 11, 107, 108, 109
    ownership inequality, 110
Law Society of Kenya (LSK), 214
legislative elections
    competitive constituencies, 13
    party violence, 44
    subnational, 44
    Zimbabwe, 13
Levitsky, Steven, 35
Liberal Democratic Party (LDP), 88
Likoni constituency
    1997 violence, 112–114
    avoidance of conflict, 116
    demographics, 110
    interview data, 18
    KANU electoral losses, 112
    KANU pursuit of votes, 113
    marginalization, 86
    parliamentary elections, 114
    party replacement, 115
    patterns of violence, 100
    peace, 115
    site of conflict, 110
    subnational research site, 98, 100, 110, 116
    transient parties, 117
Lindberg, Staffan, 174
Lok Dal (LKD), 161
Lok Sabha
    1957 replacement rates, 156
    1967 elections, 133
    1980 elections, 137
    1982 party volatility, 157
    1984 election, 148
    1984 party replacement, 159
    1989 replacement volatility, 150
    AIMIM/MIM electoral gains, 148
    BJP electoral performance, 209
    election conflict, 158
    election-related violence, 161, 168
    party replacement, 146
    party volatility, 164
    replacement volatility, 137, 138, 169
low-intensity conflict, 16, 41, 42, 48, 130, 140, 141, 171, 189
Loxton, James, 35
Luhya
    churches, 218
    demographics, 110
    KADU membership, 56

Index

Moi coalition, 66
ODM leaders, 89
violence against, 84
Luo
   churches, 218
   coalitional politics, 87
   colonial laborers, 54
   conflict with Kikuyu, 89
   deaths, 115
   demographics, 110
   elites, 123
   ethnic coalition, 90
   Jomo Kenyatta patronage, 70
   KANU domination, 56
   leaders, 68
   marginalization, 85
   nongovernmental organizations (NGOs), 211
   ODM support, 92
   violence against, 84
Lupu, Noam, 34, 199
Lynch, Gabrielle, 76, 78, 87, 95, 220

Maasai, 84
Macwana, Shailesh, 129
Madhya Pradesh, 139
mahapanchayat, 3, 167
Maharaj, Sakshi, 130
Maharashtra, 129, 145
Mahendra, K. L., 145
Maina, Wachira, 220
Mainwaring, Scott, 25
majimbo, 111
majoritarian parties, 6
majoritarian voting rules, 10
Malawi, 5, 191
Mampilly, Zachariah, 205
manipulation
   autocratic, 15
   electoral, 13, 47, 178
   ethnic, 89
   illegal, 16
   utilization, 17
marginalization
   historic, 110
   historical, 85, 86, 110, 117
   mechanisms of restraint, 40
   narratives, 11
   overestimation in violence, 117
   persistent, 18
Martin, Pilly, 118
Marxist-Leninist Armed Propaganda Union (MLSPB), 183

mass media, 11
Masumbuko, Omar, 113
Matiba, Kenneth, 83, 111
Matuga constituency, 113, 114
Mau Mau (Land and Freedom Army), 54, 55, 57, 59, 68
Mbeere, 89
Mboya, Tom, 59, 69
McLane, John, 57
media, 11, 31, 38, 42
Meerut
   1939 violence, 155
   1946 violence, 155
   1961 riots, 155, 157
   1982 violence, 158, 161
   communal conflict, 166
   communal violence, 142
   comparison to Hyderabad, 155
   decline in violence, 164
   demographics, 157, 164
   frequency of violence, 155, 169
   Gian Prakash Committee, 160
   Hashimpura massacres (1987), 43, 139, 155, 159–164, 170
   Hindu–Muslim clashes, 164
   Hindu–Muslim conflict, 168
   interview data, 43, 67, 135, 170, 202, 203, 208, 222
   low-intensity conflict, 166
   mohalla samitis, 222
   Muslims, 136, 165
   parliamentary elections, 156, 161
   party violence, 142
   patterns of riot violence, 29
   research data, 211
   riot system, 155, 157, 158, 165
   Shahghasa, 158
   site for use of violence, 157
   subnational research site, 141, 142
   support for Hindu nationalists, 159
   trajectories of Hindu–Muslim violence, 21, 124
   vulnerabilities to violence, 165
Mijikenda
   demographics, 110
   Digo, 112, 114
   land politics, 110
   leaders, 18, 56
   Moi coalition, 66
military elites, 40
militias
   ethnic, 92
   informal, 6

militias (cont.)
  Kalenjin, 104
  non-state actors, 30
  Orma, 2
  pro-government, 184
Millî Nizam Partisi (MNP), 183
Millî Selâmet Partisi (MSP), 183, 184
Milliyetçi Hareket Partisi (MHP), 183, 184
Mishra, Kapil, 129
Misoi, Joseph, 106, 107
Misra, Sripati, 157, 158
Mitra, Anirban, 24
mobilization
  caste-based, 163
  communal, 130, 135, 138, 154, 157, 166
  communal identity, 8
  demobilization, 5, 10
  dynamics, 10
  ethnic, 27, 62, 64, 67, 134
  high incentives, 12
  Hindu nationalist, 166
  incentives, 212
  land politics, 11, 84, 104
  logics, 20
  mass, 57, 63
  narratives, 199
  nationalist, 53
  ordinary individuals, 7
  religious, 73, 138
  scholarship, 7
  theories, 9
  uneven, 59
  versus containment, 10
  violence, 188
  voter, 96, 108
mobs
  Hindu, 160, 161
  provocation, 30
modalities of conflict and violence, 6, 16, 28, 171
moderation, 51, 135
Modi, Narendra, 153, 166, 169
Moi, Daniel arap
  accumulation of wealth, 81
  assassinations, 70
  autocratic regime, 70–72, 84, 218
  challenges of multipartyism, 81, 84
  clientelism, 65, 66, 72
  comparison to Nehru, 68, 73
  constitutional reform (1966), 72
  constitutional reform (1988), 72
  coup attempt against, 72
  deaths associated with, 215
  dissent, 70
  electoral defeat, 115
  ethnic coalition, 65
  exit from politics, 87
  failure on material concerns, 111
  KADU membership, 56
  KANU leadership, 69, 70, 72, 80, 81, 85, 113
  land allocation, 81
  NGO growth, 214, 216
  one-party state, 18, 65, 110
  opposition to, 85, 86, 88, 103, 111
  opposition to KANU organization, 81
  patronage system, 65
  re-election, 84, 86
  regulation of NGOs, 214, 215, 220
  relationship to civil society, 214
  support for, 111
  term limits, 87, 216
  time horizons, 81, 82
  use of coercion, 81
  utilization of ethnic conflict, 204
  utilization of violence, 78, 84, 87
Molo constituency
  1992 violence, 102
  1997 violence, 103
  2007 violence, 103
  avoidance of violence, 104
  circumstances for conflict, 106
  demographics, 101
  ethnic conflict, 103
  Kalenjin-Kikuyu violence, 103
  lack of conflict, 106
  land politics, 104, 105, 108
  party replacement, 101
  party violence, 104
  subnational research site, 100, 105
Mombasa County
  1997 violence, 112
  2007 violence, 21
  avoidance of conflict, 116
  cosmopolitan, 110
  interview data, 21, 66, 115, 123, 202, 203
  interviews, 203
  marginalization, 110
  opposition stronghold, 116, 117
  party divisions, 113
  party instability, 121
  party volatility, 116
  patterns of violence, 101
  rise in conflict, 117
  subnational research site, 21, 28, 100, 110
  utilization of violence, 85, 91

Index

Moradabad
  communal violence, 170
  INC, 137
  Muslims, 136
  riots (1980), 128, 135–137
Morishita, Michiaki Nagatani, 45
Morris-Jones, W. H., 62
Morse, Yonatan, 13–15, 17, 26, 32, 80
Motherland Party (ANAP), 184
Mount Elgon, 78
Movimiento Nacionalista Revolucionario (MNR), 36, 37, 45. *See also* Bolivia
Msambweni constituency, 113
Mubarak, Hosni, 17
Mudavadi, Musalia, 89
Mueller, Susanne, 76
Muge, Alexander Kipsang, 215
Mukherjee, Syama Prasad, 132
Muliro, Masinde, 56
Müller-Crepon, Carl, 10, 39
multiparty competition, 50–52, 74, 76, 78, 101, 104, 107, 111, 173, 174, 181
multiparty democracy, 47
multiparty elections, 47, 81, 83, 110, 173
multiparty system, 77, 81–86, 101, 102, 105, 118, 122, 177, 186, 214, 220
Mumias County, 95
Mungai, John, 103
Murumbi, Joseph, 56, 60
Muslim League (ML), 136, 137
Muslims (India)
  accused of attacks, 139
  alliances with Hindus, 166
  attacks against, 130, 134, 143, 144, 158, 160, 161, 169, 171
  attempts to control, 161
  Babri Masjid, 138, 140, 153, 159
  blamed for violence, 137
  clashes with law enforcement, 136
  colonial-era oppression, 213
  disillusionment with INC, 133
  economic specialization, 222
  holy sites, 158
  importance to INC, 157
  increase in violence toward, 166
  insecurity, 131
  Miladun-Nabi, 154
  mobilization, 163
  Nizams, 144
  party support, 136
  positioned as villains, 209
  prosperity, 136, 137
  religious holidays, 136, 159, 165
  religious processions, 148
  targeted by violence, 156
  threats to, 154
  Urdu, 144
  violence against Hindus, 156
  voters, 167
  women, 145
Muslims (Kenya), 118. *See also* Islamic Party of Kenya (IPK)
Mutunga, Willy, 2
Muzaffarnagar
  2013 conflict, 3, 188
  agrarian decline, 166
  attacks against Muslims, 141
  BJP involvement, 167
  communal conflict, 3
  emerging site of violence, 166
  ethnic conflict, 11
  interview data, 202, 208, 209
  parliamentary elections, 168
  party losses due to violence, 14
  riots, 209
  rural, 3
  rural violence, 143, 169
  strengthening of BJP, 168
  subnational research site, 23, 29
Mwahima, Mwalimu Masoud, 114
Mwamzandi, Kassim, 113
Mwidau, Hashim, 112, 114

Naik, Sudhakar Rao, 129
Nairobi, 17, 21, 55, 69, 90, 95, 202, 216
Naivasha, 92
Nakuru County
  avoidance of violence, 104
  circumstances for conflict, 106
  interview data, 43, 83, 94, 202
  Kikuyu-majority, 101
  lack of conflict, 106
  land politics, 104, 105, 108
  party instability, 121
  party violence, 91, 104
  patterns of party conflict, 21
  patterns of party violence, 104
  research data, 109
  subnational research site, 21, 28, 100, 105
Naqvi, Saba, 3, 146
Narok, 84
Narok North constituency, 84
narratives
  conflicting, 150

narratives (cont.)
  contentious, 104
  elite, 86
  land, 11
  utilization for conflict, 11
  utilization to mobilize, 199
Nasong'o, Shadrick, 216
Nath, Suman, 140
Nathan, Noah, 176, 179
National Assembly (Kenya), 37, 69, 121
National Cohesion and Integration Act (Kenya), 219
National Cohesion and Integration Commission (NCIC) (Kenya), 219
National Council of Churches of Kenya (NCCK), 214
National Democratic Congress (NDC), 176, 177
National Democratic Party (NDP), 184
National Movement Simeon II (NSDV), 37. See also Bulgaria
National Order Party (NOP). See Millî Nizam Partisi (MNP)
National People's Party (NPP), 176, 177, 180
National Rainbow Coalition (NaRC), 86–89, 94, 95, 114, 115, 118, 123
National Salvation Party. See Millî Selâmet Partisi (MSP)
National Super Alliance (NASA), 95, 116
nationalist movement (India), 53, 58–60, 74, 213
Nationalist Movement Party (NAP). See Milliyetçi Hareket Partisi (MHP)
Native Reserves, 54
nativism, 40
Navalkar, Pramod, 129
Ndung'u, Njuguna, 102
Nehru, Jawaharlal
  avoidance of riots, 132
  challenges from communal elites, 132
  comparison to Indira Gandhi, 133
  comparison to Moi, 68
  connections to Kenya, 53
  constituent forums, 61, 62
  constitutional ideology, 73
  death, 133
  democratization, 73
  establishment of Sunderlal Committee (1949), 144
  INC party independence, 73
  INC party neglect, 62
  incentives for peace, 131

limits of secularization, 133
Nehruvian period, 133
response to Partition, 131
Nepal, 46
networks
  clientelist, 72
  cross-community, 58
  indigenous institutions, 212
  institutional, 176
  intercommunal, 129
  kin, 186, 212
  local, 178
  party, 180
  social, 48
New Delhi
  interview data, 23
New York Times, 62
News24 (Ghana), 178
Ngala, Ronald, 56
Ngilu, Charity, 86, 89
Nigeria, 4, 5, 10, 40
Njonjo, Charles, 72
nongovernmental organizations (NGOs)
  apolitical, 215
  Business Associations, 217
  conflict with the state, 214
  constraints, 212
  cooperation, 216
  development activities, 216
  diversity of, 217
  ethnic composition (Kenya), 211
  growth during Moi regime, 214
  growth in India, 217
  growth under Moi regime, 216
  Hyderabad network, 217
  impact on citizenship, 216
  lack of state control, 214
  lack of state funding, 216
  nonreligious, 220
  Press Clubs, 217
  proliferation of, 217
  provision of services (Kenya), 214
  relative power to state, 211
  subordination to political society, 223
non-state actors
  churches, 218
  local, 221
  party activities, 30
  peace-oriented, 220
  state cooperation, 9
nonviolent communities, 40
Ntimama, William Ole, 84, 107

Index

Nueva Fuerza Republicana (NFR), 36, 37. *See also* Bolivia
Nyaga, Joseph, 89
Nyandarua North constituency, 65
Nyanza County
  2007 violence, 90
  2013 conflict, 93
  utilization of violence, 85, 91
Nyeri, 60, 61

Odinga, Oginga, 68, 69
Odinga, Raila, 78, 86, 88–92, 95–97, 115, 116
Omolo, Ken, 65
Opalo, Ken, 48, 55, 56, 60, 61, 96
opposition politicians, 40, 81, 90
opposition strongholds, 13
Orange Democratic Movement (ODM), 89–92, 98, 99, 104, 107, 114–117
Orma, 1, 2, 118–121, 188
Other Backward Classes, 64
Ouko, Robert, 70
outsourcing, 12
Owaisi, Akbaruddin (Akbar), 152
Owaisi, Asaduddin (Asad), 149, 152
Owaisi, Sultan Salahuddin, 146–149, 152

Pai, Sudha, 127, 130, 133, 140, 166, 190
Pakistan, 4, 12
partisan conflict, 4, 17, 49
Partition of Bengal (1905), 58
party birth, 24, 25, 36, 37, 45–47, 88, 164, 169, 176, 182–184, 194
party birth volatility, 25
party coherence, 176, 177
party collapse, 35, 45
party death, 24, 25, 32, 36, 45–47, 88, 164, 169, 182–184
party death volatility, 25
party decline, 35, 43
party deterioration, 191
party development, 27, 50, 52, 53
party discipline, 194
party entry volatility, 25, 45, 141, 157, 194, 198
party exit, 36, 45, 157
party exit volatility, 25, 37, 193
party finances, 60, 74
party fragility, 19, 35, 76, 98, 171
party instability
  alternative frameworks, 211
  alternative measures, 193, 194, 196, 198
  as institutional deterioration, 191

conditioning factor, 7, 19, 25, 27, 31, 34, 38, 44, 77, 78, 117, 128, 171–173, 186, 188
conflict risk assessment, 16
cost reduction of conflict, 17
decline, 150
decrease, 192
elite decision-making, 14, 15
elite incentives for violence, 16
elite time horizons, 127, 189
factor in elite time horizons, 31, 34
falling, 130
framework, 16, 34, 41, 47, 48, 171
high, 110, 116, 117, 121, 170
incentivizing conflict, 29, 49, 97, 99, 100, 124, 141, 173
increase, 86, 88, 89, 107, 146, 169, 171
levels, 47, 48, 50, 105, 106, 109, 223
low, 142, 154
party death, 32
party system variations, 48
persistent, 123
primacy, 48
relationship to violence, 26, 124, 142, 170, 175
replacement volatility as measure, 23, 24, 35, 37, 128
rising, 130, 135, 137
subnational data, 100
threats to hegemonic parties, 137
variations, 45
varying, 15
versus democratic age, 175, 186
party institutionalization, 173, 175, 178, 179, 185, 186, 189
party lifespan, 27, 45
party longevity, 46, 49, 75, 189
Party of National Unity (PNU), 78, 83, 89–92, 95, 98, 99, 104, 116, 123
party organization (PO)
  comparison between Kenya and India, 68, 71, 217
  Ghana, 177
  India, 61, 137, 148
  interview data, 203
  Kenya, 61, 117
  measure of party instability, 196
  measures, 193
  relationship to election-related violence, 192
  relationship to replacement volatility, 25
  Turkey, 181
party organizational capacity, 8, 12, 60–62, 74

Index

party regulation, 176
party replacement
  Andhra Pradesh, 150
  comparison between Kenya and India, 169
  contrast to vote-switching volatility, 46
  contributing factors, 35
  data, 142
  Garsen constituency, 120
  Ghana, 176
  high levels, 28, 77
  Hyderabad, 151, 154
  India, 124, 128, 135, 141, 157, 159, 171, 193
  Kapseret constituency, 109
  Kenya, 82, 93, 100
  Likoni constituency, 116
  measure of party survival, 77
  Molo constituency, 101
  Nakuru County, 104
  relationship to party birth, 46
  shifts in levels, 25
  Turkey, 185
  Uasin Gishu County, 107
  Uttar Pradesh, 159, 169
party stability, 29, 41, 127, 150, 164, 173, 180, 190
party stabilization, 151, 169
party strength (PS). *See also* Fjelde, Hanne
  data, 194
  India, 58
  Kenya, 57
  measures, 193
  negative correlation to replacement volatility, 194
  relationship to election-related violence, 174
  relationship to replacement volatility, 25
  subnational party branches, 194
party subleaders, 176
party survival, 27, 77, 88, 137, 173
party system instability, 25, 37
party system volatility, 14, 24, 37, 184, 193, 194, 198
party violence
  alternative explanations, 45–47, 200
  blame, 104, 204
  consequences, 17
  data variations, 23
  direct, 17
  disincentives, 171
  distinct from election-related violence, 6, 15
  dominant party systems, 16
  elite decision-making, 12, 53, 121, 200, 206
  elite escalation, 110
  elite participation, 78
  ethnic conflict, 20, 24
  evidence of involvement, 207
  incentives, 19, 59, 71, 75, 139, 148, 150, 169, 188, 212
  incitement, 91
  indirect, 17
  intra-and inter-, 5
  logics, 21
  low rates, 93
  newer forms, 143
  normalization, 184
  patterns, 77, 211
  policy implications, 15, 189, 190, 192
  prevention, 218
  relationship to democratic age, 48, 174
  relationship to democratic longevity, 29
  relationship to electoral violence, 4
  relationship to party instability, 117, 173, 186
  relationship to party replacement, 104, 128
  relationship to populism, 191
  relationship to voter sanctioning, 168
  risks, 76, 171
  scale, 35, 180
  shifts, 166
  strategies, 14
  subnational analyses, 99
  subnational patterns, 28, 100
  subnational variables, 100
  supply, 7
  trajectories, 19, 20, 148, 171, 203
  transformations, 130
  variations, 45, 173, 222
  vulnerability, 47, 175
  waves, 78
party volatility, 35, 48, 78, 118, 128, 132, 135, 141, 142, 182, 185
pastoralism
  benefits of violence, 188
  communal conflict, 1
  community neglect, 120
  conflict with farmers, 118, 120
  demographics, 118
  displacement, 1, 54
  herders, 1, 119
patronage-based systems
  building loyalty, 65
  building party base, 65
  central to KANU, 81
  comparison between Kenya and India, 68
  distinct from party violence, 81

Index

ethnic, 11
Ghana comparison to India, 180
Global South, 67
land politics, 107
leveraging, 214
limited by electoral politics, 67
logics, 60
Moi utilization, 72
monopoly, 66
networks, 8, 11
party-state, 66
patronage democracy, 67
reliance on, 64
time horizons, 33
weakened accountability, 190
Pearlman, Wendy, 205
peasants, 60, 182
Pedersen index, 24, 25. *See also* Pedersen volatility
Pedersen volatility, 24, 37, 193, 194, 198
pehlwans (strongmen), 151
Peisakhin, Leonid, 199
Peru, 36, 37
Pinto, Pio Gama, 69
Pipeline Camp for Internally Displaced Persons, 43
plantations, 54
Pokomo, 1, 2, 118–121
polarization, 10, 90, 140, 148, 152–154, 163, 166, 168, 181
policymakers, 77
political competition, 27, 64, 176
political instability, 82
political institutions
  maturity, 96
political uncertainty, 81, 89
population growth, 54
populism, 133, 190, 191
Populist Party (HP), 184
Prakash, Gian, 160. *See also* Meerut
Prasad, Neeraj, 5
pre-election riots, 10, 129
pre-election violence, 13
Presbyterian Church of East Africa (PCEA), 215
Preservation of Public Security Act (1966) (Kenya), 71
presidential elections, 13, 25, 70, 78, 99, 116, 204
programmatic parties, 32, 33, 58, 194
property damage, 31
proportional representation, 10, 67
protests, 58, 96, 145, 183

Provincial Administration (PA) (Kenya), 48, 52, 55, 56. *See also* Kenya African National Union (KANU)
Provincial Armed Constabulary (PAC), 136, 139, 158, 160–162
Provisional Village Guards (GKK), 184
public opinion, 30, 122, 160, 170
punishment
  appropriate target, 43, 44
  direct, 115
  future, 7, 31, 188
  inconsistent, 98
  judicial, 17, 31, 187
  opposition party, 78
  shared, 171
  voter, 17, 34, 42, 44, 49, 97, 152, 189
  voter difficulty, 43
  willingness, 125
Punjab, 73
Pye, Lucian, 33

race-based policies, 53
Raffensberger, Brad, 191
Rajya Sabha, 139
Rana, Kadir, 167
Rana, Sanjay, 130
Rana, Vishal, 130
Ranchi, 133
Rao, N. T. Rama, 149
Rao, Neena, 146
rath, 128, 135, 138
rath yatra, 128, 135, 138, 139
Rauschenbach, Mascha, 13–15
Ray, Debraj, 24
Ray-Mitra dataset, 24, 128, 206
rebel groups, 46
rebel-to-party transformations, 46
Reddy, Chenna, 146, 150, 207
Reddy, N. Janardhan, 151
regime stability, 52
regime type, 53, 60, 71, 74, 217
religious elites, 26, 77, 128, 200, 204
replacement volatility
  alternative terms, 25
  Andhra Pradesh, 142, 148, 150
  Bolivia, 35
  case studies, 37
  contrast to vote-switching volatility, 32, 37
  correlation to party strength (PS), 193, 194
  correlation to Pedersen volatility, 37, 193, 194
  data, 194

280 *Index*

replacement volatility (cont.)
  Garsen constituency, 118
  high levels, 37
  India, 138, 169, 196, 198
  Kapseret constituency, 107, 109
  Kenya, 82, 86, 95, 121
  Likoni constituency, 112, 115
  measure of party instability, 23–25, 35, 37
  measures, 25
  Molo constituency, 101, 106
  Mombasa County, 116
  Peru, 35
  Uasin Gishu County, 108
  Uttar Pradesh, 137, 138, 169
Republican Party (United States), 190, 191
Republican People's Party. *See* Cumhuriyet Halk Partisi (CHP)
resources
  access, 118
  competition, 39
  concentration, 66
  dearth, 220
  direction, 35
  domination, 120
  elite, 34
  financial, 34, 53, 113, 123
  lack of, 34
  patronage-based systems, 33
  protection, 111
  scarce, 8, 14
  state, 180
  variable, 40
restraint of violence, 7, 38
revenue losses, 17
Revolutionary Way (DEV-YOL), 183
Riedl, Rachel, 175
Rift Valley
  1991 violence, 83
  1991 violence, 84
  2007 violence, 90
  2013 conflict, 93, 95
  church leaders, 217
  coalitional politics, 93
  colonial forced migration, 54
  communal conflict, 39, 105
  comparison to Coast Province, 92, 116
  consequences of violence, 122, 123
  elite-orchestrated violence, 101, 124
  ethnic conflict, 204, 207
  interview data, 26, 43, 98, 109, 116, 122, 204
  KANU-sponsored conflict, 78, 85, 113
  Kikuyu marginalization, 101

  Kikuyu voters, 111
  land politics, 105, 106
  militias, 102, 104
  party conflict, 103
  party replacement, 107
  party violence, 104, 110
  patronage-based system, 107
  state-society partnerships, 96
  subnational research site, 21, 28, 99, 100
  utilization of violence, 85, 91
riot incidents, 128, 129, 133, 143, 149
riot production, 8, 206
riot violence
  communal conflict, 138
  containment, 9
  data, 142
  declines, 21, 75
  escalation, 28
  failure to quell, 149
  incentivized, 146
  intensity, 128
  interview data, 209
  patterns, 29
  political party involvement, 209
  relationship to party instability, 124, 142
  role of elites, 129
  subnational trajectories, 141
  Uttar Pradesh, 138
risks
  acceptable, 147
  discounting, 34
  effects of civil society, 220
  efforts to reduce, 38
  elite decision-making, 16, 127, 135, 141, 171
  judicial, 17
  management, 178, 186
  minimization, 13
  prohibitive, 28
  reduction, 13
  relationship to party instability, 14, 48
  research participants, 199
  strategic, 148
rival parties, 5, 10, 151, 204
Robinson, Amanda, 54
robust media, 17
Rosberg, Carl, 59
Rosenthal, A. M., 62
Rosenzweig, Steven, 6, 13–15, 17, 84
RSS, 158, 159, 161, 213
rule of law, 7, 190
ruling elites, 33, 39, 79, 131, 212

Index

ruling parties, 13, 53, 180
rumors, 9, 48, 134, 200
rural
  civil society organizations (CSOs), 214
  communal violence, 140
  elections, 156
  exposure to riots, 168
  Hindu–Muslim violence, 28, 48, 127, 141, 166, 171
  instrumentalization of violence, 16
  migration to urban areas, 183
  voters, 63, 169
Ruto, William, 78, 89, 92–96
Rutten, Marcel, 103
Rwanda, 200

Sahay, K. B., 133
Sajjad, Rashid, 114
Samajwadi Party (SP), 3, 167, 171
Sangh Parivar, 159, 166
Sanyukt Vyapar Sangh (Joint Business Association), 222
Sardhana constituency, 165, 168
Savkova, Lyubka, 37
Scheduled Caste(s) (SC), 64, 67, 73, 163
Scheduled Tribe(s) (ST), 64, 67
Schiff, Adam, 190
Scully, Timothy, 25
sectarian conflicts, 117
secularism
  India, 73, 131–135, 137
  Turkey, 174
Serb Democratic Party, 4
settlers
  European, 54, 55, 212
  Kikuyu, 101
  plantations, 54
severe violence
  avoidance, 2, 48
  communal grievances, 41
  incompatibility with clientelism, 180
  Kenya, 77, 124
  Likoni constituency, 116
  Mombasa County, 116
  Nakuru County, 104
  party maturity, 186
  relationship to party instability, 49, 123
  voter sanctioning, 20
Shakombo, Suleiman Rashid, 98, 114, 115
Shamli
  2013 conflict, 3
  agrarian decline, 166
  attacks against Muslims, 141
  BJP involvement, 167
  communal conflict, 3
  emerging site of violence, 166
  ethnic conflict, 11
  interview data, 202, 208
  party losses due to violence, 14
  riots, 209
  rural violence, 143, 169
  strengthening of BJP, 168
  subnational research site, 23, 29
Sharma, Nagendar, 129
Shirikisho Party (SPK), 114
Shiv Sena, 129, 133, 138
shutdowns, 17
Siaya County, 95
Siddiqui, Hafed Ahmed, 137
Siddiqui, Niloufer, 4, 6, 12–15
Sikhs
  conflict with Hindus, 137
  mobilization, 73
  separatists, 74
  threat to Congress ideology, 73
Singh, Mulayam, 139
Singh, V. P., 137
Singh, Vir Bahadur, 161
social capital, 17
Social Conflict Analysis Database (SCAD), 175, 179
Socialist Party (SP), 188
socioeconomic inequality, 5, 117, 122, 140
Som, Sangeet, 165, 167, 168
Sotik, 92
South Africa, 16, 31
South Asian diaspora, 53
South-South exchange, 53
speeches
  anti-Muslim, 129
  divisive, 30
  incendiary, 158, 167
  inflammatory, 84, 120
Sri Lanka, 5
stabilization of parties, 20, 128
stable parties
  correlation to intensity of violence, 39
  democratic maturity, 48, 175
  disincentivizing violence, 15, 20, 42, 44, 52, 175, 187
  frequency of violence, 19
  impact on time horizons, 41
  India, 48
  organizational continuity, 196

stable parties (cont.)
    policy implications, 38
    shifts in violence, 171
    voter accountability, 171
    voter sanctioning, 43, 49, 98
stable party contexts, 31, 142
stable party volatility, 35, 37
Staniland, Paul, 57, 64, 73
state capacity, 174
state informalization, 81
Steeves, Jeffrey, 65, 84
Straus, Scott, 40
subleaders
    competition, 135
    importance of subnational context, 142
    incentives for violence, 34
    instability, 105, 107, 124
    long-term consideration, 34
    party accountability, 17
    strength, 35
    strong reputations, 34
    utilization of violence, 120
subnational
    comparisons between Kenya and India, 21
    datasets, 196
    demographics, 49, 124
    distribution of violence, 39
    elites, 35
    grievances, 85, 220
    patterns of party violence, 28
    political influence, 147
    research sites, 26, 29, 39, 40, 78, 99, 100, 123, 124, 142, 169, 171, 198, 200, 211, 223
    sites of violence, 41
    violence, 13
Suhas, Prashant, 14, 15
Sunderlal, Pandit, 144
supply of violence, 6, 15, 38, 49, 50
supply-side model of violence, 14, 15, 32
Supreme Court (Kenya), 20, 78, 95, 96, 99, 123, 189
Suryanarayan, Pavithra, 193, 196
Swadeshi movement, 58
Swahilis, 110
swaraj, 53

Tamilnad Congress, 73
Tana River County
    2002 violence, 88, 118
    2013 conflict, 21
    2013 violence, 93, 118
    attacks on Pokomo, 120
    avoidance of violence, 118
    comparison to Uttar Pradesh, 4
    devolution, 120, 121, 124
    ethnic conflict, 2
    farmer-herder conflict, 121
    land politics, 1
    patterns of violence, 101
    politically effective violence, 2
    state aid, 119
    subnational research site, 21, 28, 100, 110, 120
Tandon, Purshottamdas, 70
Tanzania, 13
Telangana, 147, 154
Telugu Desam Party (TDP), 148, 149, 151, 194
Thaha, Abdul, 146
the Congress. *See* Indian National Congress (INC)
The Standard (Kenya), 114
thresholds, 10
Throup, David, 65, 72
time horizons
    clientelism, 33
    conditioning factor, 38, 45
    correlation to replacement volatility, 25
    effects, 32
    elite, 16, 128
    erosion, 41
    impact of party instability, 23
    legacy, 34, 199
    lengthy, 31, 32, 34, 141, 153, 188
    longer, 7, 13
    party instability, 34, 41
    party lifespan, 45
    patronage-based systems, 33
    relationship to party credibility, 33
    shadows of the future, 32, 33, 45, 77, 189
    short, 16, 32, 85, 89, 110, 113, 141, 175, 188, 190
    shortening, 31, 49, 97, 127, 190
    sources, 27, 31, 37
    term limits, 33, 34, 87, 92
    truncated, 7, 14, 31–33, 36–38, 77, 81, 82, 89, 99, 117
Times of India, 24, 144, 146, 152, 161
trade unions, 8, 71, 145
transient parties, 38, 41, 49, 122, 181, 186
transnational connections, 53
Trump, Donald, 17, 190, 191
Truth Power Party. *See* Doğru Yol Partisi (DYP)
Tudor, Maya, 48, 52, 60

Index

Türk Silahlı Kuvvetleri (TSK), 182, 184
Turkey
  anarşi, 29, 48, 173, 175, 181, 183–186
  Association of Idealist Youth, 183
  case study, 48, 172–174, 186
  challenges to democracy, 181
  comparison to Ghana, 29, 180
  comparison to India, 186
  comparison to Kenya, 181, 183
  coups, 181, 182, 184
  elections, 184
  freedom of speech, 182
  Islamism, 183
  Kemalist system, 181, 182
  "Kurdish question," 184
  Kurds, 184
  leftist groups, 173, 183, 185
  mature party system, 186
  military in politics, 182
  multiparty system, 181
  nationalism, 181
  one-party state, 182
  party instability, 181
  party system, 182
  party volatility, 184
  political conflict, 175
  political insecurity, 181
  political trajectory, 185
  populism, 181
  republicanism, 181
  revolutionism, 181
  right-wing groups, 183, 185
  secularism, 174, 181
  ultranationalist groups, 173, 183
  urban areas, 173, 183
  violence against Kurds, 184
Turkish Armed Forces. See Türk Silahlı Kuvvetleri (TSK)
Turkish People's Liberation Army (THKO), 183
Turkish People's Liberation Party-Front (THKO-C), 183
Turkish Worker Peasant Liberation Army (TIKKO), 183

Uasin Gishu County
  ethnic conflict, 108
  interview data, 106, 217, 218
  Kikuyu settlement, 106
  land politics, 107, 108
  party instability, 121
  party replacement, 107
  patterns of party conflict, 21
  peace accord (2022), 218
  research data, 109
  subnational research site, 21, 28, 100
Uganda, 191
uhuru, 53
United Democratic Forum Party (UDFP), 86
United States, 4, 17, 39, 183, 190, 191, 203
unstable parties
  challenges to accountability, 44
  coalitional politics, 77, 105
  elites', 38
  incentivizing violence, 20, 34, 40, 106, 121, 123, 220
  relationship to unstable governments, 182
  subleaders, 34
  truncated time horizons, 38, 77, 99, 190
  vulnerability to violence, 76
unstable party contexts, 14, 17, 19, 25, 31, 39–41, 43, 87, 127, 128
unstable party systems, 36, 37, 117, 171, 175, 186
untouchable community (India), 57, 64, 213
utility of conflict, 52, 128, 142
Uttar Pradesh
  2013 conflict, 3
  attacks against Muslims, 143
  Babri Masjid, 153
  BJP electoral success, 3
  BJP growth, 164
  BJP incitement, 139, 157
  BSP electoral defeat, 3, 4
  BSP emergence, 159
  communal conflict, 138
  communal division, 167
  communal polarization, 3
  communal violence, 143, 157
  Dadri, 130
  government role in Meerut violence, 161
  Hindu nationalism, 70, 159
  Hindu–Muslim alliance, 166
  Hindu–Muslim conflict, 135
  INC strategy, 136
  interview data, 67, 203
  law and order, 158
  Muslim politics, 136
  parliamentary elections, 159, 164, 209
  party instability, 138
  party replacement, 159
  party violence, 142
  party volatility, 157
  patterns of riot violence, 29

Uttar Pradesh (cont.)
  polarization, 158
  police, 168
  reactions to violence, 168
  replacement volatility, 137, 142, 156
  riot violence, 138
  rural areas, 168
  rural conflict, 140
  Sangh Parivar, 159
  state assembly, 159
  state assembly elections, 164
  subnational research site, 128, 155, 193, 196, 198
  subnational voter data, 170
  trajectories of Hindu–Muslim violence, 21, 124
  United Provinces (colonial), 213
  volatility trajectories, 124

Vaishnav, Milan, 168, 180
van de Walle, Nicolas, 30
Van Dyck, Brandon, 35
Vargas Llosa, Mario, 36
Varieties of Democracy (V-Dem), 175, 179
Varshney, Ashutosh, 9, 24, 39, 48, 49, 64, 129, 150, 169, 211, 217, 223
Varshney-Wilkinson dataset, 24, 128, 136, 143, 150, 206
Venezuela, 5, 35
vernacular journalism, 8, 11
VHP, 138, 140, 158, 161
victimization
  minority, 144
  narratives, 11
  utilization for mobilization, 20
Vidhan Sabha
  1957 replacement rates, 156
  1962 elections, 147
  1980 elections, 137
  1989 replacement volatility, 150
  1990 Hyderabad riots, 151
  2014 replacement rate, 154
  AIMIM/MIM electoral gains, 148
  AIMIM/MIM party seats, 149
  election results, 193
  election-related violence, 129
  party replacement, 146
  replacement volatility, 138, 169
  replacement volatility data, 142
vigilantism, 154
  attacks against Kikuyu, 117
  attacks on ethnic minorities, 127

cow-related, 130, 166
non-state actors, 30
party links, 6
village republics (India), 212
violence specialists
  communal conflict, 8
  complement to militias, 92
  conflict organization, 13
  death squads, 184, 185
  disincentivizing conflict, 180
  election-related conflict, 177
  interview data, 179, 210
  party intermediaries, 180
  political ambitions, 179
  role in political conflict, 12
vote-buying, 16
voter sanctioning
  case study, 45
  challenges in unstable party contexts, 17, 28, 43, 44, 77, 98, 100, 123, 124
  coalitional politics, 43, 98
  cross-regional comparison, 14
  disincentivizing conflict, 7
  effective deterrent to violence, 153, 187, 189
  elite decision-making, 29, 31, 38, 49, 98, 124, 125, 141, 143, 168
  interview data, 23, 152, 188
  party entry volatility, 45
  relationship to time horizons, 27, 31, 36, 37, 45, 99
  response to violence, 38, 43
  targets, 44
vote-switching volatility, 32, 35, 37, 46, 193
  Bulgaria, 35
vulnerabilities
  comparison between Kenya and India, 47
  ethnic conflict, 39
  Hindu–Muslim conflict, 142
  party weakness, 174
  to party violence, 175
Vyakweli, Mbaruku, 115

wabara, 122
Wachanga, D. Ndirangu, 11
Waki Commission (Kenya), 92
wananchi, 123
Wardei, 1, 2, 118–121, 188
weak parties, 52, 57, 81, 189
West Bengal, 133, 139, 140
Western Province, 78, 85, 91, 93
White Highlands. *See* settlers
Whitfield, Lindsay, 176

Index

Widner, Jennifer, 69, 70, 71, 80
Wilkinson, Steven, 5, 9, 14, 24, 38, 87
Wolf, Tom, 89
women
  activism, 146
  contribution to postconflict rebuilding, 20
  instrumentalization of violence against, 209
  Mau Mau participants, 54
  Muslim, 145
  narratives of victimization, 3, 150
  police, 161
  politicization of bodies, 54
  rights, 213

Wood, Elisabeth, 199, 200
World Values Surveys, 181

Yadav, Akhilesh, 3, 168
Yadav, Laloo Prasad, 139
Yadav, Mulayam Singh, 139
Young Kavirondo Association (YKA), 212
Yugoslavia, 4

Zambia, 5
Zila Shanti Samiti (District Peace Committee), 221
Zimbabwe, 13

Printed in the United States
by Baker & Taylor Publisher Services